-FAKE-

VOLUME ONE

BY SANAMI MATOH

ALSO AVAILABLE FROM 🐱 TOKYOPOP®

MANGA

ANGELIC LAYER*
BABY BIRTH* (September 2003)
BATTLE ROYALE*
BRAIN POWERED* (June 2003)
BRIGADOON* (August 2003)
CARDCAPTOR SAKURA
CARDCAPTOR SAKURA: MASTER OF THE CLOW*
CLAMP SCHOOL DETECTIVES*
CHOBITS*
CHRONICLES OF THE CURSED SWORD (July 2003)
CLOVER
CONFIDENTIAL CONFESSIONS* (July 2003)
CORRECTOR YUI
COWBOY BEBOP*
COWBOY BEBOP: SHOOTING STAR* (June 2003)
DEMON DIARY (May 2003)
DIGIMON
DRAGON HUNTER (June 2003)
DRAGON KNIGHTS*
DUKLYON: CLAMP SCHOOL DEFENDERS* (September 2003)
ERICA SAKURAZAWA* (May 2003)
ESCAFLOWNE* (July 2003)
FAKE*(May 2003)
FLCL* (September 2003)
FORBIDDEN DANCE* (August 2003)
GATE KEEPERS*
G-GUNDAM* (June 2003)
GRAVITATION* (June 2003)
GTO*
GUNDAM WING
GUNDAM WING: ENDLESS WALTZ*
GUNDAM: THE LAST OUTPOST*
HAPPY MANIA*
HARLEM BEAT
INITIAL D*
I.N.V.U.
ISLAND
JING: KING OF BANDITS* (June 2003)
JULINE
KARE KANO*
KINDAICHI CASE FILES* (June 2003)
KING OF HELL (June 2003)

KODOCHA*
LOVE HINA*
LUPIN III*
MAGIC KNIGHT RAYEARTH* (August 2003)
MAGIC KNIGHT RAYEARTH II* (COMING SOON)
MAN OF MANY FACES* (May 2003)
MARMALADE BOY*
MARS*
MIRACLE GIRLS
MIYUKI-CHAN IN WONDERLAND* (October 2003)
MONSTERS, INC.
NIEA_7* (August 2003)
PARADISE KISS*
PARASYTE
PEACH GIRL
PEACH GIRL: CHANGE OF HEART*
PET SHOP OF HORRORS* (June 2003)
PLANET LADDER
PLANETS* (October 2003)
PRIEST
RAGNAROK
RAVE MASTER*
REAL BOUT HIGH SCHOOL*
REALITY CHECK
REBIRTH
REBOUND*
SABER MARIONETTE J* (July 2003)
SAILOR MOON
SAINT TAIL
SAMURAI DEEPER KYO* (June 2003)
SCRYED*
SHAOLIN SISTERS*
SHIRAHIME-SYO* (December 2003)
THE SKULL MAN*
SORCERER HUNTERS
TOKYO MEW MEW*
UNDER THE GLASS MOON (June 2003)
VAMPIRE GAME* (June 2003)
WILD ACT* (July 2003)
WISH*
X-DAY* (August 2003)
ZODIAC P.I.* (July 2003)

CINE-MANGA™

AKIRA*
CARDCAPTORS
JIMMY NEUTRON (COMING SOON)
KIM POSSIBLE
LIZZIE McGUIRE
SPONGEBOB SQUAREPANTS (COMING SOON)
SPY KIDS 2

NOVELS

SAILOR MOON
KARMA CLUB (COMING SOON)

TOKYOPOP KIDS

STRAY SHEEP (September 2003)

ART BOOKS

CARDCAPTOR SAKURA*
MAGIC KNIGHT RAYEARTH*

ANIME GUIDES

GUNDAM TECHNICAL MANUALS
COWBOY BEBOP
SAILOR MOON SCOUT GUIDES

-FAKE-

TABLE OF CONTENTS

Translator - Nan Rymer
English Adaption - Stuart Hazleton
Editor - Julie Taylor
Contributing Editor - Jodi Bryson
Retouch and Lettering - Rob Steen
Cover Artist - Raymond Makowski

Managing Editor - Jill Freshney
Production Coordinator - Antonio DePietro
Production Manager - Jennifer Miller
Art Director - Matthew Alford
Director of Editorial - Jeremy Ross
VP of Production & Manufacturing - Ron Klamert
President & C.O.O. - John Parker
Publisher & C.E.O. - Stuart Levy

Email: editor@TOKYOPOP.com
Come visit us online at www.TOKYOPOP.com

A ⊕ TOKYOPOP® Manga
TOKYOPOP® is an imprint of Mixx Entertainment, Inc.
5900 Wilshire Blvd. Suite 2000, Los Angeles, CA 90036

ISBN: 1-59182-326-9

First TOKYOPOP® printing: May 2003

10 9 8 7 6 5 4 3 2 1

Printed in the USA

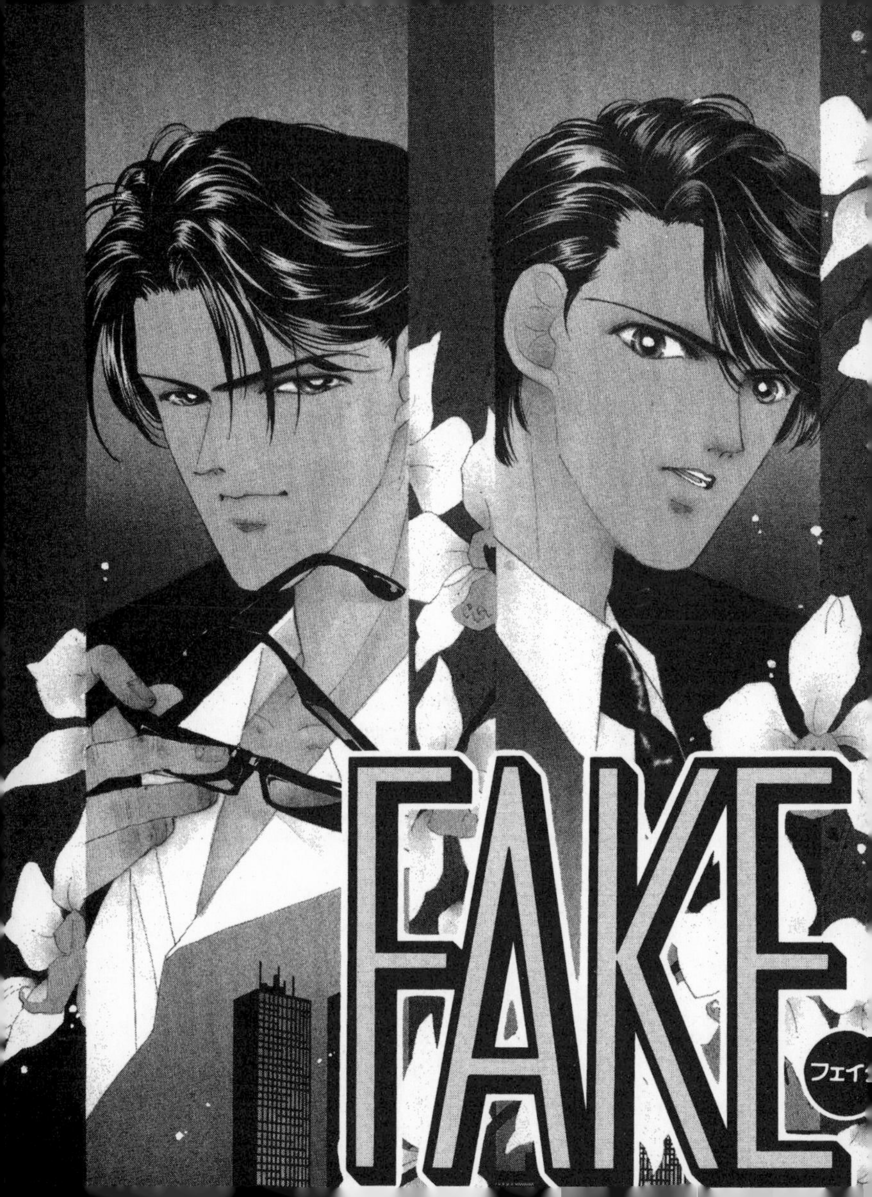
FAKE
フェイ

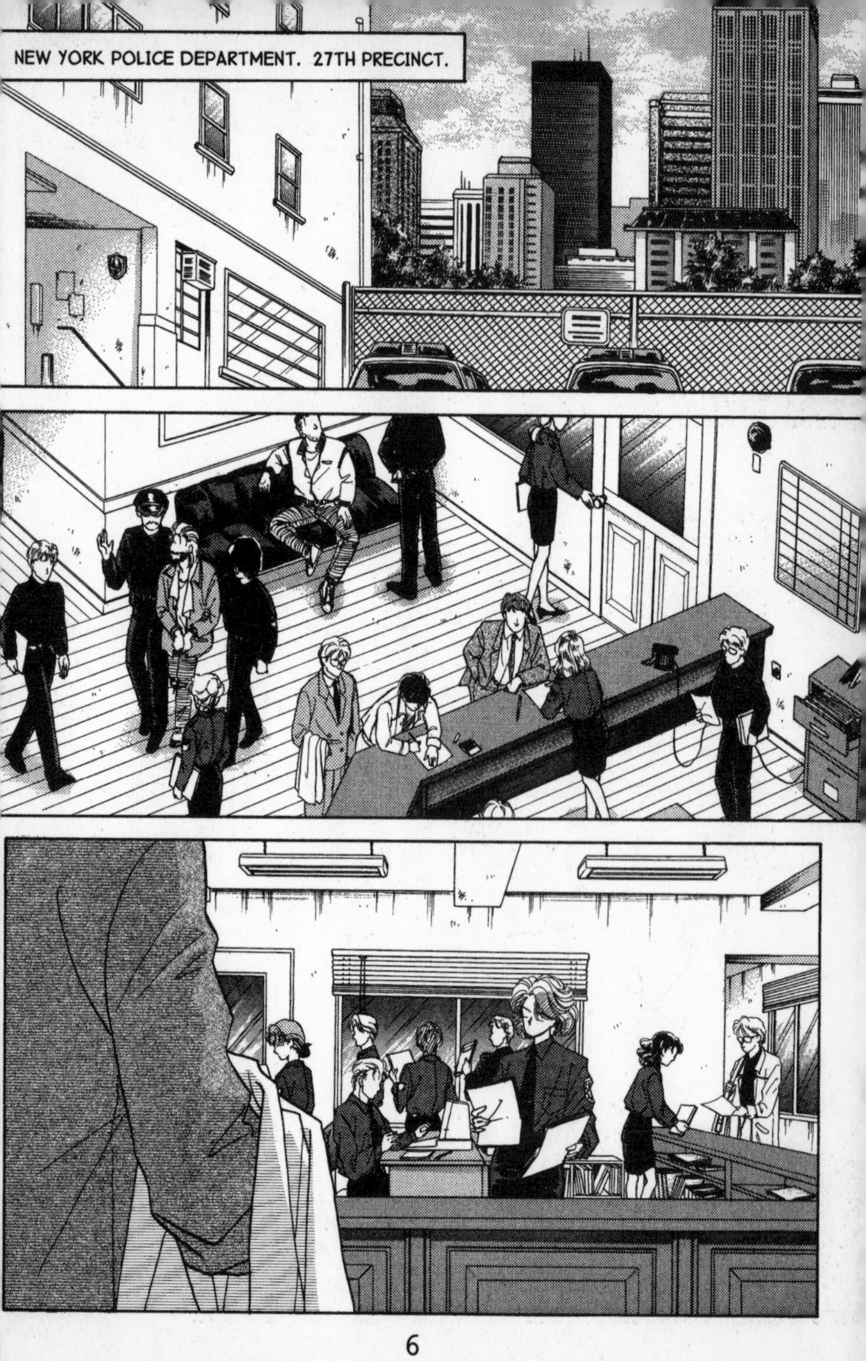
NEW YORK POLICE DEPARTMENT. 27TH PRECINCT.

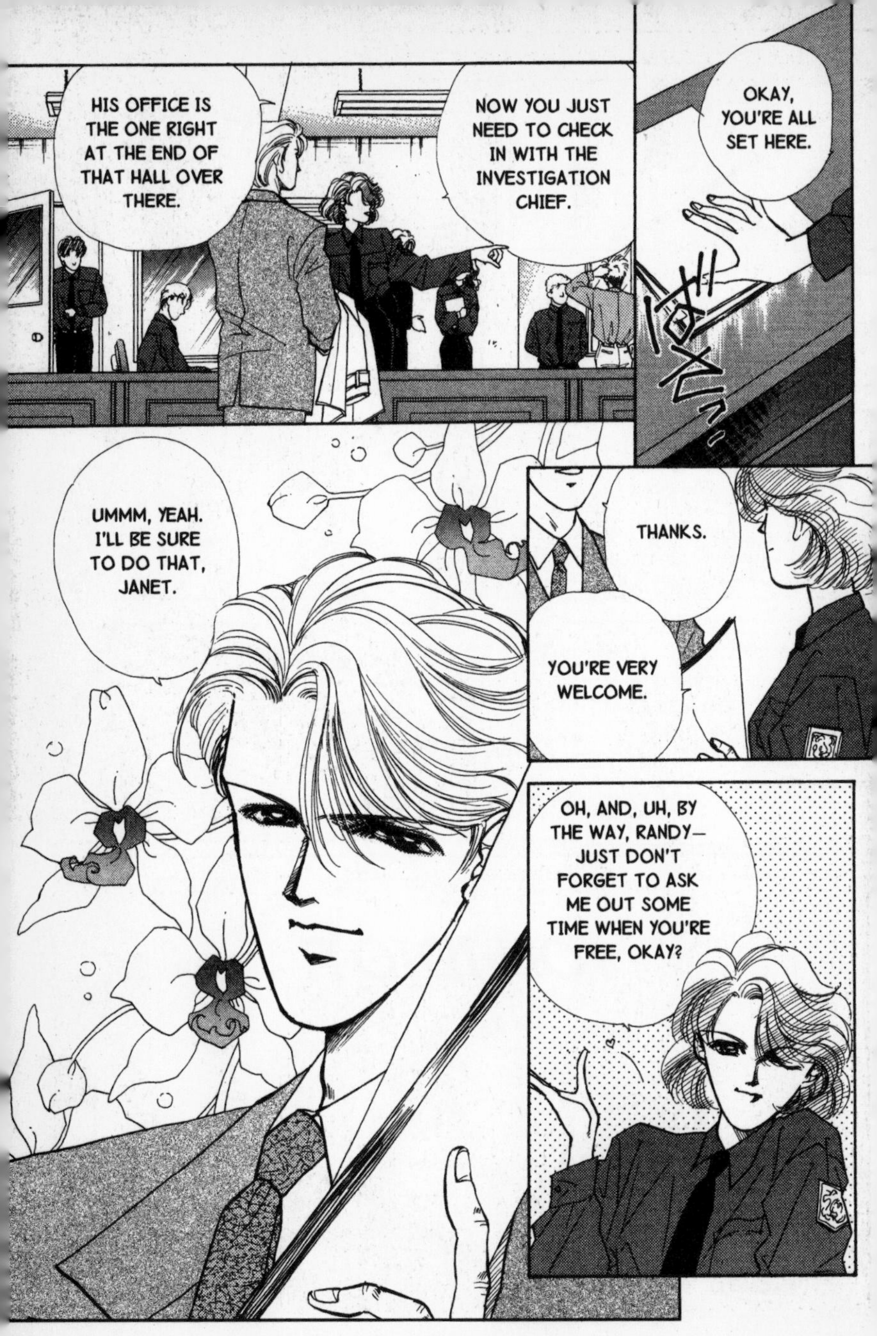
OKAY, YOU'RE ALL SET HERE.
NOW YOU JUST NEED TO CHECK IN WITH THE INVESTIGATION CHIEF.
HIS OFFICE IS THE ONE RIGHT AT THE END OF THAT HALL OVER THERE.
THANKS.
YOU'RE VERY WELCOME.
OH, AND, UH, BY THE WAY, RANDY— JUST DON'T FORGET TO ASK ME OUT SOME TIME WHEN YOU'RE FREE, OKAY?
UMMM, YEAH. I'LL BE SURE TO DO THAT, JANET.

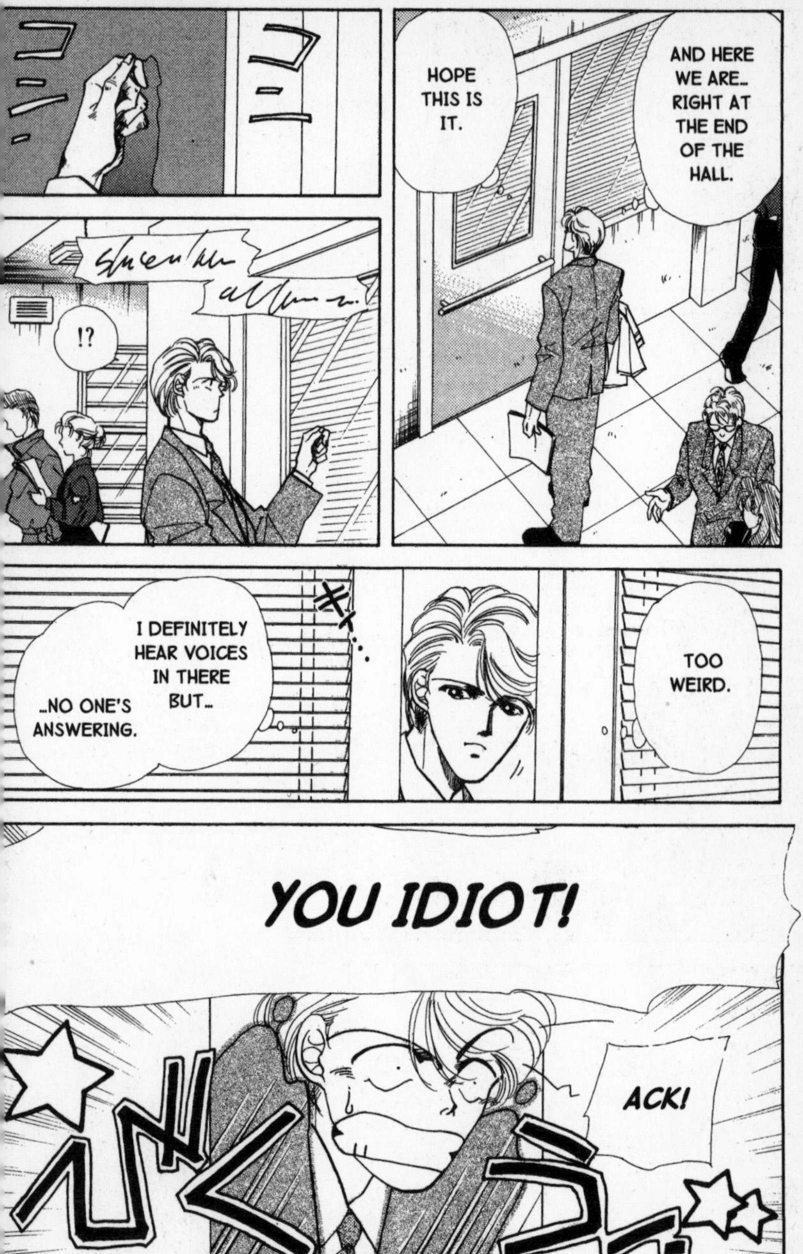
AND HERE WE ARE.. RIGHT AT THE END OF THE HALL.
HOPE THIS IS IT.
!?
TOO WEIRD.
I DEFINITELY HEAR VOICES IN THERE BUT...
...NO ONE'S ANSWERING.
YOU IDIOT!
ACK!

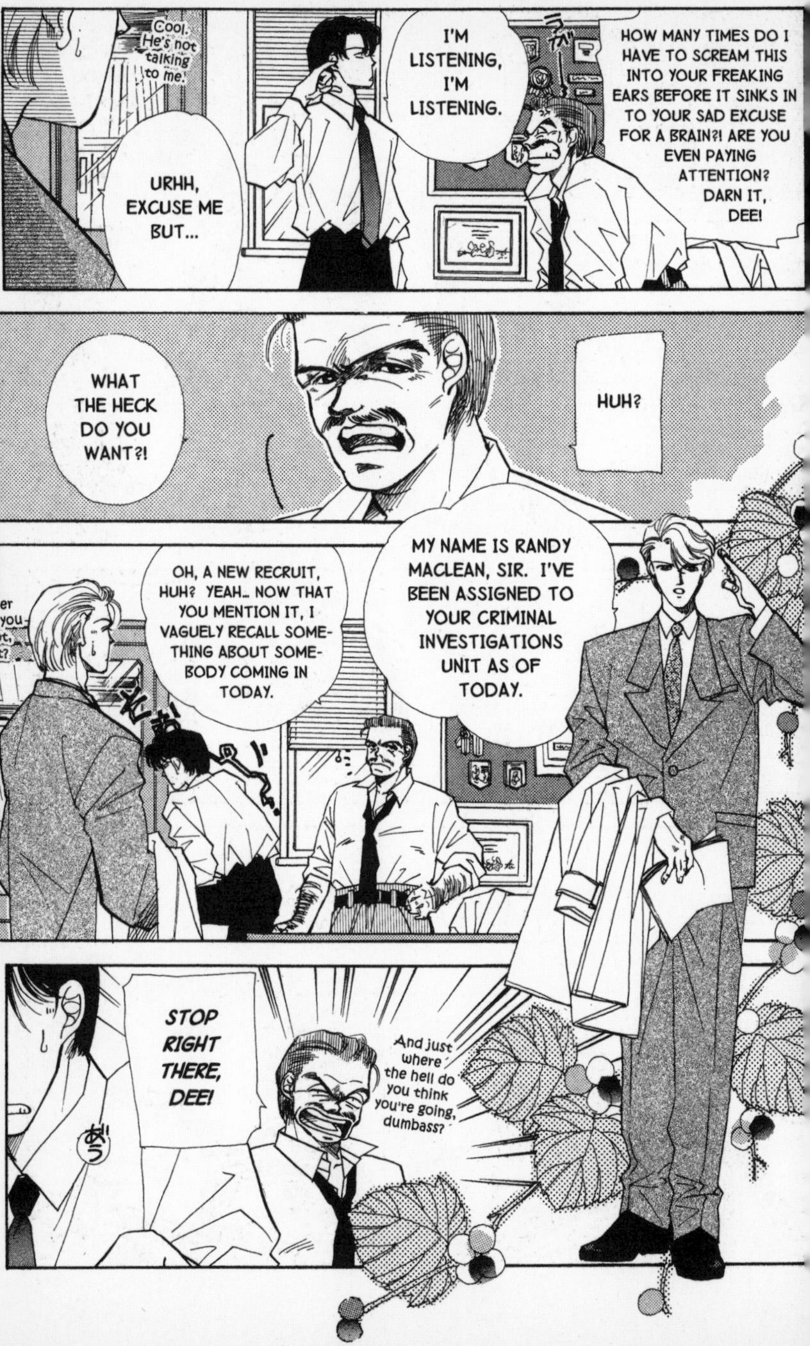

HOW MANY TIMES DO I HAVE TO SCREAM THIS INTO YOUR FREAKING EARS BEFORE IT SINKS IN TO YOUR SAD EXCUSE FOR A BRAIN?! ARE YOU EVEN PAYING ATTENTION? DARN IT, DEE!
I'M LISTENING, I'M LISTENING.
Cool. He's not talking to me.
URHH, EXCUSE ME BUT...
HUH?
WHAT THE HECK DO YOU WANT?!
MY NAME IS RANDY MACLEAN, SIR. I'VE BEEN ASSIGNED TO YOUR CRIMINAL INVESTIGATIONS UNIT AS OF TODAY.
OH, A NEW RECRUIT, HUH? YEAH.. NOW THAT YOU MENTION IT, I VAGUELY RECALL SOMETHING ABOUT SOMEBODY COMING IN TODAY.
In other words, you forgot, right?
And just where the hell do you think you're going, dumbass?
STOP RIGHT THERE, DEE!

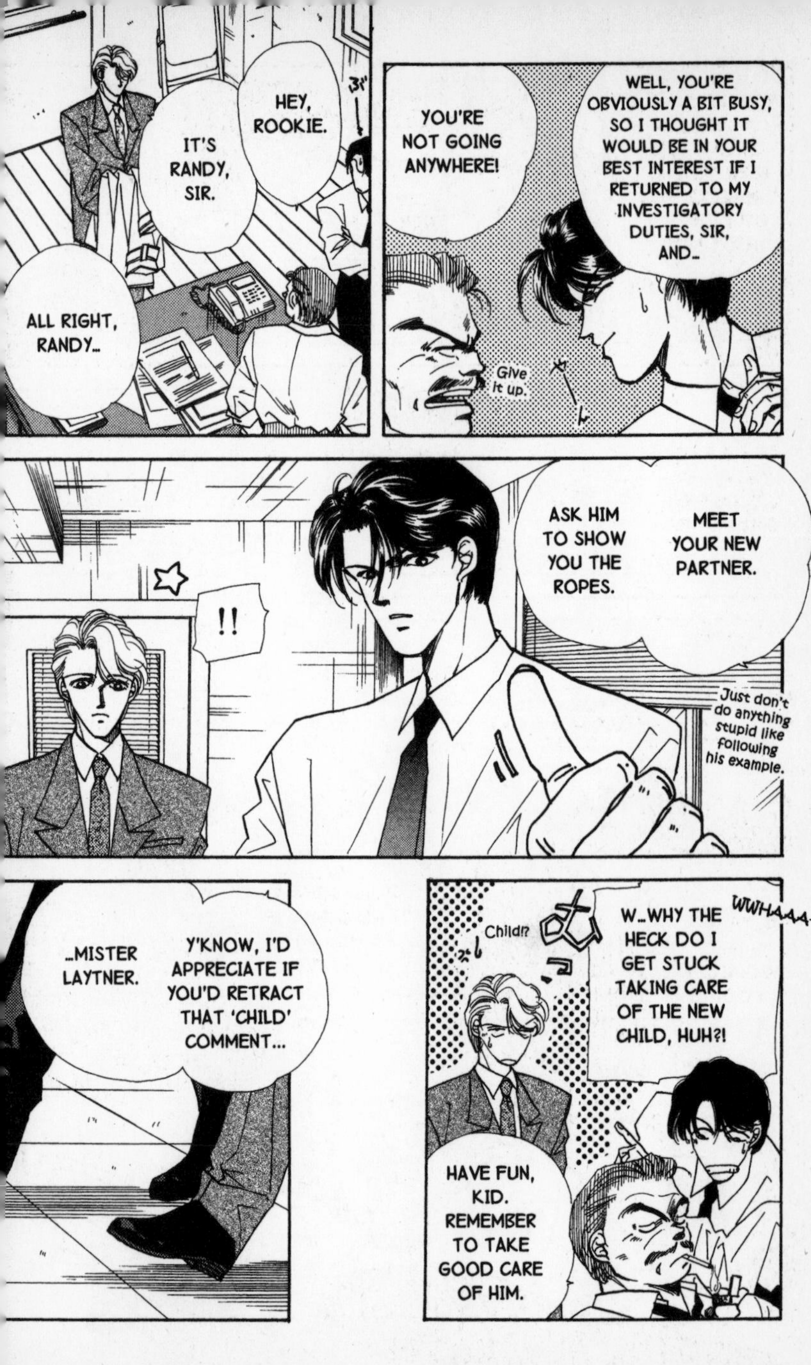
WELL, YOU'RE OBVIOUSLY A BIT BUSY, SO I THOUGHT IT WOULD BE IN YOUR BEST INTEREST IF I RETURNED TO MY INVESTIGATORY DUTIES, SIR, AND..
YOU'RE NOT GOING ANYWHERE!
Give it up.
HEY, ROOKIE.
IT'S RANDY, SIR.
ALL RIGHT, RANDY..
MEET YOUR NEW PARTNER.
ASK HIM TO SHOW YOU THE ROPES.
Just don't do anything stupid like following his example.
!!
WWHAAA—!?
W..WHY THE HECK DO I GET STUCK TAKING CARE OF THE NEW CHILD, HUH?!
Child!?
HAVE FUN, KID. REMEMBER TO TAKE GOOD CARE OF HIM.
Y'KNOW, I'D APPRECIATE IF YOU'D RETRACT THAT 'CHILD' COMMENT...
..MISTER LAYTNER.

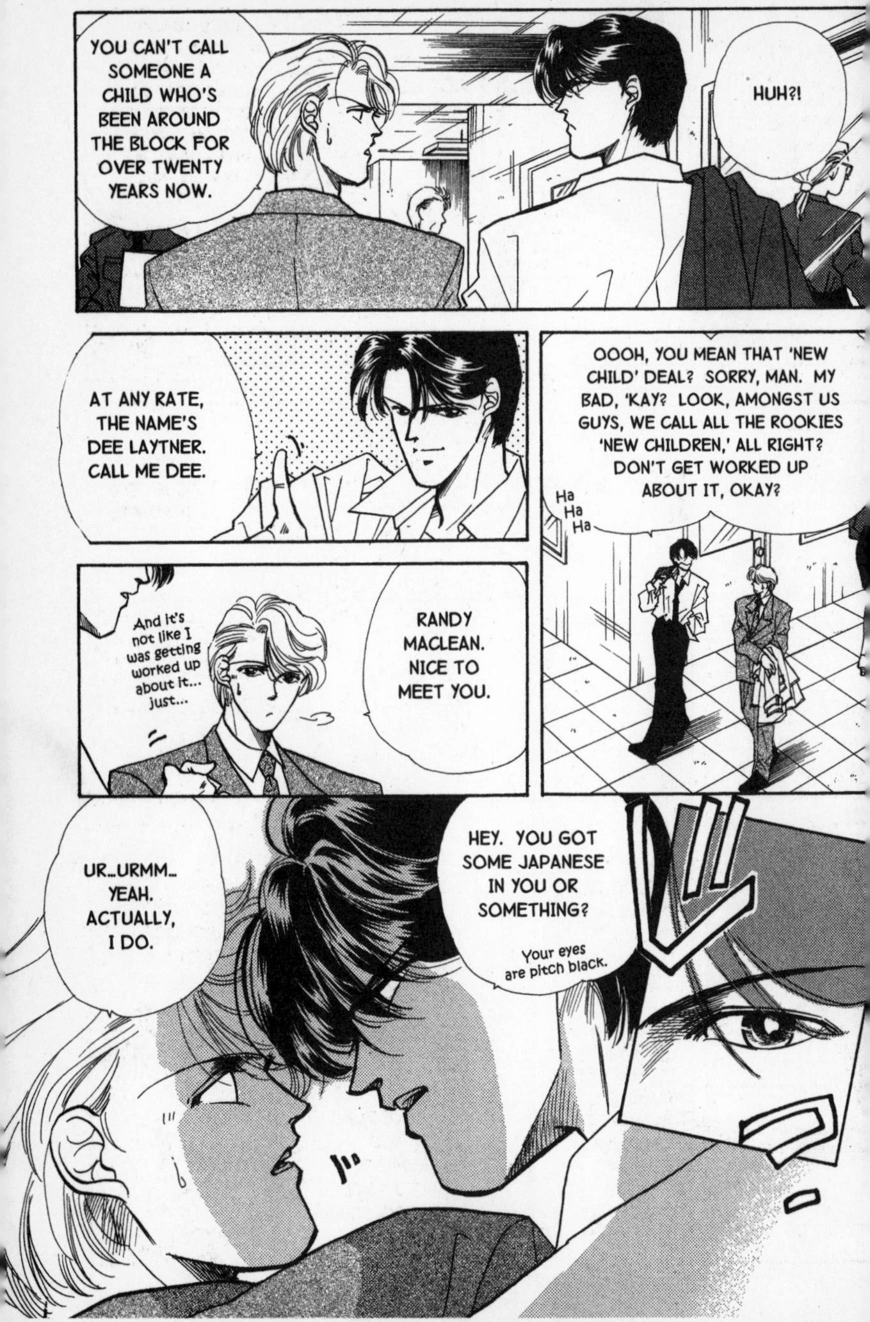
HUH?!
YOU CAN'T CALL SOMEONE A CHILD WHO'S BEEN AROUND THE BLOCK FOR OVER TWENTY YEARS NOW.
OOOH, YOU MEAN THAT 'NEW CHILD' DEAL? SORRY, MAN. MY BAD, 'KAY? LOOK, AMONGST US GUYS, WE CALL ALL THE ROOKIES 'NEW CHILDREN,' ALL RIGHT? DON'T GET WORKED UP ABOUT IT, OKAY?
Ha Ha Ha
AT ANY RATE, THE NAME'S DEE LAYTNER. CALL ME DEE.
RANDY MACLEAN. NICE TO MEET YOU.
And it's not like I was getting worked up about it... just...
HEY. YOU GOT SOME JAPANESE IN YOU OR SOMETHING?
Your eyes are pitch black.
UR...URMM... YEAH. ACTUALLY, I DO.

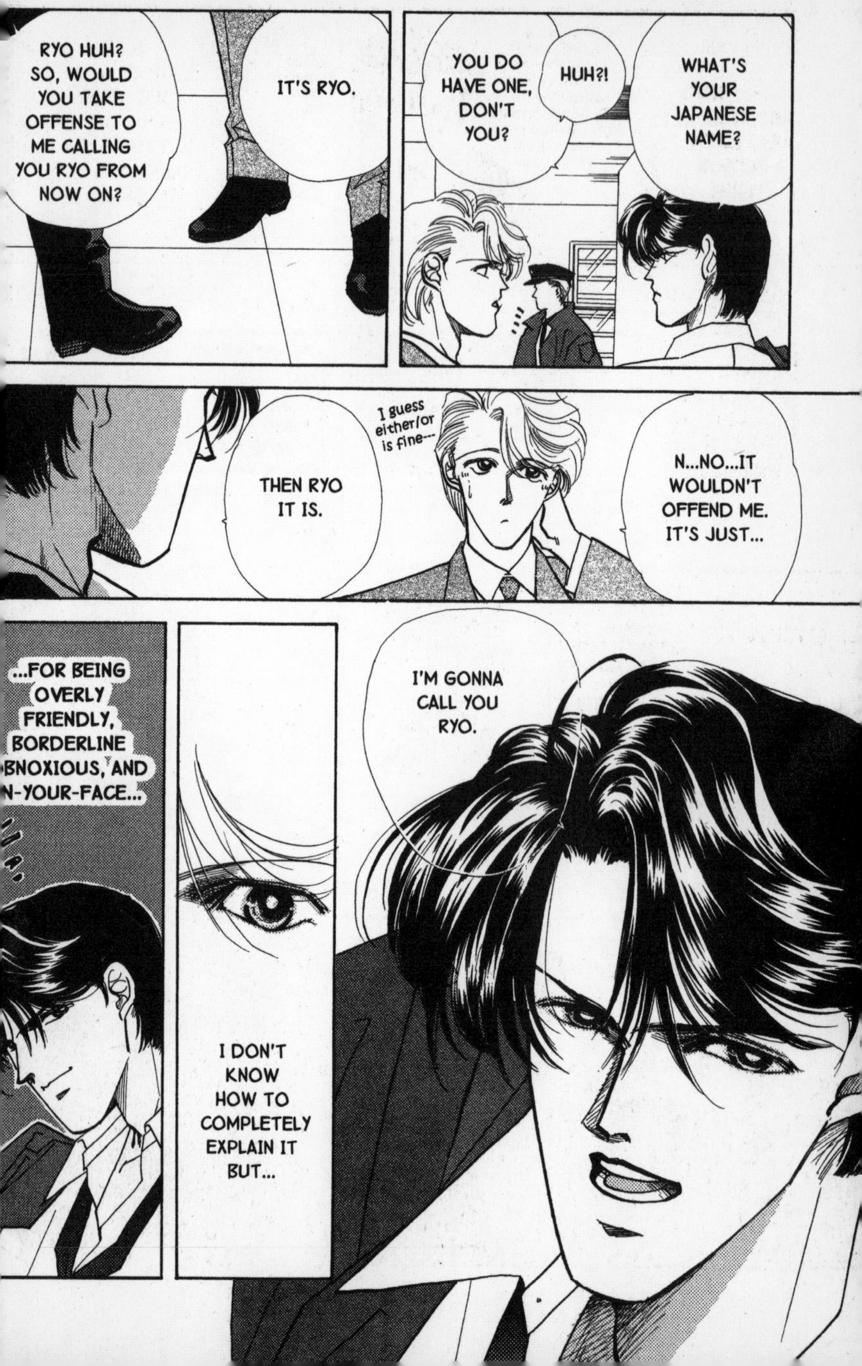
WHAT'S YOUR JAPANESE NAME?
HUH?!
YOU DO HAVE ONE, DON'T YOU?
IT'S RYO.
RYO HUH? SO, WOULD YOU TAKE OFFENSE TO ME CALLING YOU RYO FROM NOW ON?
N...NO...IT WOULDN'T OFFEND ME. IT'S JUST...
I guess either/or is fine---
THEN RYO IT IS.
I'M GONNA CALL YOU RYO.
I DON'T KNOW HOW TO COMPLETELY EXPLAIN IT BUT...
...FOR BEING OVERLY FRIENDLY, BORDERLINE BNOXIOUS, AND N-YOUR-FACE...

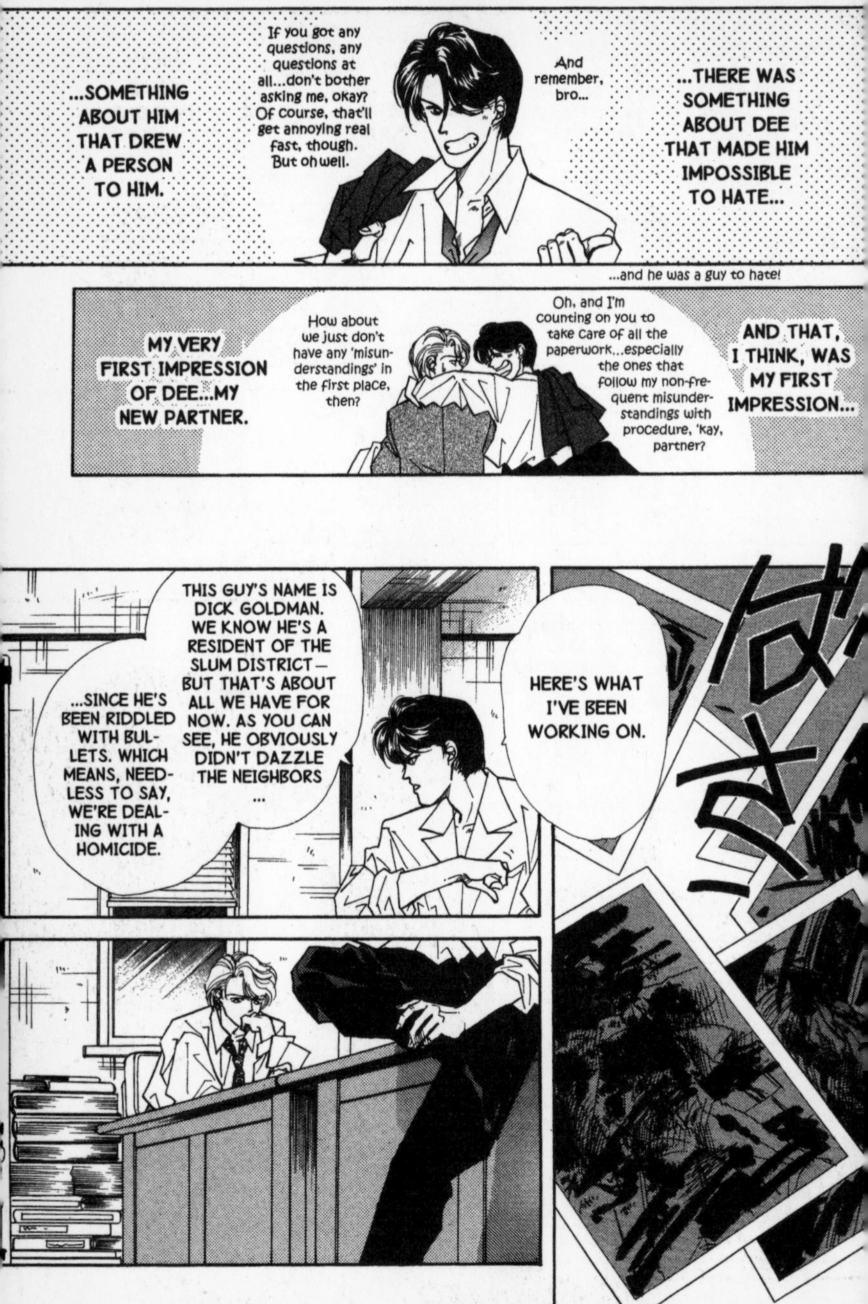
...THERE WAS SOMETHING ABOUT DEE THAT MADE HIM IMPOSSIBLE TO HATE...
And remember, bro...
If you got any questions, any questions at all...don't bother asking me, okay? Of course, that'll get annoying real fast, though. But oh well.
...SOMETHING ABOUT HIM THAT DREW A PERSON TO HIM.
...and he was a guy to hate!
AND THAT, I THINK, WAS MY FIRST IMPRESSION...
Oh, and I'm counting on you to take care of all the paperwork...especially the ones that follow my non-frequent misunderstandings with procedure, 'kay, partner?
How about we just don't have any 'misunderstandings' in the first place, then?
MY VERY FIRST IMPRESSION OF DEE...MY NEW PARTNER.
HERE'S WHAT I'VE BEEN WORKING ON.
THIS GUY'S NAME IS DICK GOLDMAN. WE KNOW HE'S A RESIDENT OF THE SLUM DISTRICT— BUT THAT'S ABOUT ALL WE HAVE FOR NOW. AS YOU CAN SEE, HE OBVIOUSLY DIDN'T DAZZLE THE NEIGHBORS ...
...SINCE HE'S BEEN RIDDLED WITH BUL-LETS. WHICH MEANS, NEED-LESS TO SAY, WE'RE DEAL-ING WITH A HOMICIDE.

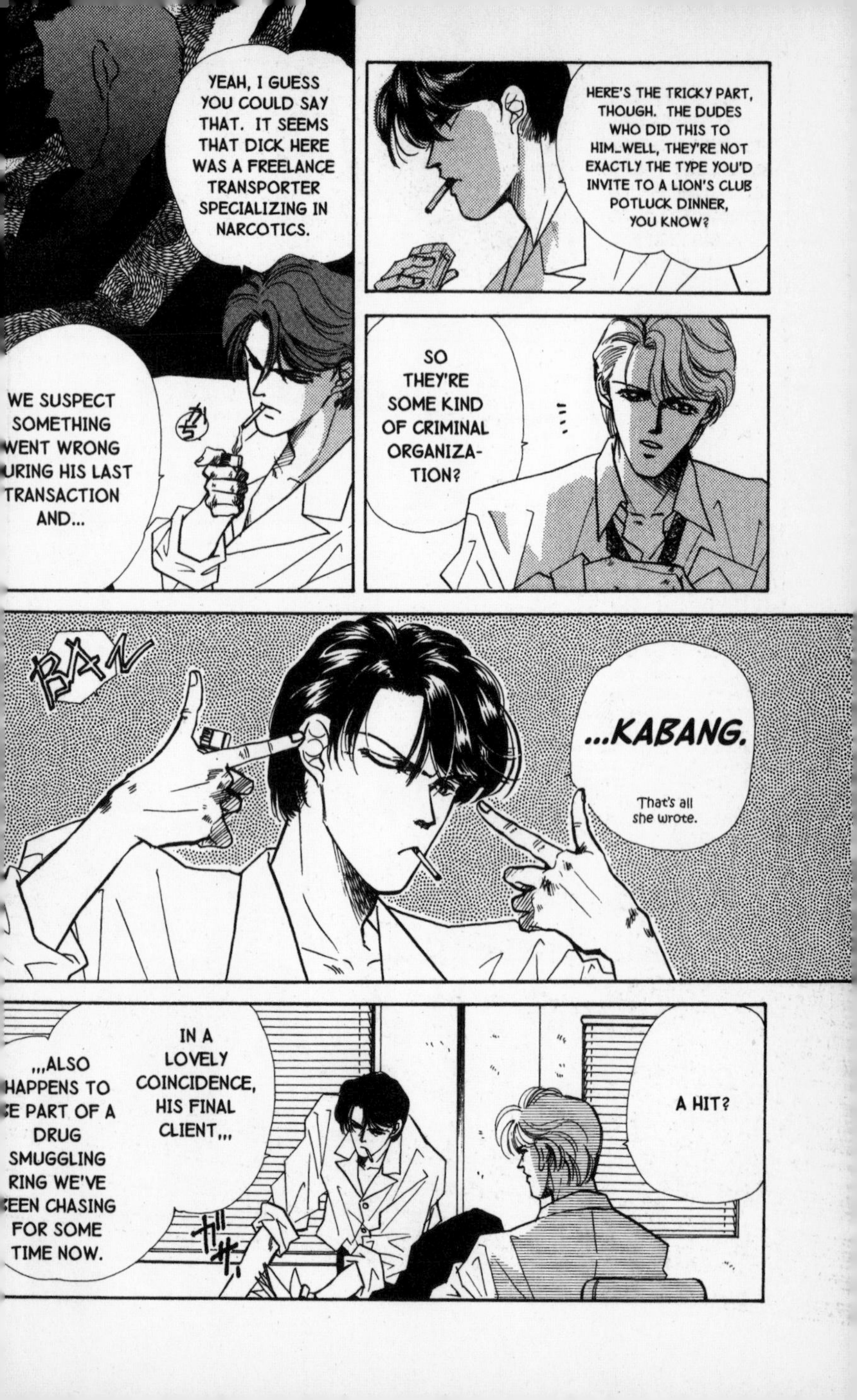
HERE'S THE TRICKY PART, THOUGH. THE DUDES WHO DID THIS TO HIM...WELL, THEY'RE NOT EXACTLY THE TYPE YOU'D INVITE TO A LION'S CLUB POTLUCK DINNER, YOU KNOW?
SO THEY'RE SOME KIND OF CRIMINAL ORGANIZA-TION?
YEAH, I GUESS YOU COULD SAY THAT. IT SEEMS THAT DICK HERE WAS A FREELANCE TRANSPORTER SPECIALIZING IN NARCOTICS.
WE SUSPECT SOMETHING WENT WRONG URING HIS LAST TRANSACTION AND...
...KABANG.
That's all she wrote.
BAN
A HIT?
IN A LOVELY COINCIDENCE, HIS FINAL CLIENT...
...ALSO HAPPENS TO E PART OF A DRUG SMUGGLING RING WE'VE EEN CHASING FOR SOME TIME NOW.

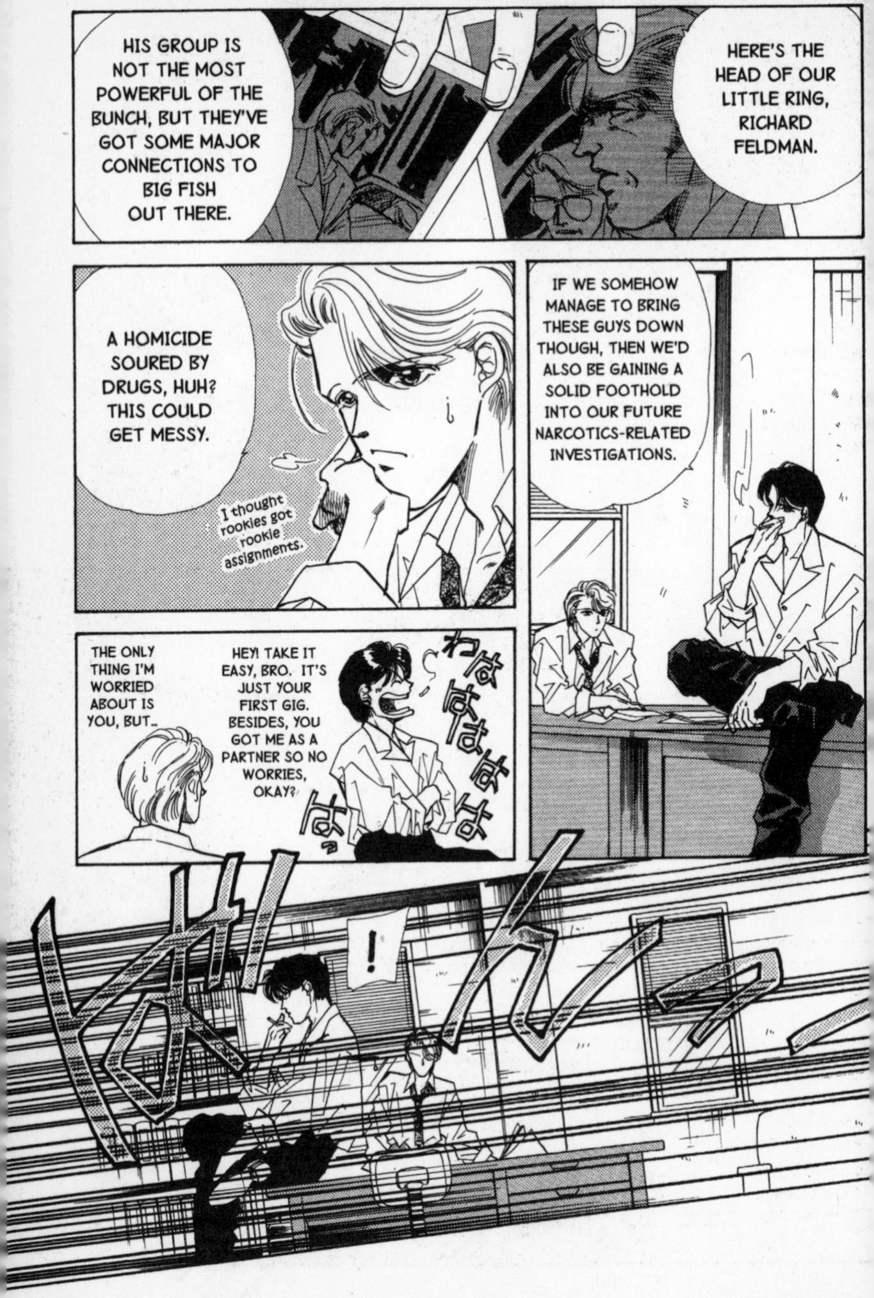
HERE'S THE HEAD OF OUR LITTLE RING, RICHARD FELDMAN.
HIS GROUP IS NOT THE MOST POWERFUL OF THE BUNCH, BUT THEY'VE GOT SOME MAJOR CONNECTIONS TO BIG FISH OUT THERE.
IF WE SOMEHOW MANAGE TO BRING THESE GUYS DOWN THOUGH, THEN WE'D ALSO BE GAINING A SOLID FOOTHOLD INTO OUR FUTURE NARCOTICS-RELATED INVESTIGATIONS.
A HOMICIDE SOURED BY DRUGS, HUH? THIS COULD GET MESSY.
I thought rookies got rookie assignments.
わはははははっ
HEY! TAKE IT EASY, BRO. IT'S JUST YOUR FIRST GIG. BESIDES, YOU GOT ME AS A PARTNER SO NO WORRIES, OKAY?
THE ONLY THING I'M WORRIED ABOUT IS YOU, BUT...
!

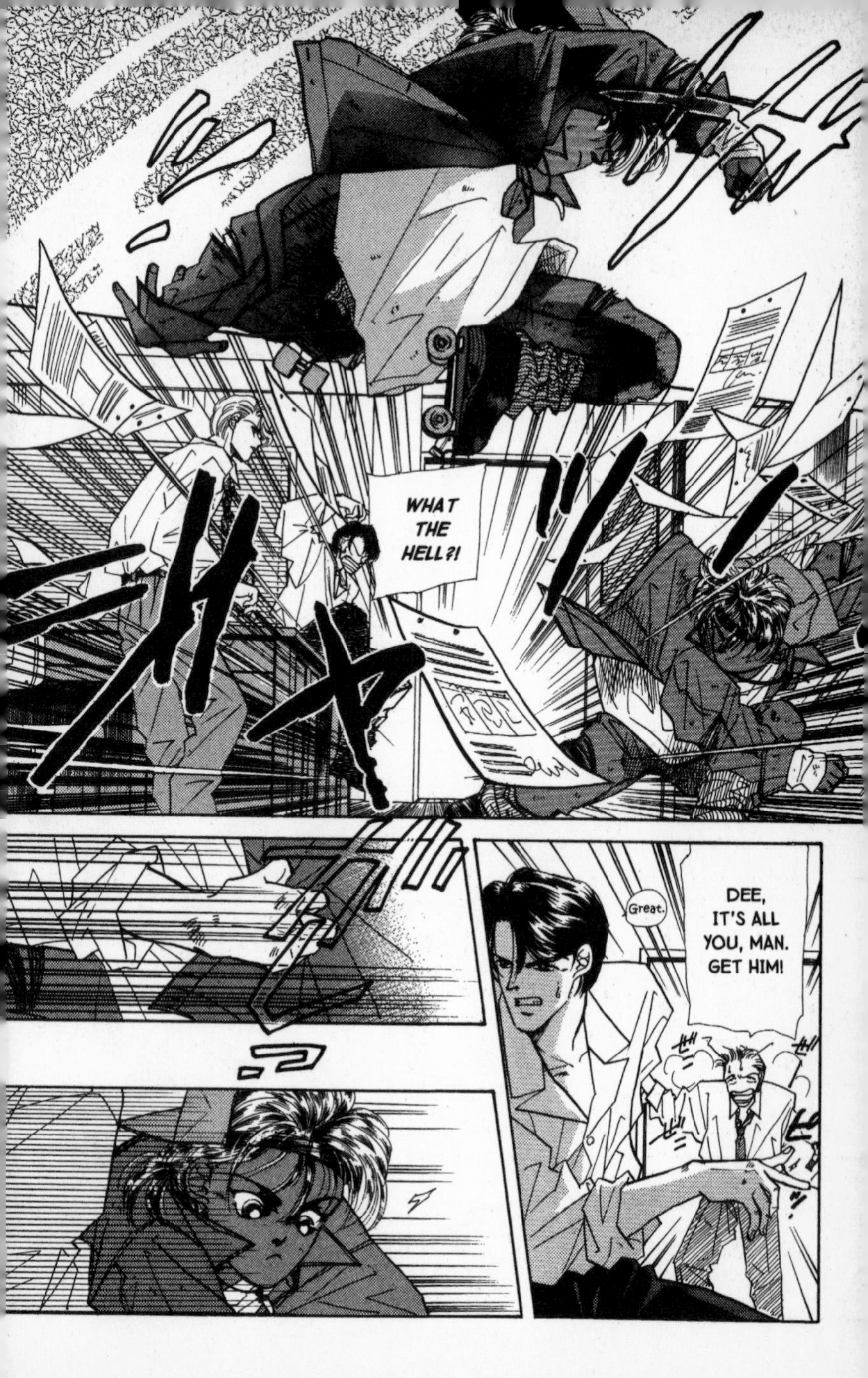
WHAT THE HELL?!
DEE, IT'S ALL YOU, MAN. GET HIM!
Great.

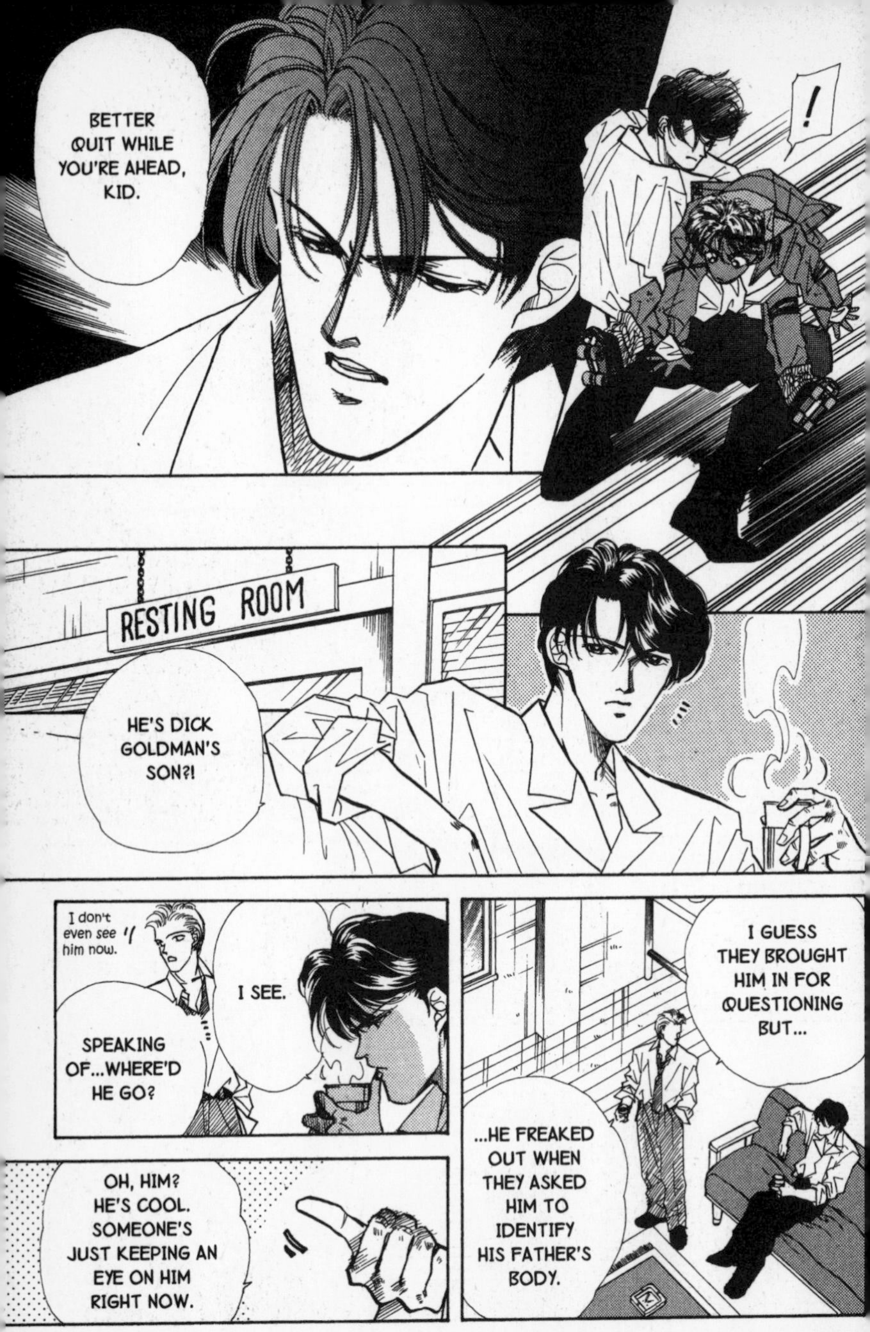
!
BETTER QUIT WHILE YOU'RE AHEAD, KID.
RESTING ROOM
HE'S DICK GOLDMAN'S SON?!
I GUESS THEY BROUGHT HIM IN FOR QUESTIONING BUT...
...HE FREAKED OUT WHEN THEY ASKED HIM TO IDENTIFY HIS FATHER'S BODY.
I SEE.
I don't even see him now.
SPEAKING OF...WHERE'D HE GO?
OH, HIM? HE'S COOL. SOMEONE'S JUST KEEPING AN EYE ON HIM RIGHT NOW.

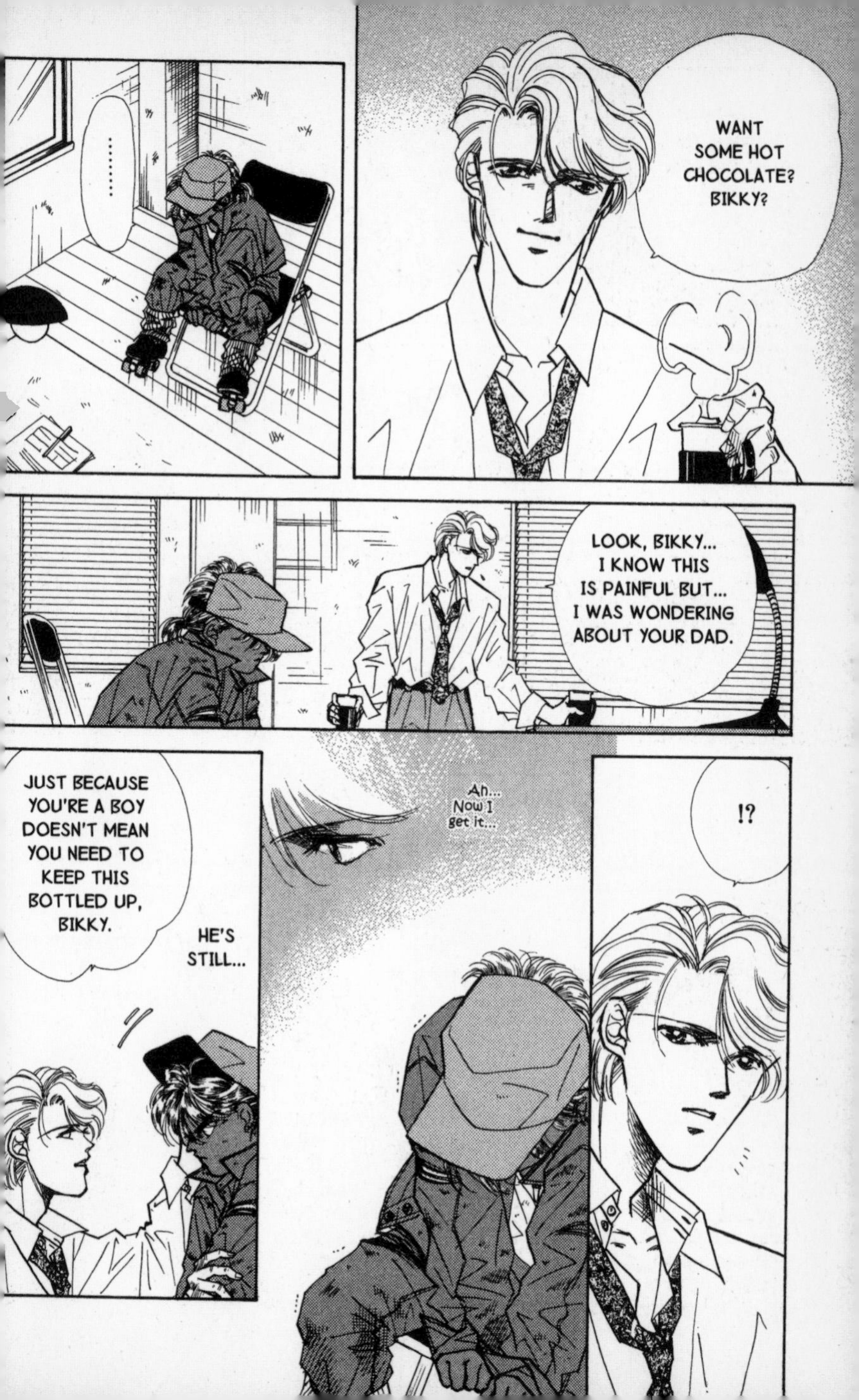
WANT SOME HOT CHOCOLATE? BIKKY?
......
LOOK, BIKKY... I KNOW THIS IS PAINFUL BUT... I WAS WONDERING ABOUT YOUR DAD.
!?
Ah... Now I get it...
HE'S STILL...
JUST BECAUSE YOU'RE A BOY DOESN'T MEAN YOU NEED TO KEEP THIS BOTTLED UP, BIKKY.

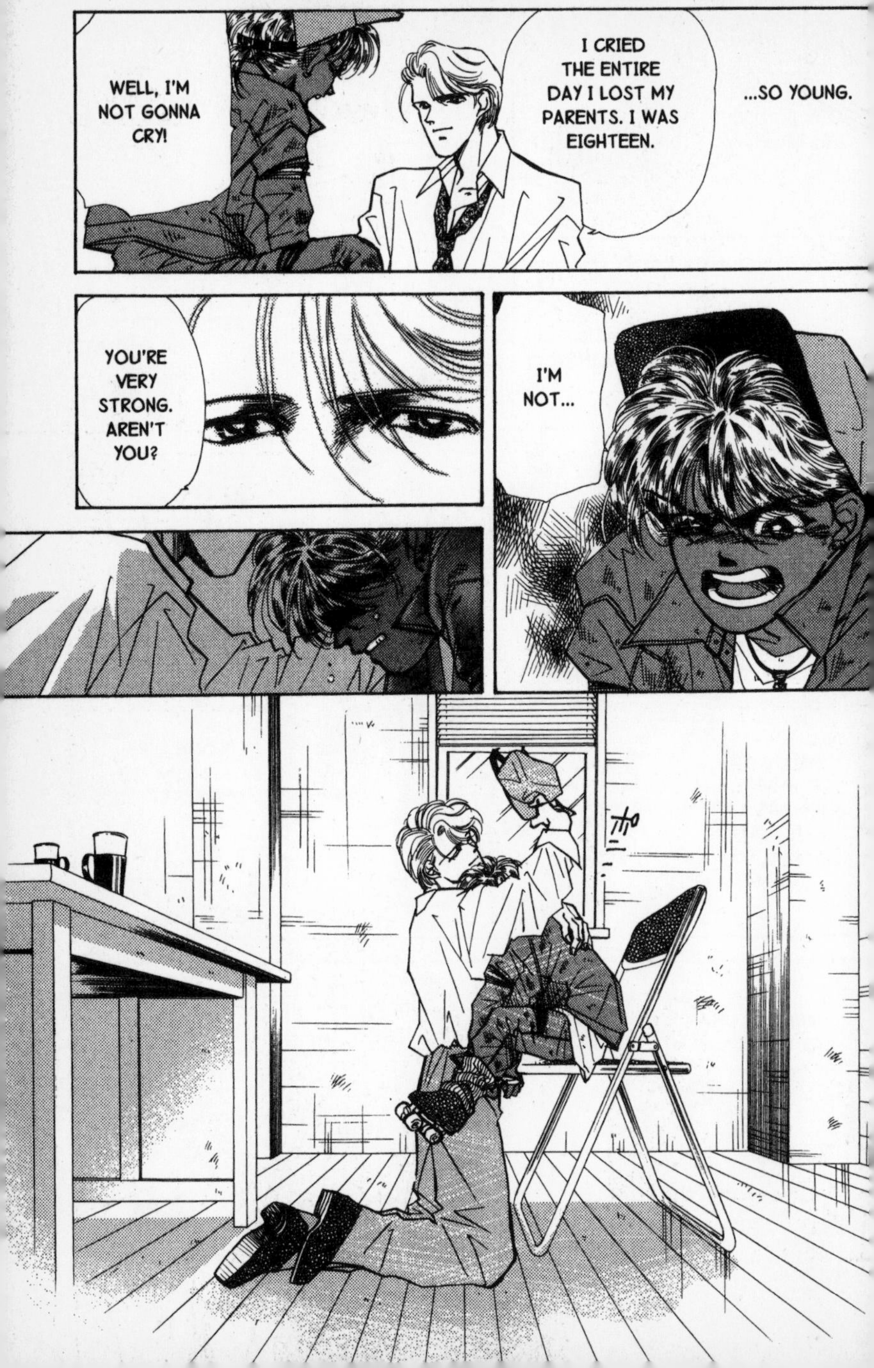
...SO YOUNG.
I CRIED THE ENTIRE DAY I LOST MY PARENTS. I WAS EIGHTEEN.
WELL, I'M NOT GONNA CRY!
I'M NOT...
YOU'RE VERY STRONG. AREN'T YOU?

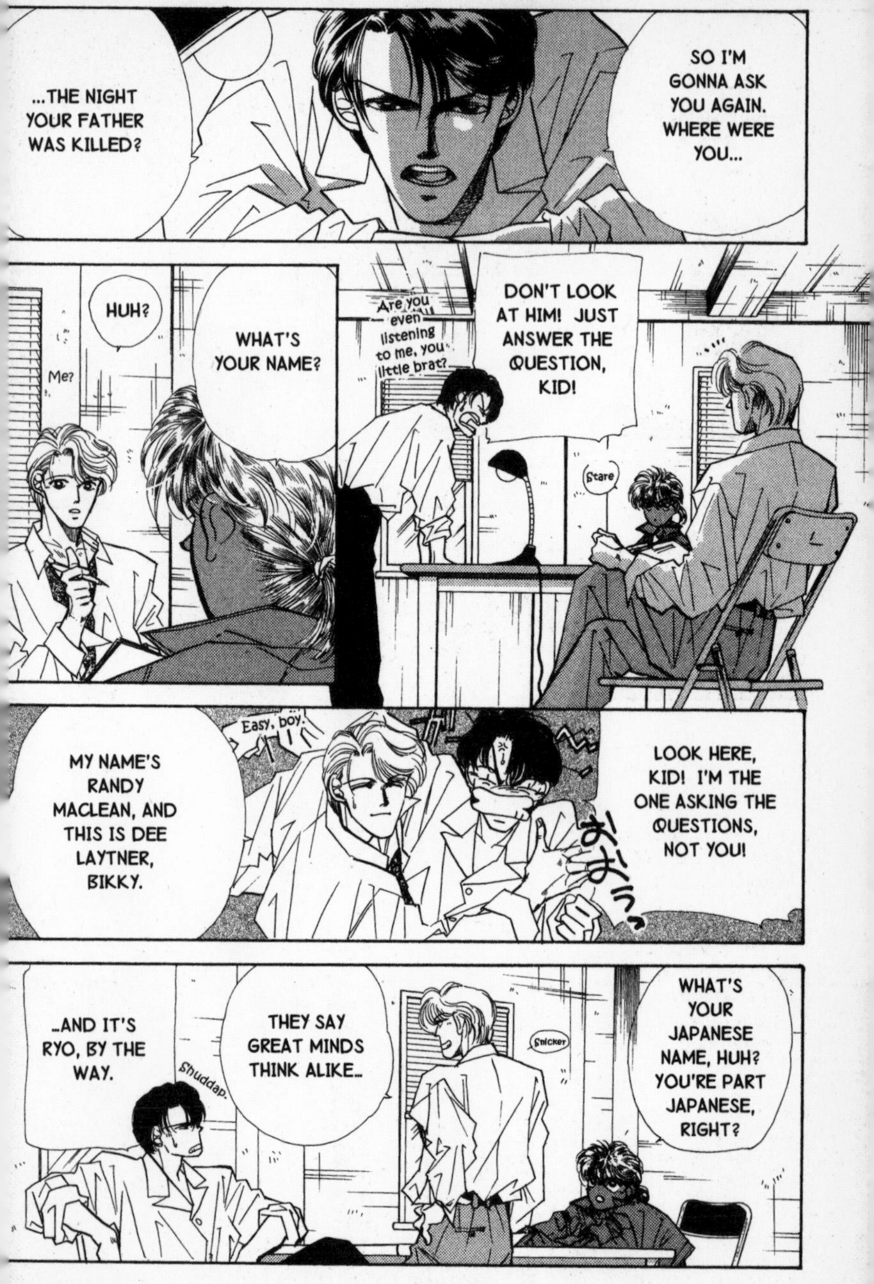
SO I'M GONNA ASK YOU AGAIN. WHERE WERE YOU...
...THE NIGHT YOUR FATHER WAS KILLED?
DON'T LOOK AT HIM! JUST ANSWER THE QUESTION, KID!
Are you even listening to me, you little brat?
Stare
WHAT'S YOUR NAME?
HUH?
Me?
LOOK HERE, KID! I'M THE ONE ASKING THE QUESTIONS, NOT YOU!
Easy, boy.
MY NAME'S RANDY MACLEAN, AND THIS IS DEE LAYTNER, BIKKY.
WHAT'S YOUR JAPANESE NAME, HUH? YOU'RE PART JAPANESE, RIGHT?
Snicker
THEY SAY GREAT MINDS THINK ALIKE...
Shuddap.
...AND IT'S RYO, BY THE WAY.

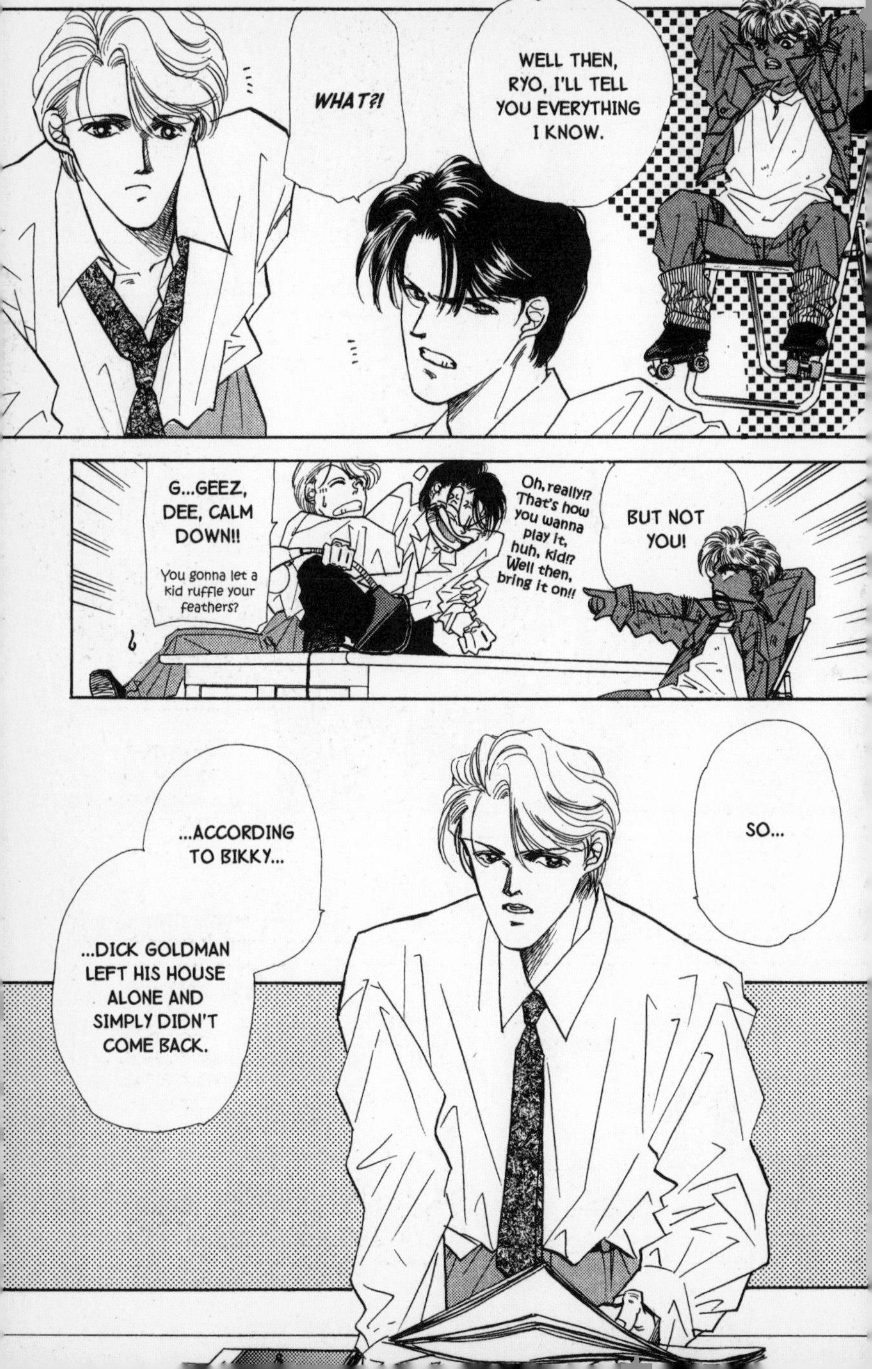
WELL THEN, RYO, I'LL TELL YOU EVERYTHING I KNOW.
WHAT?!
BUT NOT YOU!
Oh, really!? That's how you wanna play it, huh, kid!? Well then, bring it on!!
G...GEEZ, DEE, CALM DOWN!!
You gonna let a kid ruffle your feathers?
SO...
...ACCORDING TO BIKKY...
...DICK GOLDMAN LEFT HIS HOUSE ALONE AND SIMPLY DIDN'T COME BACK.

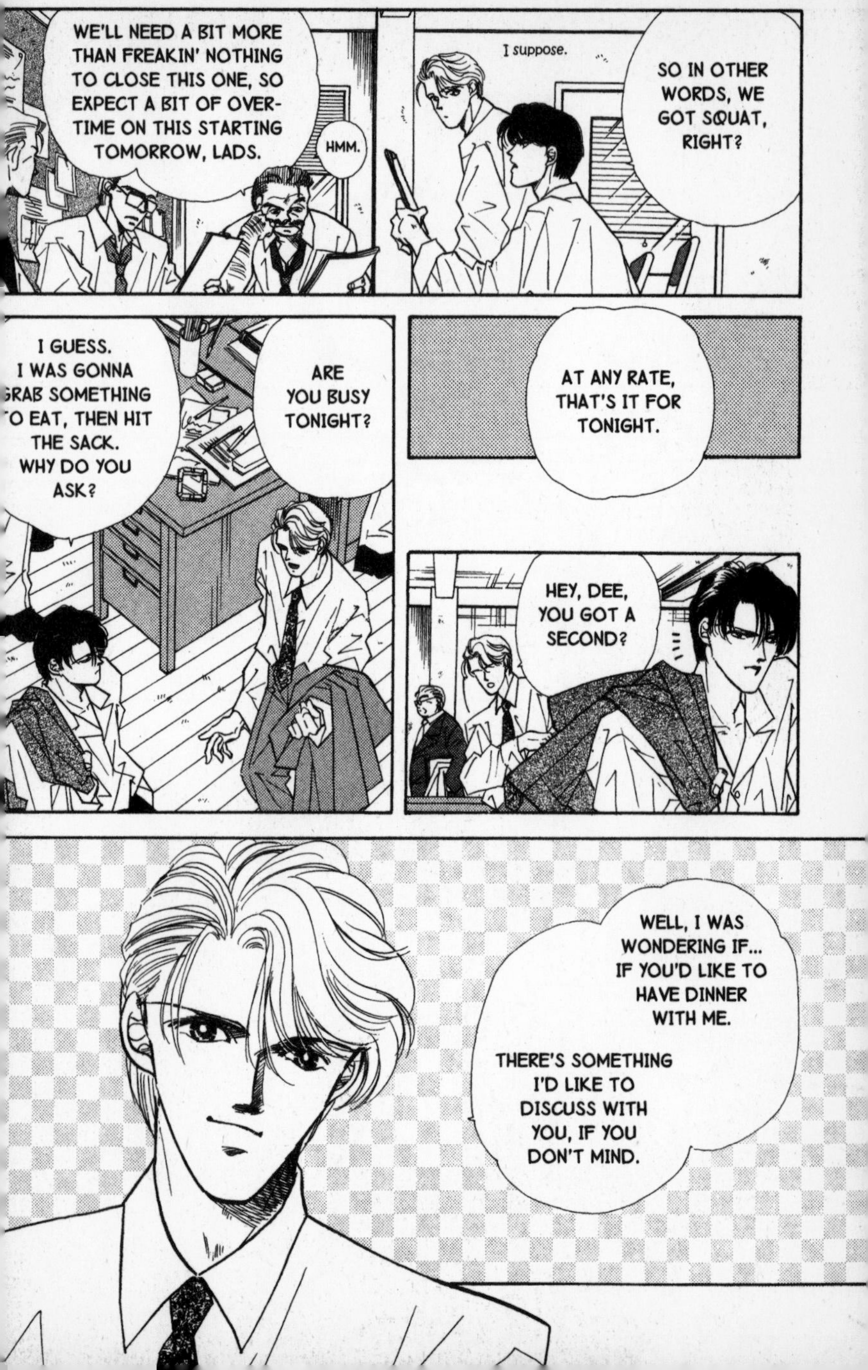
SO IN OTHER WORDS, WE GOT SQUAT, RIGHT?
I suppose.
WE'LL NEED A BIT MORE THAN FREAKIN' NOTHING TO CLOSE THIS ONE, SO EXPECT A BIT OF OVER-TIME ON THIS STARTING TOMORROW, LADS.
HMM.
AT ANY RATE, THAT'S IT FOR TONIGHT.
HEY, DEE, YOU GOT A SECOND?
ARE YOU BUSY TONIGHT?
I GUESS. I WAS GONNA GRAB SOMETHING TO EAT, THEN HIT THE SACK. WHY DO YOU ASK?
WELL, I WAS WONDERING IF... IF YOU'D LIKE TO HAVE DINNER WITH ME.
THERE'S SOMETHING I'D LIKE TO DISCUSS WITH YOU, IF YOU DON'T MIND.

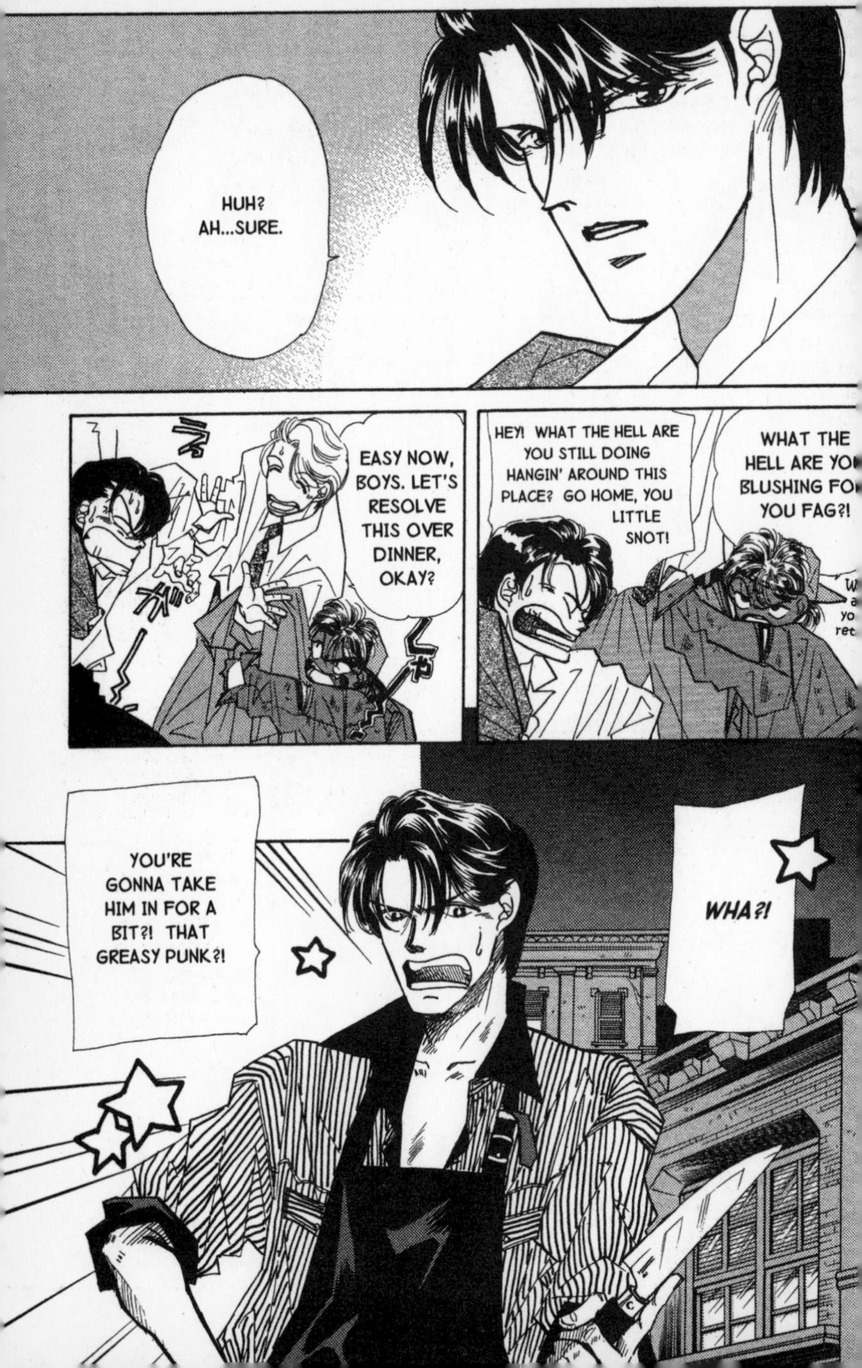
HUH? AH...SURE.
WHAT THE HELL ARE YO BLUSHING FO YOU FAG?!
HEY! WHAT THE HELL ARE YOU STILL DOING HANGIN' AROUND THIS PLACE? GO HOME, YOU LITTLE SNOT!
EASY NOW, BOYS. LET'S RESOLVE THIS OVER DINNER, OKAY?
WHA?!
YOU'RE GONNA TAKE HIM IN FOR A BIT?! THAT GREASY PUNK?!

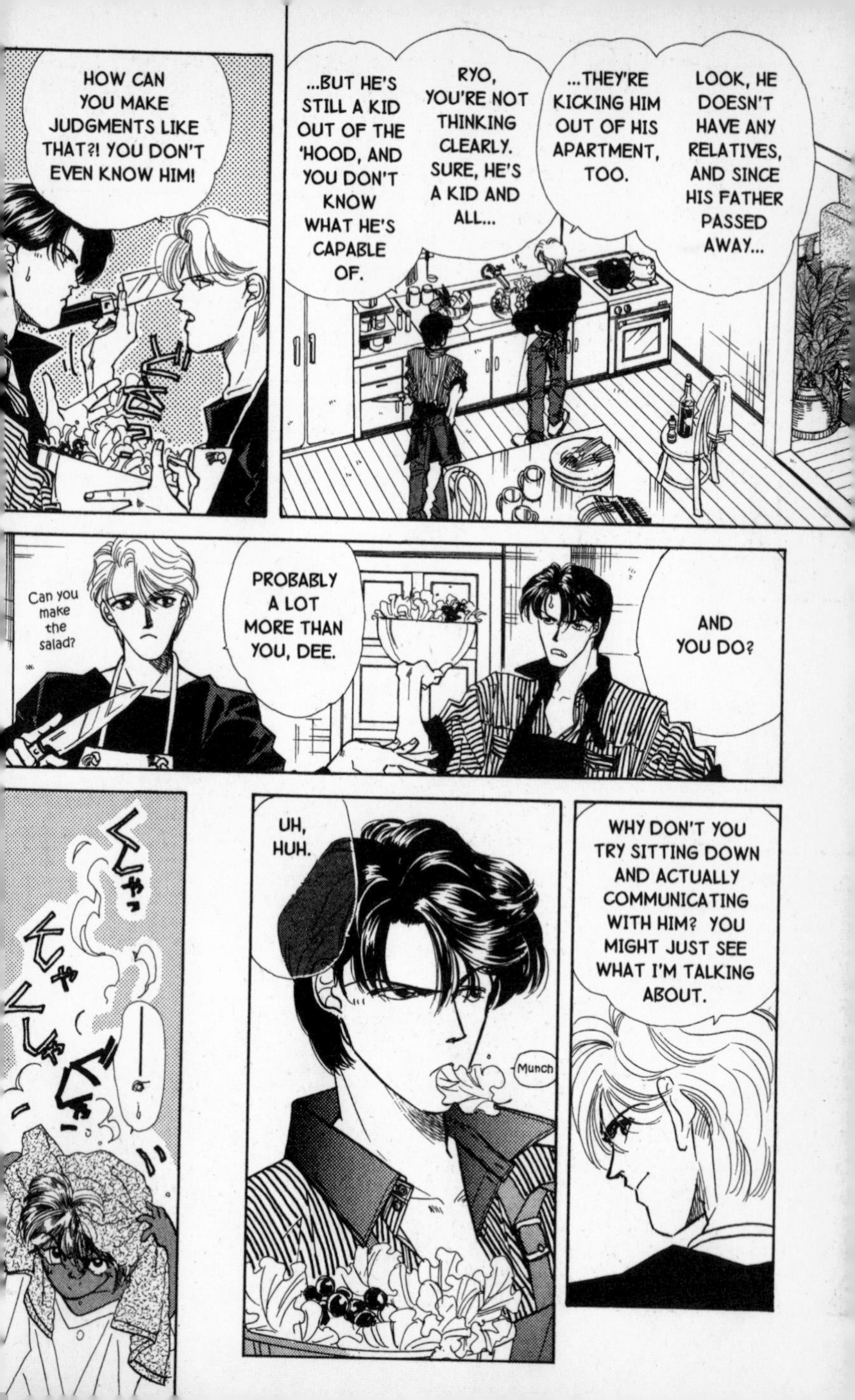

LOOK, HE DOESN'T HAVE ANY RELATIVES, AND SINCE HIS FATHER PASSED AWAY...
...THEY'RE KICKING HIM OUT OF HIS APARTMENT, TOO.
RYO, YOU'RE NOT THINKING CLEARLY. SURE, HE'S A KID AND ALL...
...BUT HE'S STILL A KID OUT OF THE 'HOOD, AND YOU DON'T KNOW WHAT HE'S CAPABLE OF.
HOW CAN YOU MAKE JUDGMENTS LIKE THAT?! YOU DON'T EVEN KNOW HIM!
AND YOU DO?
PROBABLY A LOT MORE THAN YOU, DEE.
Can you make the salad?
WHY DON'T YOU TRY SITTING DOWN AND ACTUALLY COMMUNICATING WITH HIM? YOU MIGHT JUST SEE WHAT I'M TALKING ABOUT.
UH, HUH.
Munch

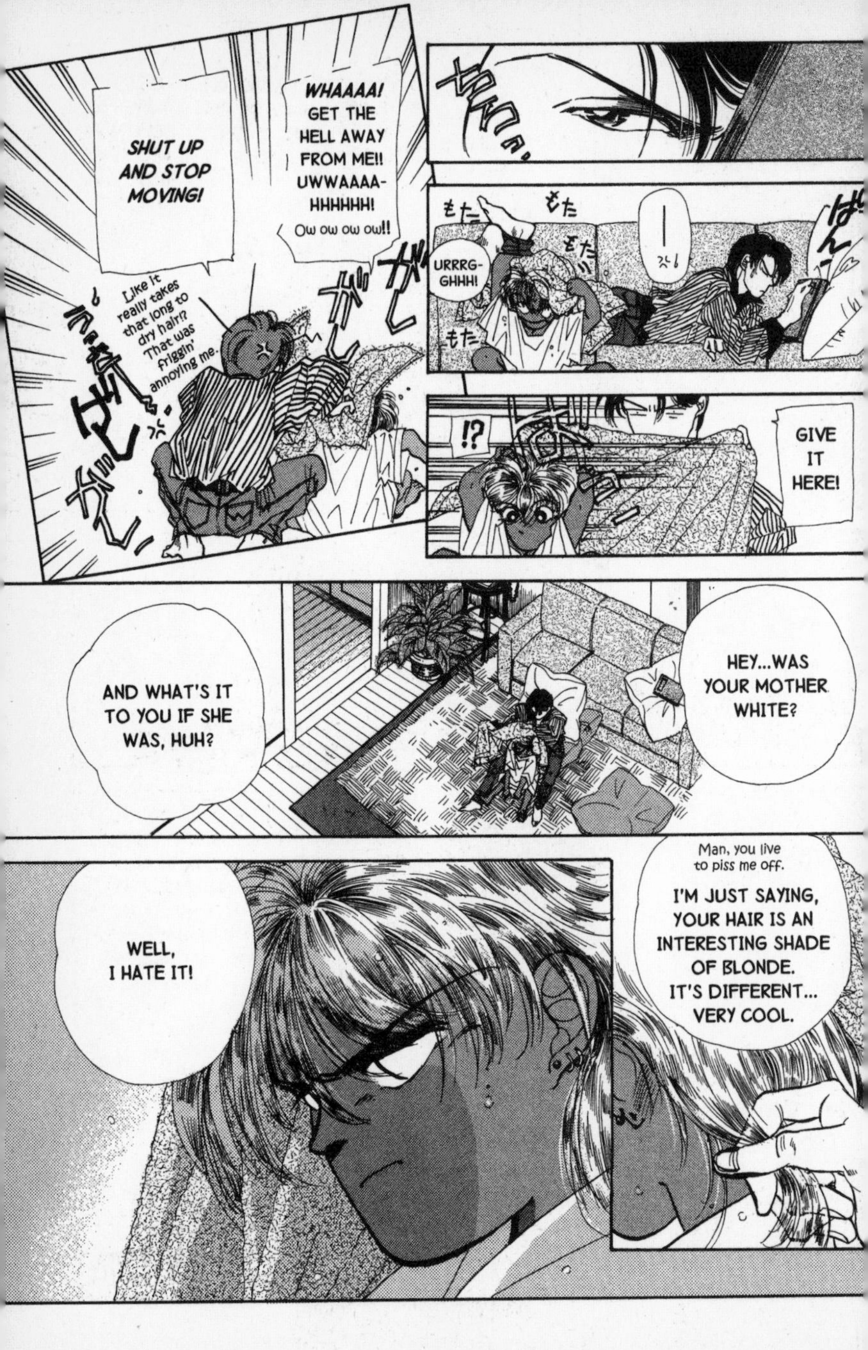

もた
もた
もた
もた
URRRG-GHHH!
!?
GIVE IT HERE!
WHAAAA! GET THE HELL AWAY FROM ME!! UWWAAAA-HHHHHH!
Ow ow ow ow!!
SHUT UP AND STOP MOVING!
Like it really takes that long to dry hair!? That was friggin' annoying me.
HEY...WAS YOUR MOTHER WHITE?
AND WHAT'S IT TO YOU IF SHE WAS, HUH?
Man, you live to piss me off.
I'M JUST SAYING, YOUR HAIR IS AN INTERESTING SHADE OF BLONDE. IT'S DIFFERENT... VERY COOL.
WELL, I HATE IT!

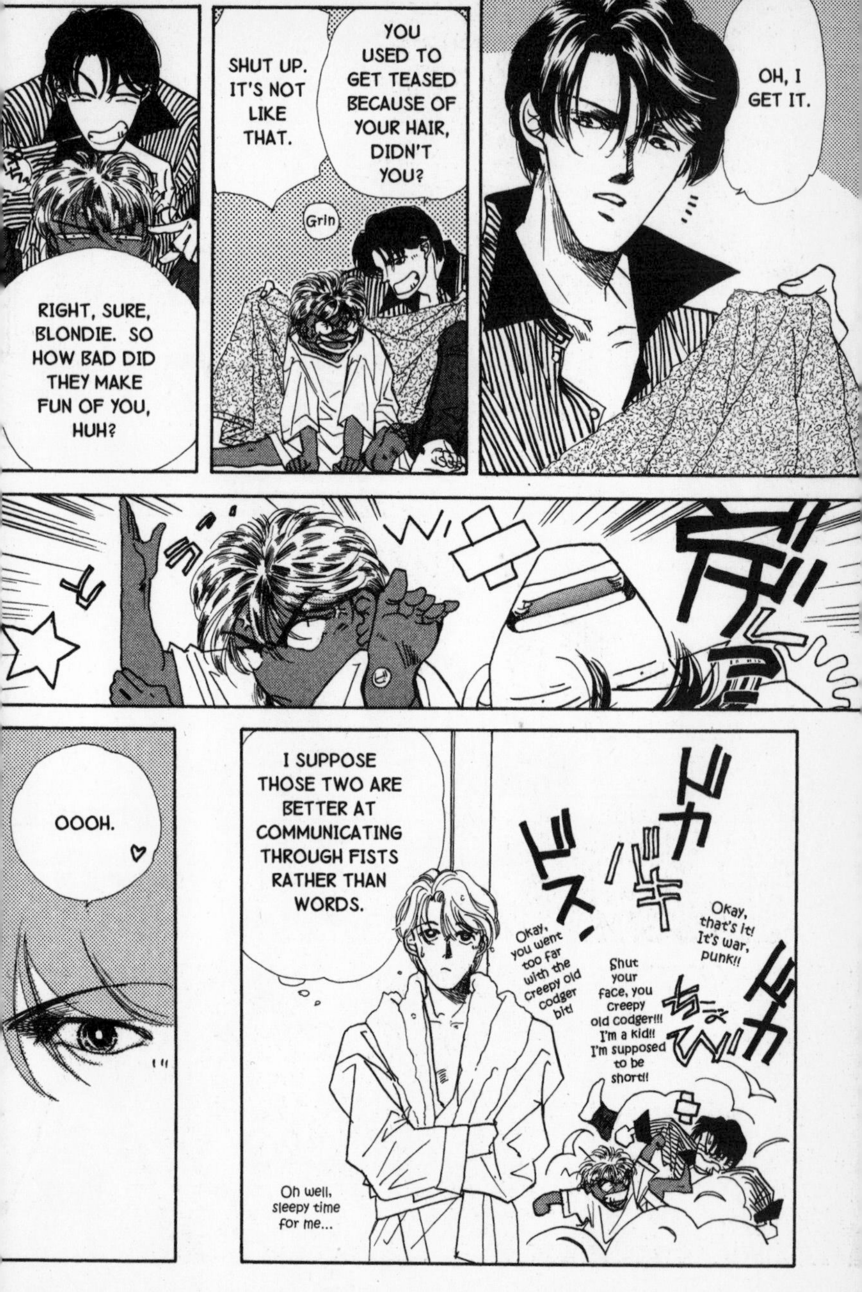
OH, I GET IT.
YOU USED TO GET TEASED BECAUSE OF YOUR HAIR, DIDN'T YOU?
SHUT UP. IT'S NOT LIKE THAT.
Grin
RIGHT, SURE, BLONDIE. SO HOW BAD DID THEY MAKE FUN OF YOU, HUH?
I SUPPOSE THOSE TWO ARE BETTER AT COMMUNICATING THROUGH FISTS RATHER THAN WORDS.
Okay, that's it! It's war, punk!!
Shut your face, you creepy old codger!!! I'm a kid!! I'm supposed to be short!!
Okay, you went too far with the creepy old codger bit!
Oh well, sleepy time for me...
OOOH. ♡

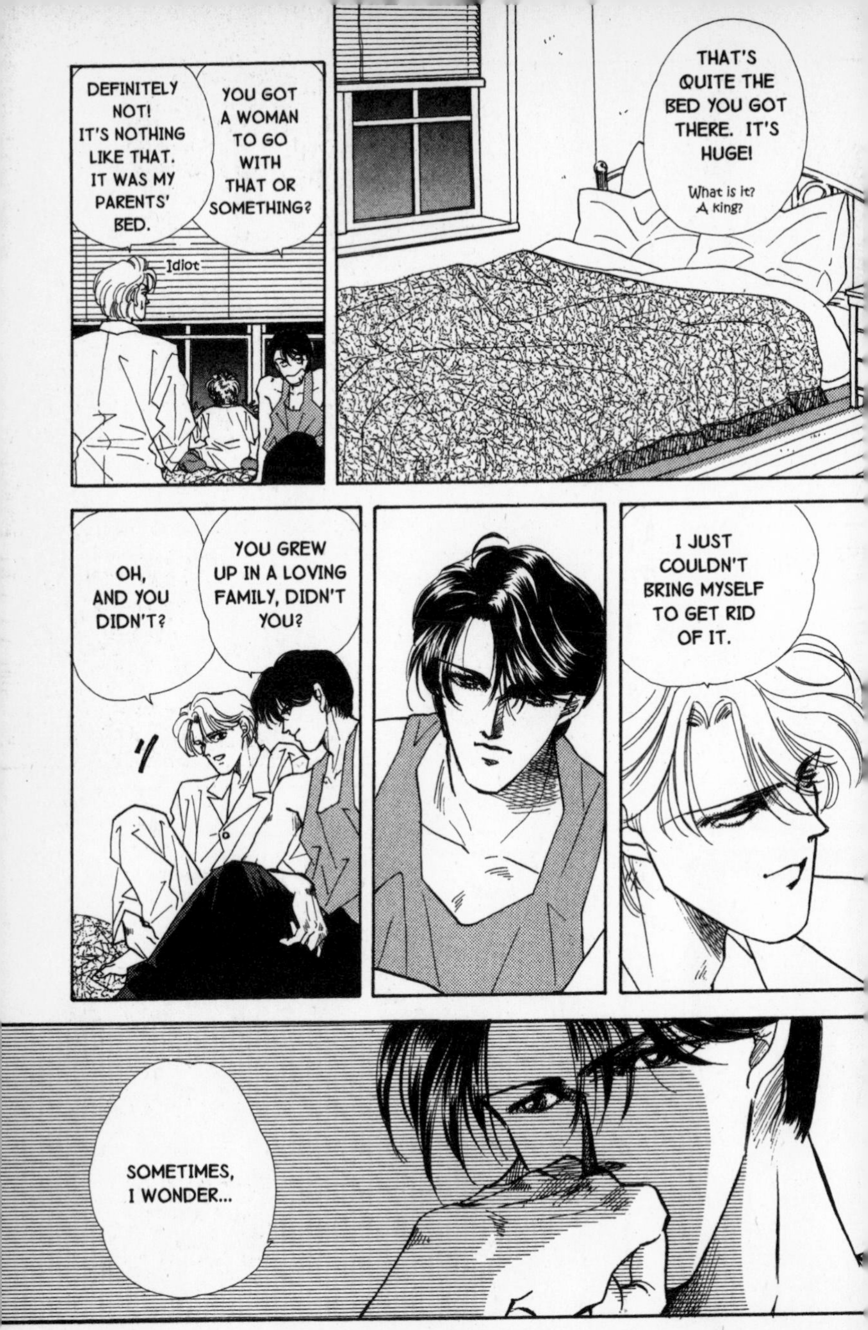
THAT'S QUITE THE BED YOU GOT THERE. IT'S HUGE!
What is it? A king?
YOU GOT A WOMAN TO GO WITH THAT OR SOMETHING?
DEFINITELY NOT! IT'S NOTHING LIKE THAT. IT WAS MY PARENTS' BED.
Idiot
I JUST COULDN'T BRING MYSELF TO GET RID OF IT.
YOU GREW UP IN A LOVING FAMILY, DIDN'T YOU?
OH, AND YOU DIDN'T?
SOMETIMES, I WONDER...

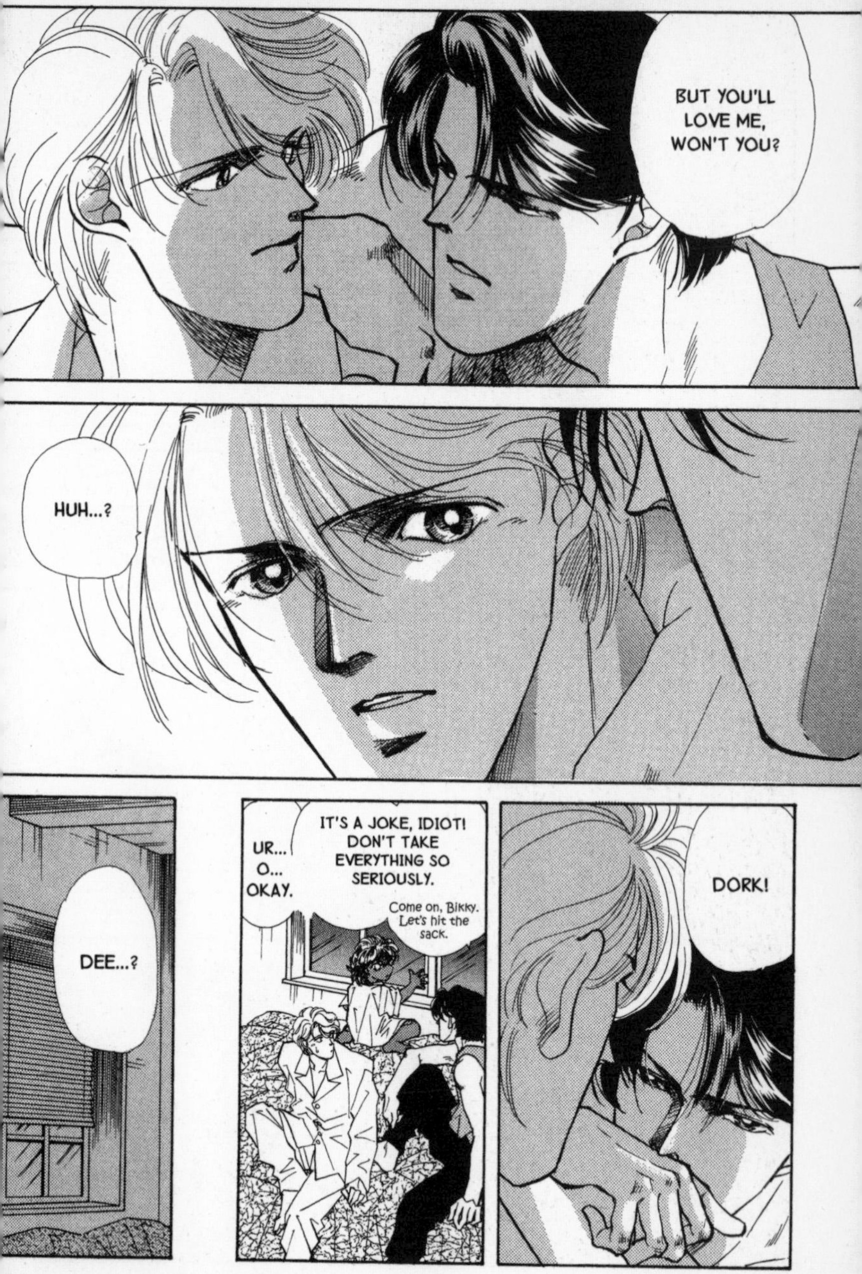
BUT YOU'LL LOVE ME, WON'T YOU?
HUH...?
DORK!
IT'S A JOKE, IDIOT! DON'T TAKE EVERYTHING SO SERIOUSLY.
UR... O... OKAY.
Come on, Bikky. Let's hit the sack.
DEE...?

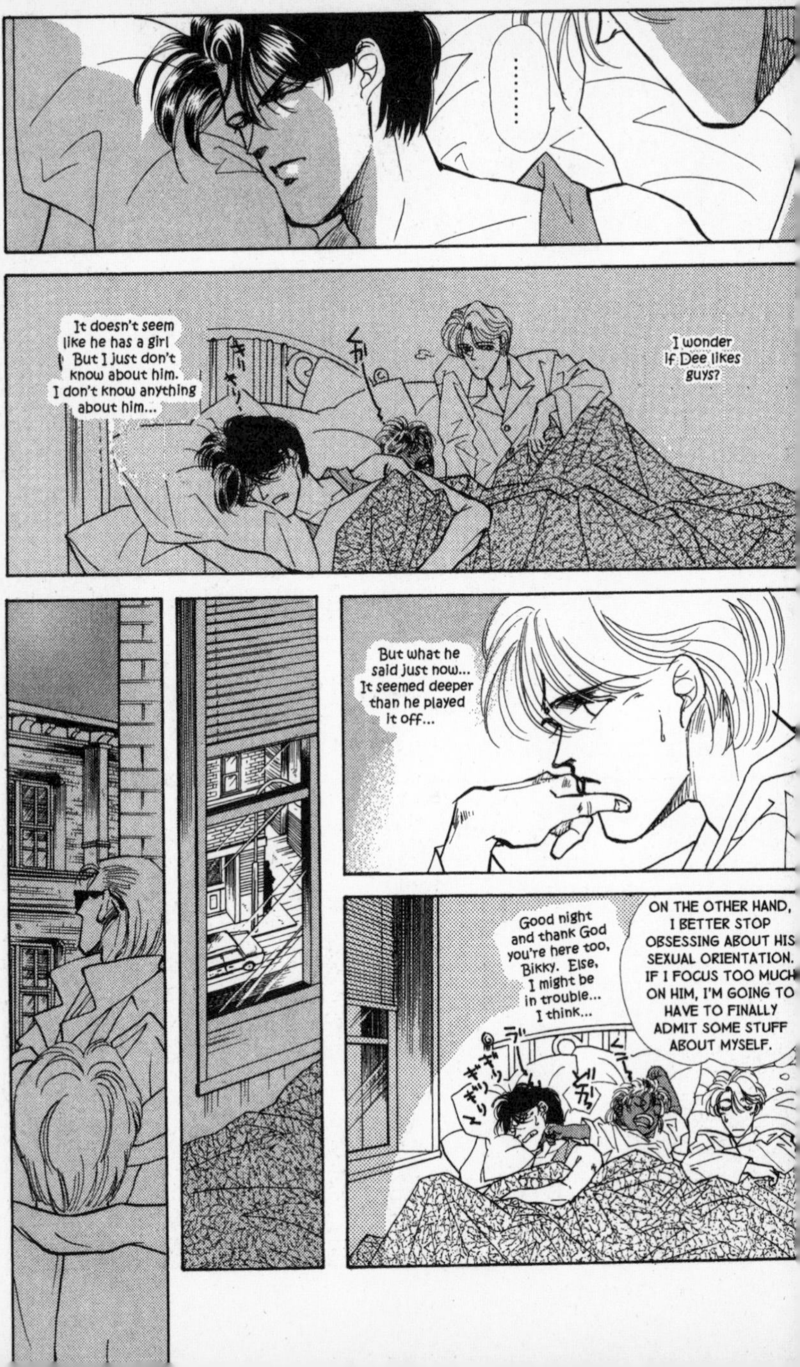
......
I wonder if Dee likes guys?
It doesn't seem like he has a girl But I just don't know about him. I don't know anything about him...
But what he said just now... It seemed deeper than he played it off...
ON THE OTHER HAND, I BETTER STOP OBSESSING ABOUT HIS SEXUAL ORIENTATION. IF I FOCUS TOO MUCH ON HIM, I'M GOING TO HAVE TO FINALLY ADMIT SOME STUFF ABOUT MYSELF.
Good night and thank God you're here too, Bikky. Else, I might be in trouble... I think...

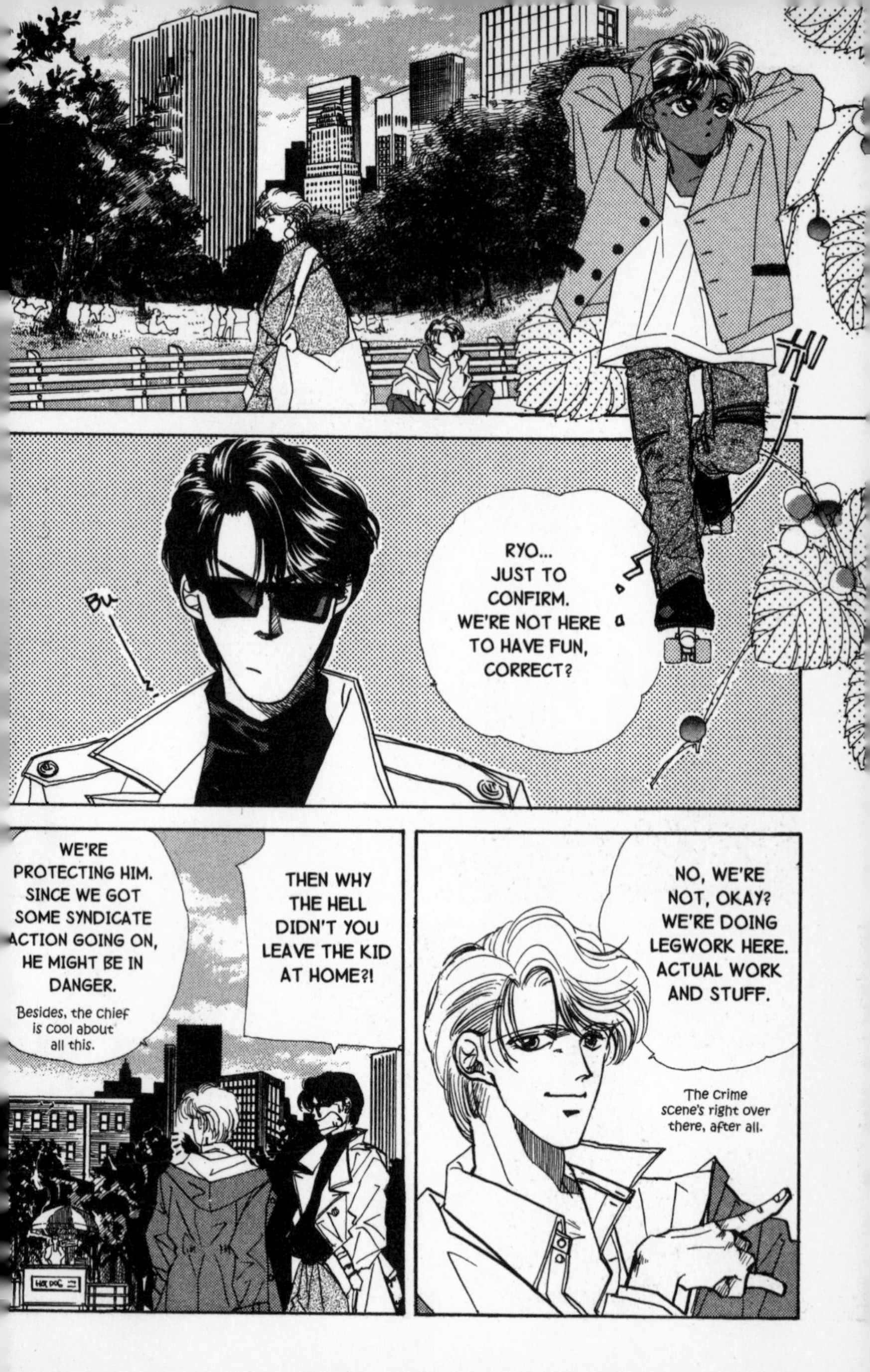
RYO... JUST TO CONFIRM. WE'RE NOT HERE TO HAVE FUN, CORRECT?
BU
NO, WE'RE NOT, OKAY? WE'RE DOING LEGWORK HERE. ACTUAL WORK AND STUFF.
The crime scene's right over there, after all.
THEN WHY THE HELL DIDN'T YOU LEAVE THE KID AT HOME?!
WE'RE PROTECTING HIM. SINCE WE GOT SOME SYNDICATE ACTION GOING ON, HE MIGHT BE IN DANGER.
Besides, the chief is cool about all this.

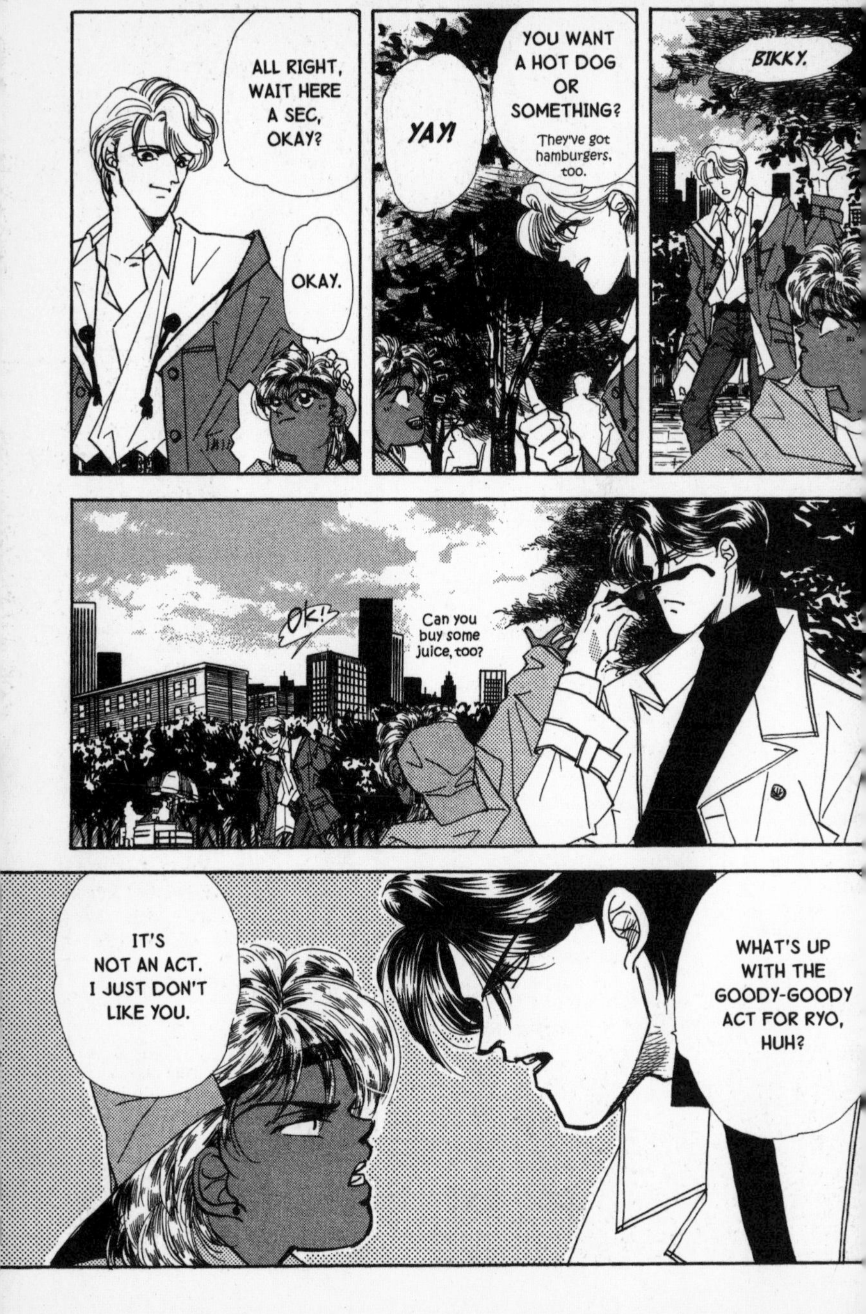
BIKKY.
YOU WANT A HOT DOG OR SOMETHING?
They've got hamburgers, too.
YAY!
ALL RIGHT, WAIT HERE A SEC, OKAY?
OKAY.
Can you buy some juice, too?
OK!
WHAT'S UP WITH THE GOODY-GOODY ACT FOR RYO, HUH?
IT'S NOT AN ACT. I JUST DON'T LIKE YOU.

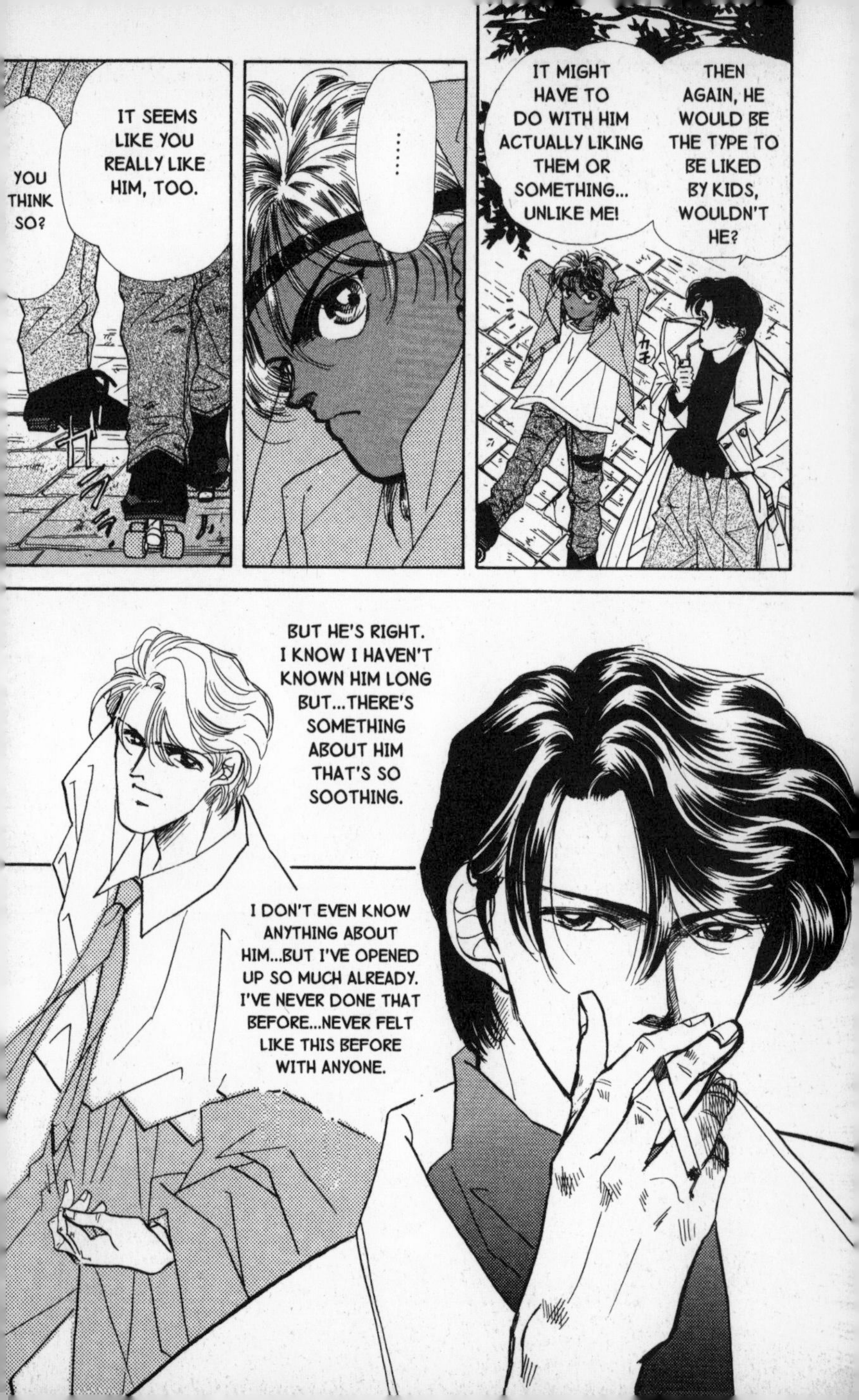
THEN AGAIN, HE WOULD BE THE TYPE TO BE LIKED BY KIDS, WOULDN'T HE?
IT MIGHT HAVE TO DO WITH HIM ACTUALLY LIKING THEM OR SOMETHING... UNLIKE ME!
......
IT SEEMS LIKE YOU REALLY LIKE HIM, TOO.
YOU THINK SO?
BUT HE'S RIGHT. I KNOW I HAVEN'T KNOWN HIM LONG BUT...THERE'S SOMETHING ABOUT HIM THAT'S SO SOOTHING.
I DON'T EVEN KNOW ANYTHING ABOUT HIM...BUT I'VE OPENED UP SO MUCH ALREADY. I'VE NEVER DONE THAT BEFORE...NEVER FELT LIKE THIS BEFORE WITH ANYONE.

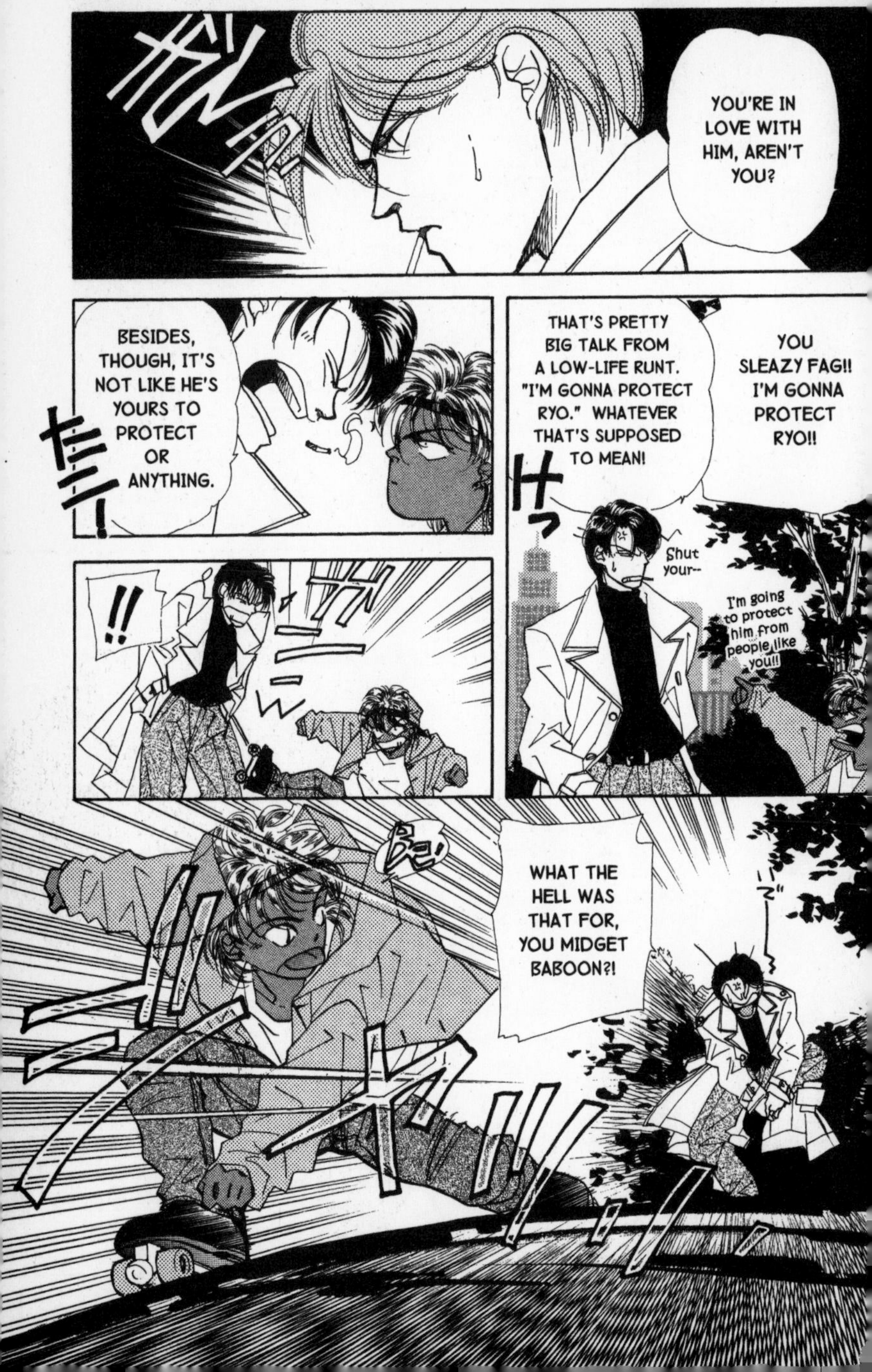

YOU'RE IN LOVE WITH HIM, AREN'T YOU?
YOU SLEAZY FAG!! I'M GONNA PROTECT RYO!!
THAT'S PRETTY BIG TALK FROM A LOW-LIFE RUNT. "I'M GONNA PROTECT RYO." WHATEVER THAT'S SUPPOSED TO MEAN!
Shut your--
I'm going to protect him from people like you!!
BESIDES, THOUGH, IT'S NOT LIKE HE'S YOURS TO PROTECT OR ANYTHING.
!!
WHAT THE HELL WAS THAT FOR, YOU MIDGET BABOON?!

AS IF.

COME BACK HERE, YOU LITTLE SNOT!

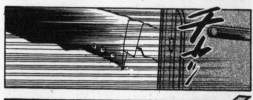

BIKKY!!

LEMME GO!! LEMME GO, YOU BASTARD!!

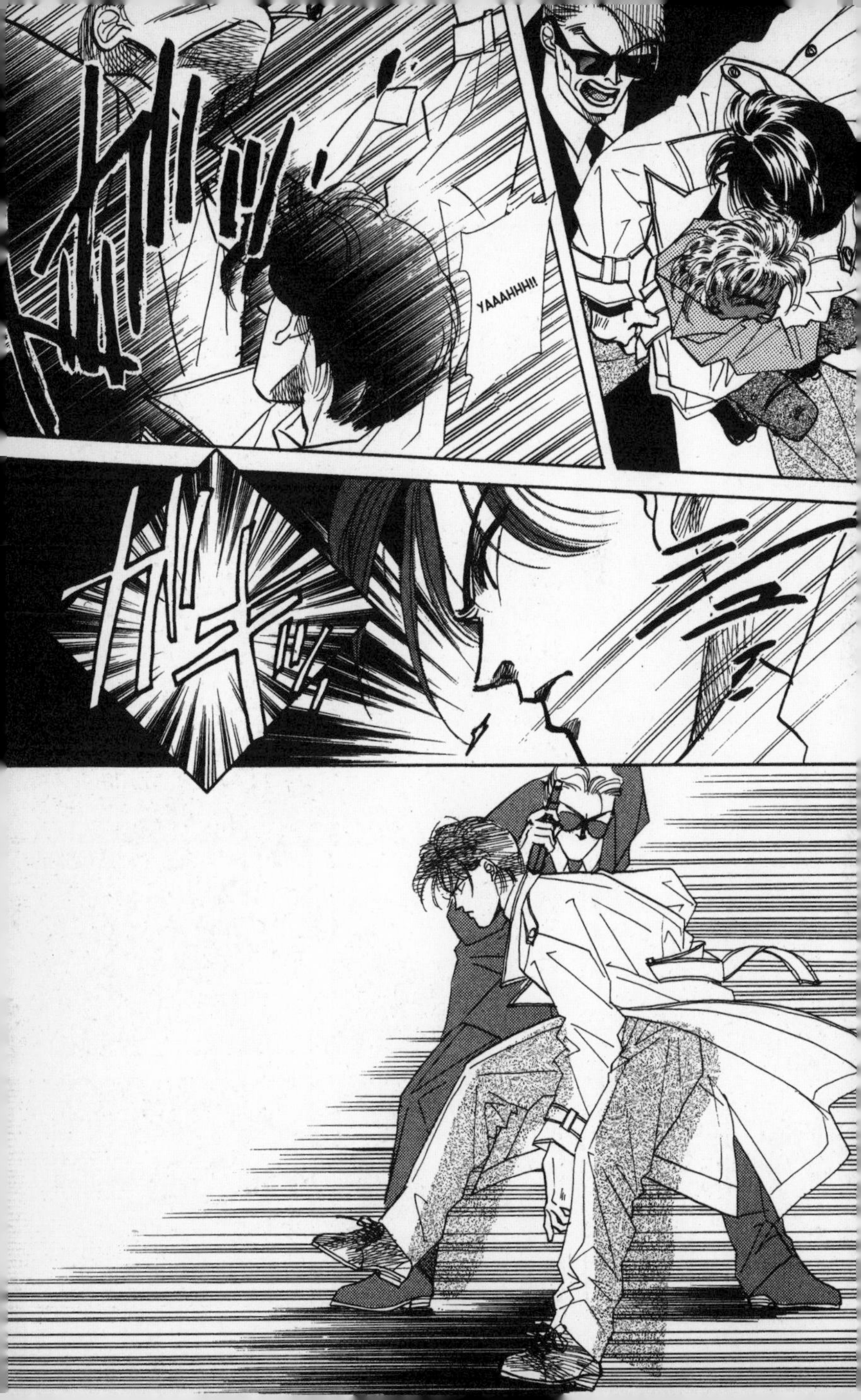
YAAAHHH!!

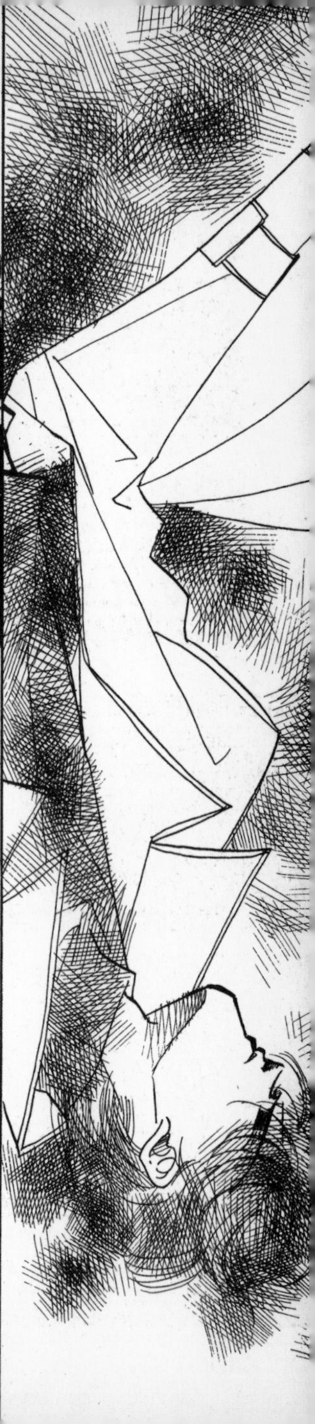

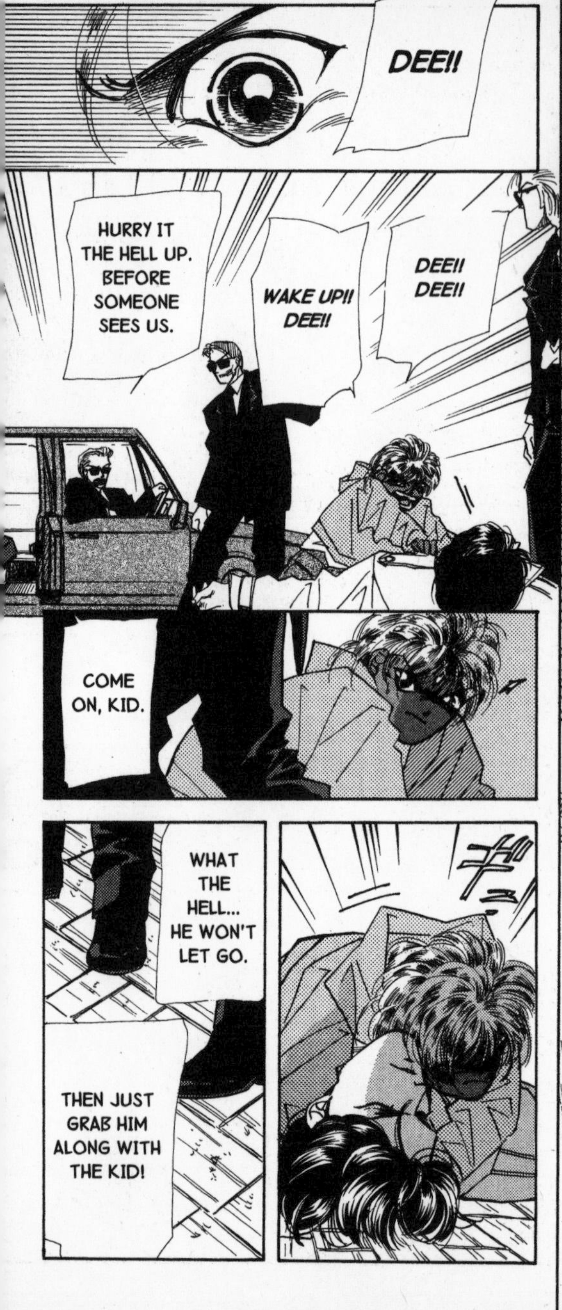

DEE!!
DEE!! DEE!!
WAKE UP!! DEE!!
HURRY IT THE HELL UP. BEFORE SOMEONE SEES US.
COME ON, KID.
WHAT THE HELL... HE WON'T LET GO.
THEN JUST GRAB HIM ALONG WITH THE KID!

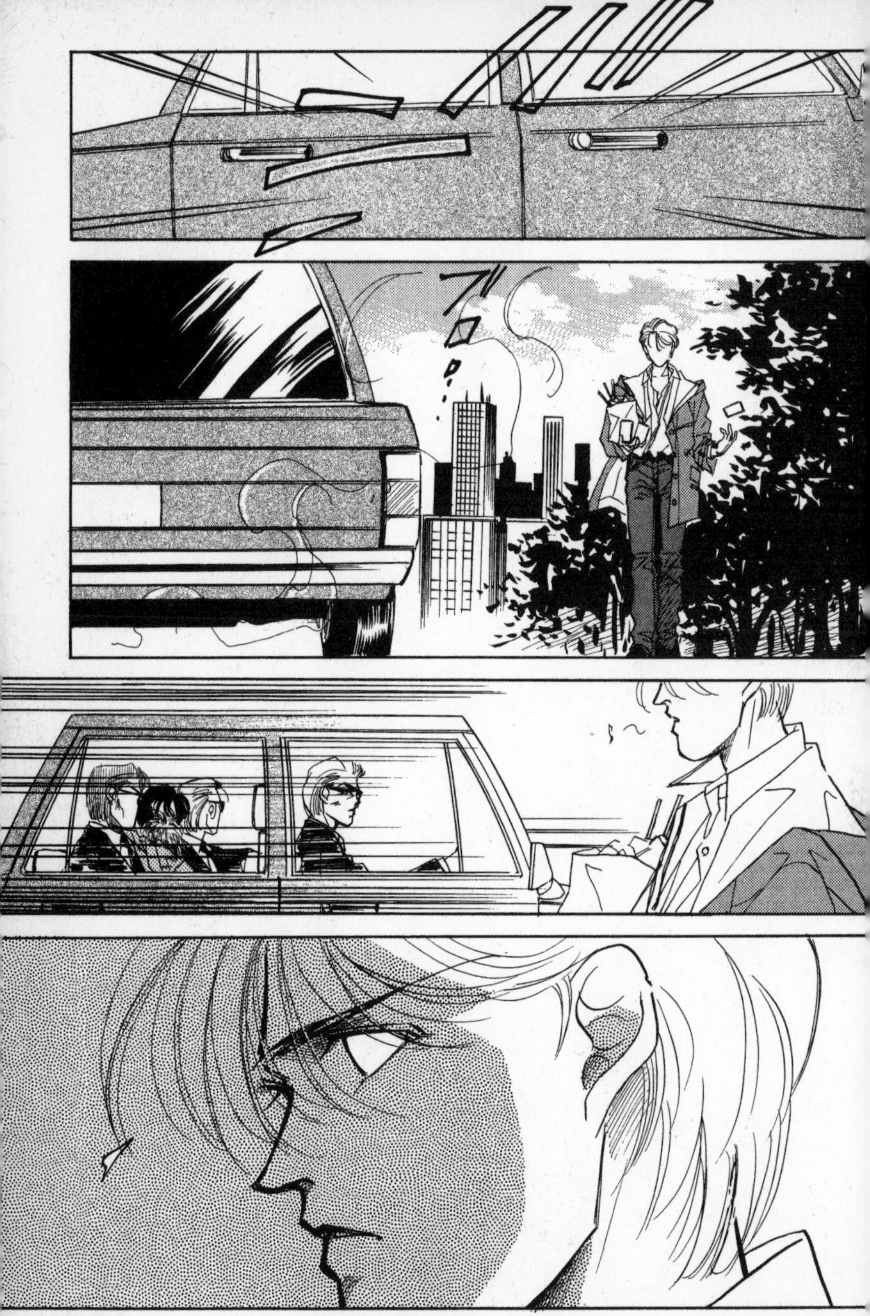
ブロ…

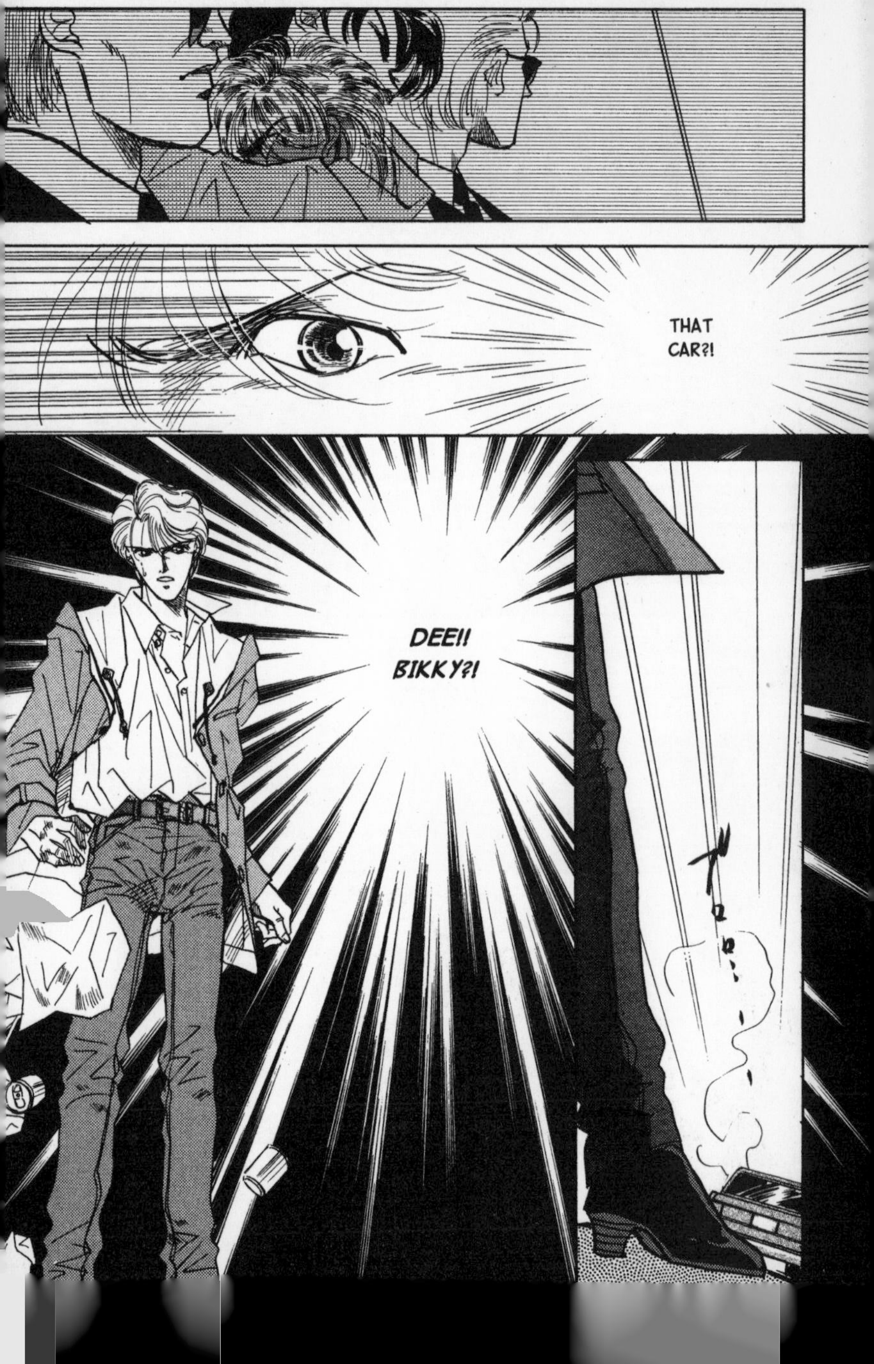
THAT CAR?!
DEE!! BIKKY?!

FAKE

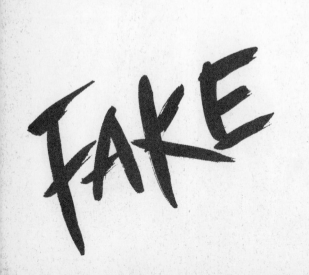

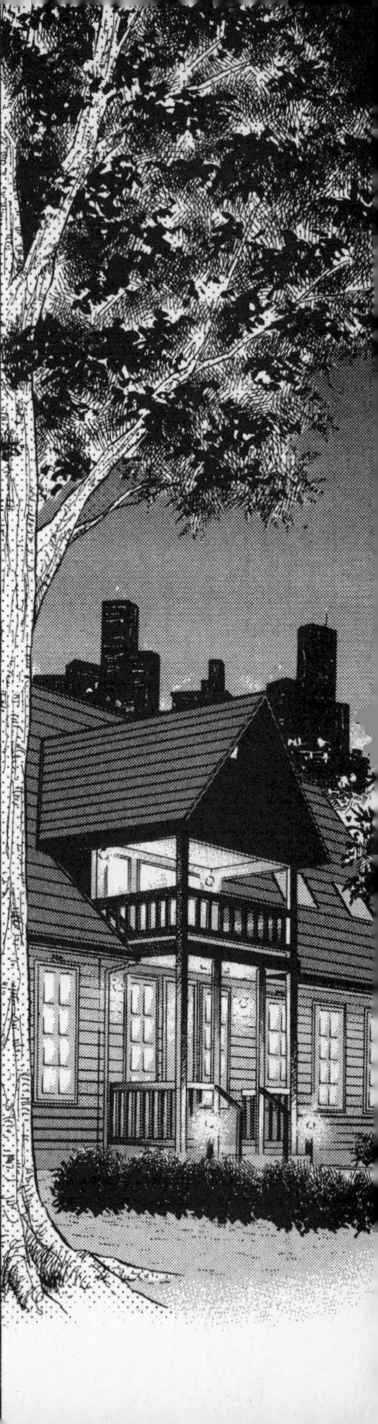

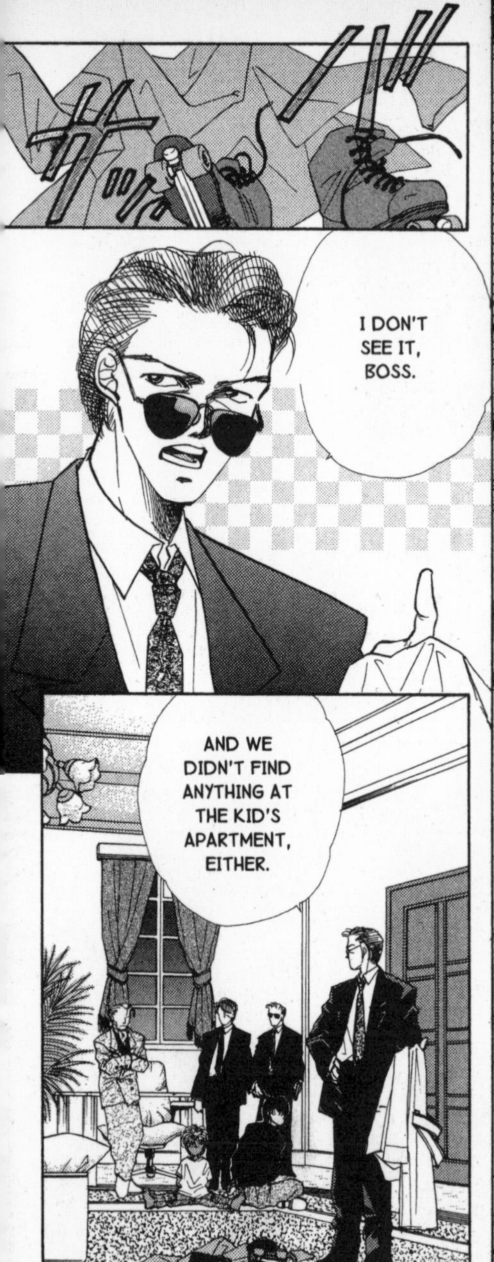

I DON'T SEE IT, BOSS.
AND WE DIDN'T FIND ANYTHING AT THE KID'S APARTMENT, EITHER.

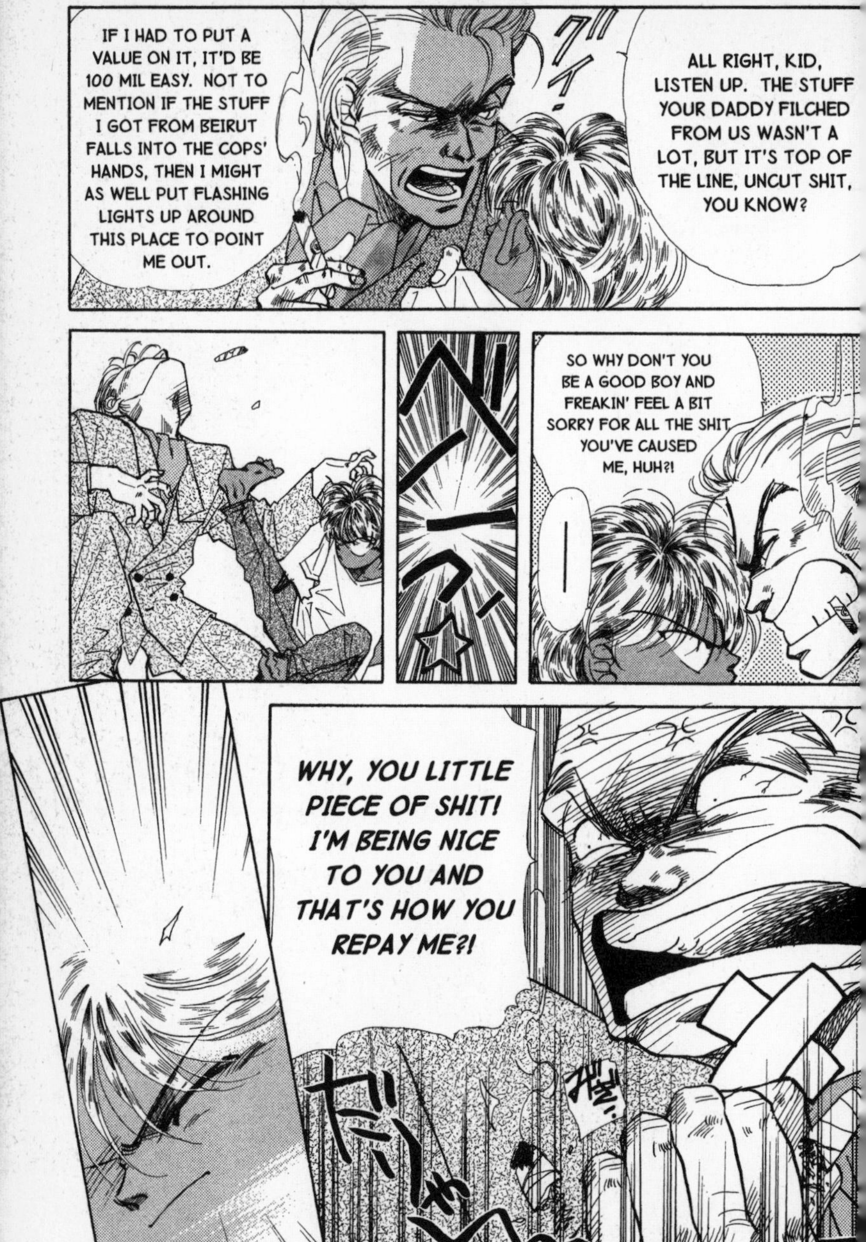
ALL RIGHT, KID, LISTEN UP. THE STUFF YOUR DADDY FILCHED FROM US WASN'T A LOT, BUT IT'S TOP OF THE LINE, UNCUT SHIT, YOU KNOW?
IF I HAD TO PUT A VALUE ON IT, IT'D BE 100 MIL EASY. NOT TO MENTION IF THE STUFF I GOT FROM BEIRUT FALLS INTO THE COPS' HANDS, THEN I MIGHT AS WELL PUT FLASHING LIGHTS UP AROUND THIS PLACE TO POINT ME OUT.
SO WHY DON'T YOU BE A GOOD BOY AND FREAKIN' FEEL A BIT SORRY FOR ALL THE SHIT YOU'VE CAUSED ME, HUH?!
WHY, YOU LITTLE PIECE OF SHIT! I'M BEING NICE TO YOU AND THAT'S HOW YOU REPAY ME?!

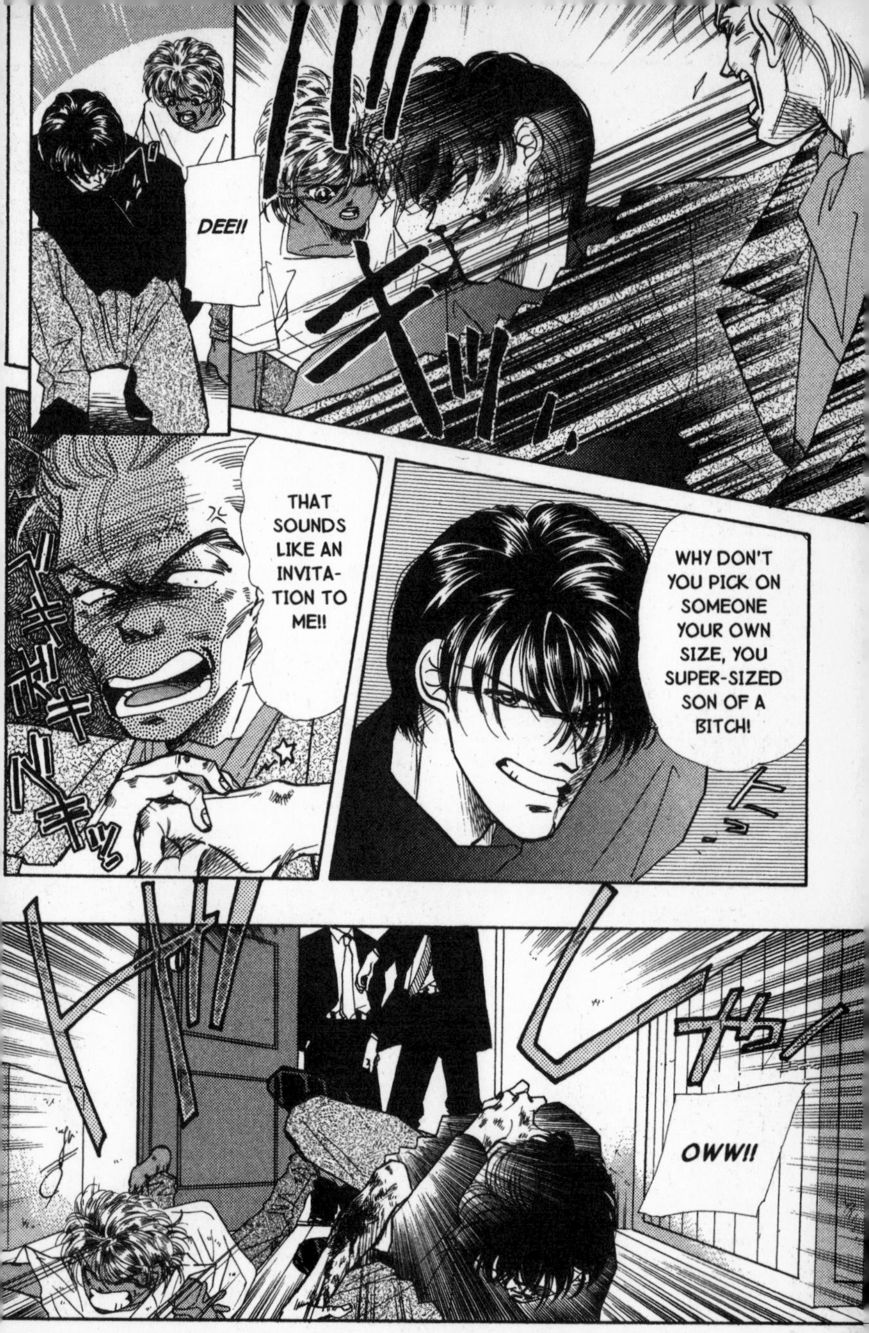
DEE!!
WHY DON'T YOU PICK ON SOMEONE YOUR OWN SIZE, YOU SUPER-SIZED SON OF A BITCH!
THAT SOUNDS LIKE AN INVITA-TION TO ME!!
OWW!!

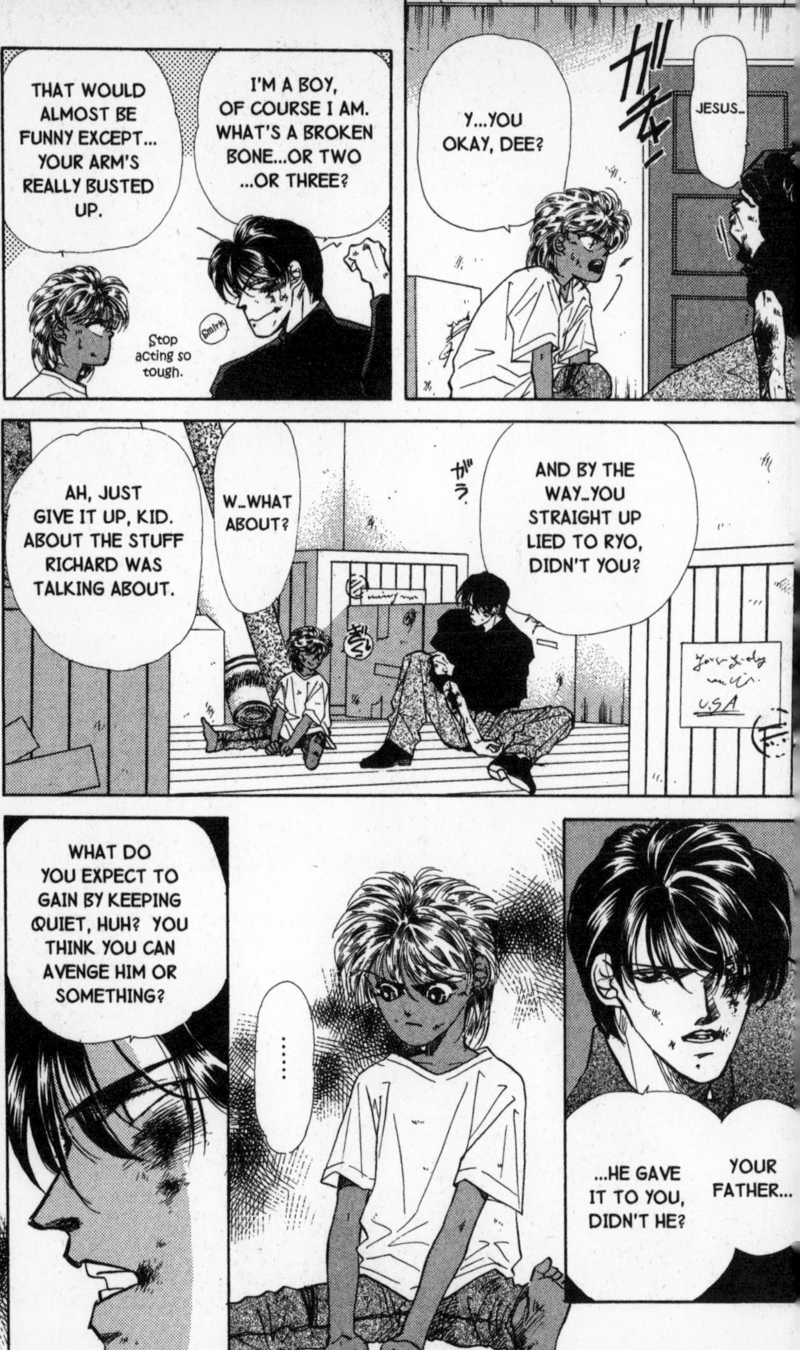
JESUS...
Y...YOU OKAY, DEE?
I'M A BOY, OF COURSE I AM. WHAT'S A BROKEN BONE...OR TWO ...OR THREE?
THAT WOULD ALMOST BE FUNNY EXCEPT... YOUR ARM'S REALLY BUSTED UP.
Smirk
Stop acting so tough.
AND BY THE WAY..YOU STRAIGHT UP LIED TO RYO, DIDN'T YOU?
W..WHAT ABOUT?
AH, JUST GIVE IT UP, KID. ABOUT THE STUFF RICHARD WAS TALKING ABOUT.
U.S.A
YOUR FATHER...
...HE GAVE IT TO YOU, DIDN'T HE?
......
WHAT DO YOU EXPECT TO GAIN BY KEEPING QUIET, HUH? YOU THINK YOU CAN AVENGE HIM OR SOMETHING?

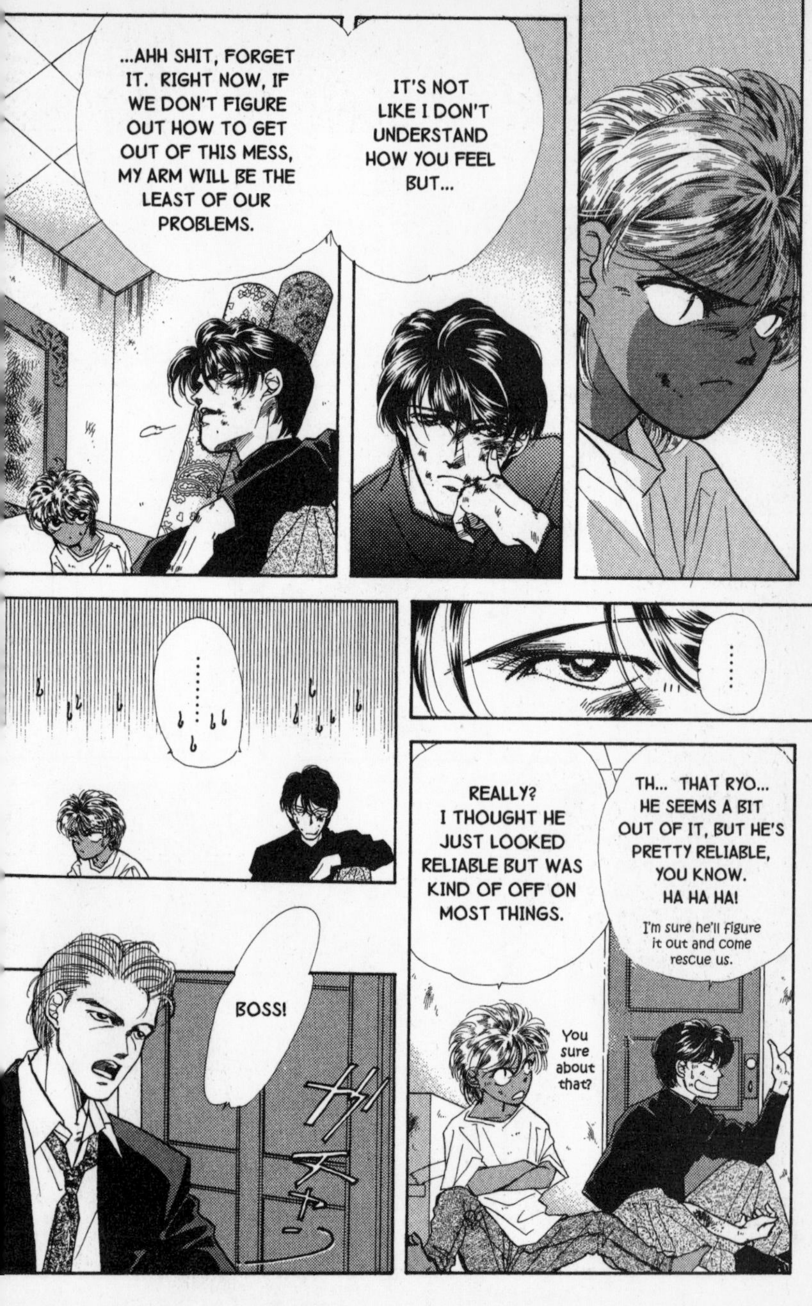
IT'S NOT LIKE I DON'T UNDERSTAND HOW YOU FEEL BUT...
...AHH SHIT, FORGET IT. RIGHT NOW, IF WE DON'T FIGURE OUT HOW TO GET OUT OF THIS MESS, MY ARM WILL BE THE LEAST OF OUR PROBLEMS.
......
......
TH... THAT RYO... HE SEEMS A BIT OUT OF IT, BUT HE'S PRETTY RELIABLE, YOU KNOW. HA HA HA!
I'm sure he'll figure it out and come rescue us.
REALLY? I THOUGHT HE JUST LOOKED RELIABLE BUT WAS KIND OF OFF ON MOST THINGS.
You sure about that?
BOSS!

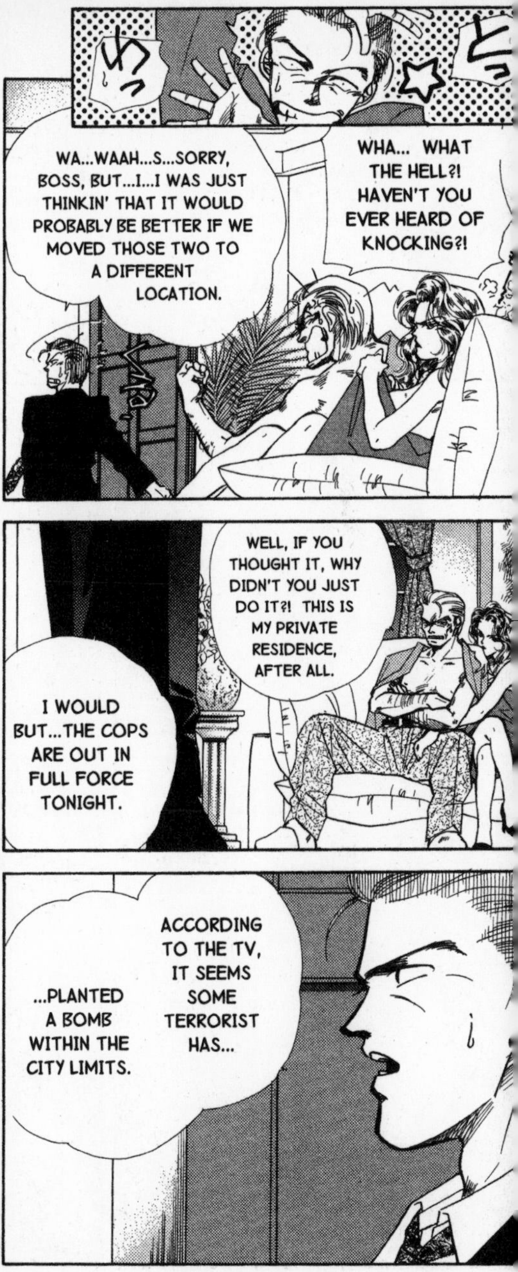
WHA... WHAT THE HELL?! HAVEN'T YOU EVER HEARD OF KNOCKING?!
WA...WAAH...S...SORRY, BOSS, BUT...I...I WAS JUST THINKIN' THAT IT WOULD PROBABLY BE BETTER IF WE MOVED THOSE TWO TO A DIFFERENT LOCATION.
WELL, IF YOU THOUGHT IT, WHY DIDN'T YOU JUST DO IT?! THIS IS MY PRIVATE RESIDENCE, AFTER ALL.
I WOULD BUT...THE COPS ARE OUT IN FULL FORCE TONIGHT.
ACCORDING TO THE TV, IT SEEMS SOME TERRORIST HAS...
...PLANTED A BOMB WITHIN THE CITY LIMITS.

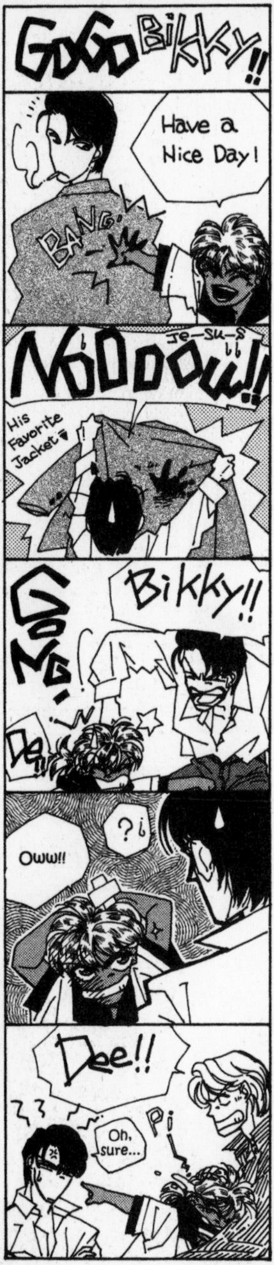
GoGo Bikky!!
Have a Nice Day!
BANG
Je-su-s
NOOOOW!!
His Favorite Jacket
Bikky!!
GONG
Oww!!
?¡
Dee!!
Oh, sure...
Pi

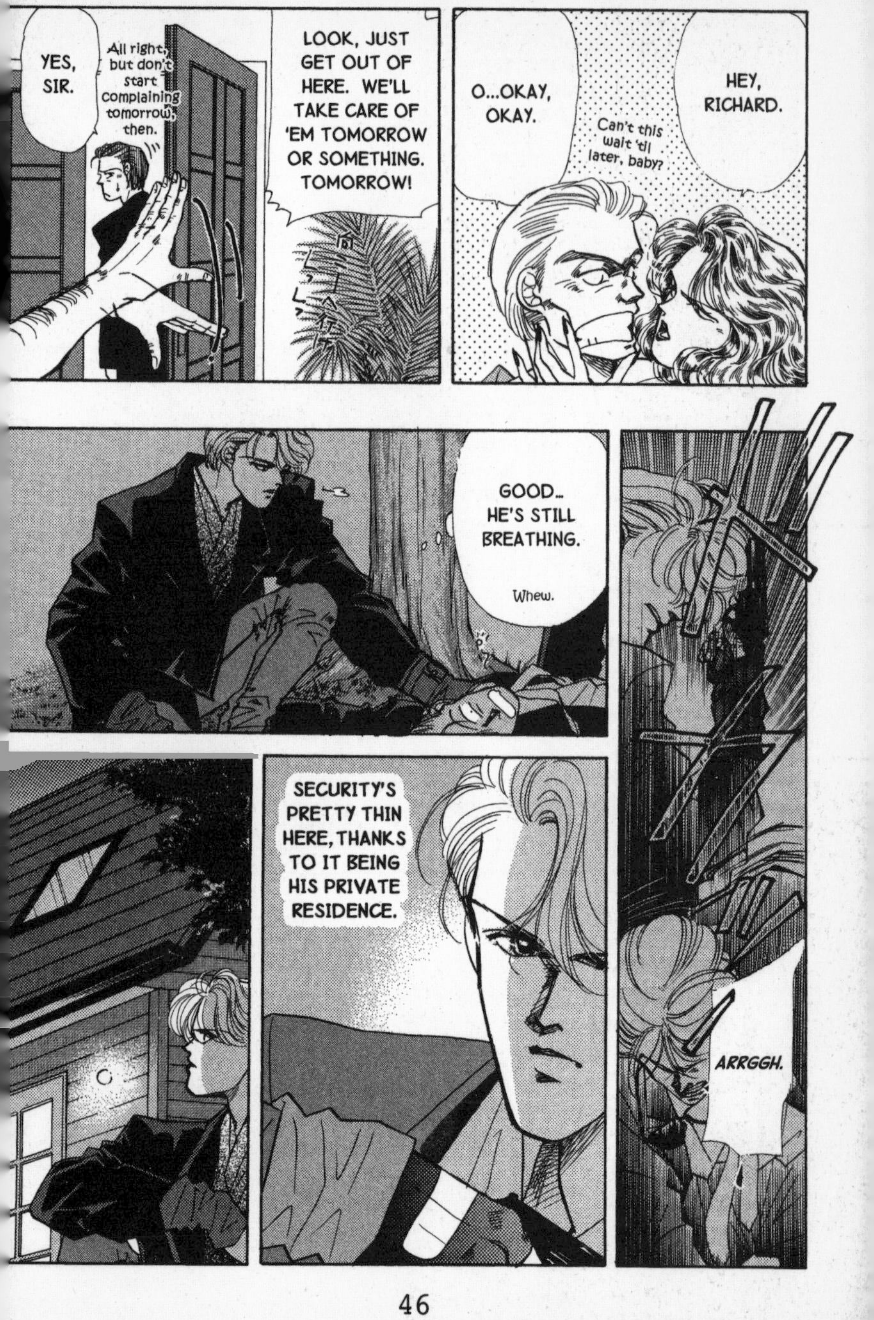
HEY, RICHARD.
Can't this wait 'til later, baby?
O...OKAY, OKAY.
LOOK, JUST GET OUT OF HERE. WE'LL TAKE CARE OF 'EM TOMORROW OR SOMETHING. TOMORROW!
All right, but don't start complaining tomorrow, then.
YES, SIR.
ARRGGH.
GOOD.. HE'S STILL BREATHING.
Whew.
SECURITY'S PRETTY THIN HERE, THANKS TO IT BEING HIS PRIVATE RESIDENCE.

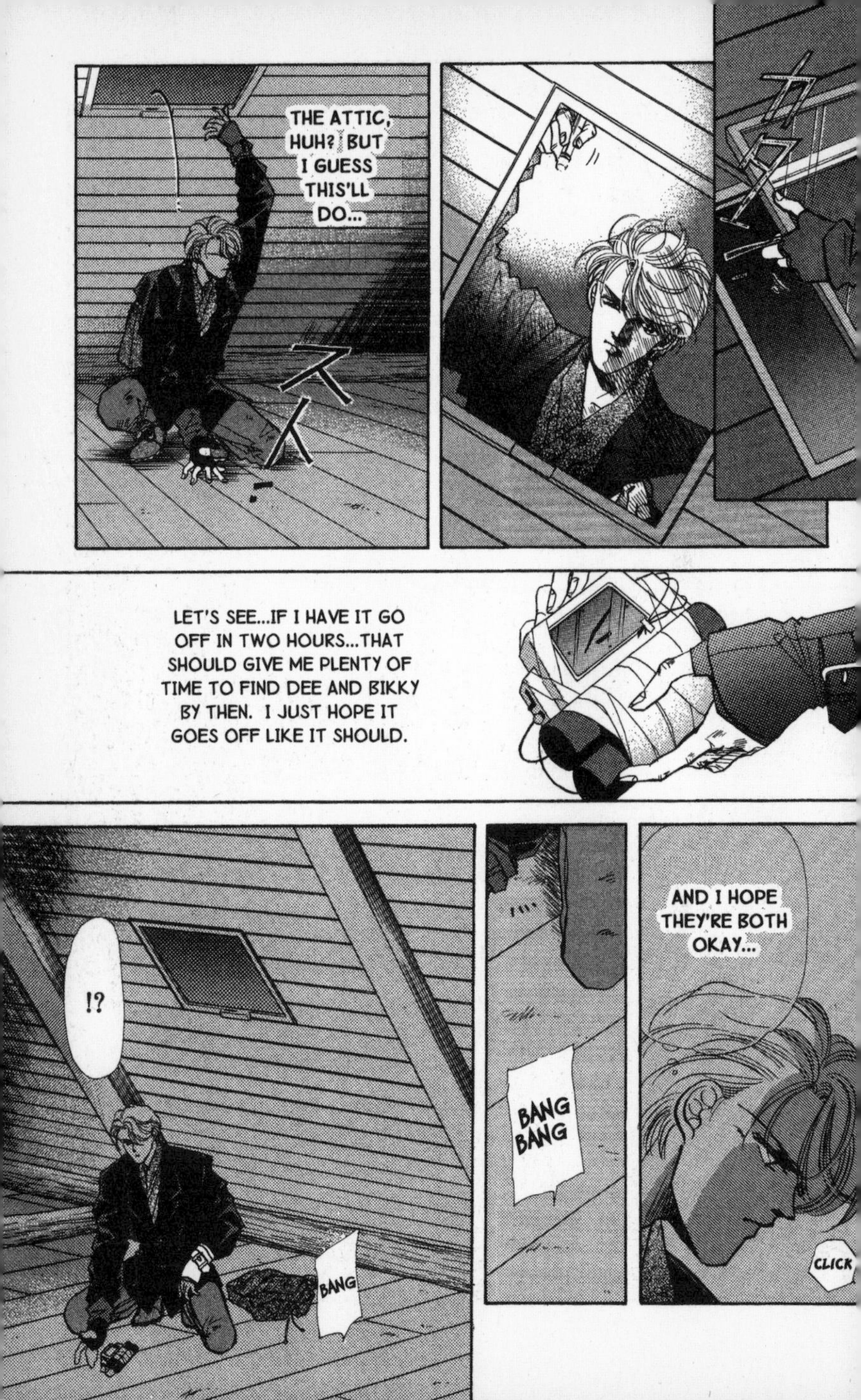
THE ATTIC, HUH? BUT I GUESS THIS'LL DO...
LET'S SEE...IF I HAVE IT GO OFF IN TWO HOURS...THAT SHOULD GIVE ME PLENTY OF TIME TO FIND DEE AND BIKKY BY THEN. I JUST HOPE IT GOES OFF LIKE IT SHOULD.
AND I HOPE THEY'RE BOTH OKAY...
CLICK
BANG BANG
!?
BANG

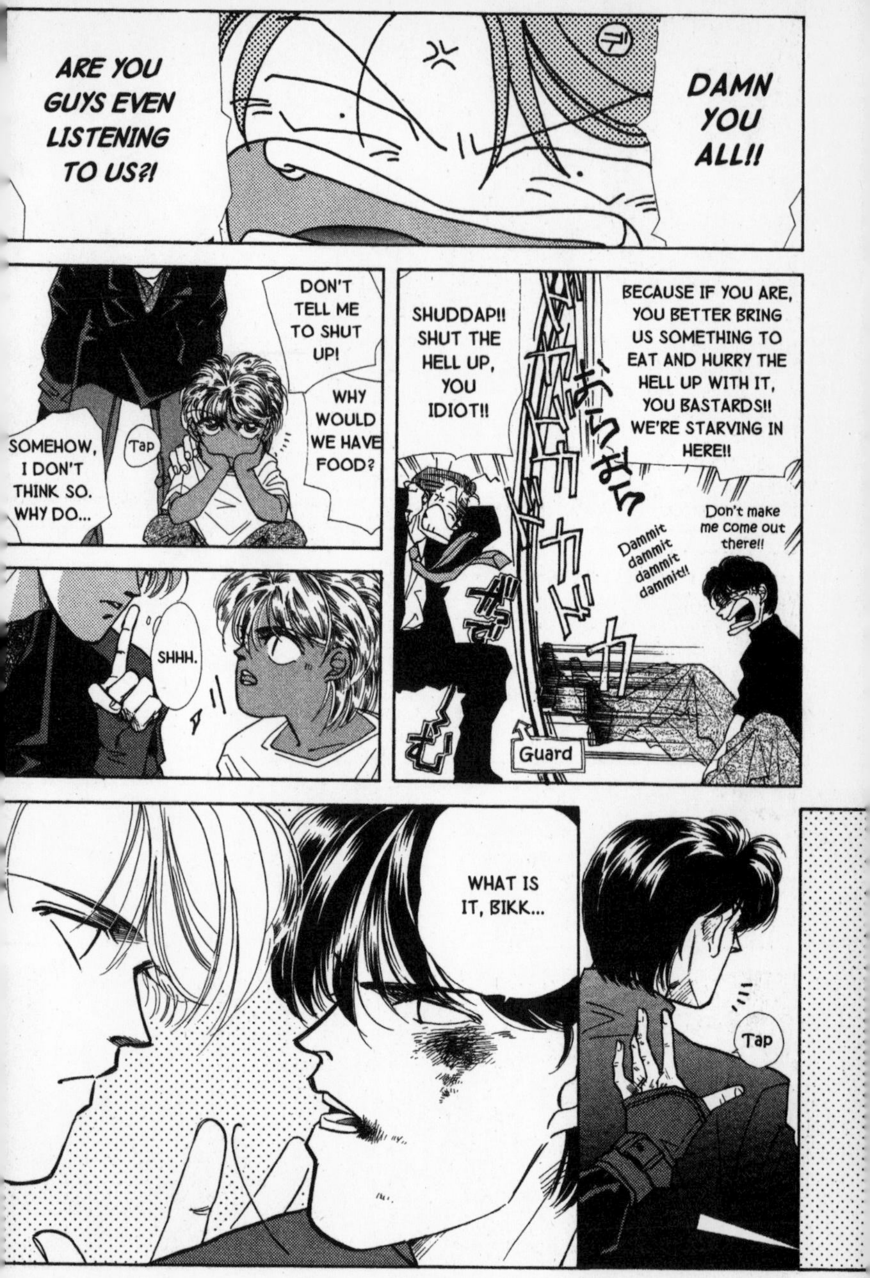
DAMN YOU ALL!!
ARE YOU GUYS EVEN LISTENING TO US?!
BECAUSE IF YOU ARE, YOU BETTER BRING US SOMETHING TO EAT AND HURRY THE HELL UP WITH IT, YOU BASTARDS!! WE'RE STARVING IN HERE!!
Don't make me come out there!!
Dammit dammit dammit dammit!!
SHUDDAP!! SHUT THE HELL UP, YOU IDIOT!!
Guard
DON'T TELL ME TO SHUT UP!
WHY WOULD WE HAVE FOOD?
Tap
SOMEHOW, I DON'T THINK SO. WHY DO...
SHHH.
Tap
WHAT IS IT, BIKK...

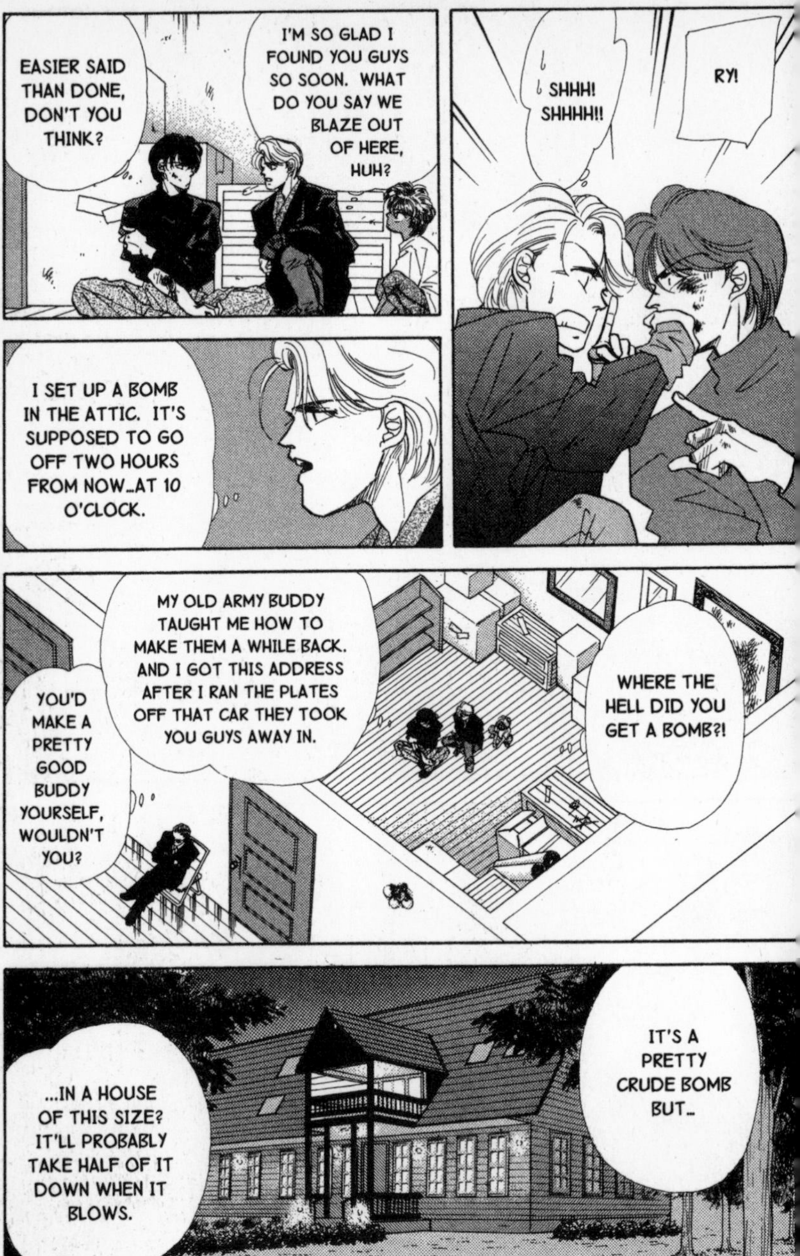
RY!
SHHH! SHHHH!!
I'M SO GLAD I FOUND YOU GUYS SO SOON. WHAT DO YOU SAY WE BLAZE OUT OF HERE, HUH?
EASIER SAID THAN DONE, DON'T YOU THINK?
I SET UP A BOMB IN THE ATTIC. IT'S SUPPOSED TO GO OFF TWO HOURS FROM NOW...AT 10 O'CLOCK.
WHERE THE HELL DID YOU GET A BOMB?!
MY OLD ARMY BUDDY TAUGHT ME HOW TO MAKE THEM A WHILE BACK. AND I GOT THIS ADDRESS AFTER I RAN THE PLATES OFF THAT CAR THEY TOOK YOU GUYS AWAY IN.
YOU'D MAKE A PRETTY GOOD BUDDY YOURSELF, WOULDN'T YOU?
IT'S A PRETTY CRUDE BOMB BUT...
...IN A HOUSE OF THIS SIZE? IT'LL PROBABLY TAKE HALF OF IT DOWN WHEN IT BLOWS.

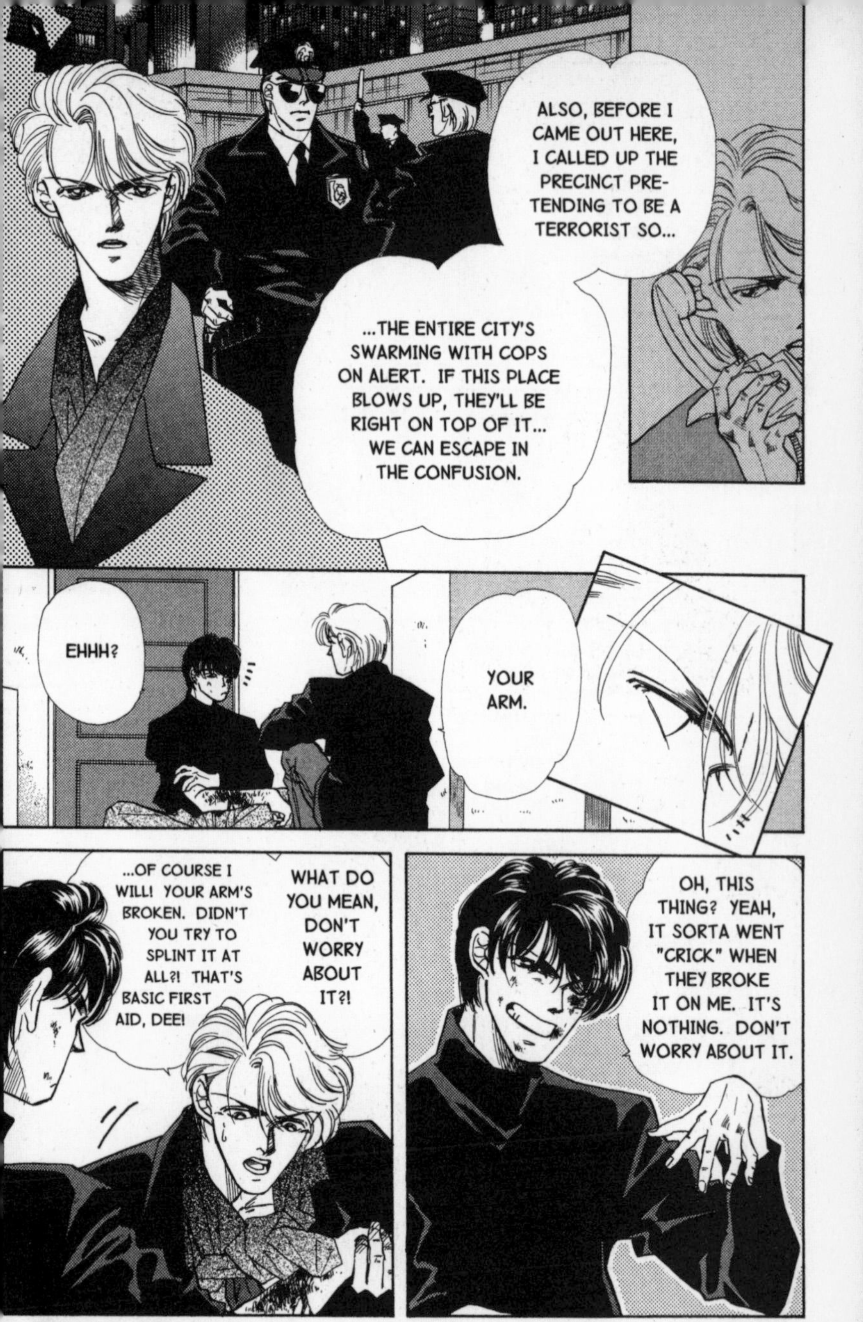
ALSO, BEFORE I CAME OUT HERE, I CALLED UP THE PRECINCT PRE-TENDING TO BE A TERRORIST SO...
...THE ENTIRE CITY'S SWARMING WITH COPS ON ALERT. IF THIS PLACE BLOWS UP, THEY'LL BE RIGHT ON TOP OF IT... WE CAN ESCAPE IN THE CONFUSION.
YOUR ARM.
EHHH?
OH, THIS THING? YEAH, IT SORTA WENT "CRICK" WHEN THEY BROKE IT ON ME. IT'S NOTHING. DON'T WORRY ABOUT IT.
WHAT DO YOU MEAN, DON'T WORRY ABOUT IT?!
...OF COURSE I WILL! YOUR ARM'S BROKEN. DIDN'T YOU TRY TO SPLINT IT AT ALL?! THAT'S BASIC FIRST AID, DEE!

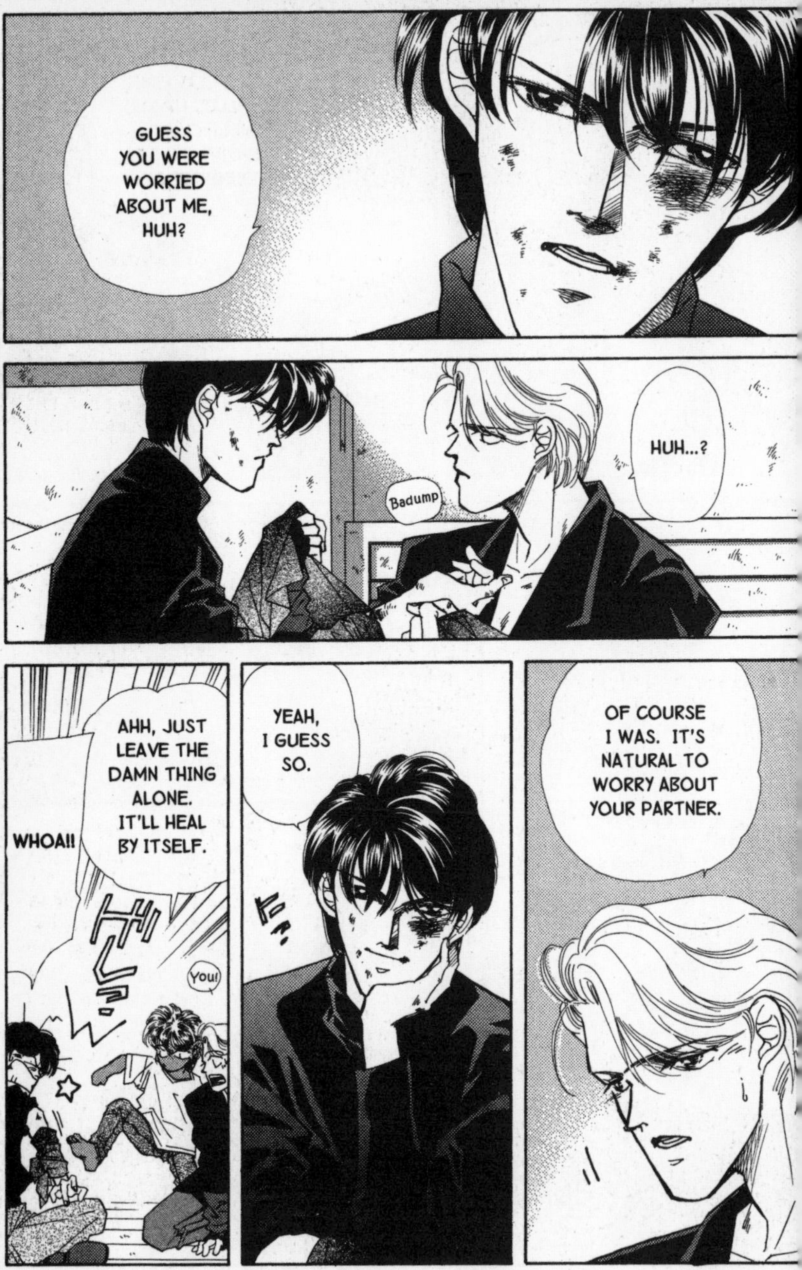
GUESS YOU WERE WORRIED ABOUT ME, HUH?
HUH...?
Badump
OF COURSE I WAS. IT'S NATURAL TO WORRY ABOUT YOUR PARTNER.
YEAH, I GUESS SO.
AHH, JUST LEAVE THE DAMN THING ALONE. IT'LL HEAL BY ITSELF.
WHOA!!
You!

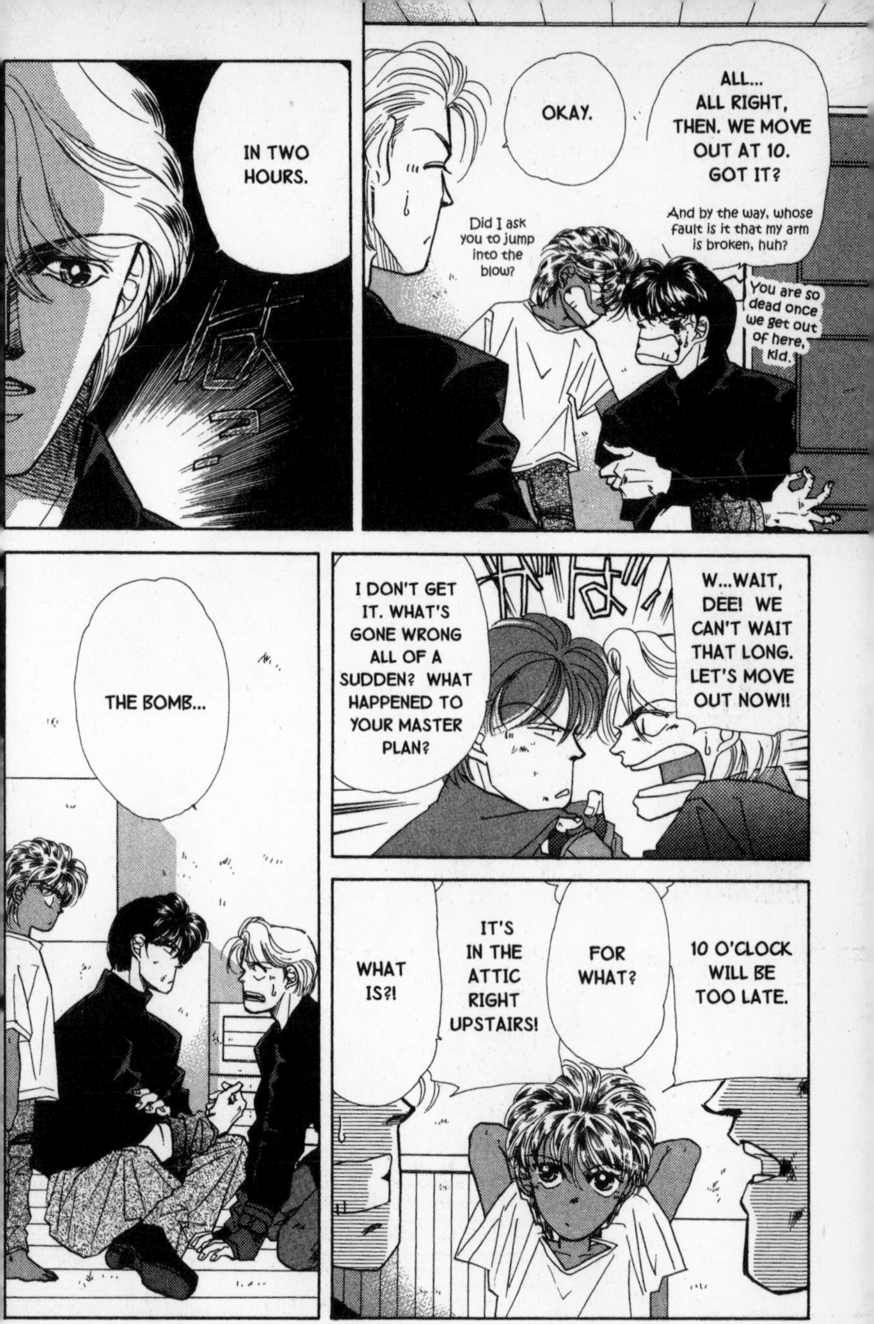
ALL... ALL RIGHT, THEN. WE MOVE OUT AT 10. GOT IT?
OKAY.
And by the way, whose fault is it that my arm is broken, huh?
Did I ask you to jump into the blow?
You are so dead once we get out of here, kid.
IN TWO HOURS.
W...WAIT, DEE! WE CAN'T WAIT THAT LONG. LET'S MOVE OUT NOW!!
I DON'T GET IT. WHAT'S GONE WRONG ALL OF A SUDDEN? WHAT HAPPENED TO YOUR MASTER PLAN?
10 O'CLOCK WILL BE TOO LATE.
FOR WHAT?
IT'S IN THE ATTIC RIGHT UPSTAIRS!
WHAT IS?!
THE BOMB...

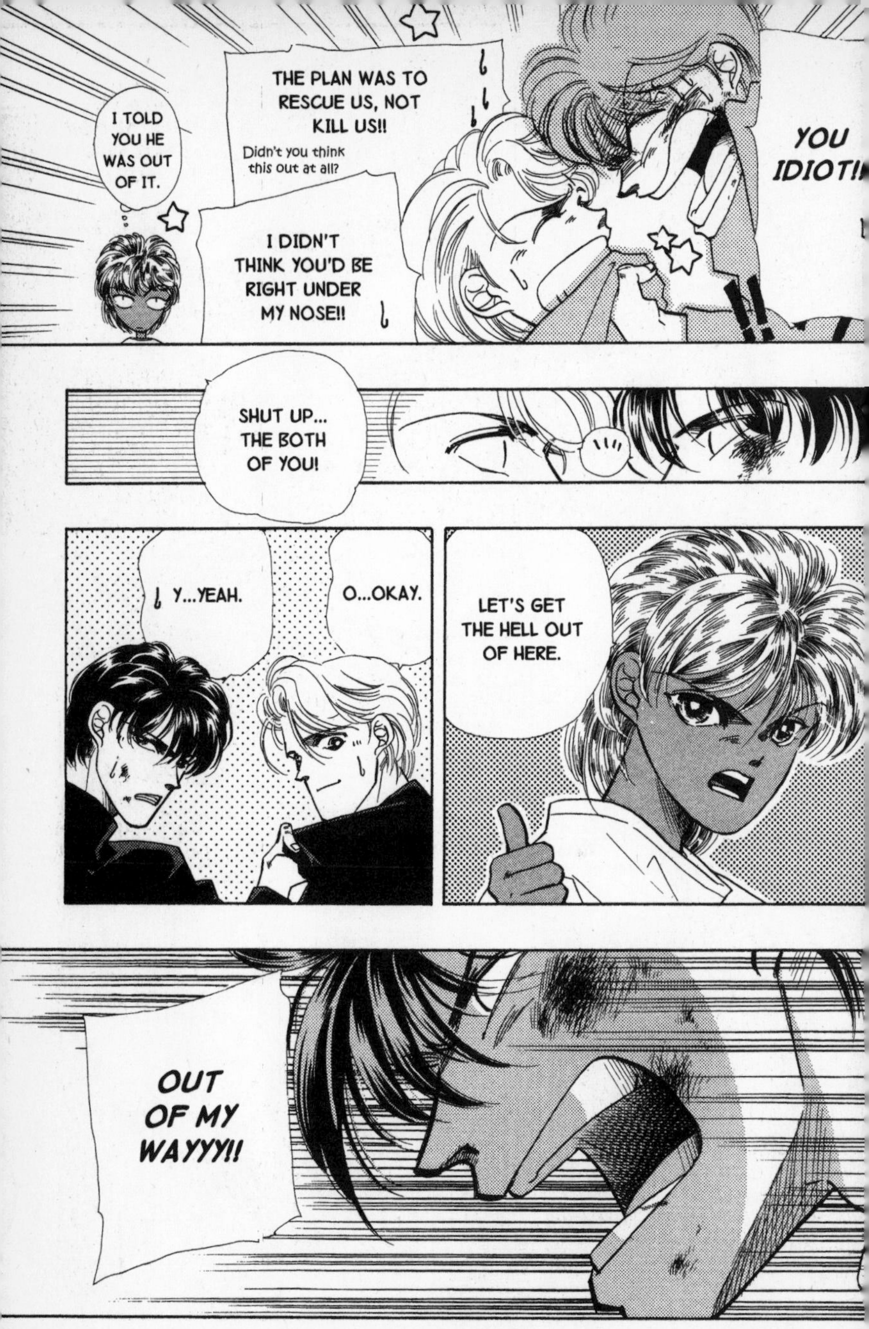
YOU IDIOT!!
THE PLAN WAS TO RESCUE US, NOT KILL US!!
Didn't you think this out at all?
I DIDN'T THINK YOU'D BE RIGHT UNDER MY NOSE!!
I TOLD YOU HE WAS OUT OF IT.
SHUT UP... THE BOTH OF YOU!
LET'S GET THE HELL OUT OF HERE.
O...OKAY.
Y...YEAH.
OUT OF MY WAYYY!!

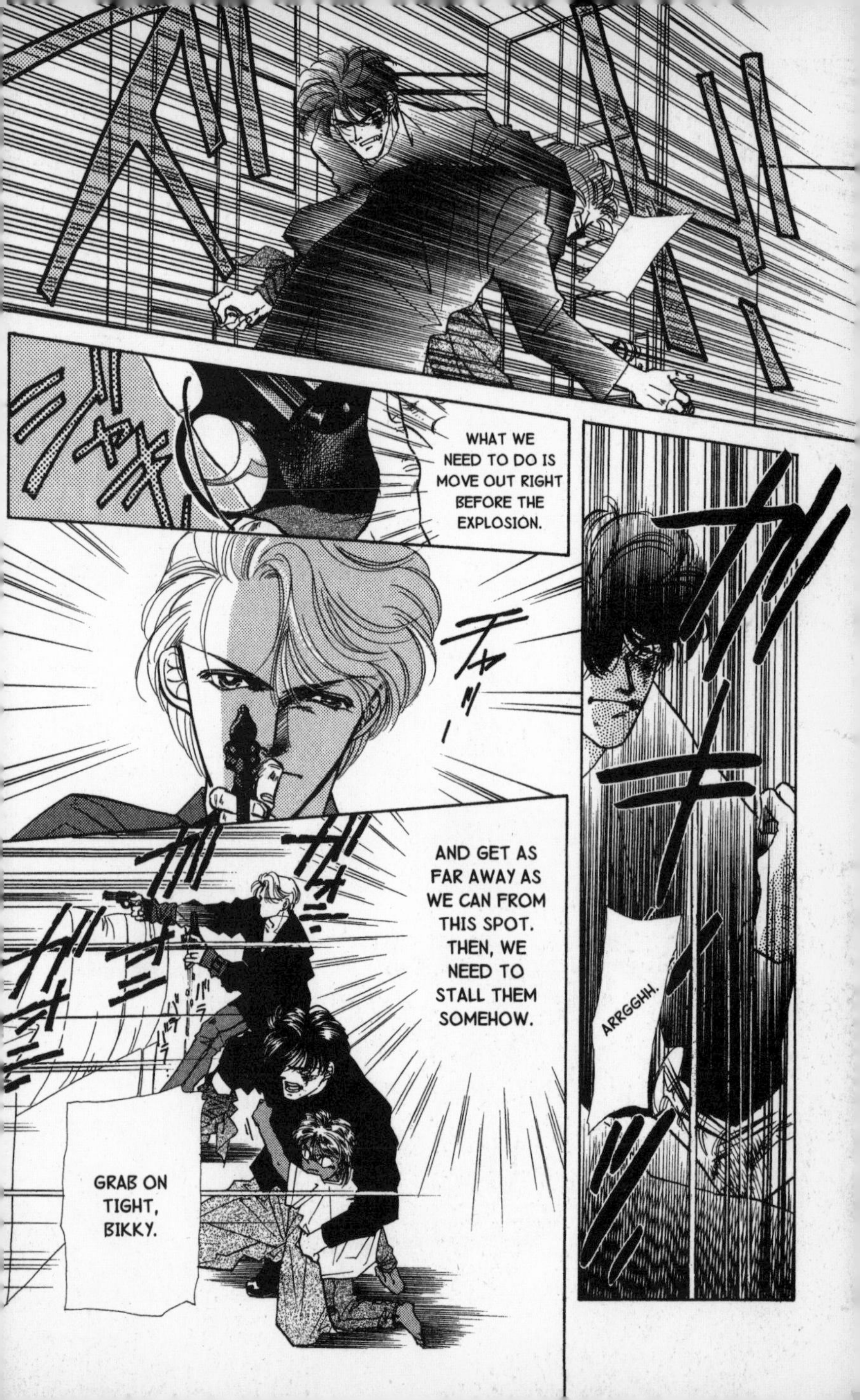
ARRGGHH.
WHAT WE NEED TO DO IS MOVE OUT RIGHT BEFORE THE EXPLOSION.
AND GET AS FAR AWAY AS WE CAN FROM THIS SPOT. THEN, WE NEED TO STALL THEM SOMEHOW.
GRAB ON TIGHT, BIKKY.

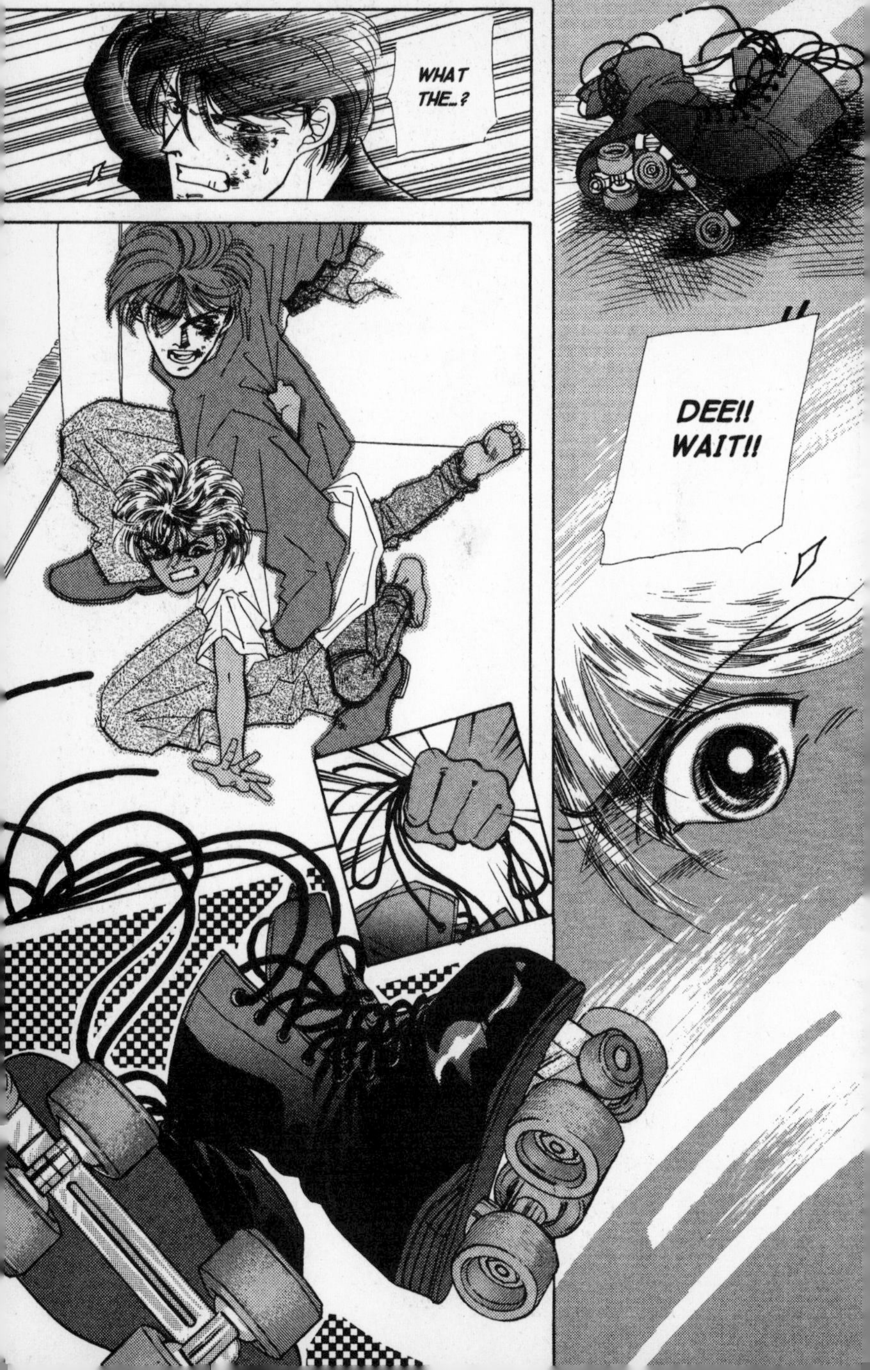
DEE!! WAIT!!
WHAT THE..?

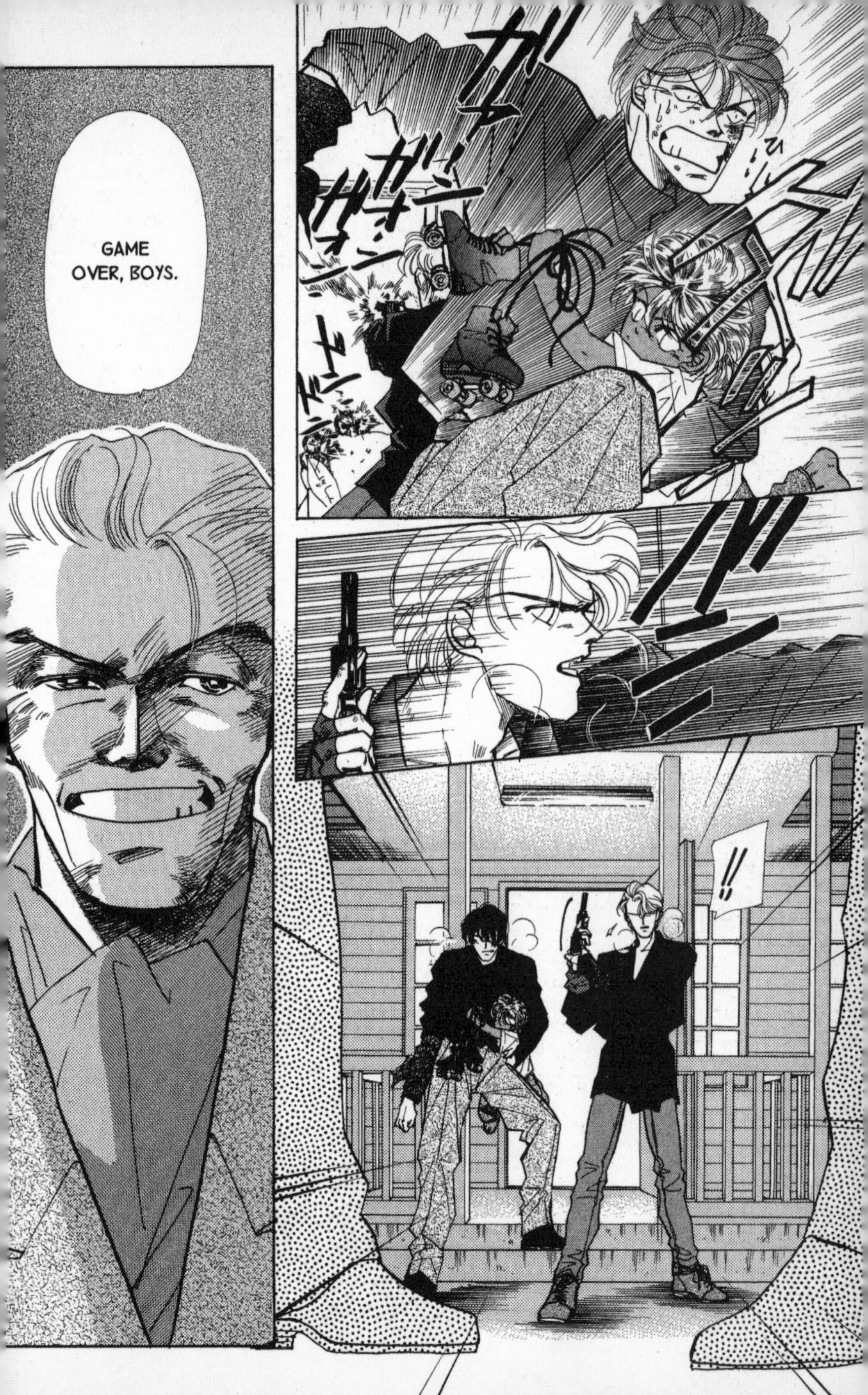
!!
GAME OVER, BOYS.

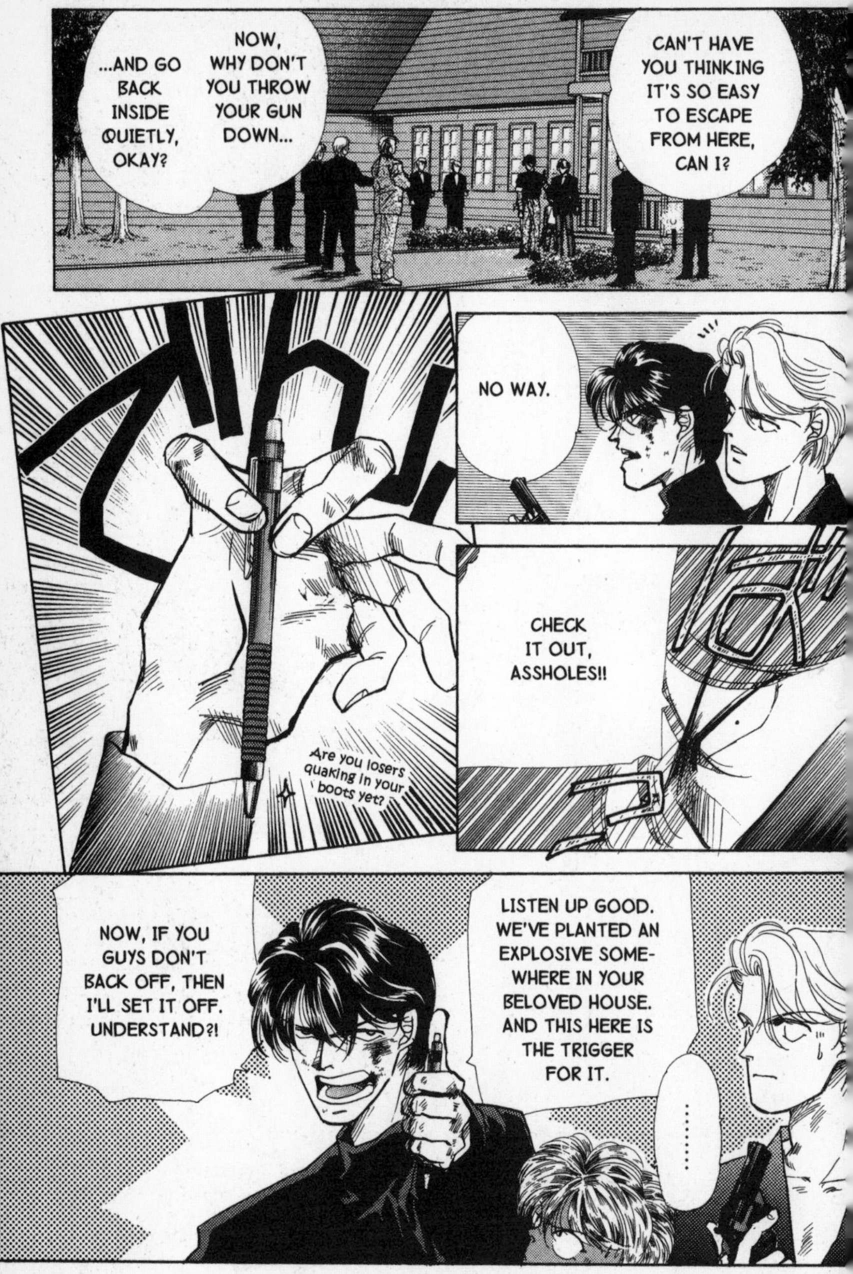
CAN'T HAVE YOU THINKING IT'S SO EASY TO ESCAPE FROM HERE, CAN I?
NOW, WHY DON'T YOU THROW YOUR GUN DOWN...
...AND GO BACK INSIDE QUIETLY, OKAY?
NO WAY.
CHECK IT OUT, ASSHOLES!!
Are you losers quaking in your boots yet?
LISTEN UP GOOD. WE'VE PLANTED AN EXPLOSIVE SOME-WHERE IN YOUR BELOVED HOUSE. AND THIS HERE IS THE TRIGGER FOR IT.
......
NOW, IF YOU GUYS DON'T BACK OFF, THEN I'LL SET IT OFF. UNDERSTAND?!

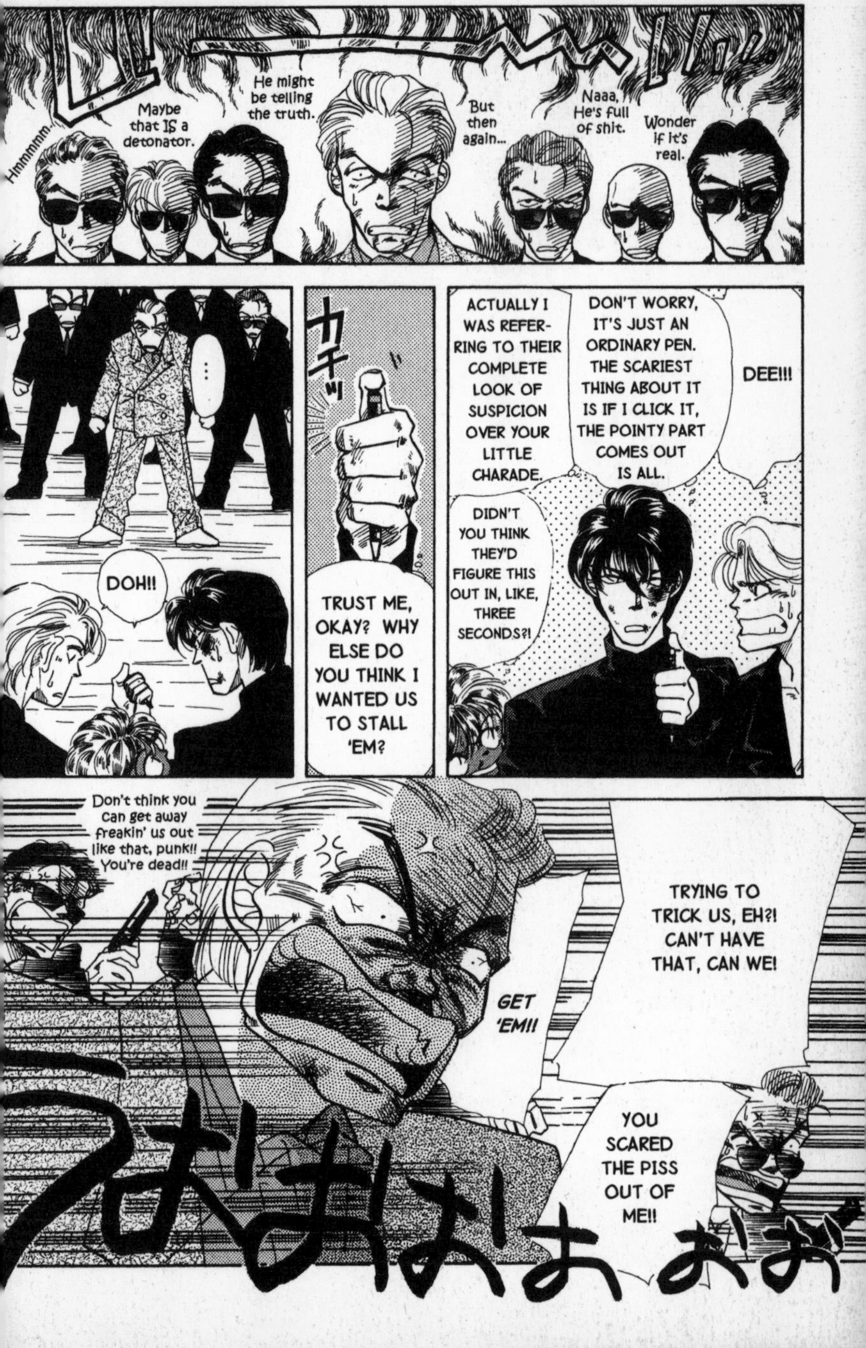
Wonder if it's real.
Naaa, He's full of shit.
But then again...
He might be telling the truth.
Maybe that IS a detonator.
Hmmmmm.
DEE!!!
DON'T WORRY, IT'S JUST AN ORDINARY PEN. THE SCARIEST THING ABOUT IT IS IF I CLICK IT, THE POINTY PART COMES OUT IS ALL.
ACTUALLY I WAS REFER-RING TO THEIR COMPLETE LOOK OF SUSPICION OVER YOUR LITTLE CHARADE.
DIDN'T YOU THINK THEY'D FIGURE THIS OUT IN, LIKE, THREE SECONDS?!
カチッ
TRUST ME, OKAY? WHY ELSE DO YOU THINK I WANTED US TO STALL 'EM?
...
DOH!!
TRYING TO TRICK US, EH?! CAN'T HAVE THAT, CAN WE!
GET 'EM!!
YOU SCARED THE PISS OUT OF ME!!
Don't think you can get away freakin' us out like that, punk!! You're dead!!

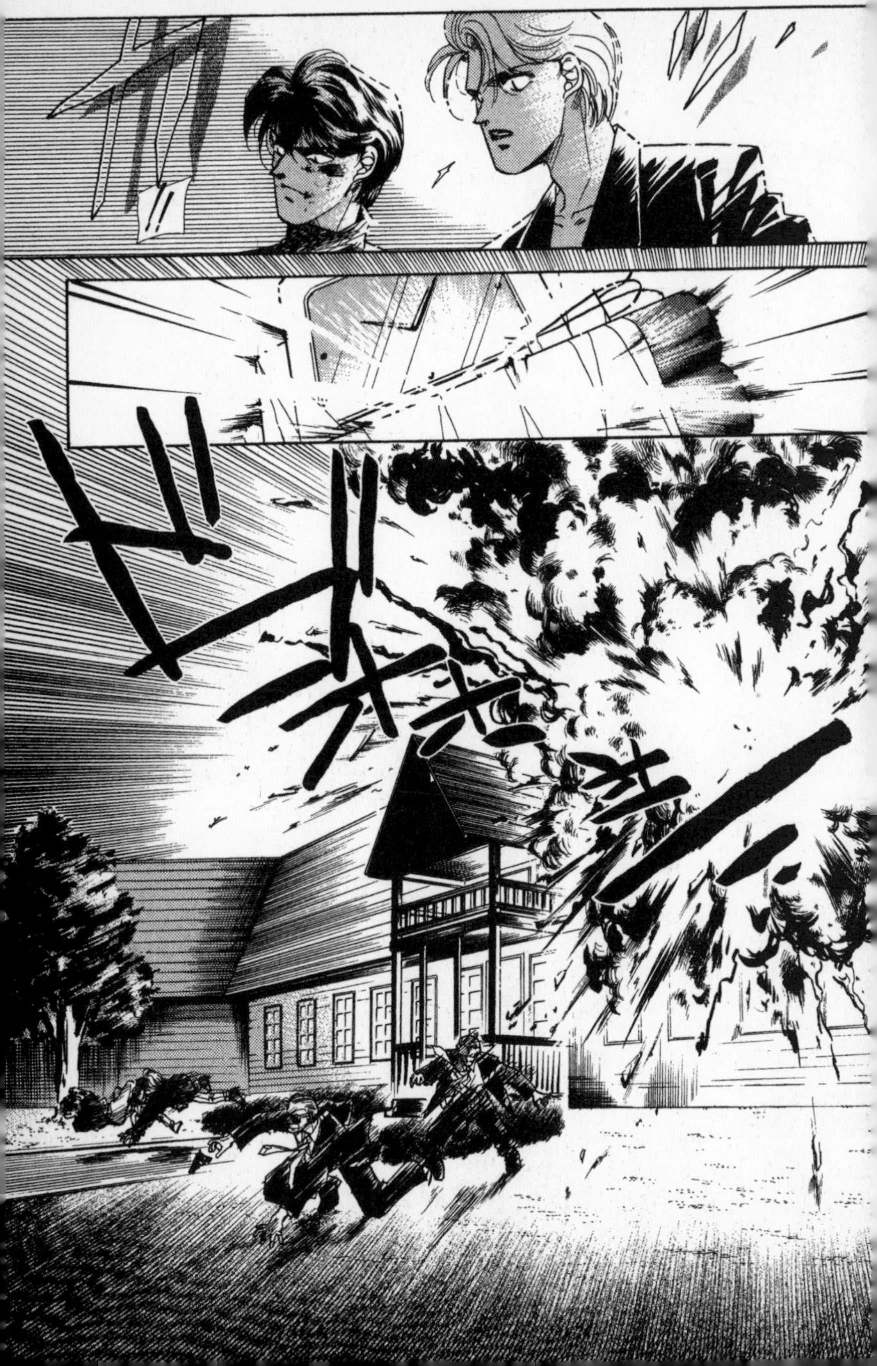

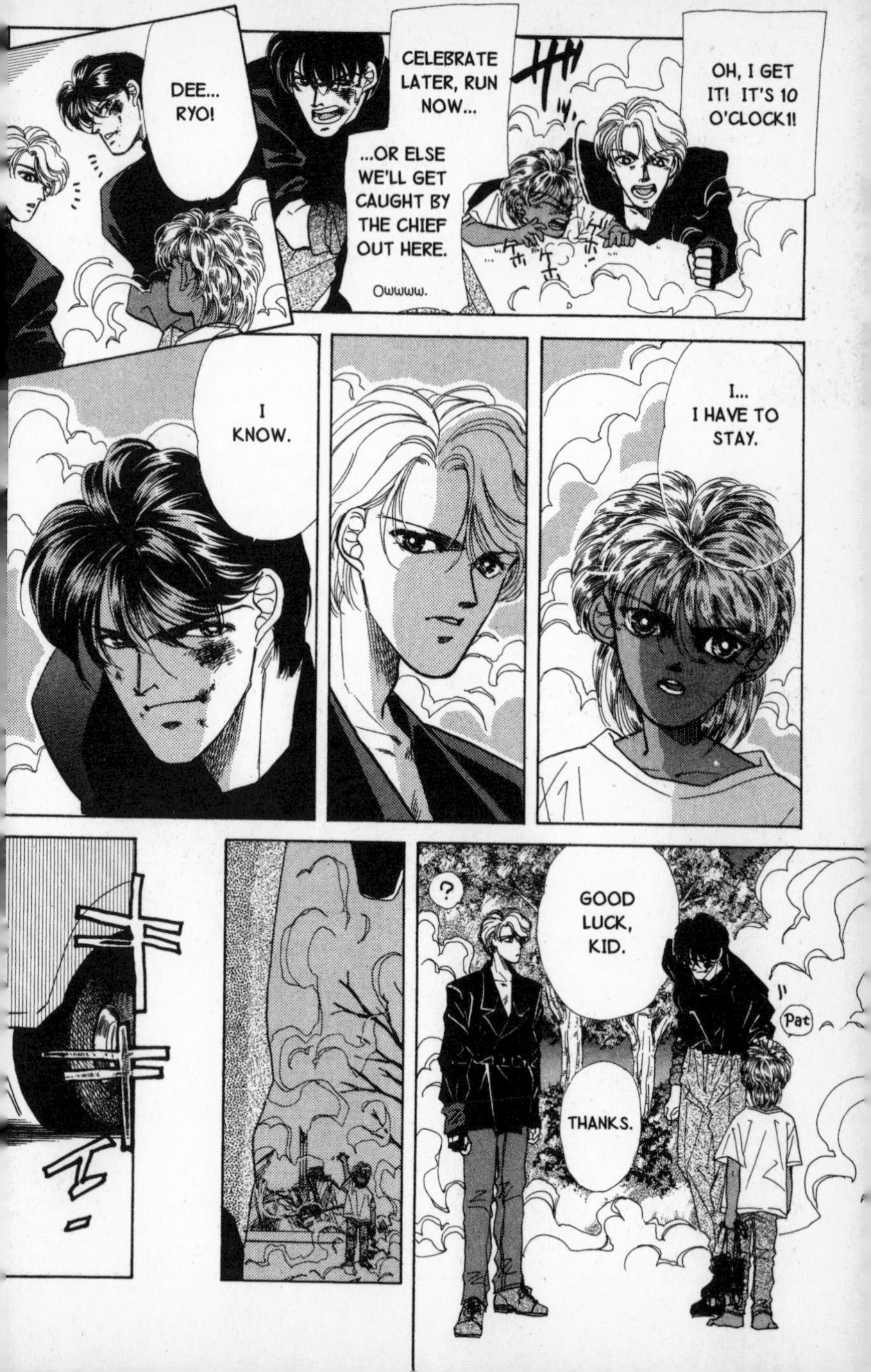
OH, I GET IT! IT'S 10 O'CLOCK!!
CELEBRATE LATER, RUN NOW...
...OR ELSE WE'LL GET CAUGHT BY THE CHIEF OUT HERE.
Owwww.
DEE... RYO!
I... I HAVE TO STAY.
I KNOW.
GOOD LUCK, KID.
Pat
THANKS.

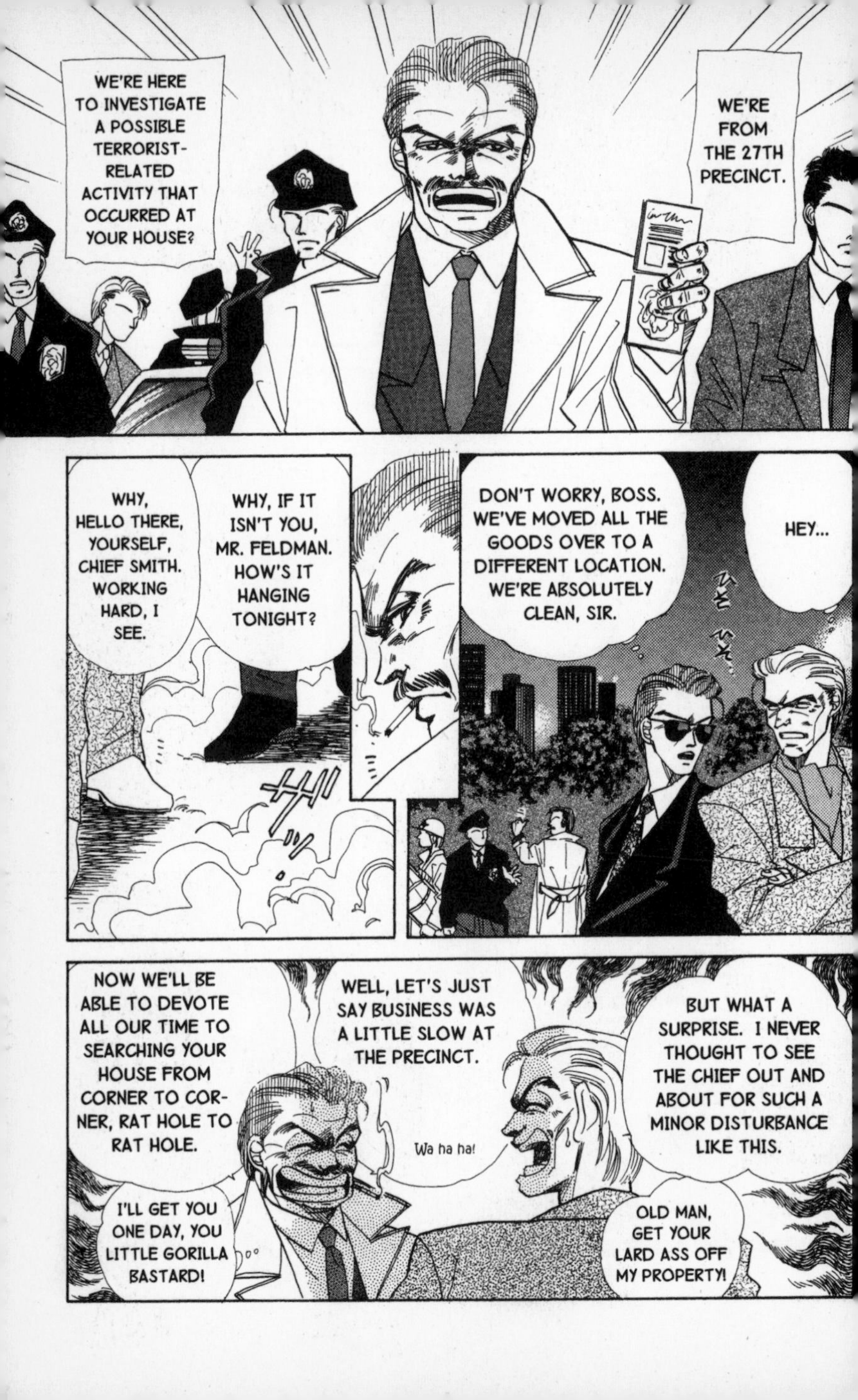
WE'RE FROM THE 27TH PRECINCT.
WE'RE HERE TO INVESTIGATE A POSSIBLE TERRORIST-RELATED ACTIVITY THAT OCCURRED AT YOUR HOUSE?
HEY...
DON'T WORRY, BOSS. WE'VE MOVED ALL THE GOODS OVER TO A DIFFERENT LOCATION. WE'RE ABSOLUTELY CLEAN, SIR.
WHY, IF IT ISN'T YOU, MR. FELDMAN. HOW'S IT HANGING TONIGHT?
WHY, HELLO THERE, YOURSELF, CHIEF SMITH. WORKING HARD, I SEE.
BUT WHAT A SURPRISE. I NEVER THOUGHT TO SEE THE CHIEF OUT AND ABOUT FOR SUCH A MINOR DISTURBANCE LIKE THIS.
OLD MAN, GET YOUR LARD ASS OFF MY PROPERTY!
WELL, LET'S JUST SAY BUSINESS WAS A LITTLE SLOW AT THE PRECINCT.
Wa ha ha!
NOW WE'LL BE ABLE TO DEVOTE ALL OUR TIME TO SEARCHING YOUR HOUSE FROM CORNER TO COR-NER, RAT HOLE TO RAT HOLE.
I'LL GET YOU ONE DAY, YOU LITTLE GORILLA BASTARD!

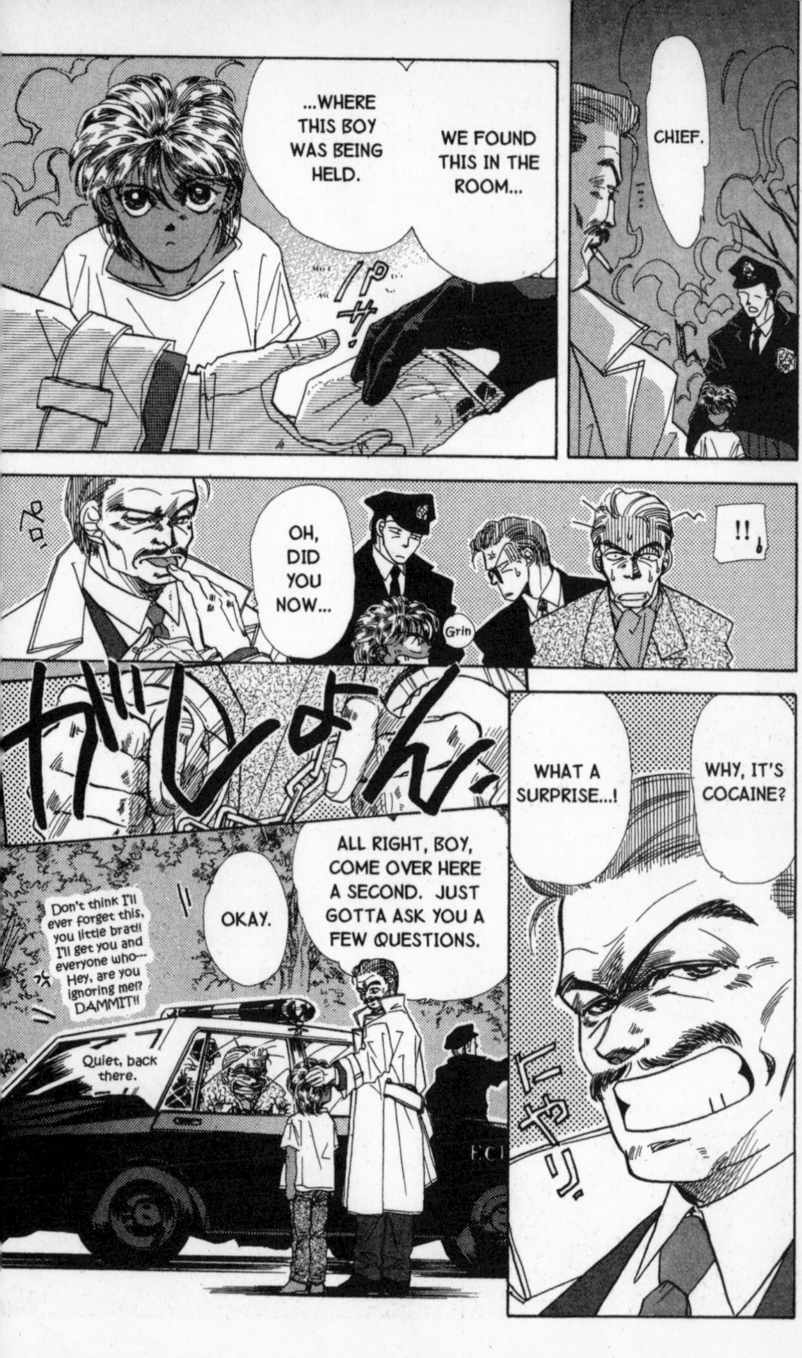
CHIEF.
WE FOUND THIS IN THE ROOM...
...WHERE THIS BOY WAS BEING HELD.
パサ!
!!
Grin
OH, DID YOU NOW...
WHY, IT'S COCAINE?
WHAT A SURPRISE...!
ニヤリ
がしゃん
ALL RIGHT, BOY, COME OVER HERE A SECOND. JUST GOTTA ASK YOU A FEW QUESTIONS.
OKAY.
Don't think I'll ever forget this, you little brat!! I'll get you and everyone who-- Hey, are you ignoring me!? DAMMIT!!
Quiet, back there.

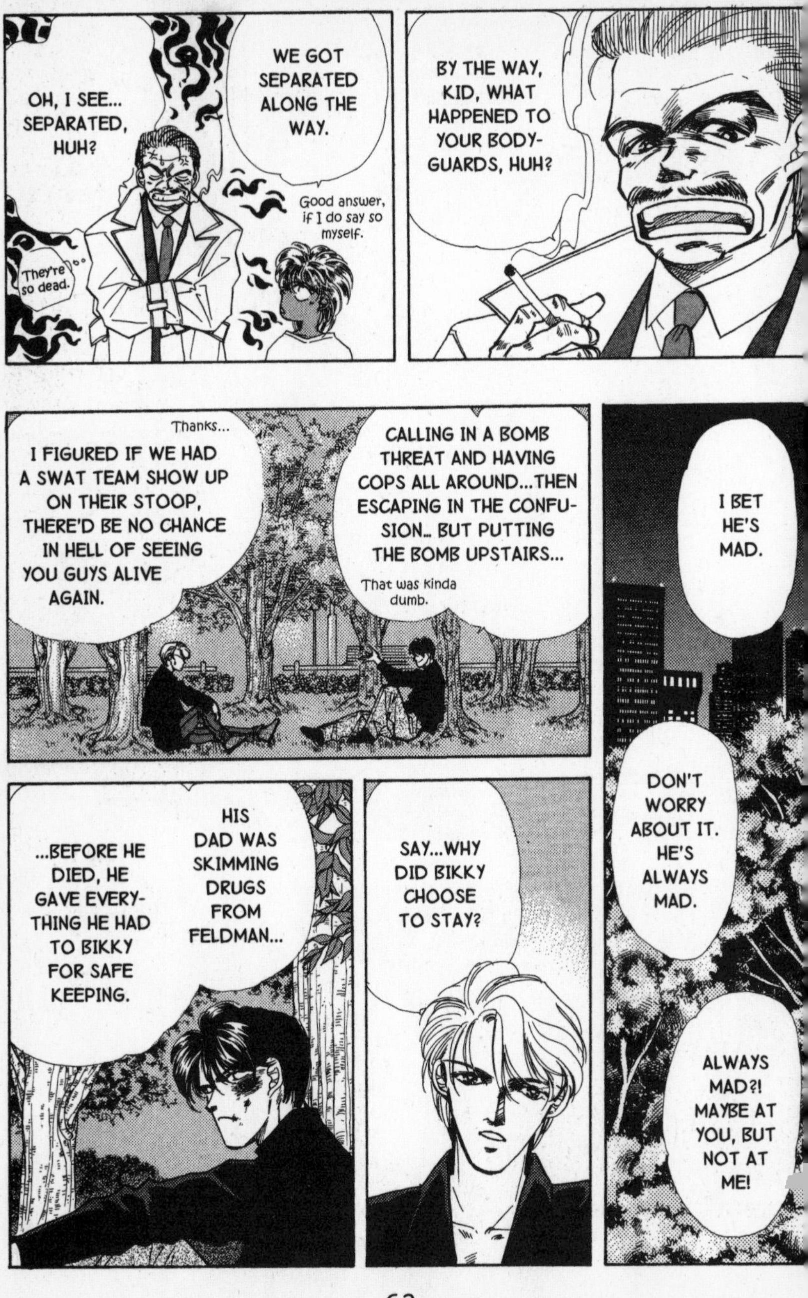
BY THE WAY, KID, WHAT HAPPENED TO YOUR BODY-GUARDS, HUH?
WE GOT SEPARATED ALONG THE WAY.
OH, I SEE... SEPARATED, HUH?
Good answer, if I do say so myself.
They're so dead.
I BET HE'S MAD.
DON'T WORRY ABOUT IT. HE'S ALWAYS MAD.
ALWAYS MAD?! MAYBE AT YOU, BUT NOT AT ME!
CALLING IN A BOMB THREAT AND HAVING COPS ALL AROUND...THEN ESCAPING IN THE CONFU-SION... BUT PUTTING THE BOMB UPSTAIRS...
That was kinda dumb.
Thanks...
I FIGURED IF WE HAD A SWAT TEAM SHOW UP ON THEIR STOOP, THERE'D BE NO CHANCE IN HELL OF SEEING YOU GUYS ALIVE AGAIN.
SAY...WHY DID BIKKY CHOOSE TO STAY?
HIS DAD WAS SKIMMING DRUGS FROM FELDMAN...
...BEFORE HE DIED, HE GAVE EVERY-THING HE HAD TO BIKKY FOR SAFE KEEPING.

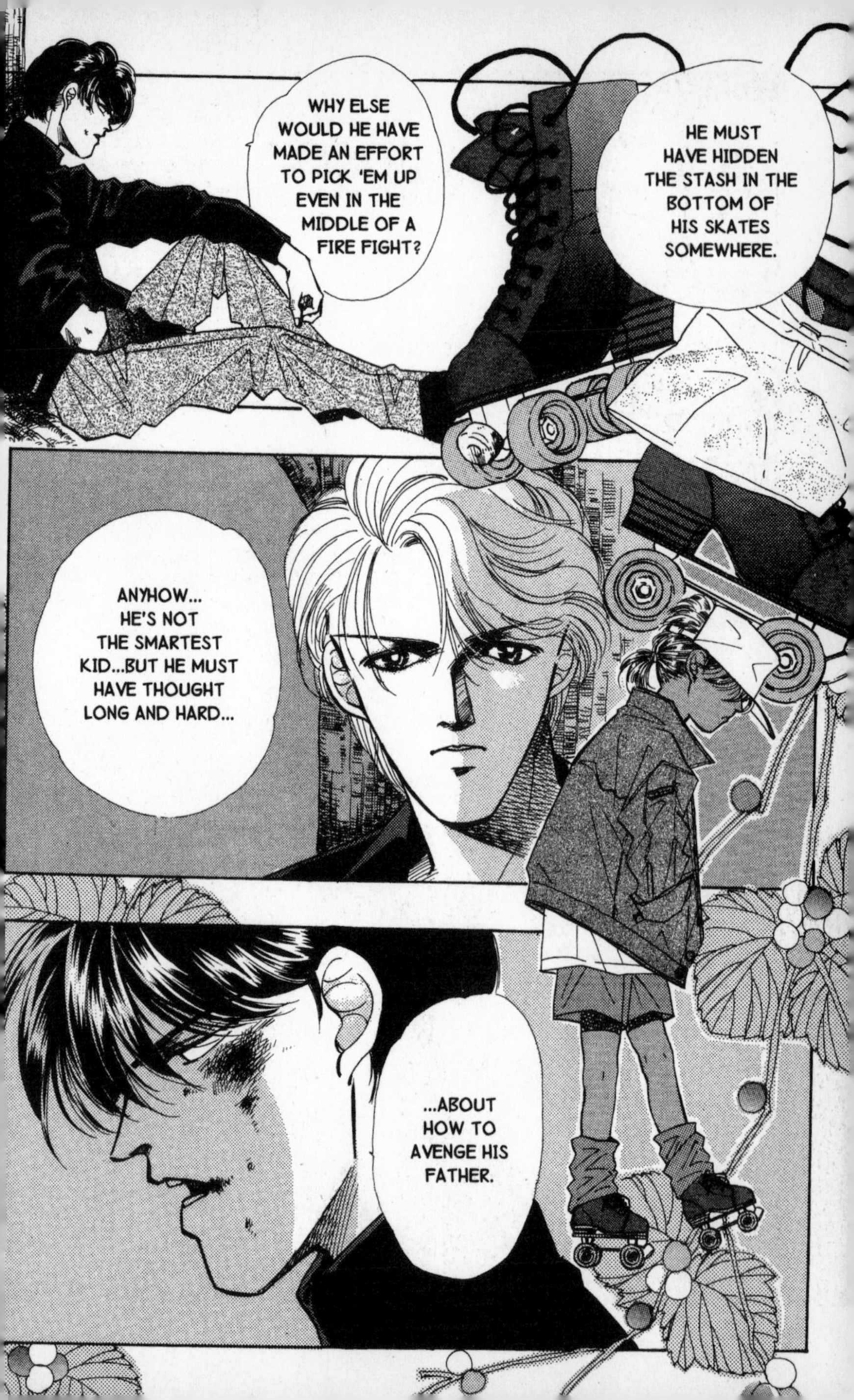
HE MUST HAVE HIDDEN THE STASH IN THE BOTTOM OF HIS SKATES SOMEWHERE.
WHY ELSE WOULD HE HAVE MADE AN EFFORT TO PICK 'EM UP EVEN IN THE MIDDLE OF A FIRE FIGHT?
ANYHOW... HE'S NOT THE SMARTEST KID...BUT HE MUST HAVE THOUGHT LONG AND HARD...
...ABOUT HOW TO AVENGE HIS FATHER.

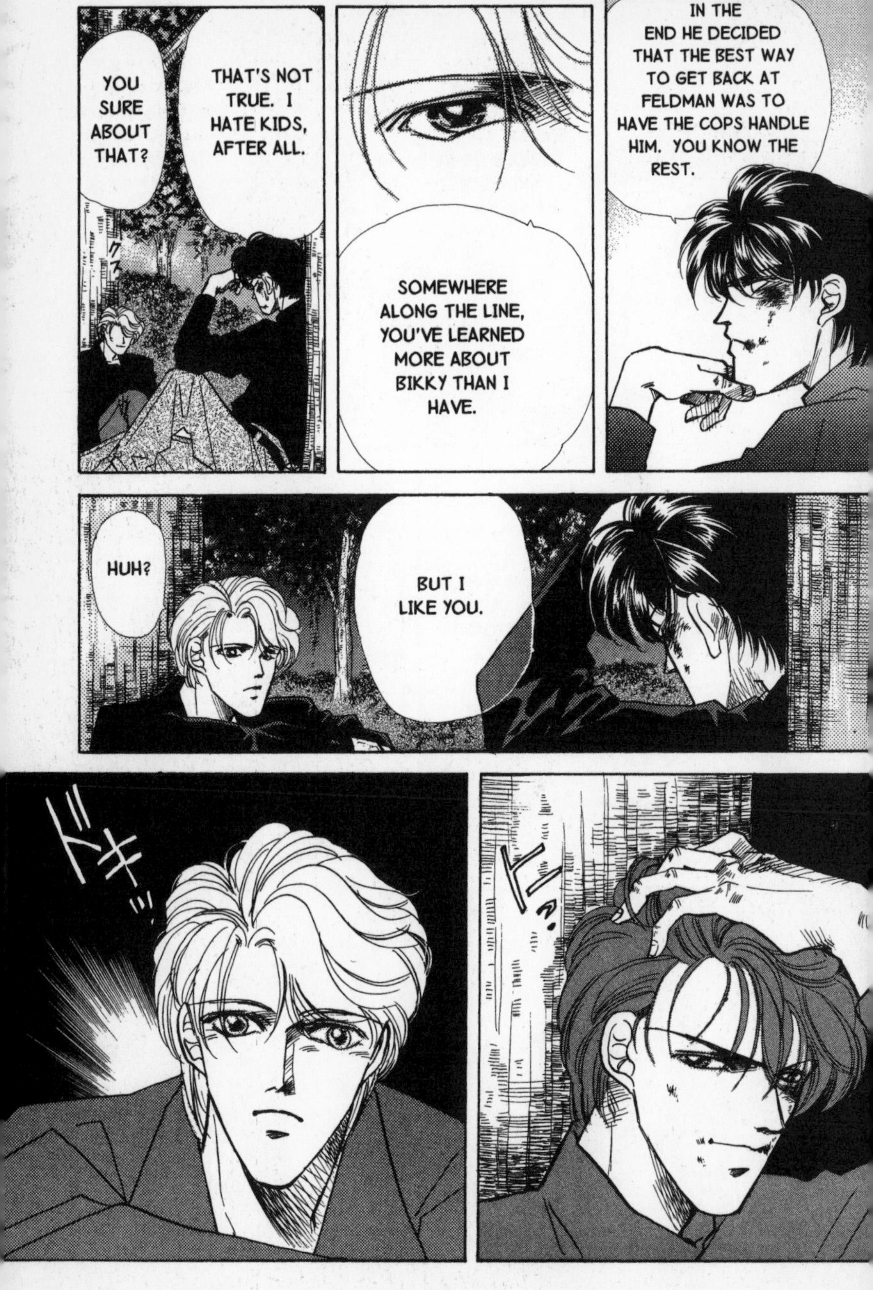
IN THE END HE DECIDED THAT THE BEST WAY TO GET BACK AT FELDMAN WAS TO HAVE THE COPS HANDLE HIM. YOU KNOW THE REST.
SOMEWHERE ALONG THE LINE, YOU'VE LEARNED MORE ABOUT BIKKY THAN I HAVE.
THAT'S NOT TRUE. I HATE KIDS, AFTER ALL.
YOU SURE ABOUT THAT?
BUT I LIKE YOU.
HUH?

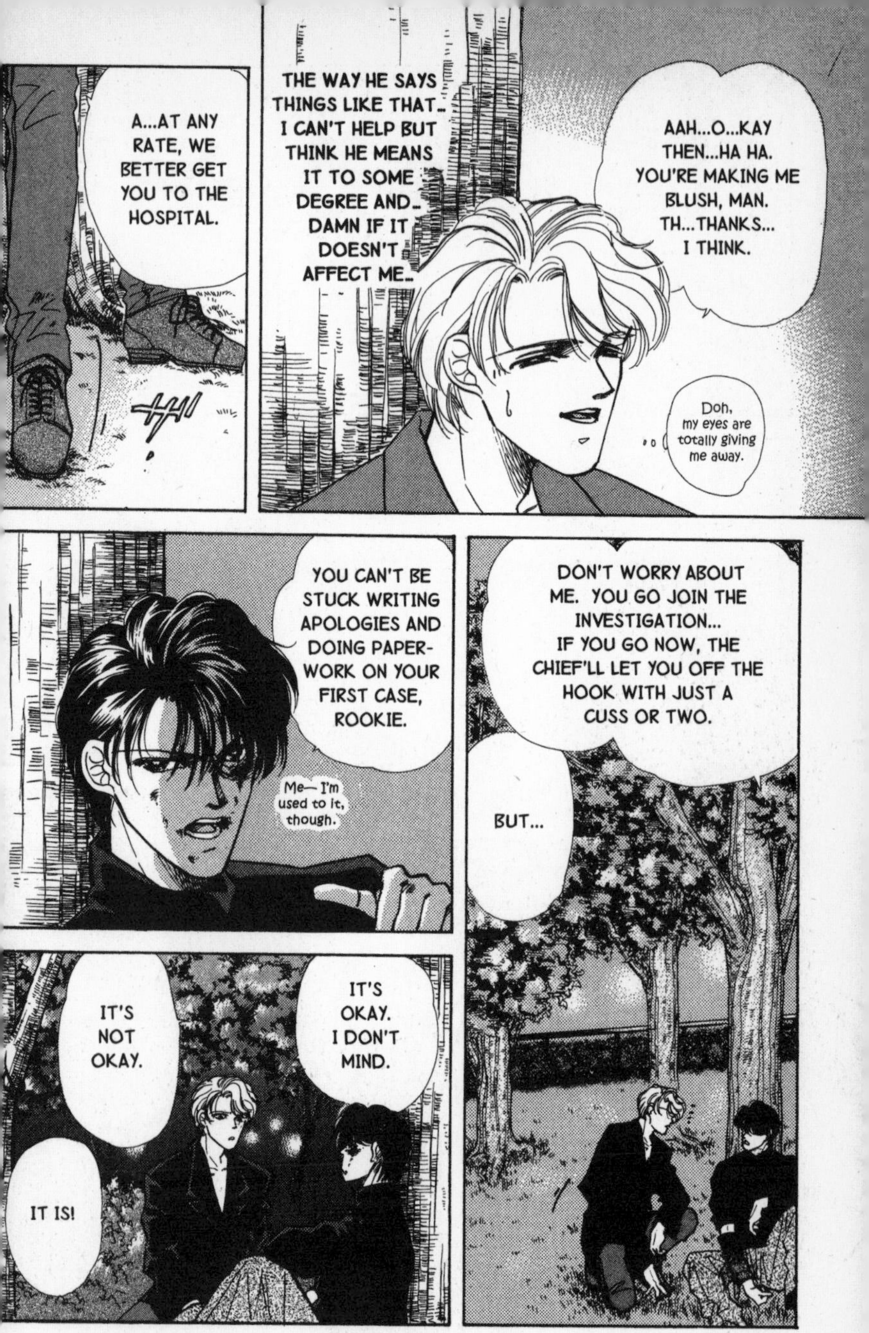
AAH...O...KAY THEN...HA HA. YOU'RE MAKING ME BLUSH, MAN. TH...THANKS... I THINK.
THE WAY HE SAYS THINGS LIKE THAT.. I CAN'T HELP BUT THINK HE MEANS IT TO SOME DEGREE AND.. DAMN IF IT DOESN'T AFFECT ME..
Doh, my eyes are totally giving me away.
A...AT ANY RATE, WE BETTER GET YOU TO THE HOSPITAL.
DON'T WORRY ABOUT ME. YOU GO JOIN THE INVESTIGATION... IF YOU GO NOW, THE CHIEF'LL LET YOU OFF THE HOOK WITH JUST A CUSS OR TWO.
BUT...
YOU CAN'T BE STUCK WRITING APOLOGIES AND DOING PAPER-WORK ON YOUR FIRST CASE, ROOKIE.
Me—I'm used to it, though.
IT'S OKAY. I DON'T MIND.
IT'S NOT OKAY.
IT IS!

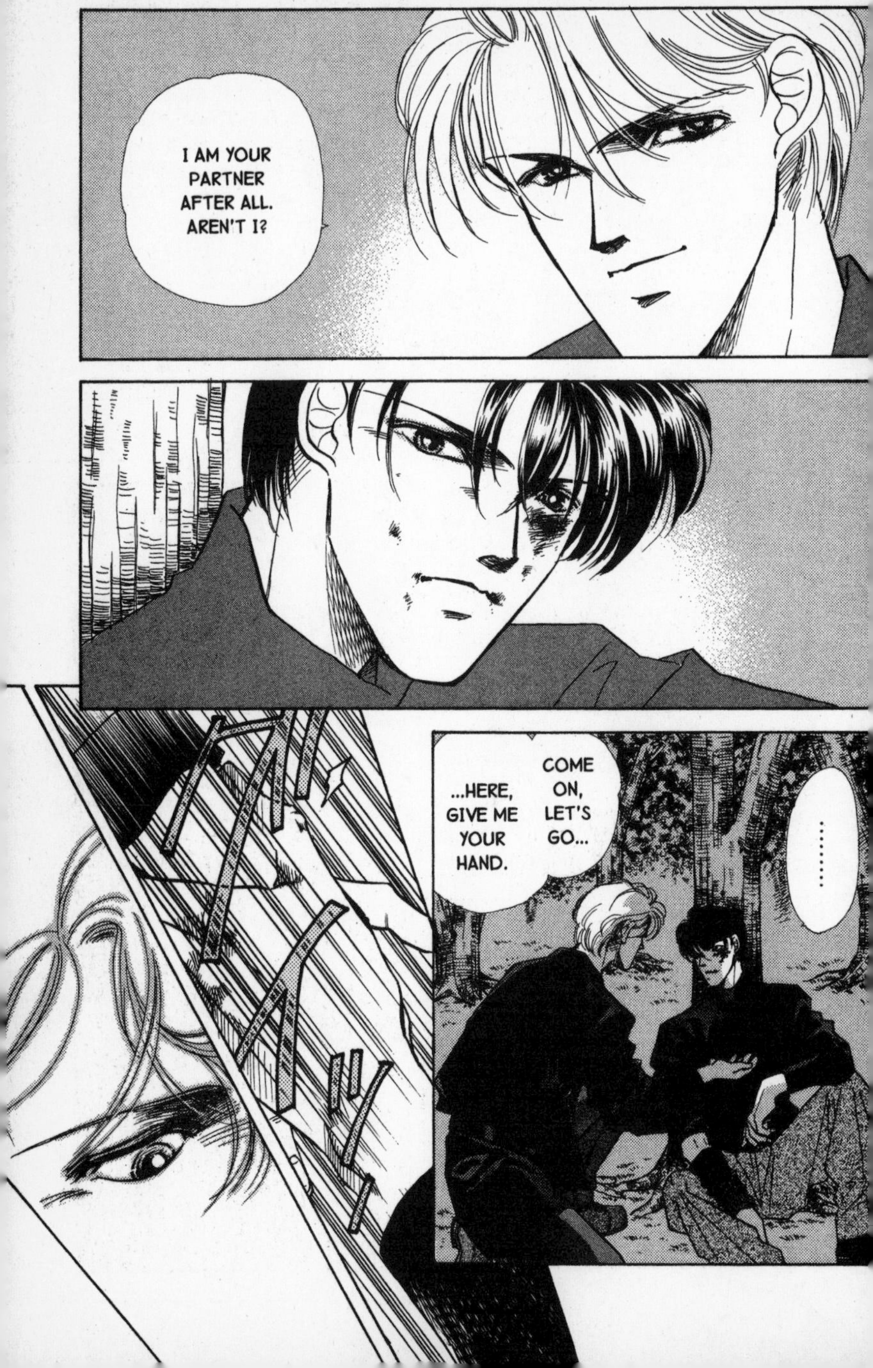
I AM YOUR PARTNER AFTER ALL. AREN'T I?
......
COME ON, LET'S GO...
...HERE, GIVE ME YOUR HAND.

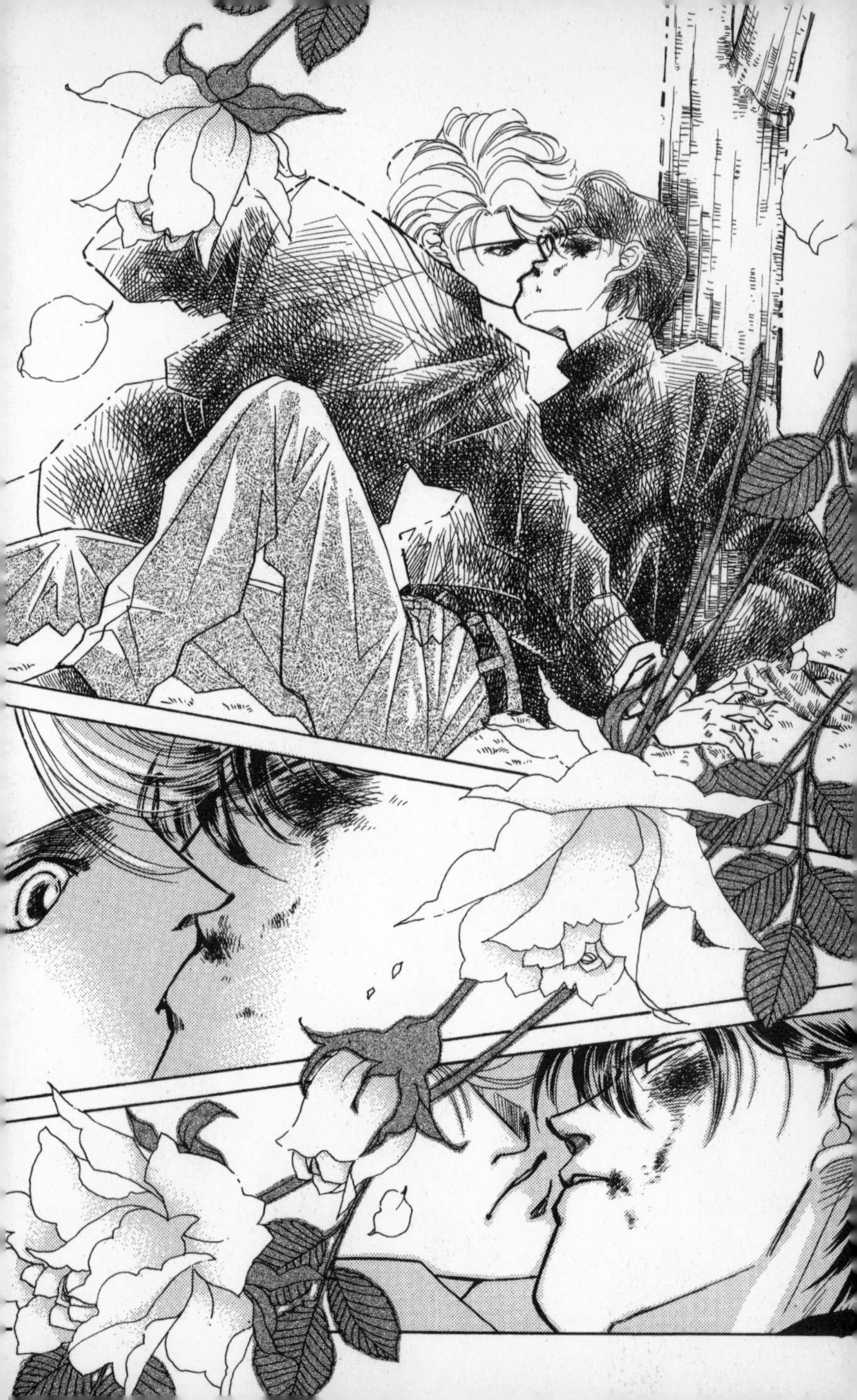

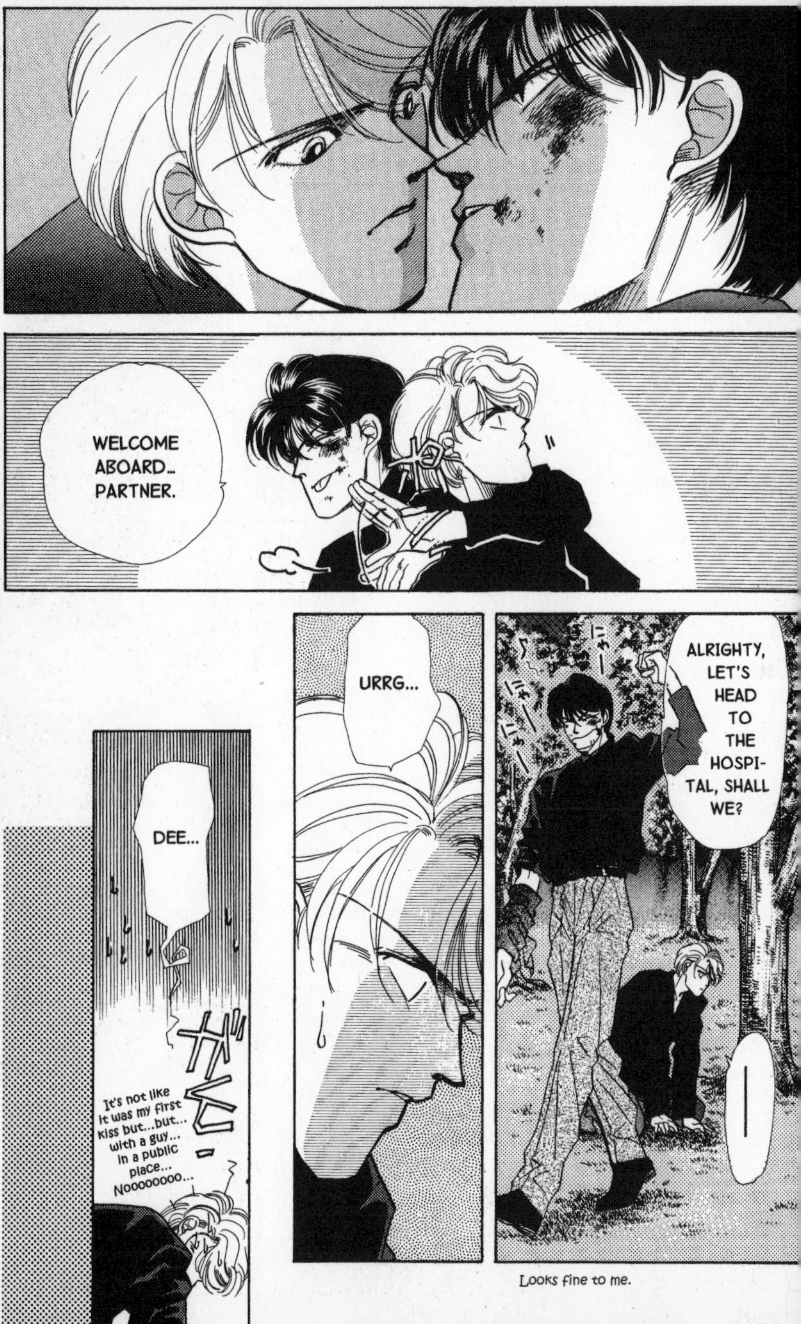

WELCOME ABOARD... PARTNER.
ALRIGHTY, LET'S HEAD TO THE HOSPI-TAL, SHALL WE?
URRG...
DEE...
It's not like it was my first kiss but...but... with a guy... in a public place... Nooooooo...

Looks fine to me.

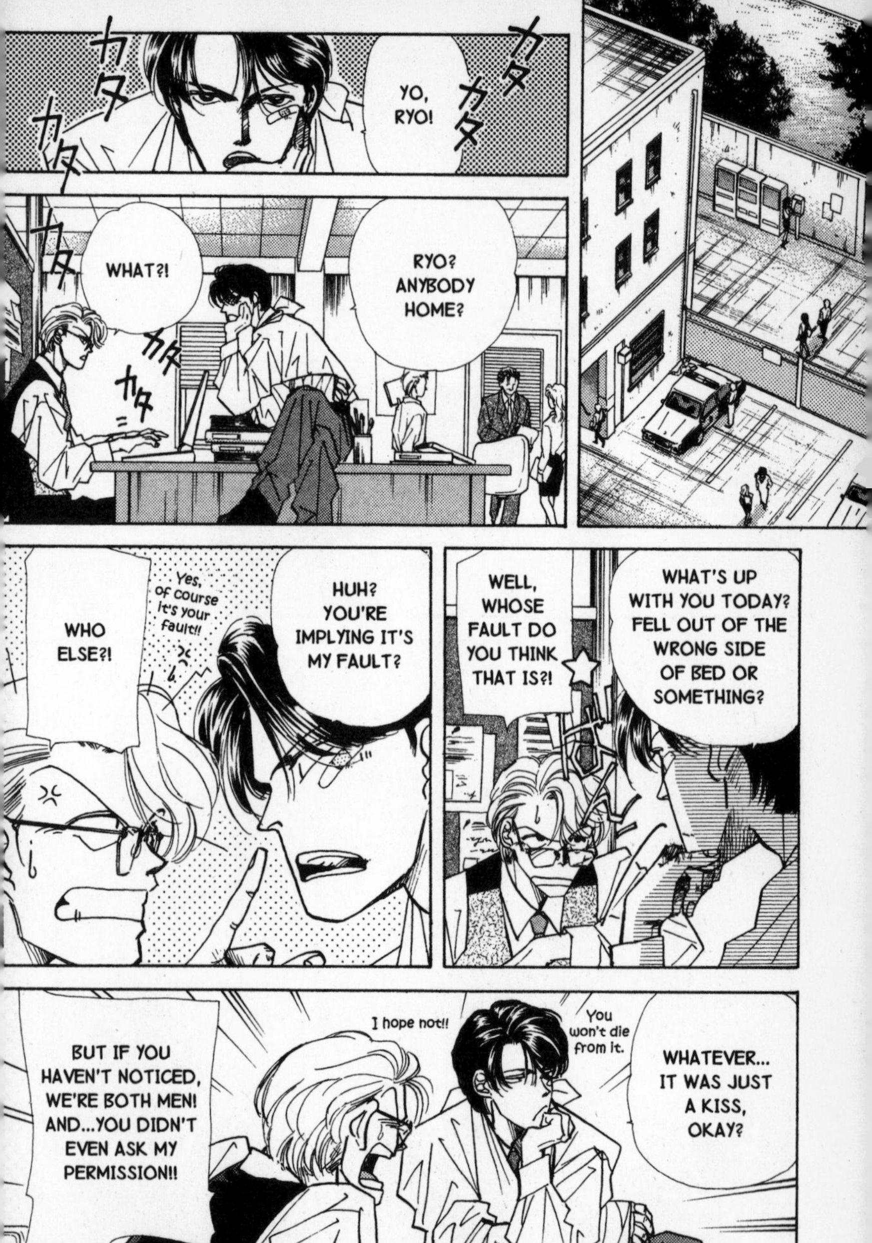

カタ
カタ
YO, RYO!
カタ
カタ
カタ
RYO? ANYBODY HOME?
WHAT?!
カタ
カタ
WHAT'S UP WITH YOU TODAY? FELL OUT OF THE WRONG SIDE OF BED OR SOMETHING?
WELL, WHOSE FAULT DO YOU THINK THAT IS?!
HUH? YOU'RE IMPLYING IT'S MY FAULT?
Yes, of course it's your fault!!
WHO ELSE?!
WHATEVER... IT WAS JUST A KISS, OKAY?
You won't die from it.
I hope not!!
BUT IF YOU HAVEN'T NOTICED, WE'RE BOTH MEN! AND...YOU DIDN'T EVEN ASK MY PERMISSION!!

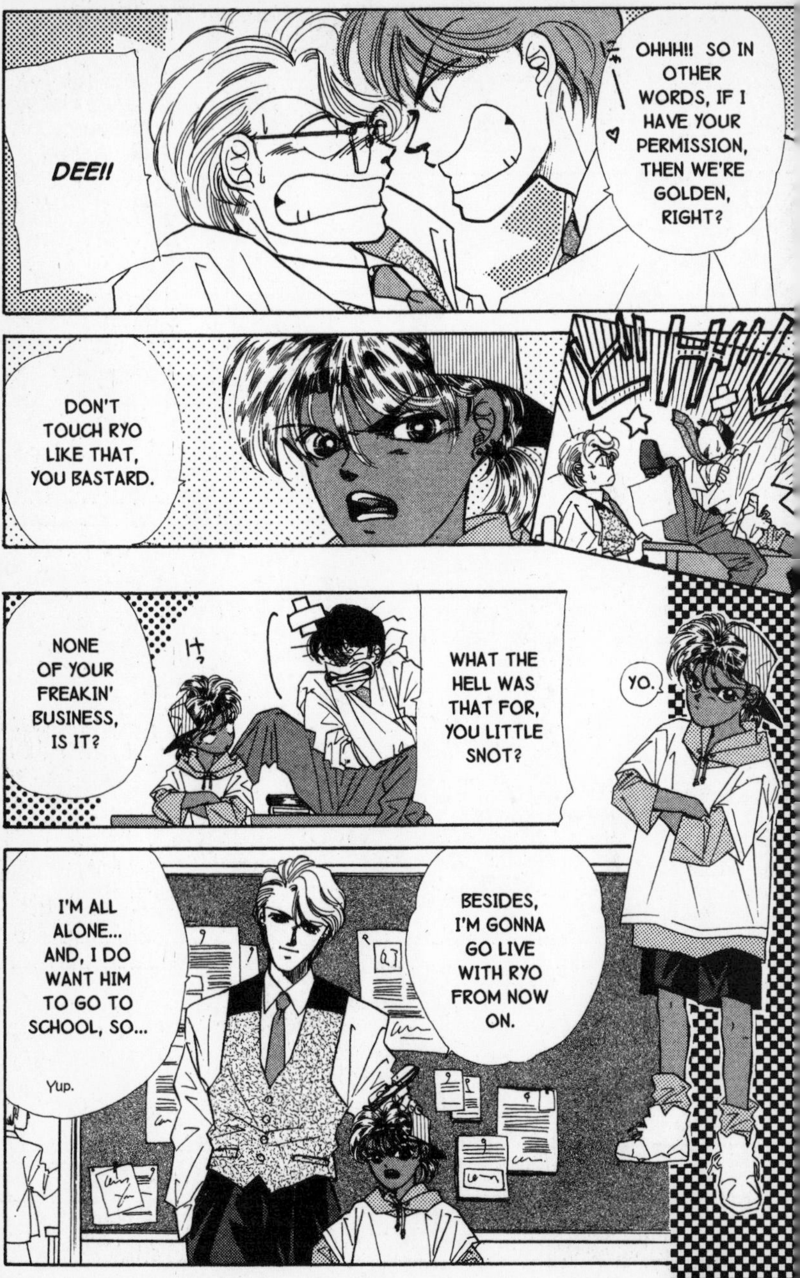
OHHH!! SO IN OTHER WORDS, IF I HAVE YOUR PERMISSION, THEN WE'RE GOLDEN, RIGHT?
DEE!!
DON'T TOUCH RYO LIKE THAT, YOU BASTARD.
YO.
WHAT THE HELL WAS THAT FOR, YOU LITTLE SNOT?
けっ
NONE OF YOUR FREAKIN' BUSINESS, IS IT?
BESIDES, I'M GONNA GO LIVE WITH RYO FROM NOW ON.
I'M ALL ALONE... AND, I DO WANT HIM TO GO TO SCHOOL, SO...
Yup.

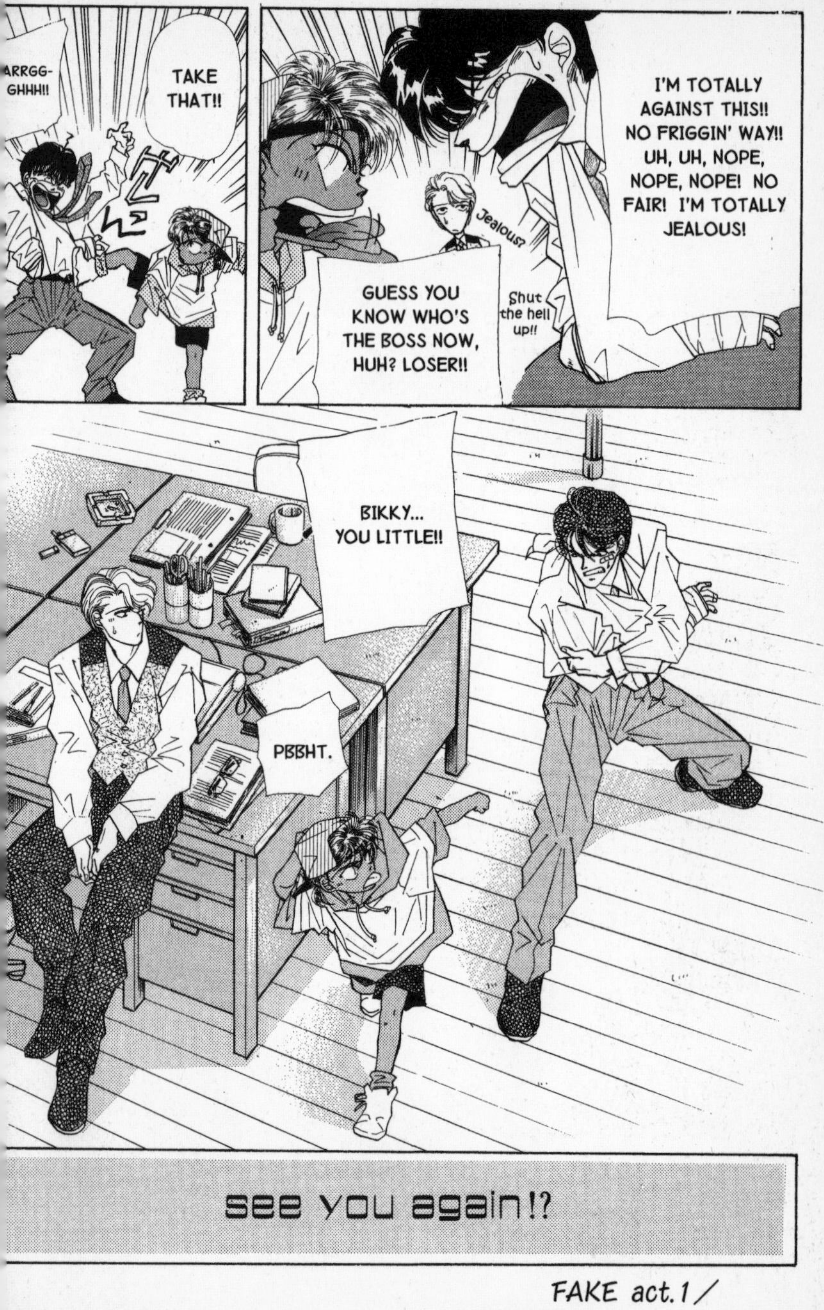
I'M TOTALLY AGAINST THIS!! NO FRIGGIN' WAY!! UH, UH, NOPE, NOPE, NOPE! NO FAIR! I'M TOTALLY JEALOUS!
Jealous?
Shut the hell up!!
GUESS YOU KNOW WHO'S THE BOSS NOW, HUH? LOSER!!
TAKE THAT!!
ARRGG-GHHH!!
BIKKY... YOU LITTLE!!
PBBHT.

see you again!?

FAKE act.1/

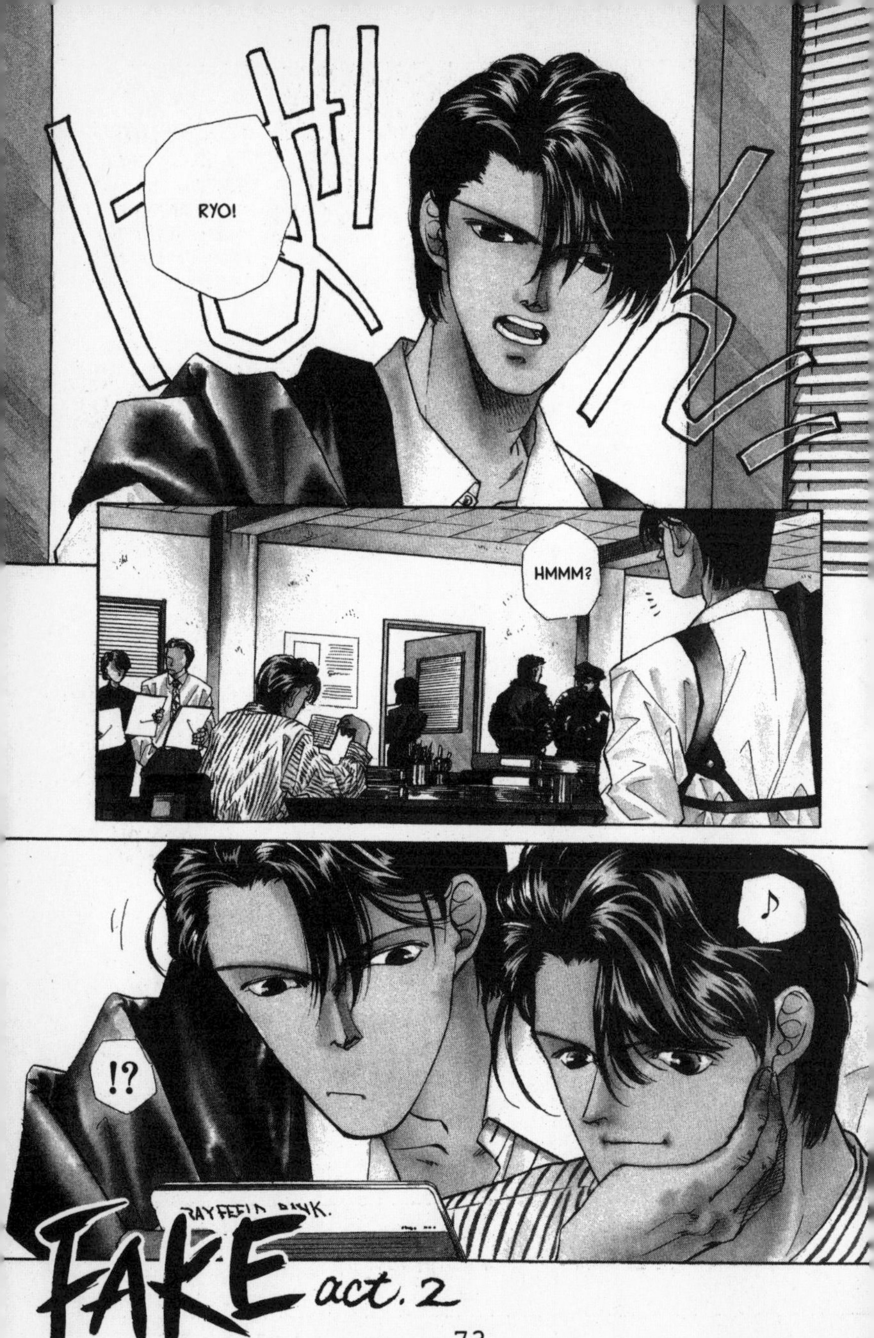
RYO!
HMMM?
♪
!?
FAKE act. 2

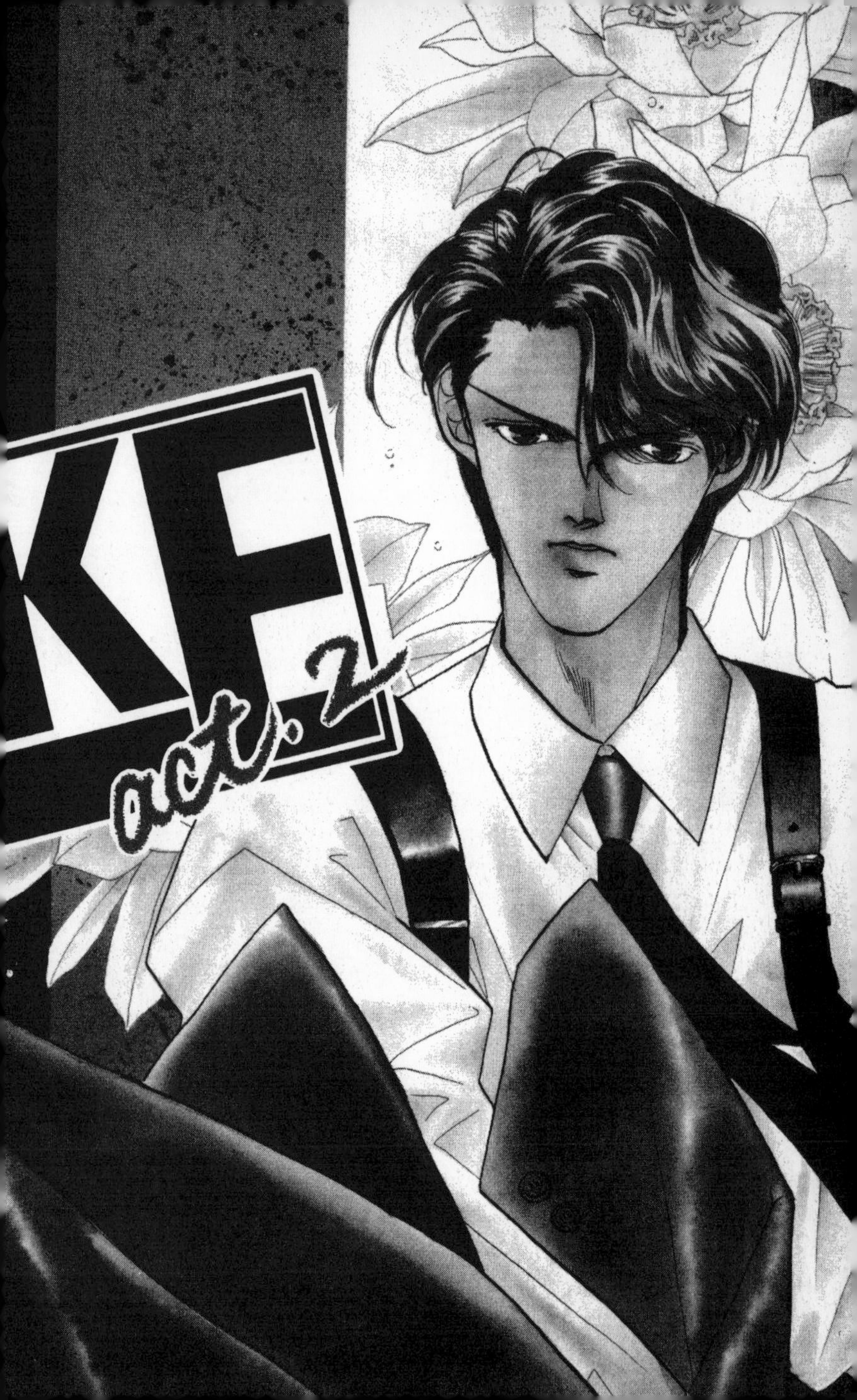
KF
act. 2

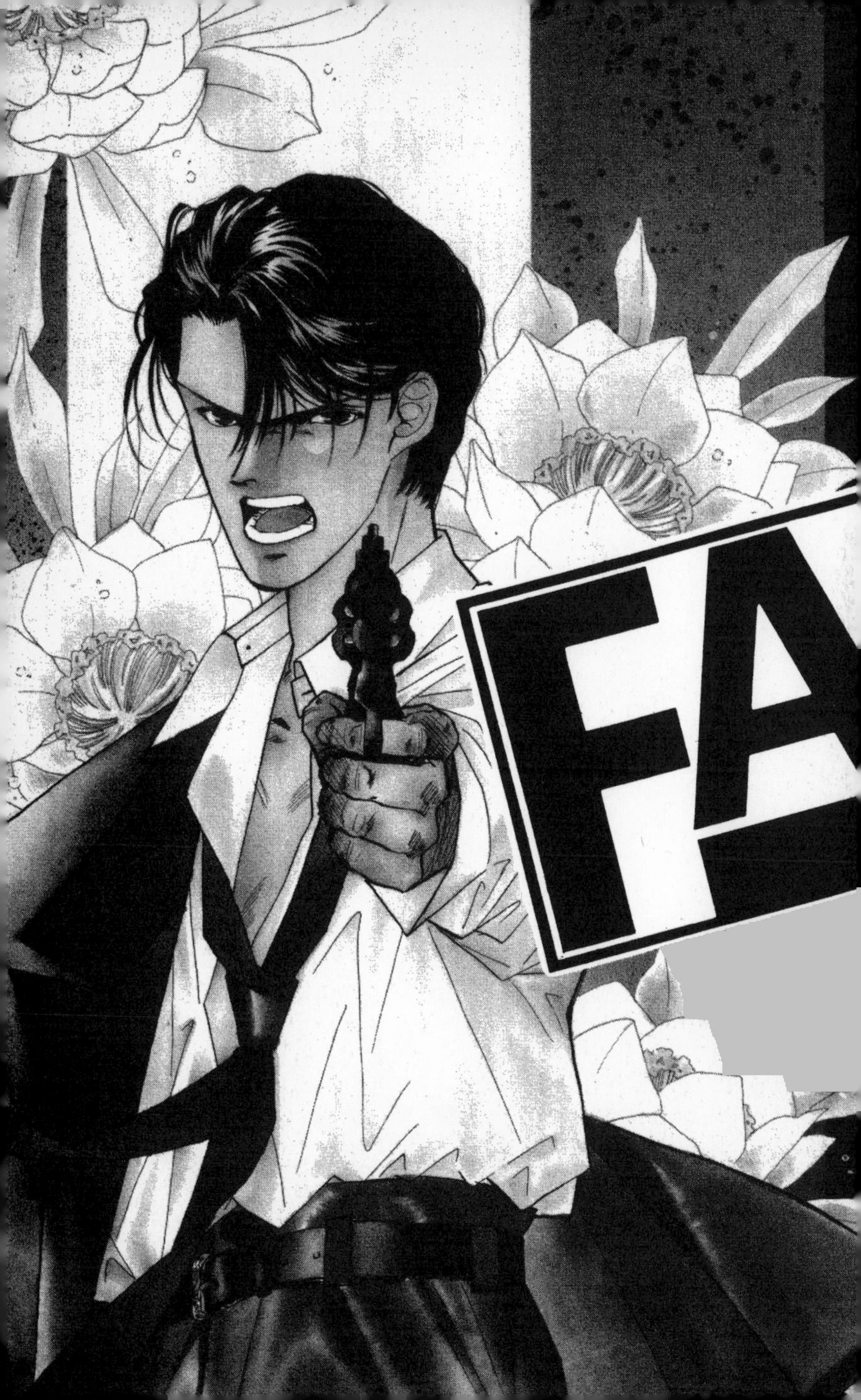
FA

FAKE

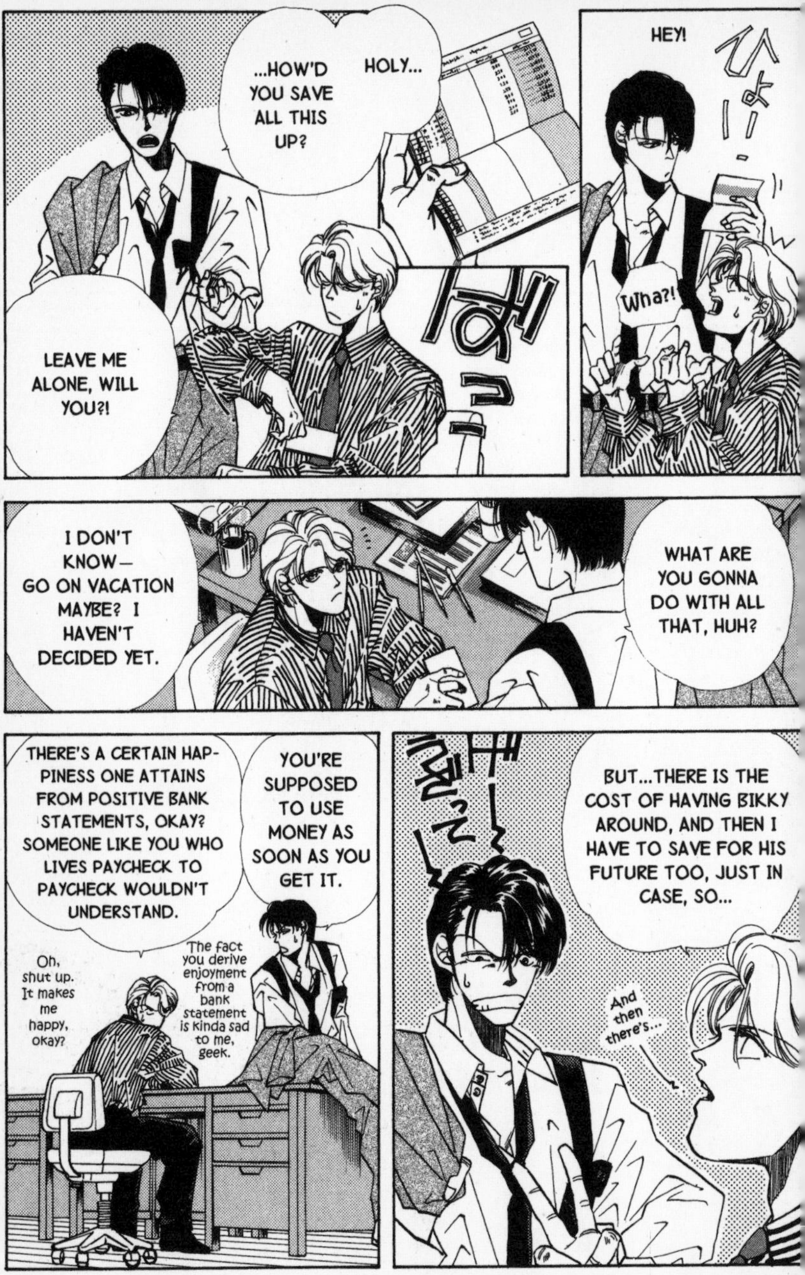
HEY!
ひょい
Wha?!
HOLY...
...HOW'D YOU SAVE ALL THIS UP?
はっ
LEAVE ME ALONE, WILL YOU?!
WHAT ARE YOU GONNA DO WITH ALL THAT, HUH?
I DON'T KNOW— GO ON VACATION MAYBE? I HAVEN'T DECIDED YET.
BUT...THERE IS THE COST OF HAVING BIKKY AROUND, AND THEN I HAVE TO SAVE FOR HIS FUTURE TOO, JUST IN CASE, SO...
And then there's...
YOU'RE SUPPOSED TO USE MONEY AS SOON AS YOU GET IT.
THERE'S A CERTAIN HAPPINESS ONE ATTAINS FROM POSITIVE BANK STATEMENTS, OKAY? SOMEONE LIKE YOU WHO LIVES PAYCHECK TO PAYCHECK WOULDN'T UNDERSTAND.
The fact you derive enjoyment from a bank statement is kinda sad to me, geek.
Oh, shut up. It makes me happy, okay?

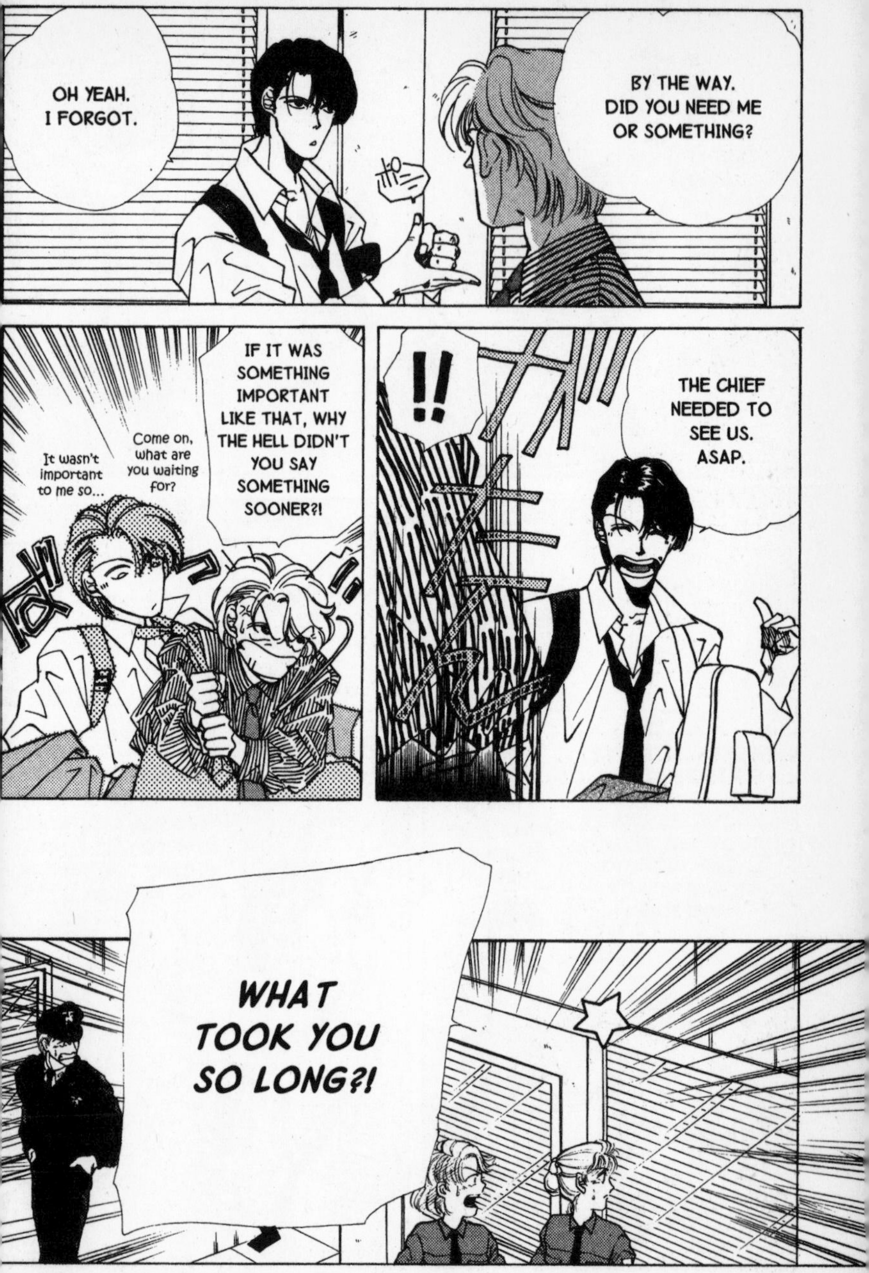
BY THE WAY. DID YOU NEED ME OR SOMETHING?
OH YEAH. I FORGOT.
THE CHIEF NEEDED TO SEE US. ASAP.
!!
IF IT WAS SOMETHING IMPORTANT LIKE THAT, WHY THE HELL DIDN'T YOU SAY SOMETHING SOONER?!
Come on, what are you waiting for?
It wasn't important to me so...
WHAT TOOK YOU SO LONG?!

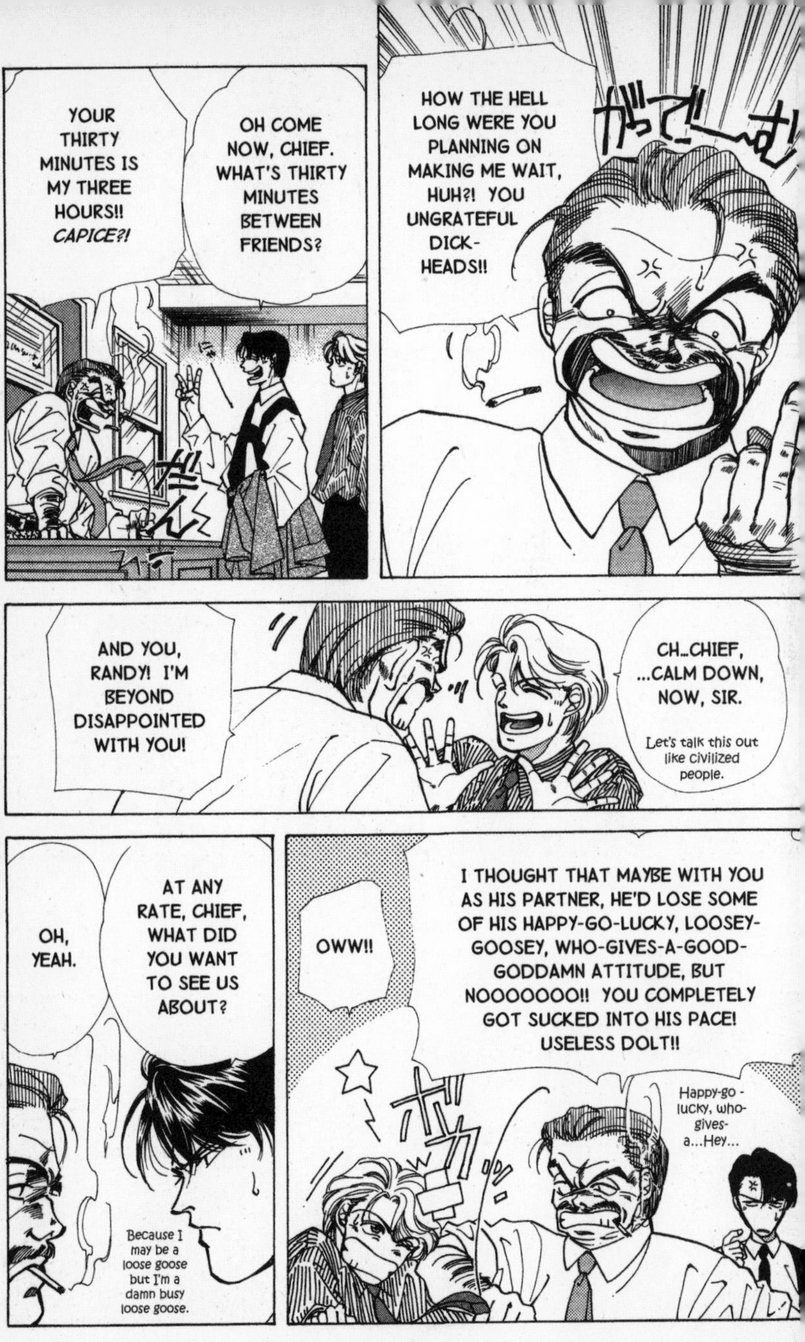
HOW THE HELL LONG WERE YOU PLANNING ON MAKING ME WAIT, HUH?! YOU UNGRATEFUL DICK-HEADS!!
OH COME NOW, CHIEF. WHAT'S THIRTY MINUTES BETWEEN FRIENDS?
YOUR THIRTY MINUTES IS MY THREE HOURS!! *CAPICE?!*
CH...CHIEF, ...CALM DOWN, NOW, SIR.
Let's talk this out like civilized people.
AND YOU, RANDY! I'M BEYOND DISAPPOINTED WITH YOU!
I THOUGHT THAT MAYBE WITH YOU AS HIS PARTNER, HE'D LOSE SOME OF HIS HAPPY-GO-LUCKY, LOOSEY-GOOSEY, WHO-GIVES-A-GOOD-GODDAMN ATTITUDE, BUT NOOOOOOO!! YOU COMPLETELY GOT SUCKED INTO HIS PACE! USELESS DOLT!!
OWW!!
Happy-go-lucky, who-gives-a...Hey...
AT ANY RATE, CHIEF, WHAT DID YOU WANT TO SEE US ABOUT?
OH, YEAH.
Because I may be a loose goose but I'm a damn busy loose goose.

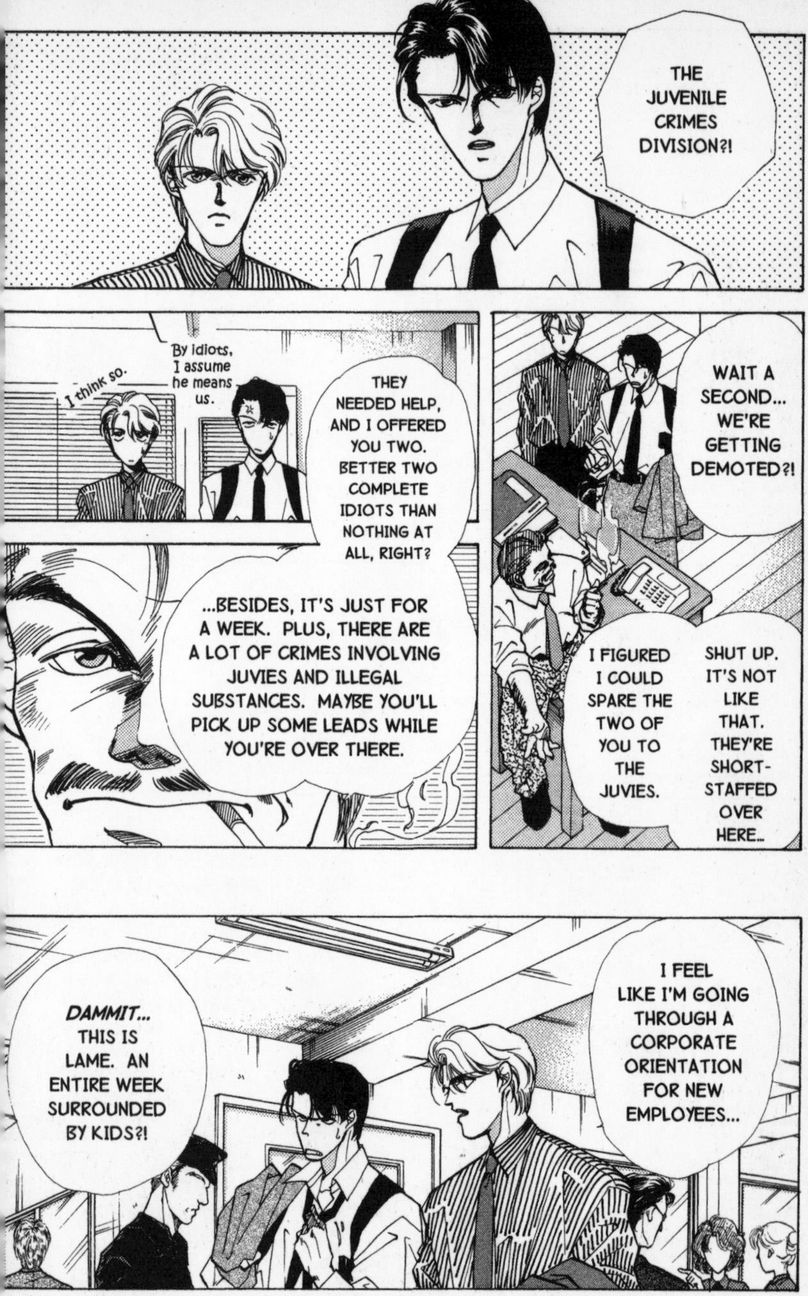

THE JUVENILE CRIMES DIVISION?!
WAIT A SECOND... WE'RE GETTING DEMOTED?!
SHUT UP. IT'S NOT LIKE THAT. THEY'RE SHORT-STAFFED OVER HERE..
I FIGURED I COULD SPARE THE TWO OF YOU TO THE JUVIES.
THEY NEEDED HELP, AND I OFFERED YOU TWO. BETTER TWO COMPLETE IDIOTS THAN NOTHING AT ALL, RIGHT?
By idiots, I assume he means us.
I think so.
...BESIDES, IT'S JUST FOR A WEEK. PLUS, THERE ARE A LOT OF CRIMES INVOLVING JUVIES AND ILLEGAL SUBSTANCES. MAYBE YOU'LL PICK UP SOME LEADS WHILE YOU'RE OVER THERE.
I FEEL LIKE I'M GOING THROUGH A CORPORATE ORIENTATION FOR NEW EMPLOYEES...
DAMMIT... THIS IS LAME. AN ENTIRE WEEK SURROUNDED BY KIDS?!

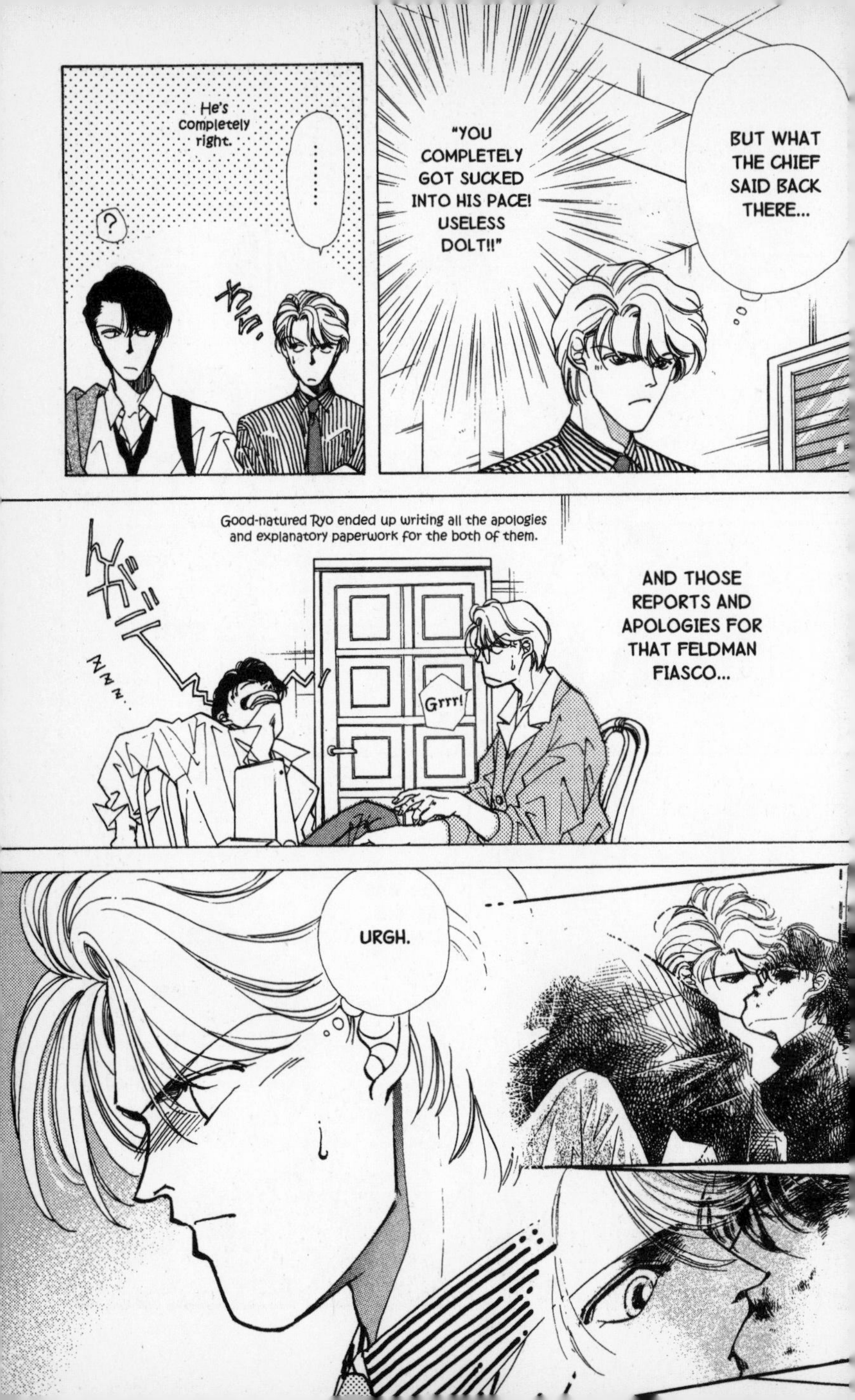
BUT WHAT THE CHIEF SAID BACK THERE...
"YOU COMPLETELY GOT SUCKED INTO HIS PACE! USELESS DOLT!!"
......
He's completely right.
?
AND THOSE REPORTS AND APOLOGIES FOR THAT FELDMAN FIASCO...
Grrr!
Good-natured Ryo ended up writing all the apologies and explanatory paperwork for the both of them.
URGH.

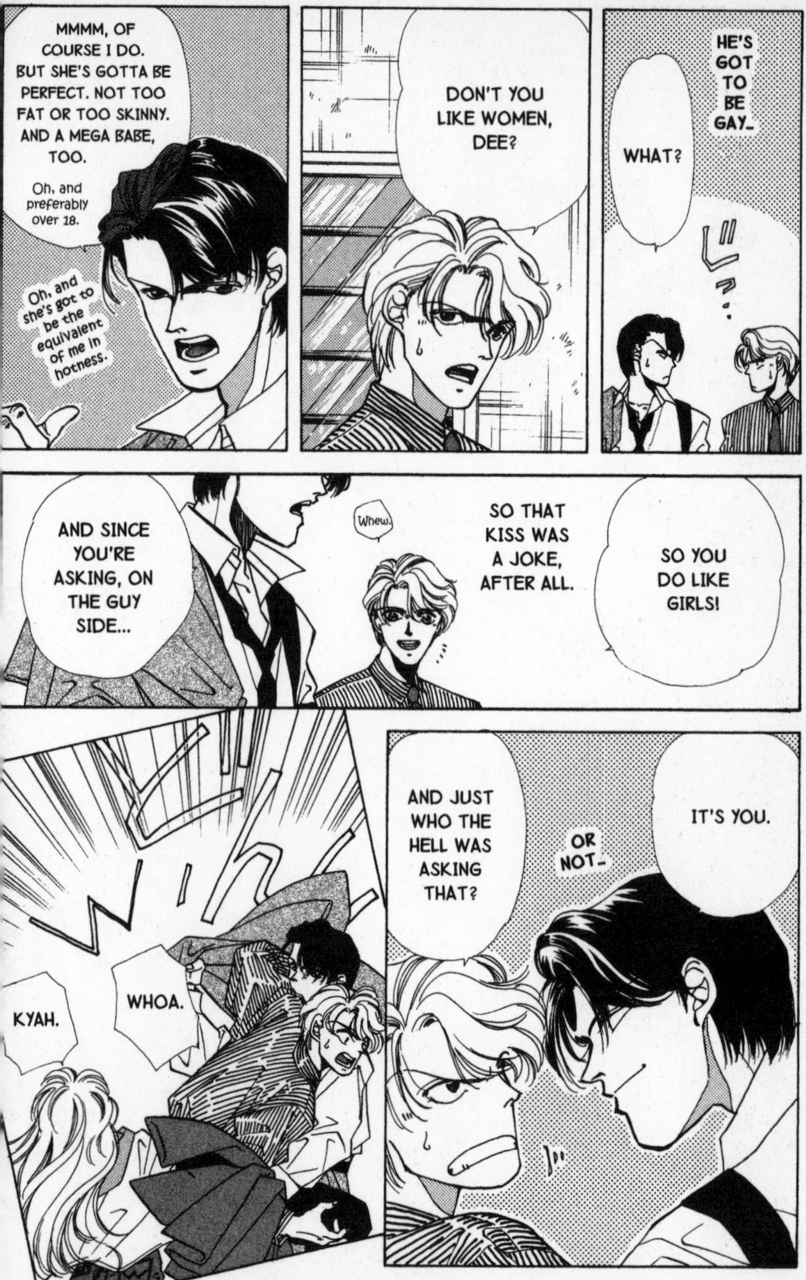
HE'S GOT TO BE GAY...
WHAT?
DON'T YOU LIKE WOMEN, DEE?
MMMM, OF COURSE I DO. BUT SHE'S GOTTA BE PERFECT. NOT TOO FAT OR TOO SKINNY. AND A MEGA BABE, TOO.
Oh, and preferably over 18.
Oh, and she's got to be the equivalent of me in hotness.
SO YOU DO LIKE GIRLS!
SO THAT KISS WAS A JOKE, AFTER ALL.
Whew.
AND SINCE YOU'RE ASKING, ON THE GUY SIDE...
IT'S YOU.
OR NOT...
AND JUST WHO THE HELL WAS ASKING THAT?
WHOA.
KYAH.

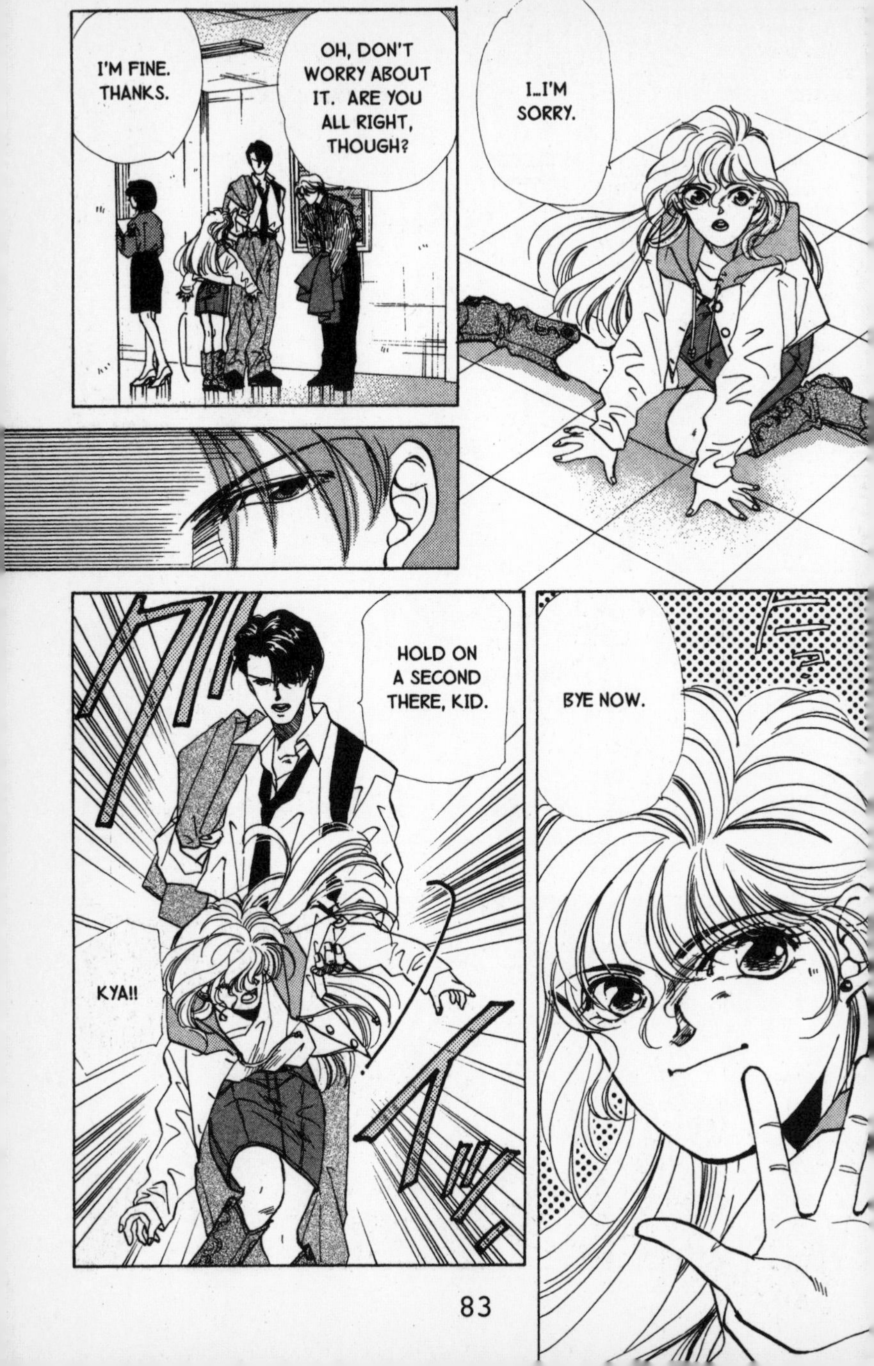
I...I'M SORRY.
OH, DON'T WORRY ABOUT IT. ARE YOU ALL RIGHT, THOUGH?
I'M FINE. THANKS.
BYE NOW.
HOLD ON A SECOND THERE, KID.
KYA!!

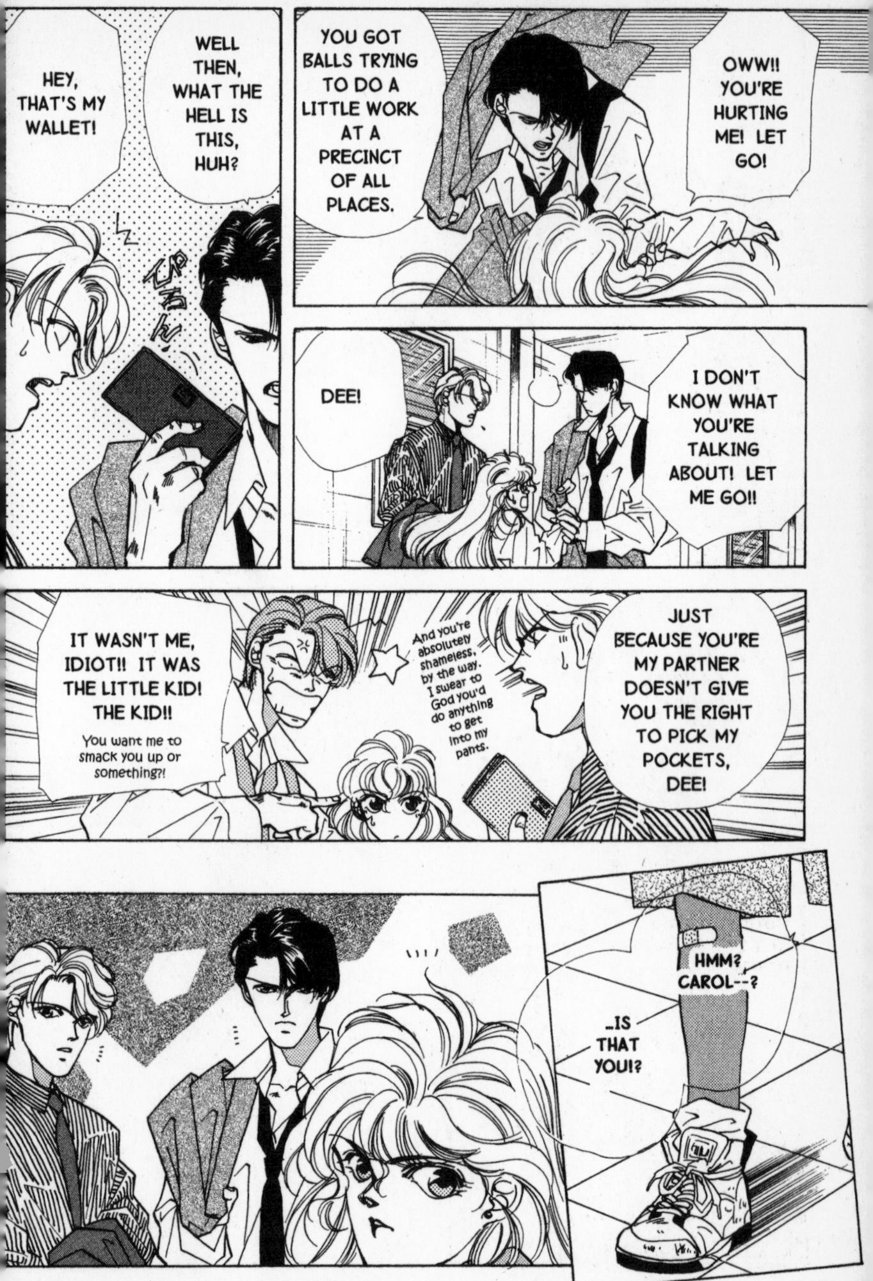
OWW!! YOU'RE HURTING ME! LET GO!
YOU GOT BALLS TRYING TO DO A LITTLE WORK AT A PRECINCT OF ALL PLACES.
I DON'T KNOW WHAT YOU'RE TALKING ABOUT! LET ME GO!!
DEE!
WELL THEN, WHAT THE HELL IS THIS, HUH?
HEY, THAT'S MY WALLET!
JUST BECAUSE YOU'RE MY PARTNER DOESN'T GIVE YOU THE RIGHT TO PICK MY POCKETS, DEE!
And you're absolutely shameless, by the way. I swear to God you'd do anything to get into my pants.
IT WASN'T ME, IDIOT!! IT WAS THE LITTLE KID! THE KID!!
You want me to smack you up or something?!
HMM? CAROL--?
..IS THAT YOU!?

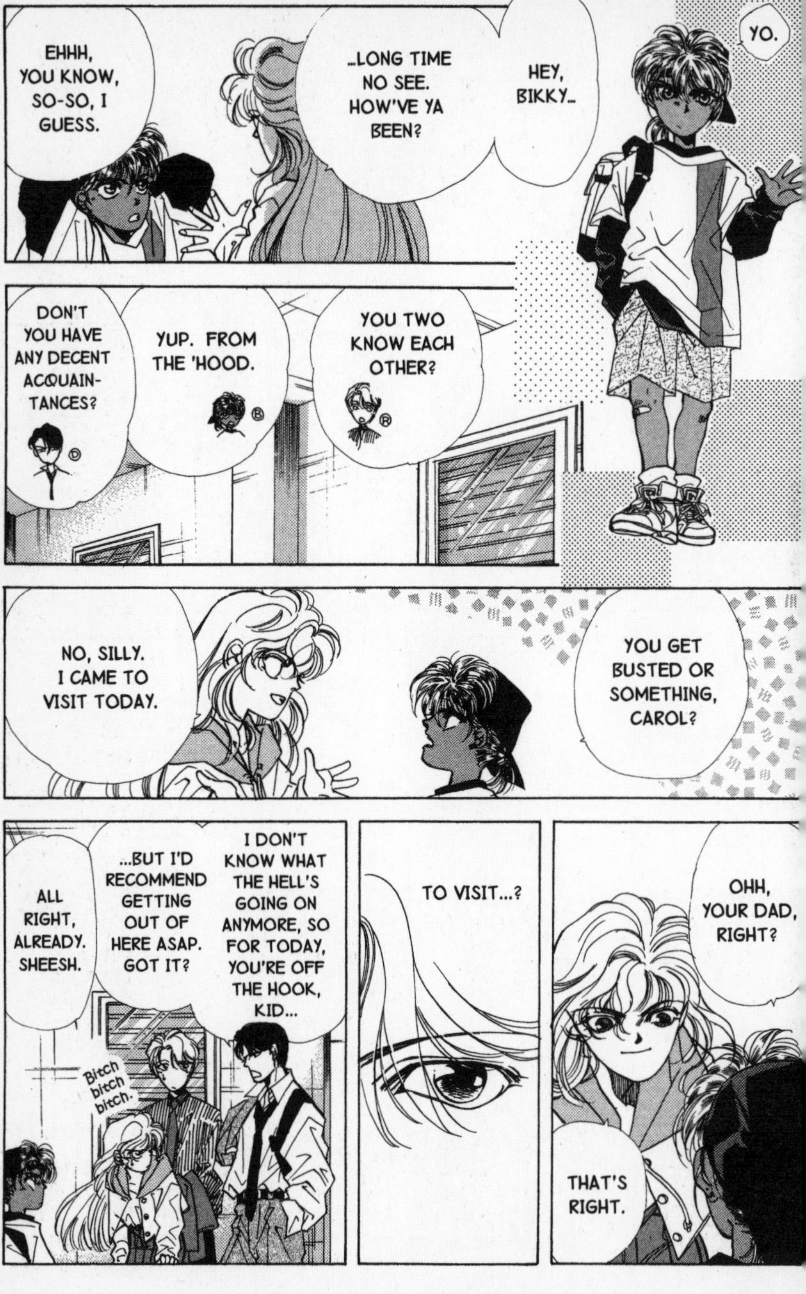
YO.
HEY, BIKKY..
..LONG TIME NO SEE. HOW'VE YA BEEN?
EHHH, YOU KNOW, SO-SO, I GUESS.
YOU TWO KNOW EACH OTHER?
YUP. FROM THE 'HOOD.
DON'T YOU HAVE ANY DECENT ACQUAIN-TANCES?
YOU GET BUSTED OR SOMETHING, CAROL?
NO, SILLY. I CAME TO VISIT TODAY.
OHH, YOUR DAD, RIGHT?
THAT'S RIGHT.
TO VISIT...?
I DON'T KNOW WHAT THE HELL'S GOING ON ANYMORE, SO FOR TODAY, YOU'RE OFF THE HOOK, KID...
...BUT I'D RECOMMEND GETTING OUT OF HERE ASAP. GOT IT?
ALL RIGHT, ALREADY. SHEESH.
Bitch bitch bitch.

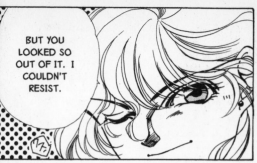

OH, AND OFFICER? I'M REALLY SORRY ABOUT YOUR WALLET.
BUT YOU LOOKED SO OUT OF IT. I COULDN'T RESIST.
THANKS FOR THE HEADS UP. I'LL TRY TO BE MORE CAREFUL FROM NOW ON.
BUH-BYE NOW.
HEY, BIKKY... ...WHAT DID SHE MEAN BY VISITING, HUH?
YOU KNOW THAT POLICE HOSPITAL NEXT DOOR?
YEAH.
HER FATHER'S A PATIENT THERE.

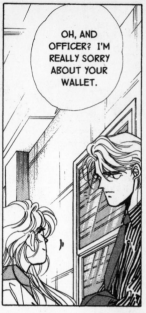

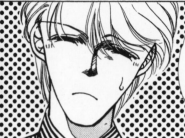

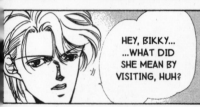

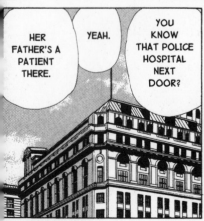

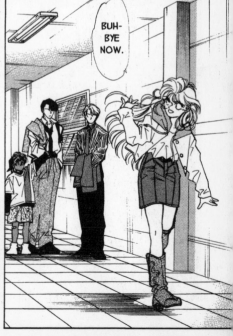

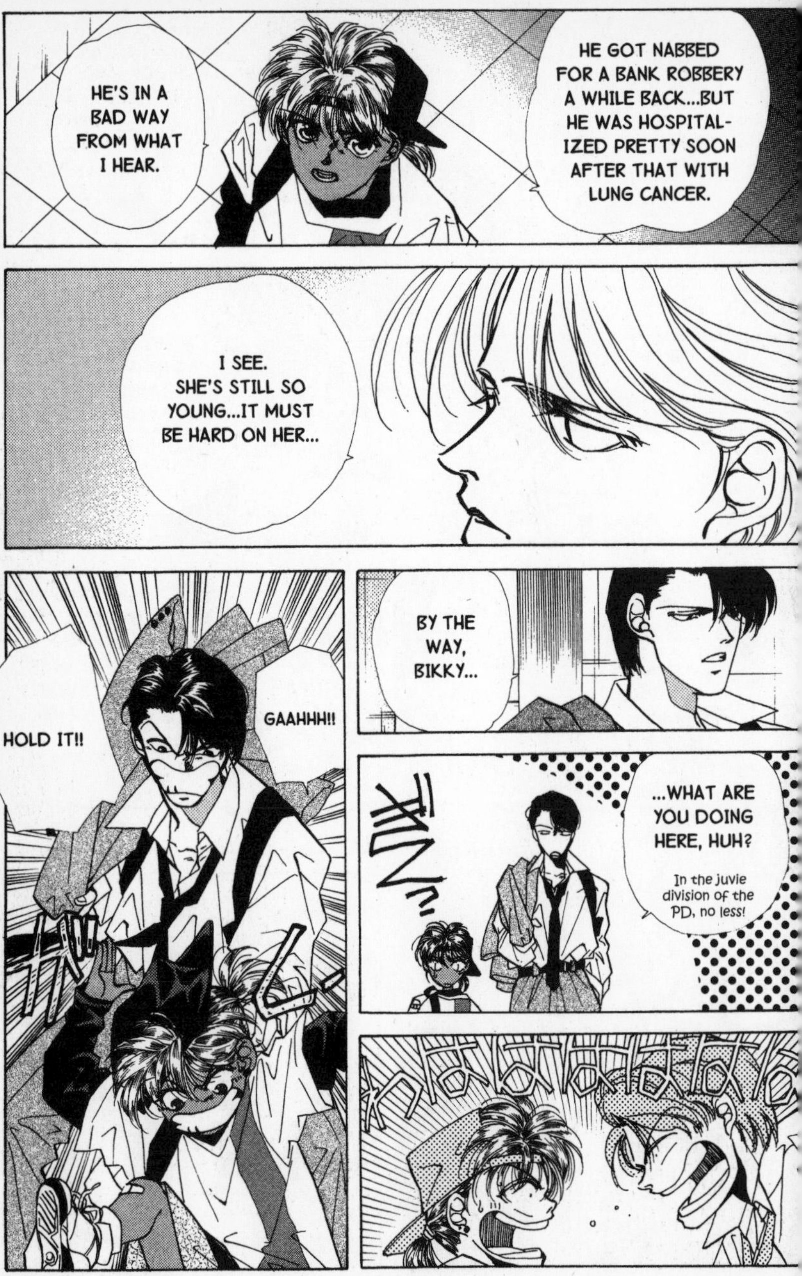
HE GOT NABBED FOR A BANK ROBBERY A WHILE BACK...BUT HE WAS HOSPITAL-IZED PRETTY SOON AFTER THAT WITH LUNG CANCER.
HE'S IN A BAD WAY FROM WHAT I HEAR.
I SEE. SHE'S STILL SO YOUNG...IT MUST BE HARD ON HER...
BY THE WAY, BIKKY...
...WHAT ARE YOU DOING HERE, HUH?
In the juvie division of the PD, no less!
GAAHHH!!
HOLD IT!!

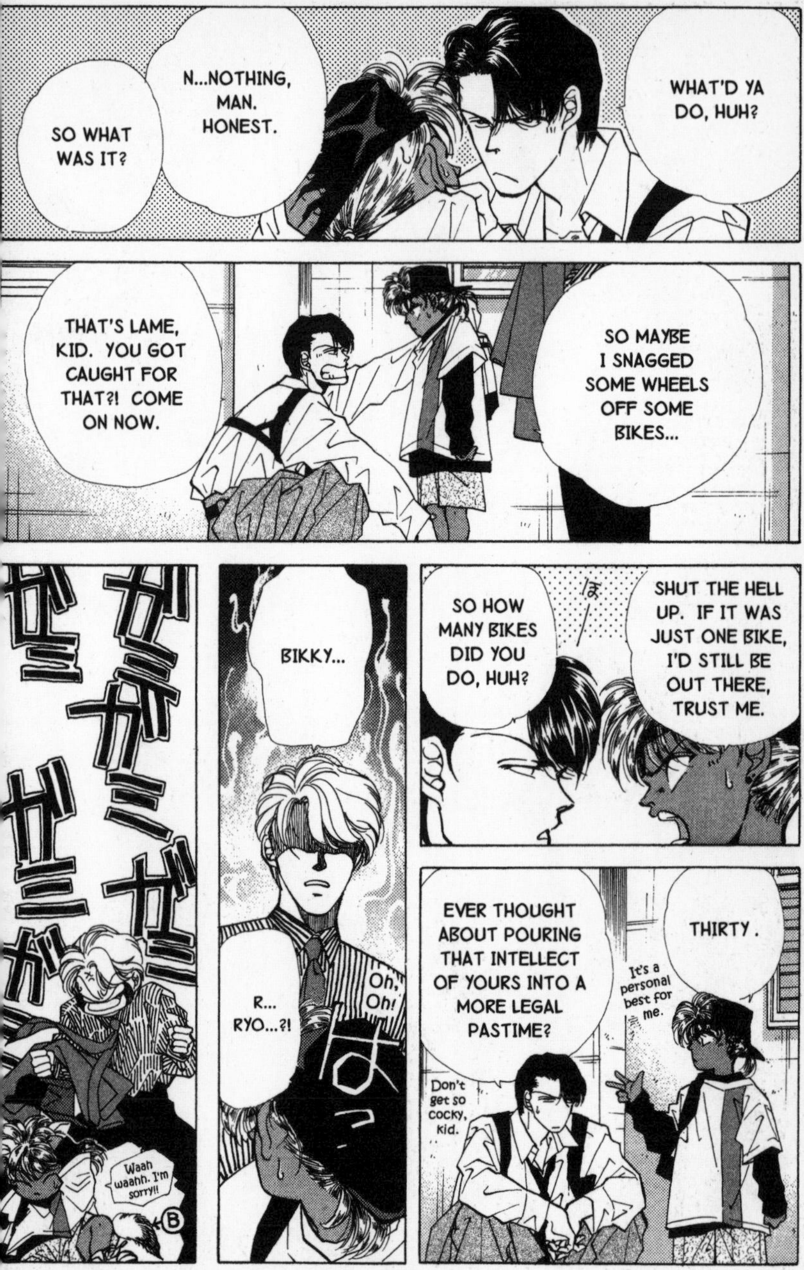
WHAT'D YA DO, HUH?
N...NOTHING, MAN. HONEST.
SO WHAT WAS IT?
SO MAYBE I SNAGGED SOME WHEELS OFF SOME BIKES...
THAT'S LAME, KID. YOU GOT CAUGHT FOR THAT?! COME ON NOW.
SHUT THE HELL UP. IF IT WAS JUST ONE BIKE, I'D STILL BE OUT THERE, TRUST ME.
SO HOW MANY BIKES DID YOU DO, HUH?
THIRTY.
It's a personal best for me.
EVER THOUGHT ABOUT POURING THAT INTELLECT OF YOURS INTO A MORE LEGAL PASTIME?
Don't get so cocky, kid.
BIKKY...
Oh, Oh!
R... RYO...?!
Waah waahh. I'm sorry!!

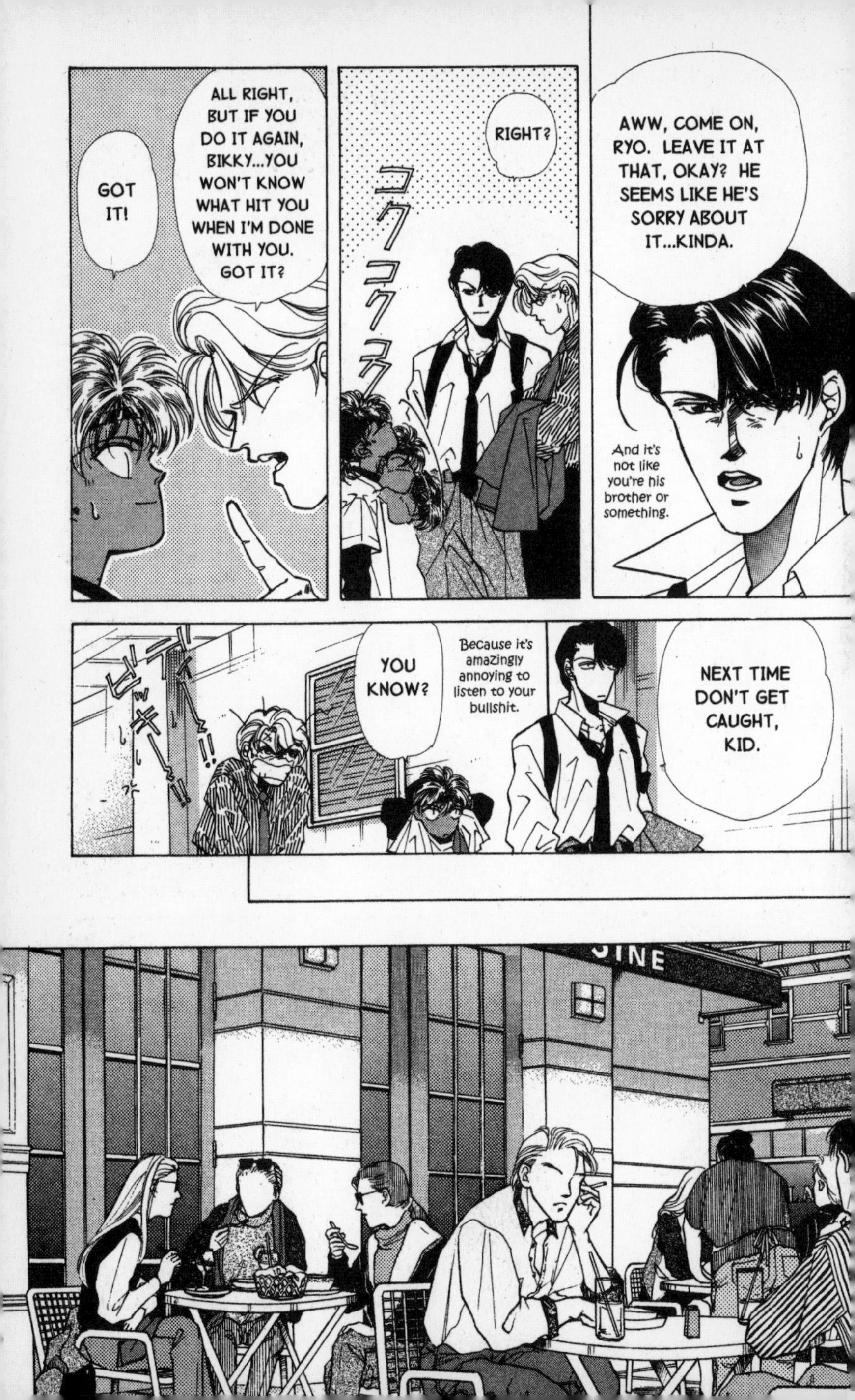
AWW, COME ON, RYO. LEAVE IT AT THAT, OKAY? HE SEEMS LIKE HE'S SORRY ABOUT IT...KINDA.
And it's not like you're his brother or something.
RIGHT?
ALL RIGHT, BUT IF YOU DO IT AGAIN, BIKKY...YOU WON'T KNOW WHAT HIT YOU WHEN I'M DONE WITH YOU. GOT IT?
GOT IT!
NEXT TIME DON'T GET CAUGHT, KID.
Because it's amazingly annoying to listen to your bullshit.
YOU KNOW?

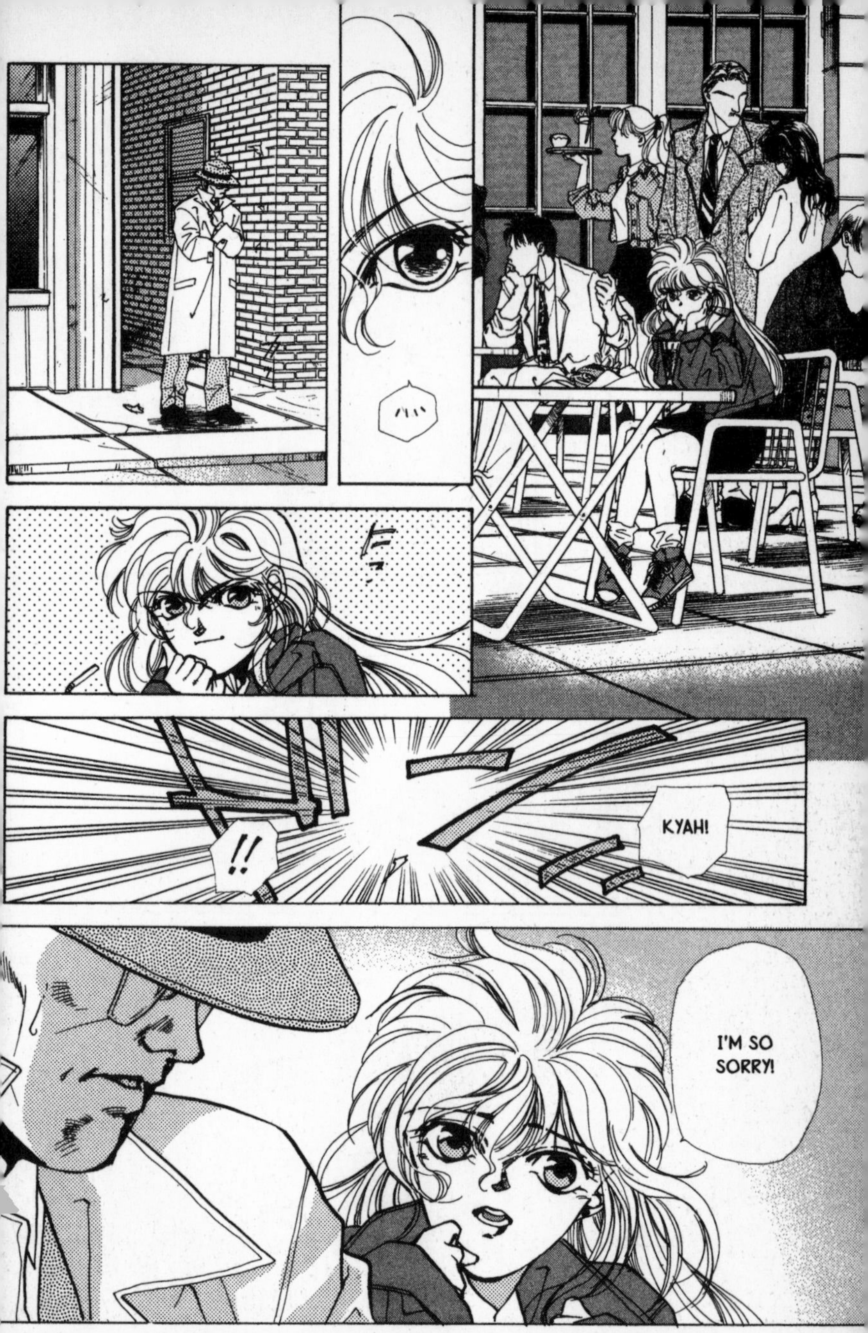
KYAH!
!!
I'M SO SORRY!

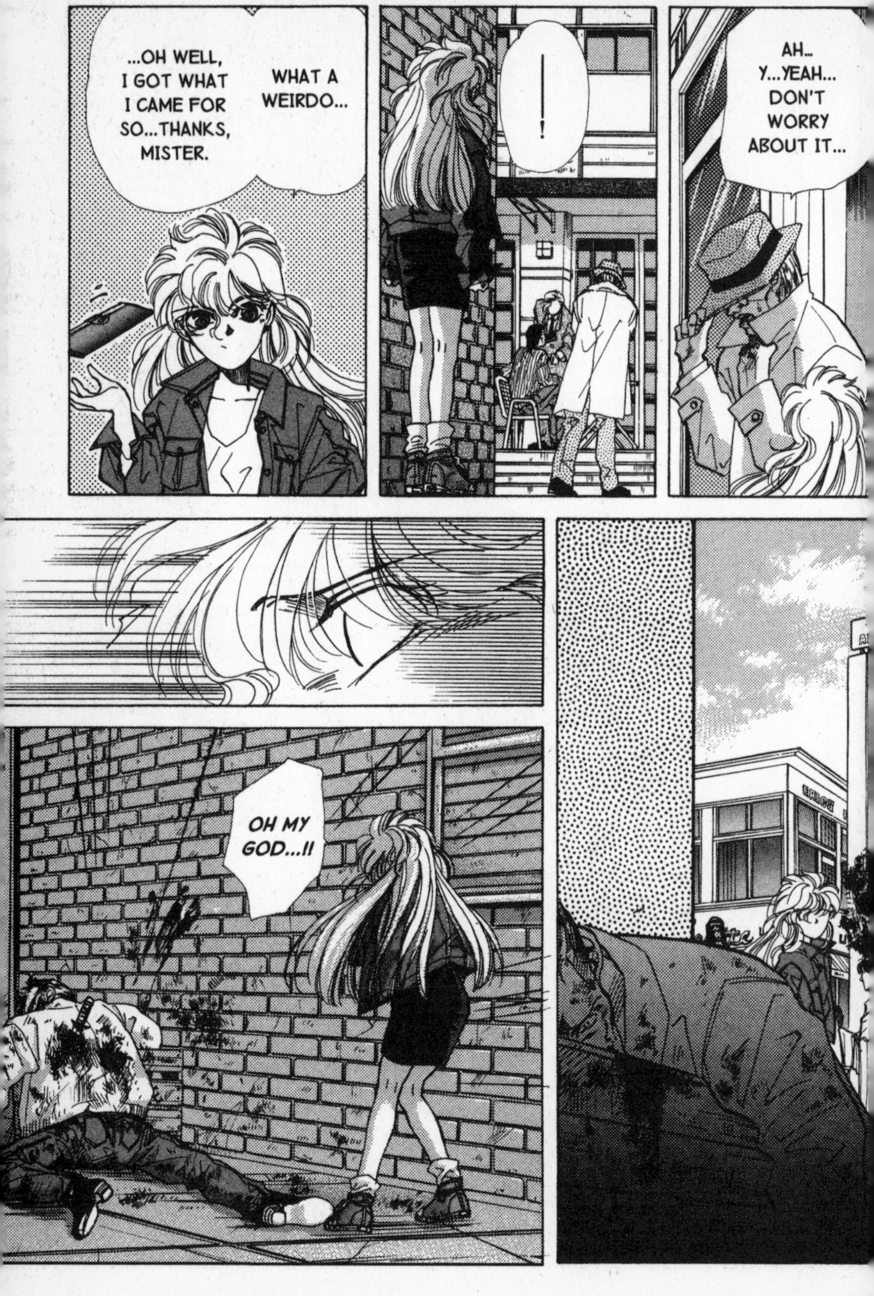

AH.. Y...YEAH... DON'T WORRY ABOUT IT...
—!
WHAT A WEIRDO...
...OH WELL, I GOT WHAT I CAME FOR SO...THANKS, MISTER.
OH MY GOD...!!

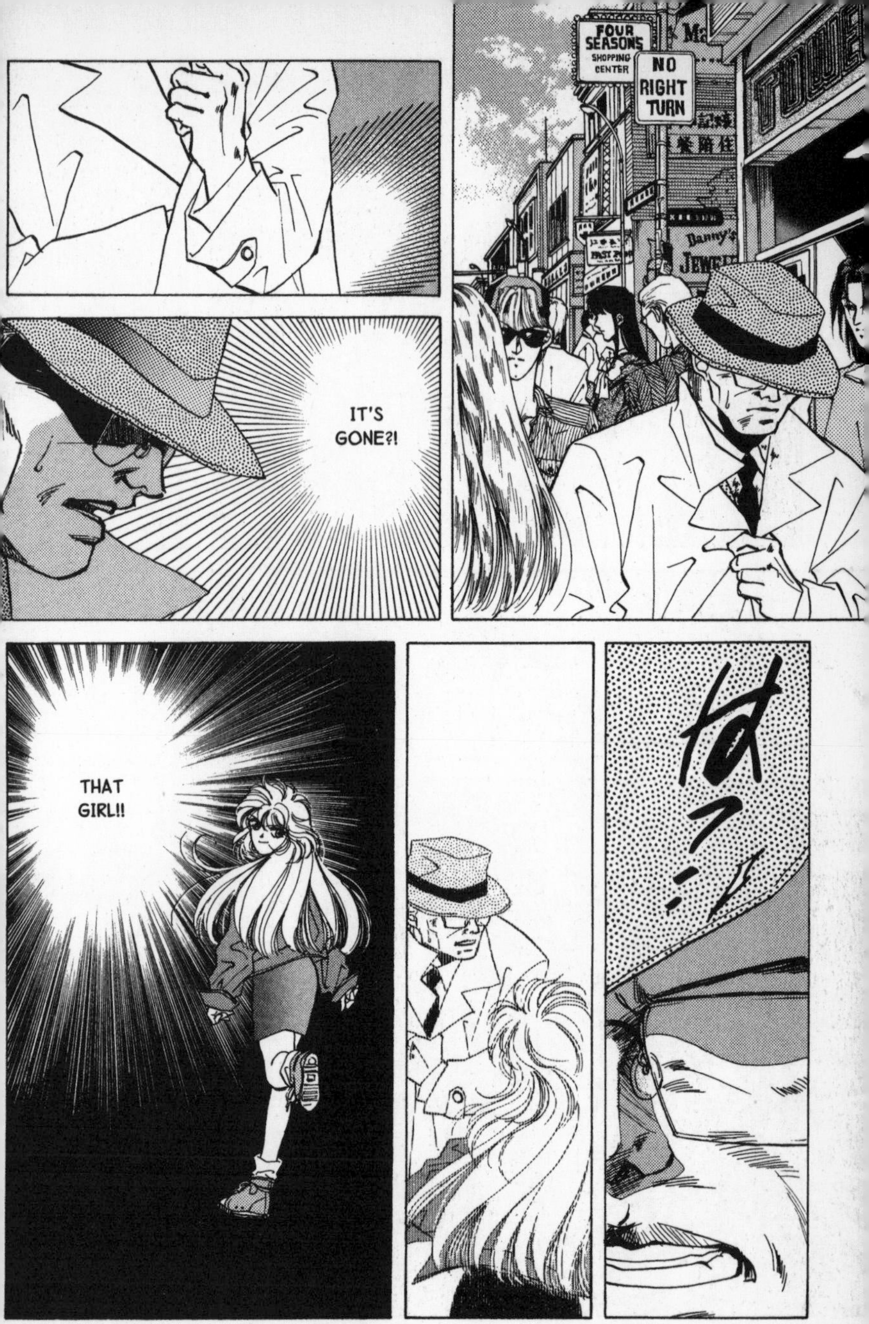
FOUR SEASONS SHOPPING CENTER
NO RIGHT TURN
IT'S GONE?!
はっ
THAT GIRL!!

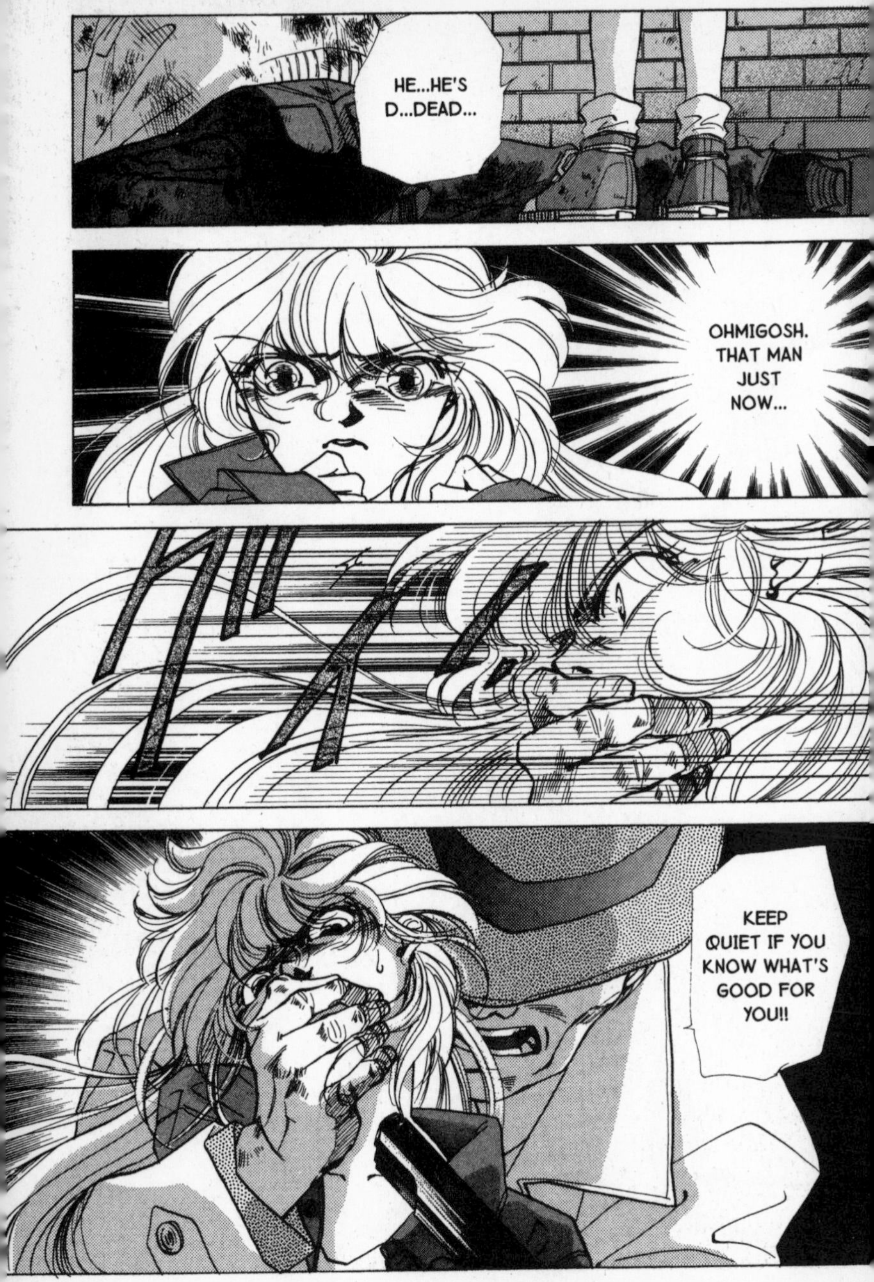
HE...HE'S D...DEAD...
OHMIGOSH. THAT MAN JUST NOW...
KEEP QUIET IF YOU KNOW WHAT'S GOOD FOR YOU!!

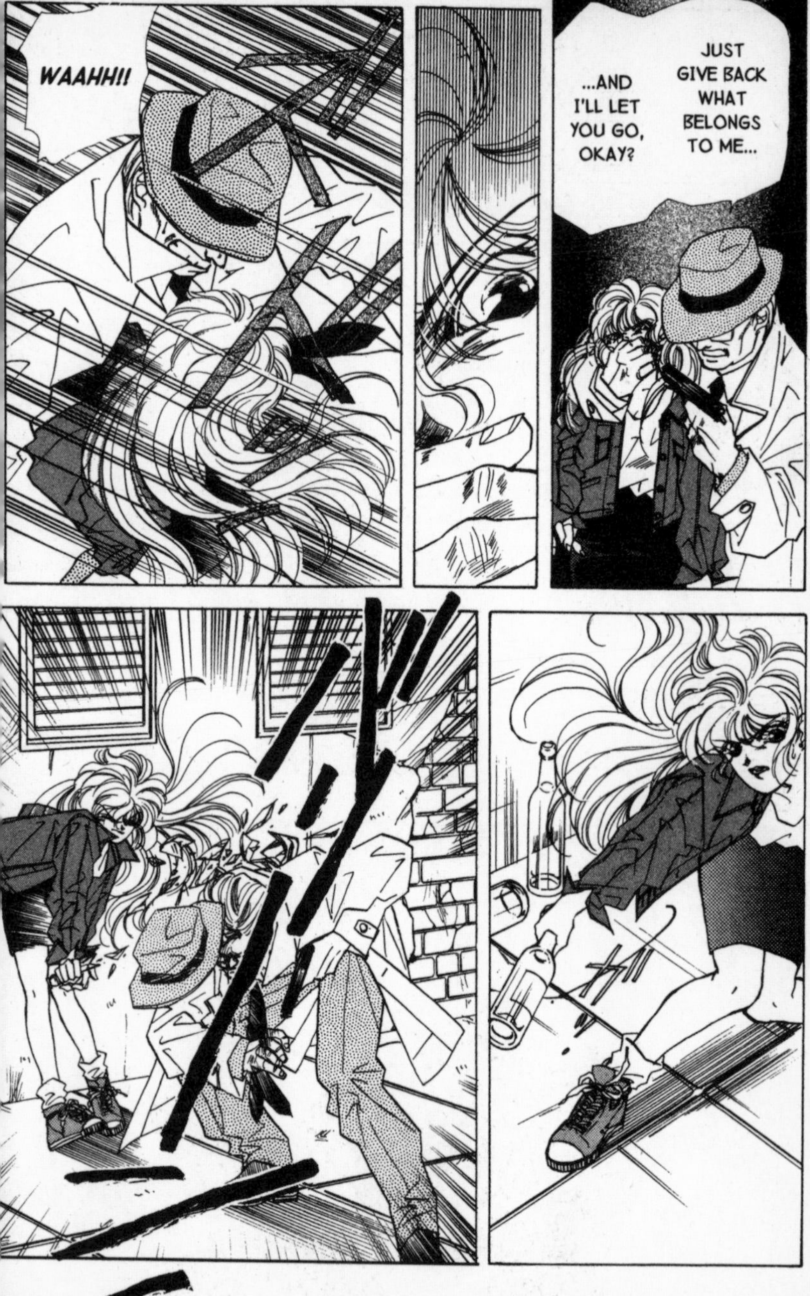
JUST GIVE BACK WHAT BELONGS TO ME...
...AND I'LL LET YOU GO, OKAY?
WAAHH!!

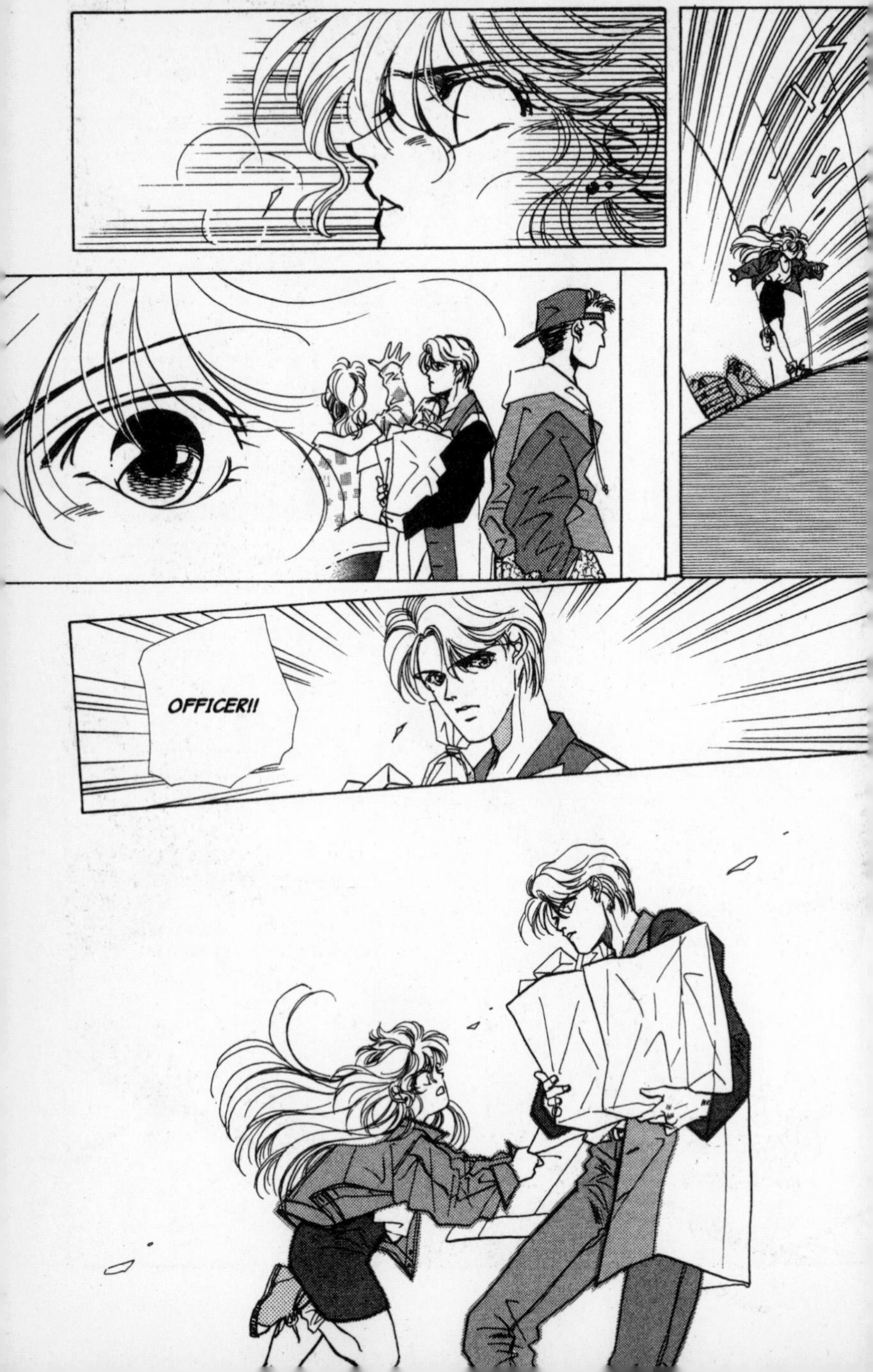
OFFICER!!

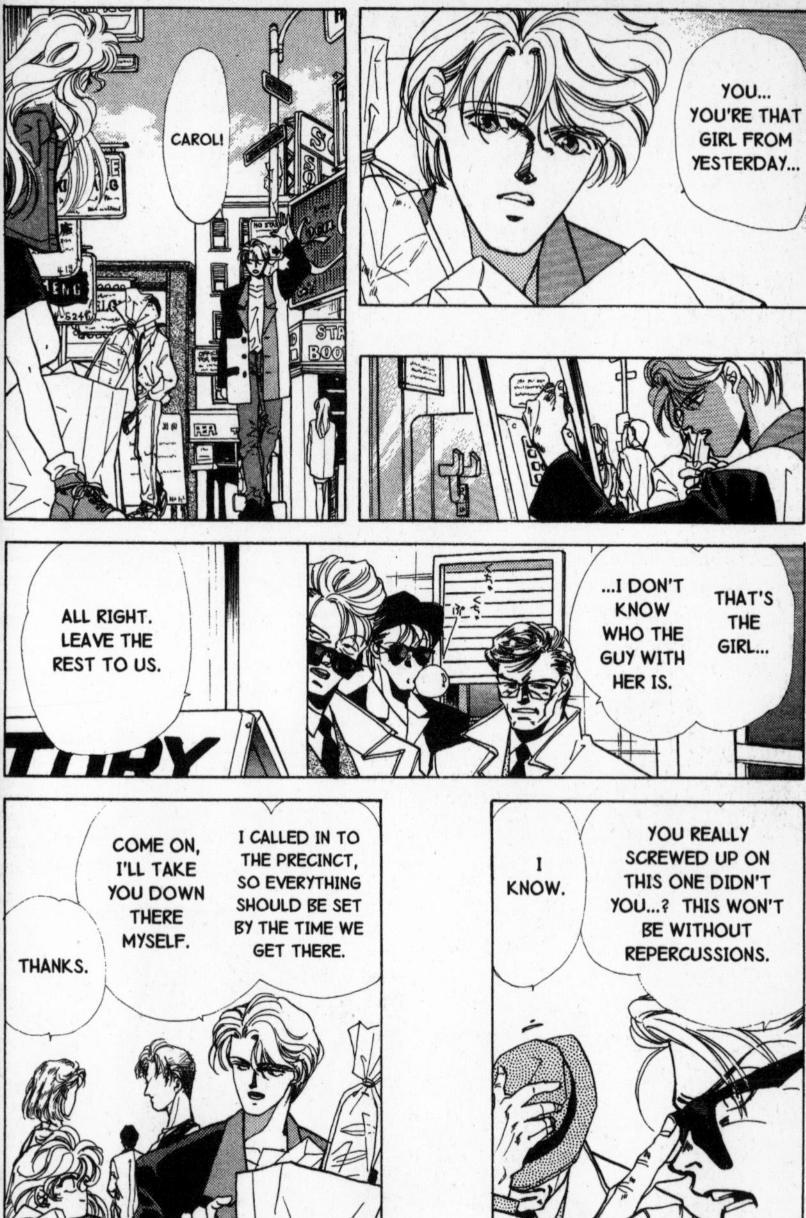
YOU... YOU'RE THAT GIRL FROM YESTERDAY...
CAROL!
THAT'S THE GIRL...
...I DON'T KNOW WHO THE GUY WITH HER IS.
ALL RIGHT. LEAVE THE REST TO US.
YOU REALLY SCREWED UP ON THIS ONE DIDN'T YOU...? THIS WON'T BE WITHOUT REPERCUSSIONS.
I KNOW.
I CALLED IN TO THE PRECINCT, SO EVERYTHING SHOULD BE SET BY THE TIME WE GET THERE.
COME ON, I'LL TAKE YOU DOWN THERE MYSELF.
THANKS.

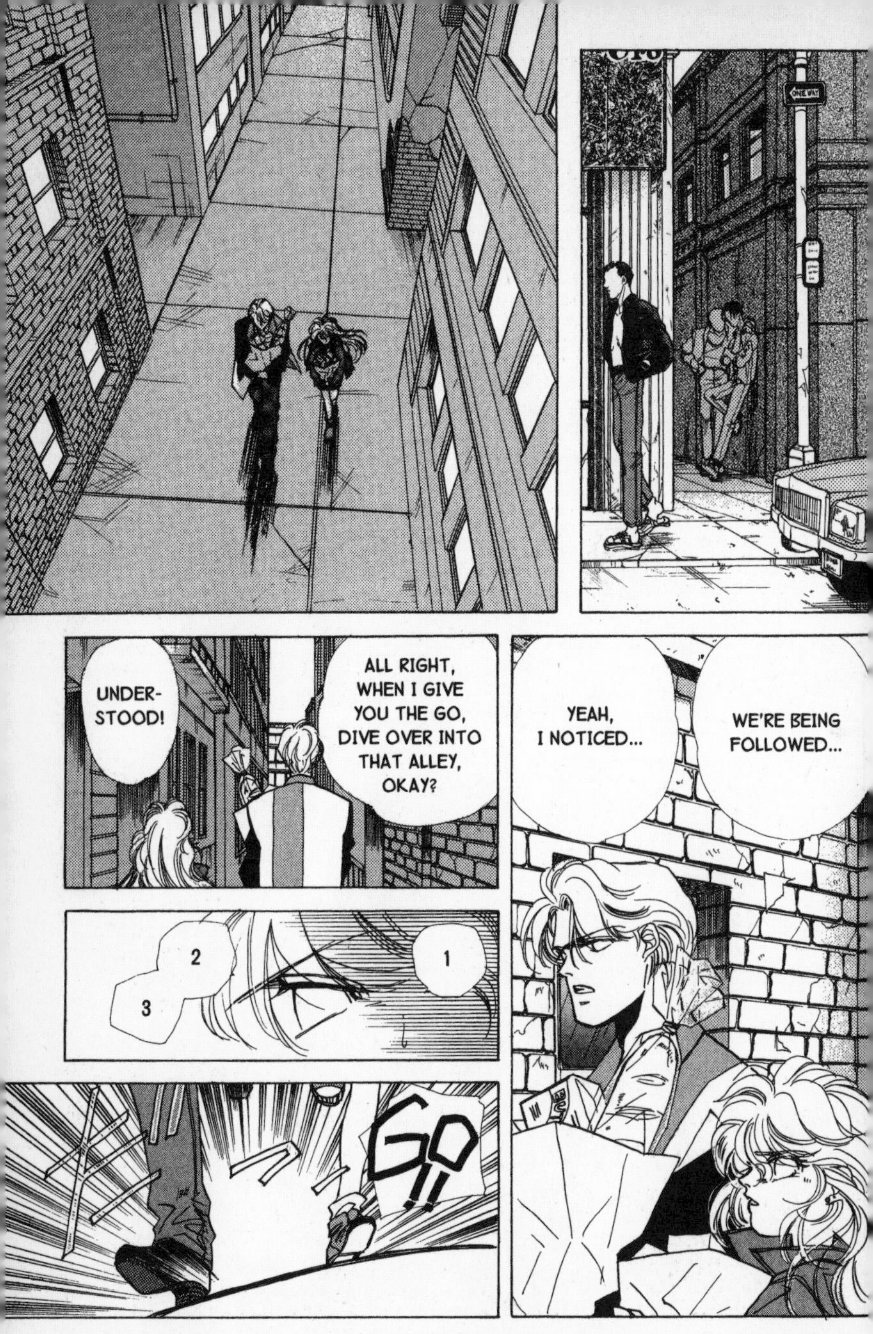
WE'RE BEING FOLLOWED...
YEAH, I NOTICED...
ALL RIGHT, WHEN I GIVE YOU THE GO, DIVE OVER INTO THAT ALLEY, OKAY?
UNDER-STOOD!
1
2
3
GO!!

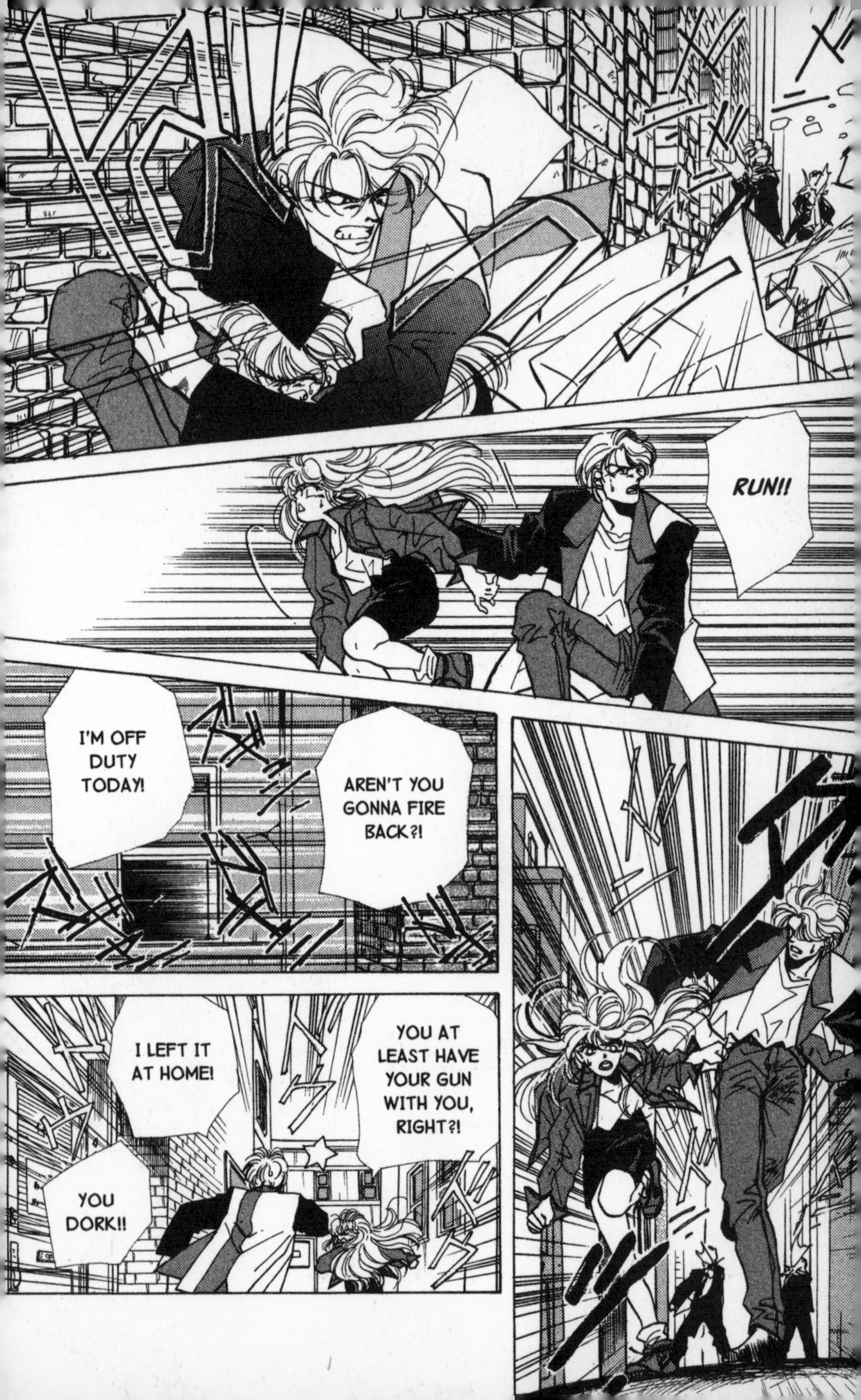
RUN!!
AREN'T YOU GONNA FIRE BACK?!
I'M OFF DUTY TODAY!
YOU AT LEAST HAVE YOUR GUN WITH YOU, RIGHT?!
I LEFT IT AT HOME!
YOU DORK!!

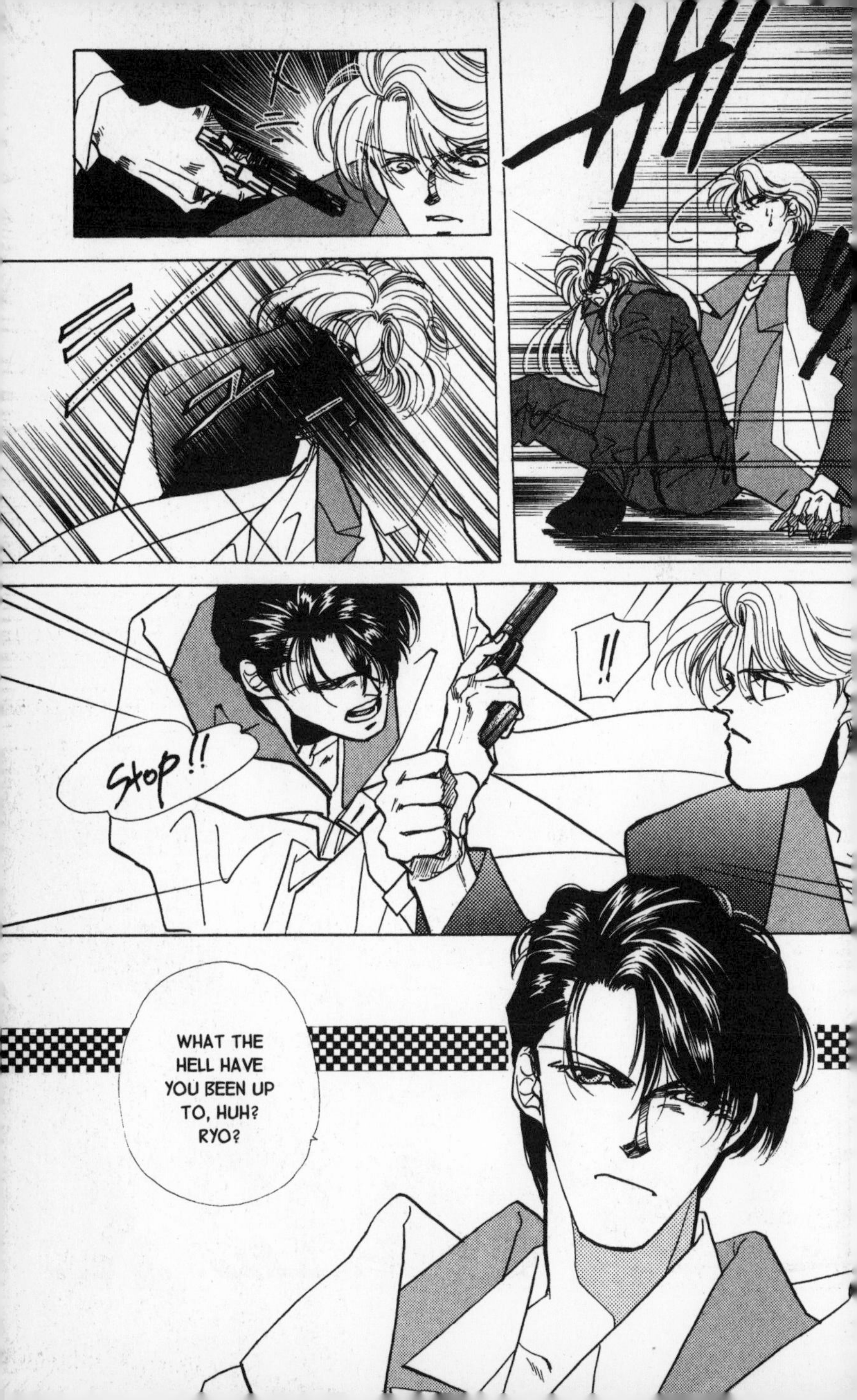
!!
Stop!!
WHAT THE HELL HAVE YOU BEEN UP TO, HUH? RYO?

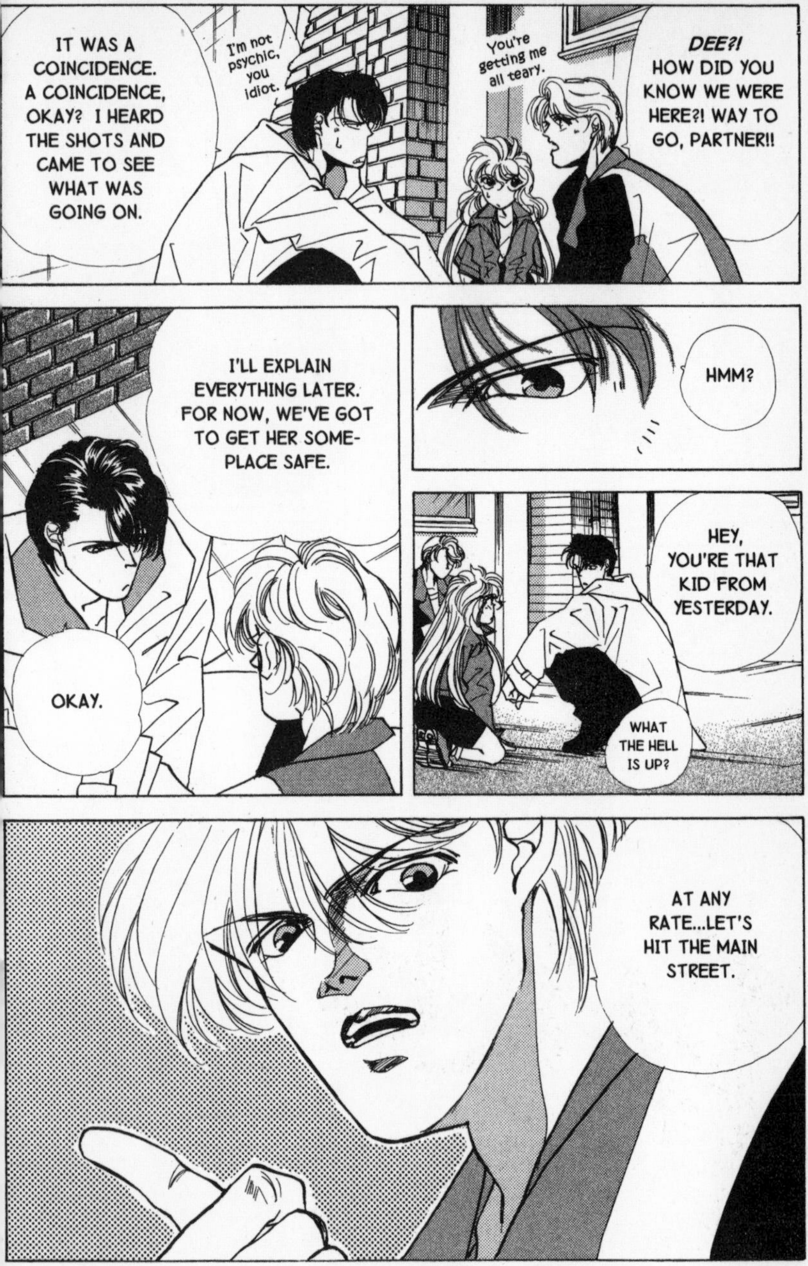
DEE?! HOW DID YOU KNOW WE WERE HERE?! WAY TO GO, PARTNER!!
You're getting me all teary.
I'm not psychic, you idiot.
IT WAS A COINCIDENCE. A COINCIDENCE, OKAY? I HEARD THE SHOTS AND CAME TO SEE WHAT WAS GOING ON.
HMM?
HEY, YOU'RE THAT KID FROM YESTERDAY.
WHAT THE HELL IS UP?
I'LL EXPLAIN EVERYTHING LATER. FOR NOW, WE'VE GOT TO GET HER SOME-PLACE SAFE.
OKAY.
AT ANY RATE...LET'S HIT THE MAIN STREET.

FAKE

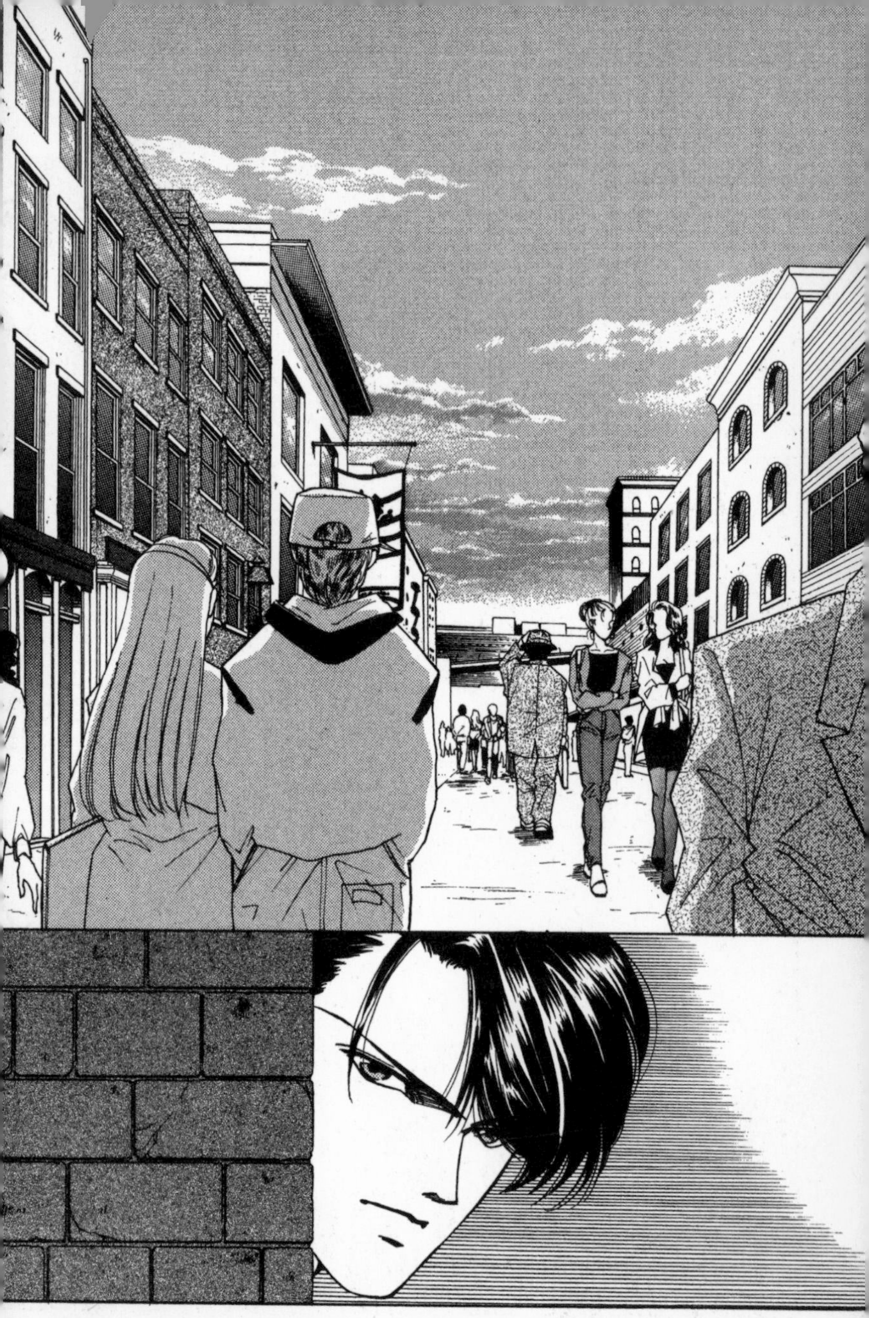

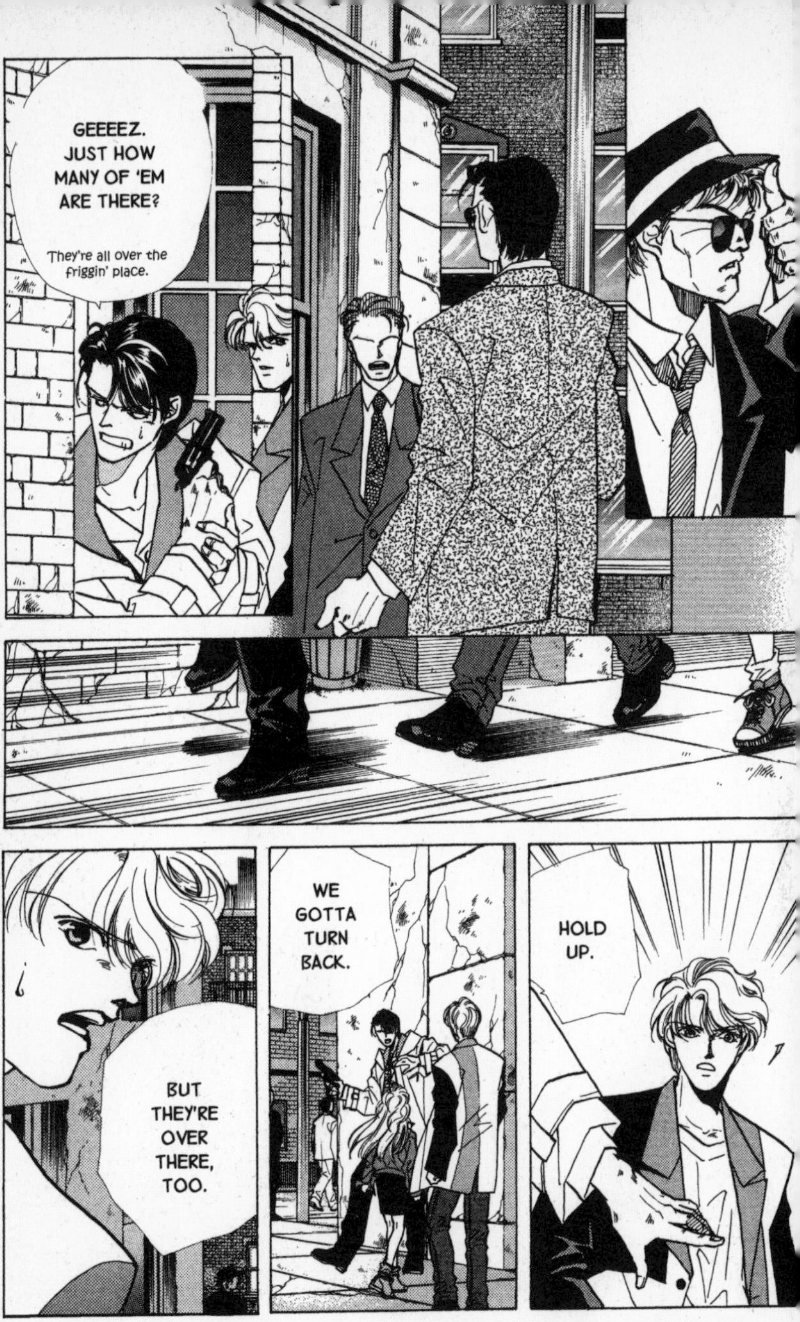
GEEEZ. JUST HOW MANY OF 'EM ARE THERE?
They're all over the friggin' place.
HOLD UP.
WE GOTTA TURN BACK.
BUT THEY'RE OVER THERE, TOO.

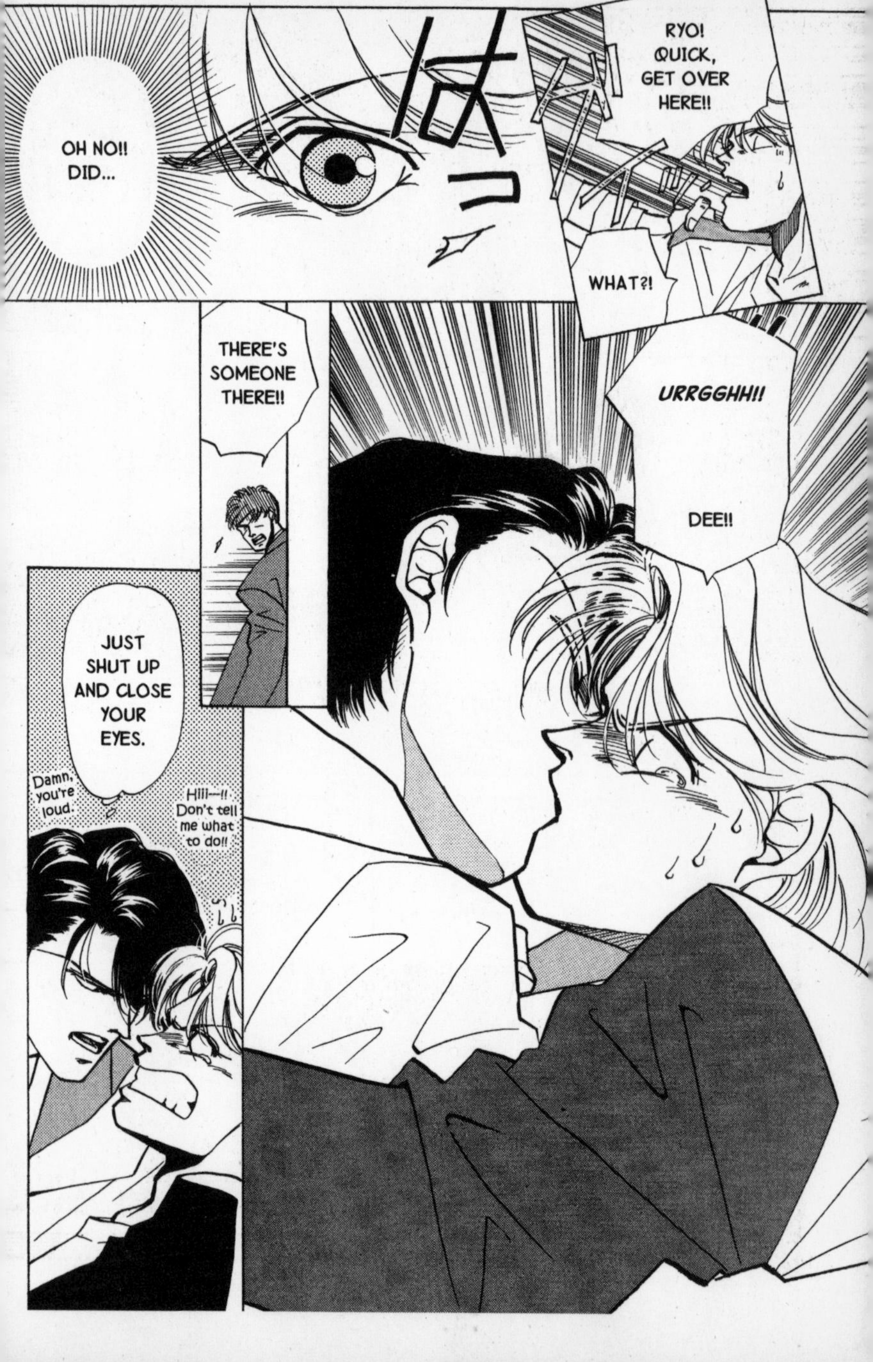
RYO! QUICK, GET OVER HERE!!
WHAT?!
OH NO!! DID...
URRGGHH!!
DEE!!
THERE'S SOMEONE THERE!!
JUST SHUT UP AND CLOSE YOUR EYES.
Hiii--!! Don't tell me what to do!!
Damn, you're loud.

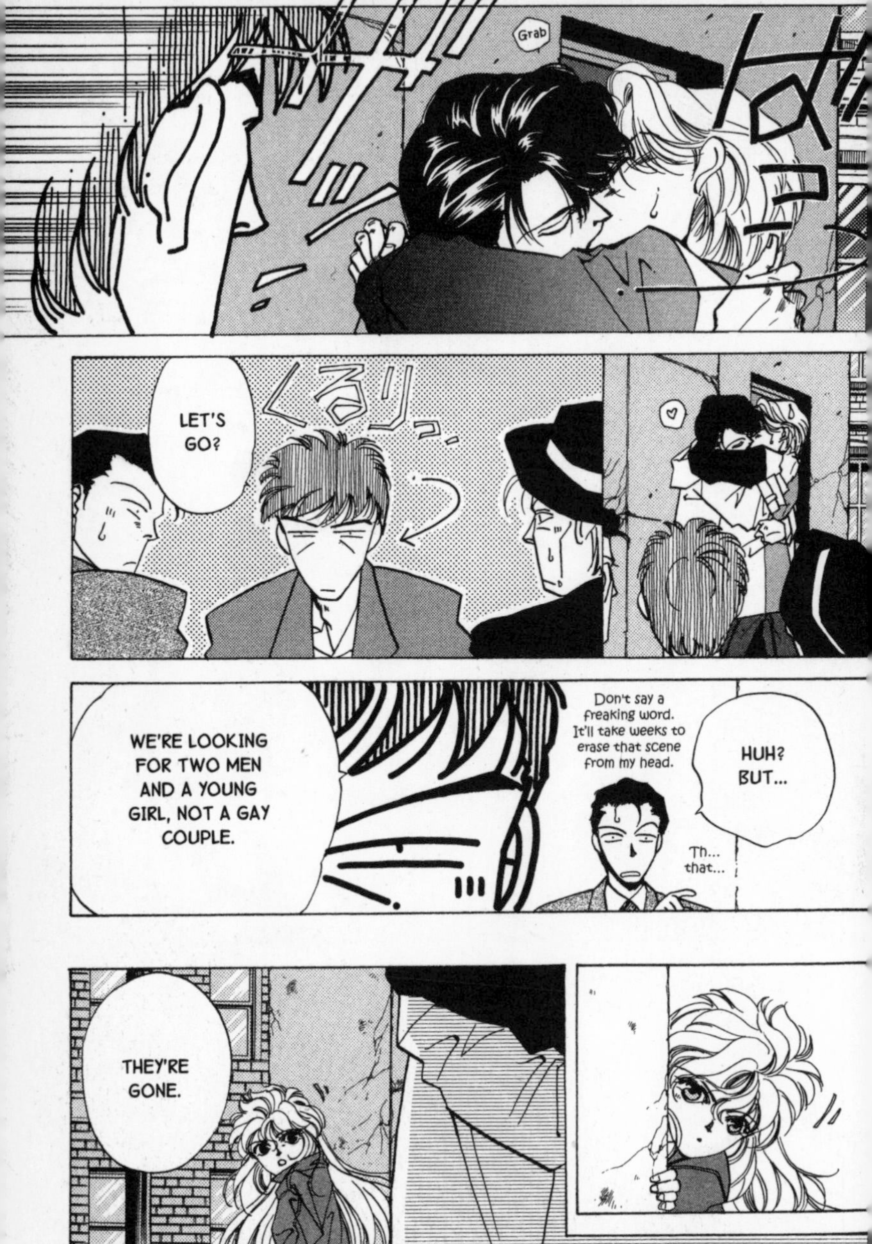
Grab
LET'S GO?
くるりっ
HUH? BUT...
Don't say a freaking word. It'll take weeks to erase that scene from my head.
Th... that...
WE'RE LOOKING FOR TWO MEN AND A YOUNG GIRL, NOT A GAY COUPLE.
THEY'RE GONE.

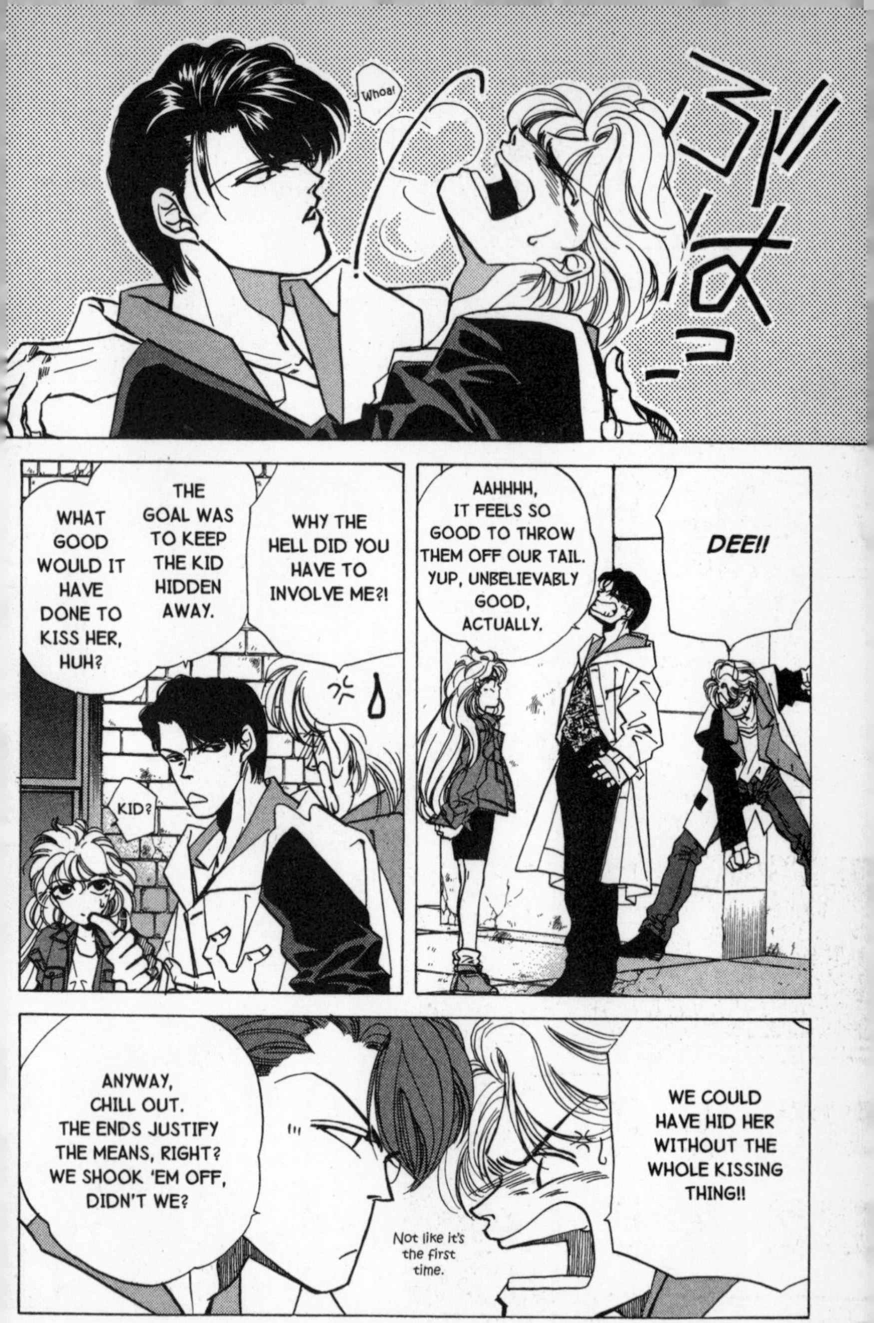
ぶはっ
Whoa!
DEE!!
AAHHHH, IT FEELS SO GOOD TO THROW THEM OFF OUR TAIL. YUP, UNBELIEVABLY GOOD, ACTUALLY.
WHY THE HELL DID YOU HAVE TO INVOLVE ME?!
THE GOAL WAS TO KEEP THE KID HIDDEN AWAY.
WHAT GOOD WOULD IT HAVE DONE TO KISS HER, HUH?
KID?
WE COULD HAVE HID HER WITHOUT THE WHOLE KISSING THING!!
Not like it's the first time.
ANYWAY, CHILL OUT. THE ENDS JUSTIFY THE MEANS, RIGHT? WE SHOOK 'EM OFF, DIDN'T WE?

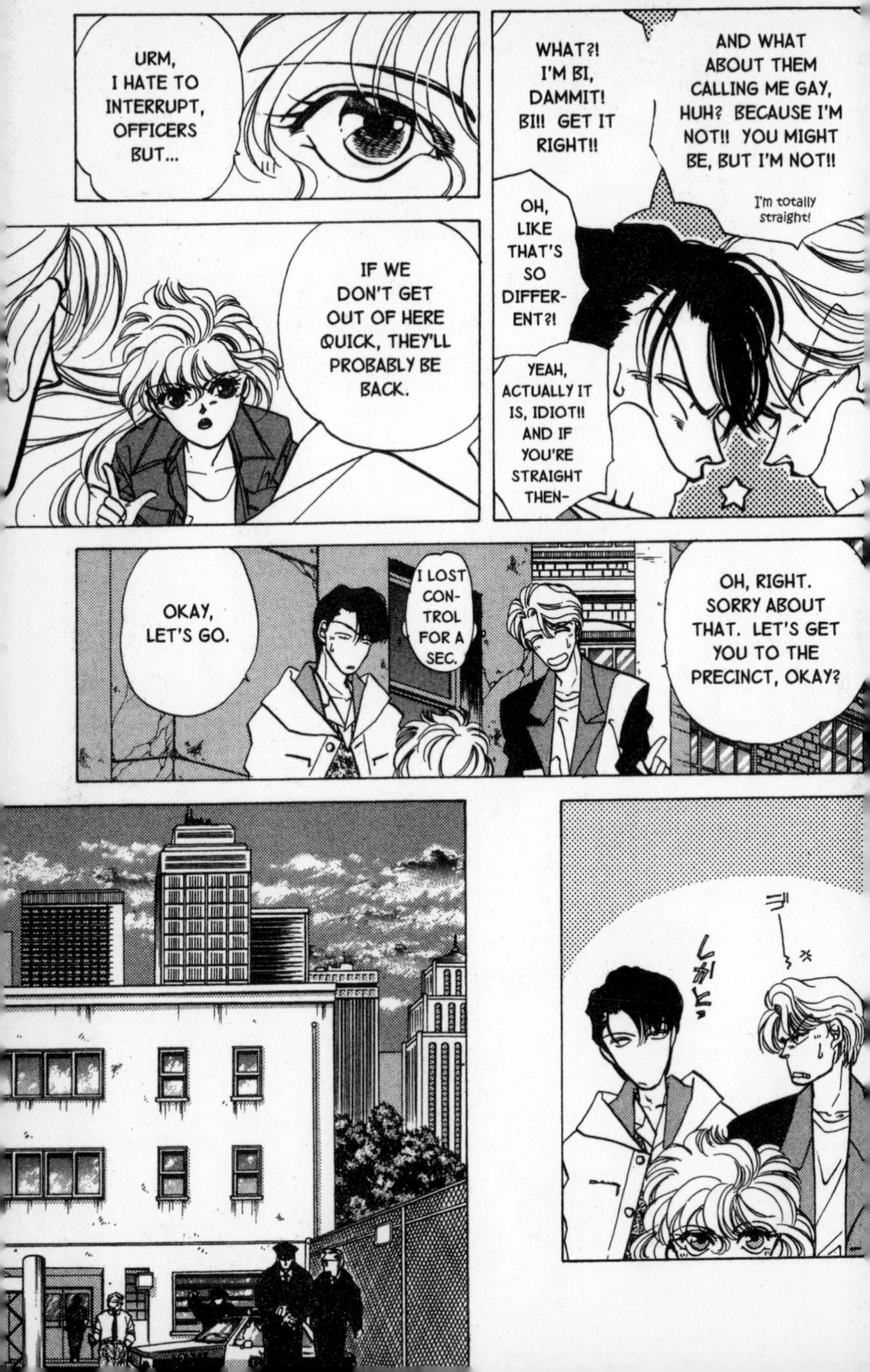
AND WHAT ABOUT THEM CALLING ME GAY, HUH? BECAUSE I'M NOT!! YOU MIGHT BE, BUT I'M NOT!!
WHAT?! I'M BI, DAMMIT! BI!! GET IT RIGHT!!
I'm totally straight!
OH, LIKE THAT'S SO DIFFER-ENT?!
YEAH, ACTUALLY IT IS, IDIOT!! AND IF YOU'RE STRAIGHT THEN-
URM, I HATE TO INTERRUPT, OFFICERS BUT...
IF WE DON'T GET OUT OF HERE QUICK, THEY'LL PROBABLY BE BACK.
OH, RIGHT. SORRY ABOUT THAT. LET'S GET YOU TO THE PRECINCT, OKAY?
I LOST CON-TROL FOR A SEC.
OKAY, LET'S GO.

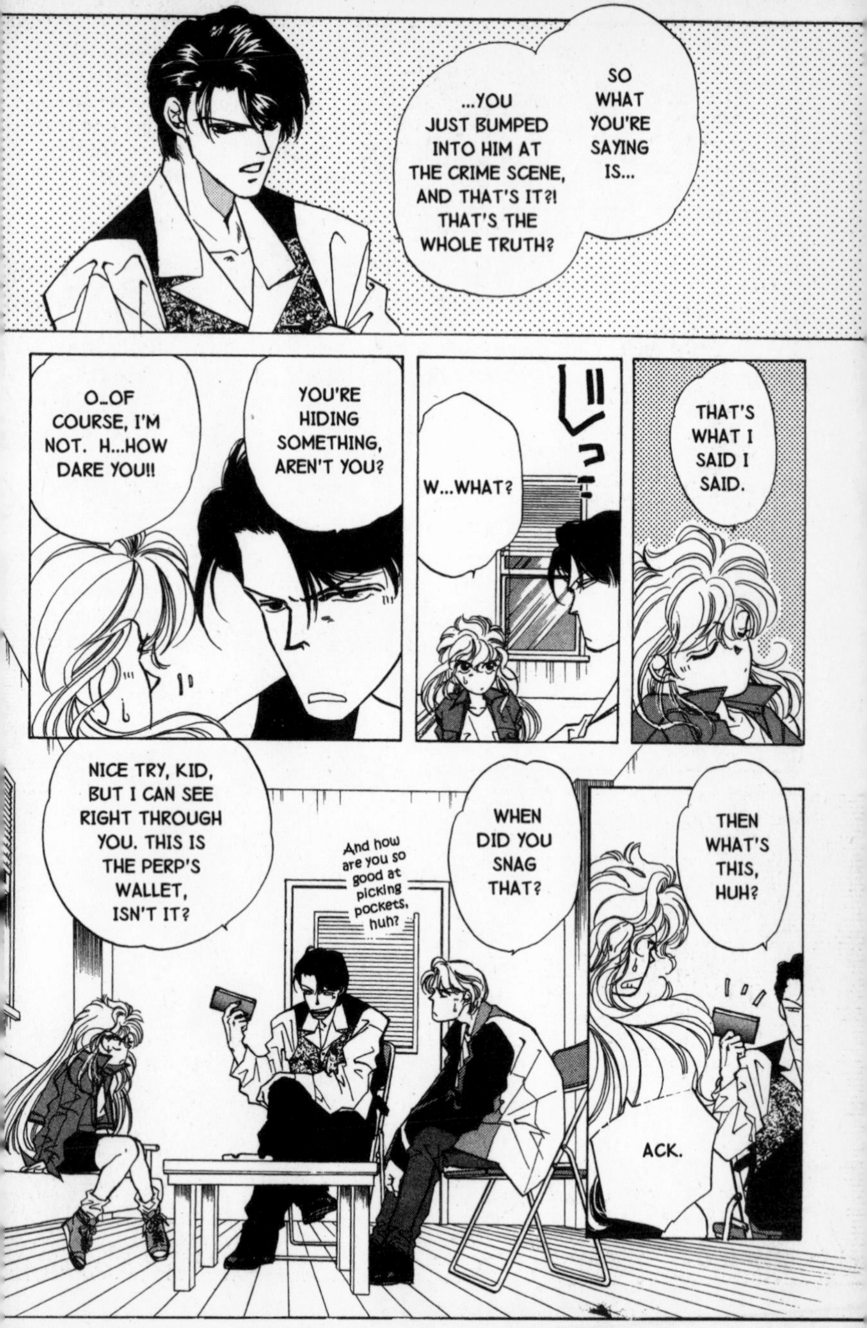
SO WHAT YOU'RE SAYING IS...
...YOU JUST BUMPED INTO HIM AT THE CRIME SCENE, AND THAT'S IT?! THAT'S THE WHOLE TRUTH?
THAT'S WHAT I SAID I SAID.
W...WHAT?
YOU'RE HIDING SOMETHING, AREN'T YOU?
O..OF COURSE, I'M NOT. H...HOW DARE YOU!!
THEN WHAT'S THIS, HUH?
ACK.
WHEN DID YOU SNAG THAT?
And how are you so good at picking pockets, huh?
NICE TRY, KID, BUT I CAN SEE RIGHT THROUGH YOU. THIS IS THE PERP'S WALLET, ISN'T IT?

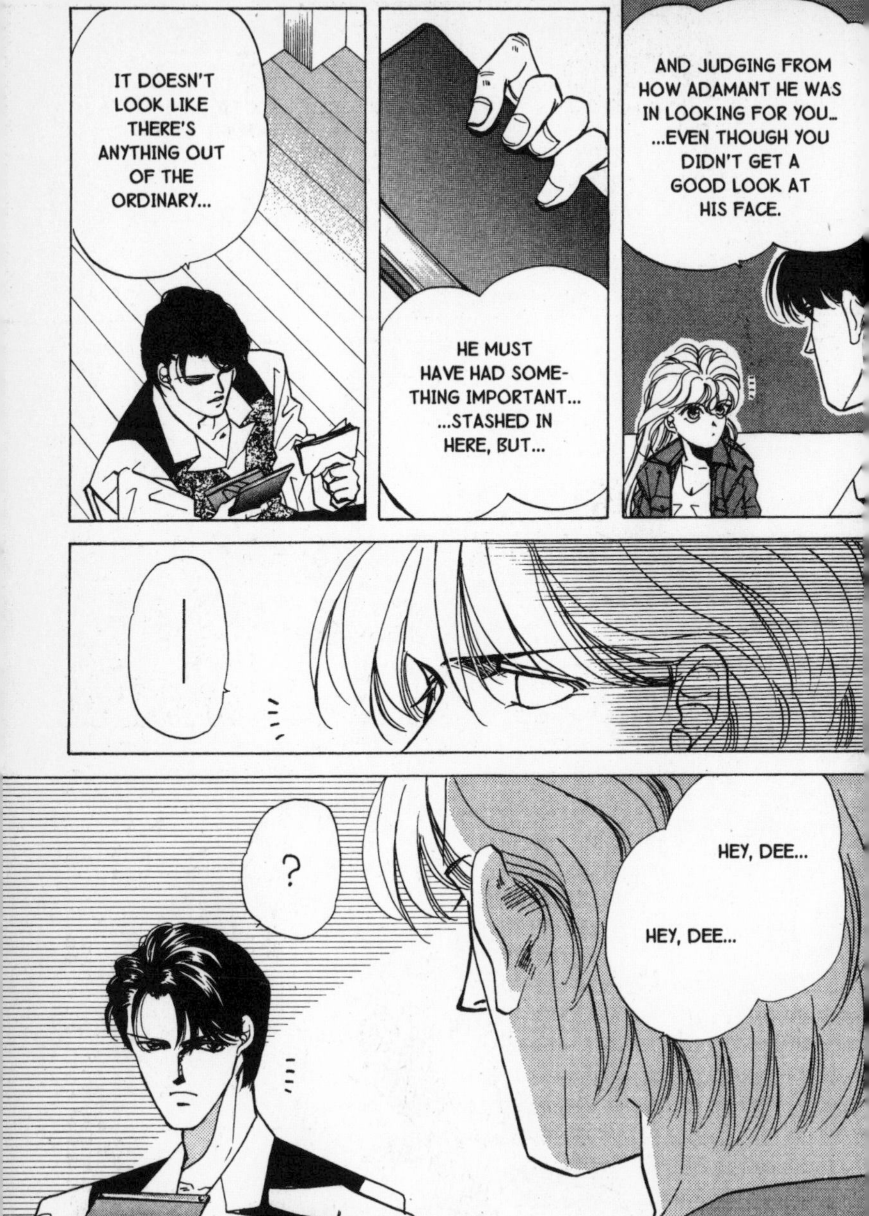
AND JUDGING FROM HOW ADAMANT HE WAS IN LOOKING FOR YOU... ...EVEN THOUGH YOU DIDN'T GET A GOOD LOOK AT HIS FACE.
HE MUST HAVE HAD SOME-THING IMPORTANT... ...STASHED IN HERE, BUT...
IT DOESN'T LOOK LIKE THERE'S ANYTHING OUT OF THE ORDINARY...
—
HEY, DEE...
HEY, DEE...
?

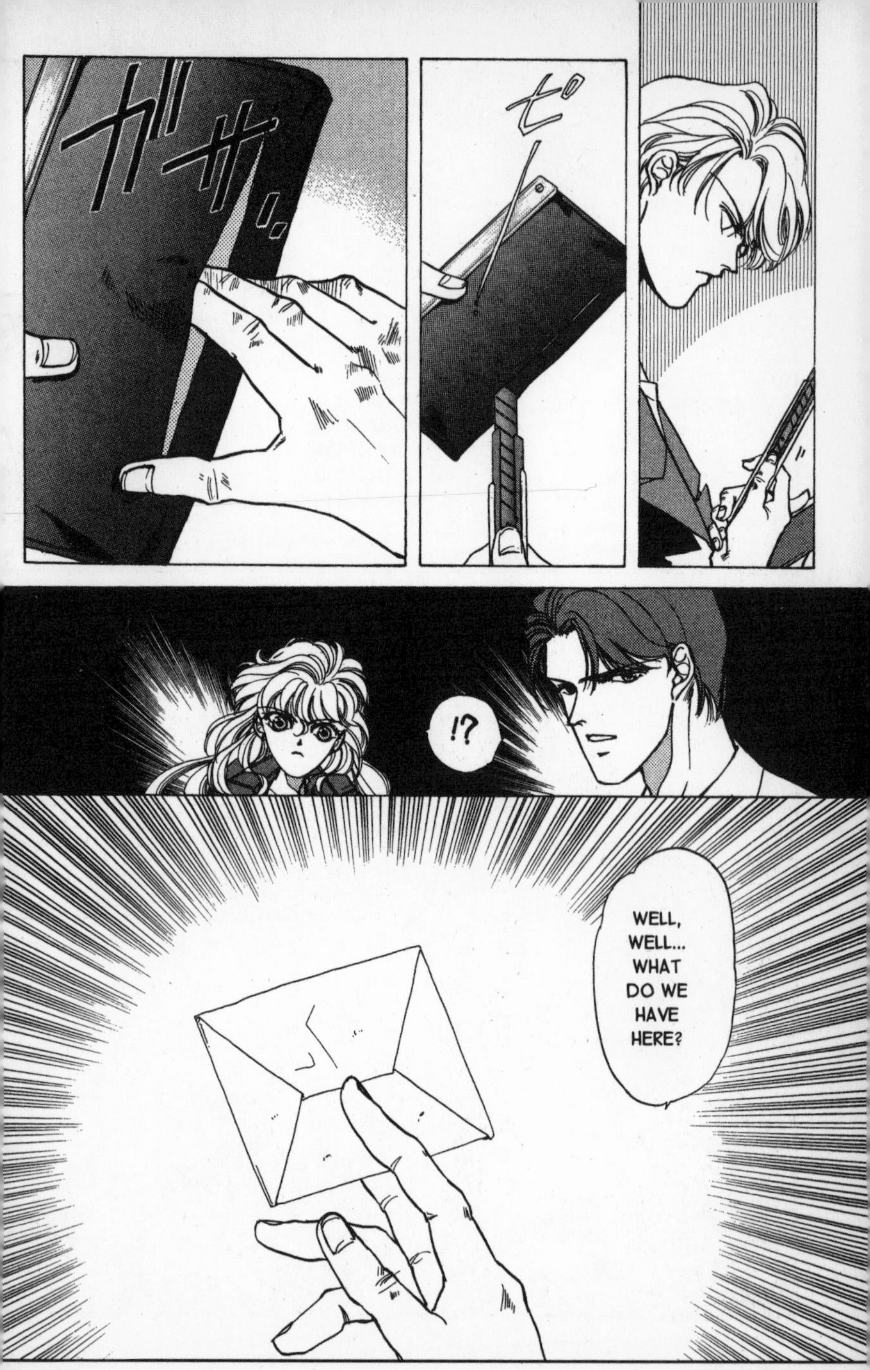
ピ
ガザッ
!?
WELL, WELL... WHAT DO WE HAVE HERE?

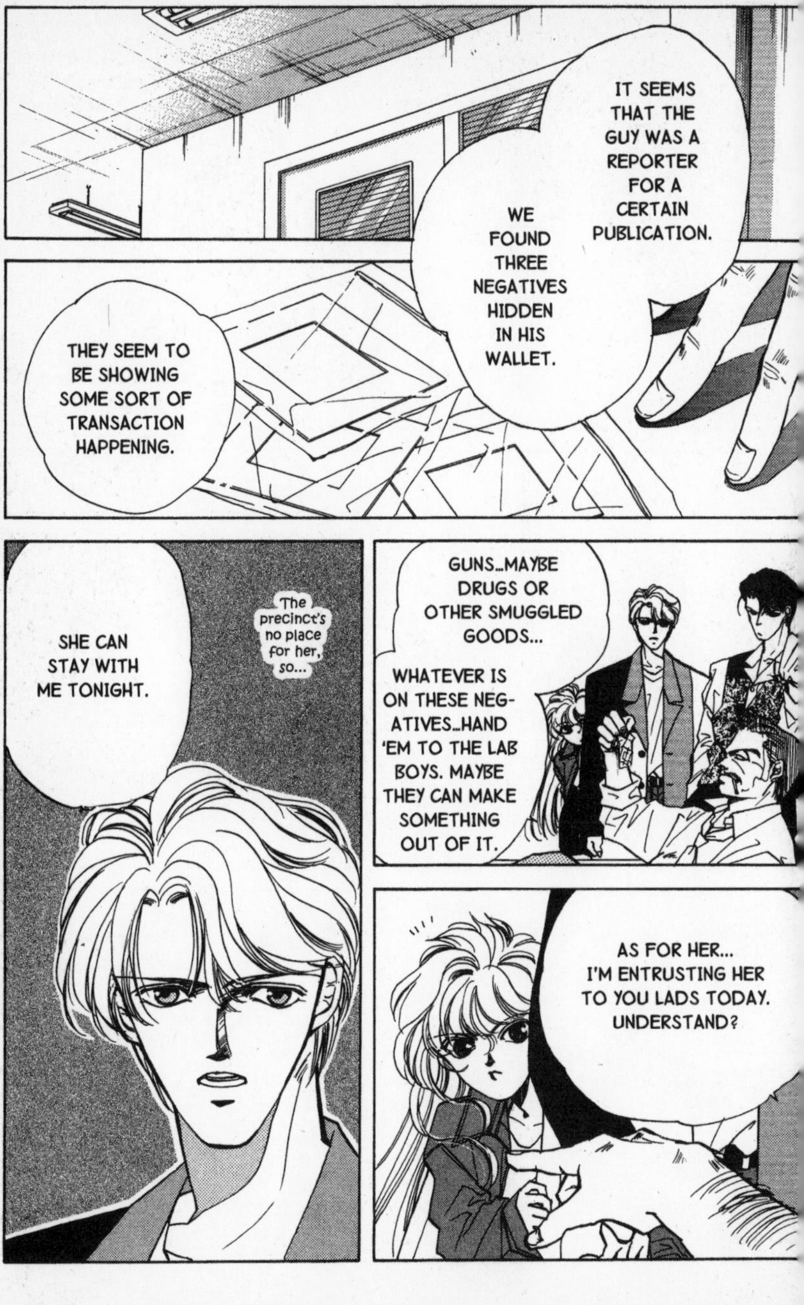
IT SEEMS THAT THE GUY WAS A REPORTER FOR A CERTAIN PUBLICATION.
WE FOUND THREE NEGATIVES HIDDEN IN HIS WALLET.
THEY SEEM TO BE SHOWING SOME SORT OF TRANSACTION HAPPENING.
GUNS...MAYBE DRUGS OR OTHER SMUGGLED GOODS...
WHATEVER IS ON THESE NEG-ATIVES...HAND 'EM TO THE LAB BOYS. MAYBE THEY CAN MAKE SOMETHING OUT OF IT.
AS FOR HER... I'M ENTRUSTING HER TO YOU LADS TODAY. UNDERSTAND?
The precinct's no place for her, so...
SHE CAN STAY WITH ME TONIGHT.

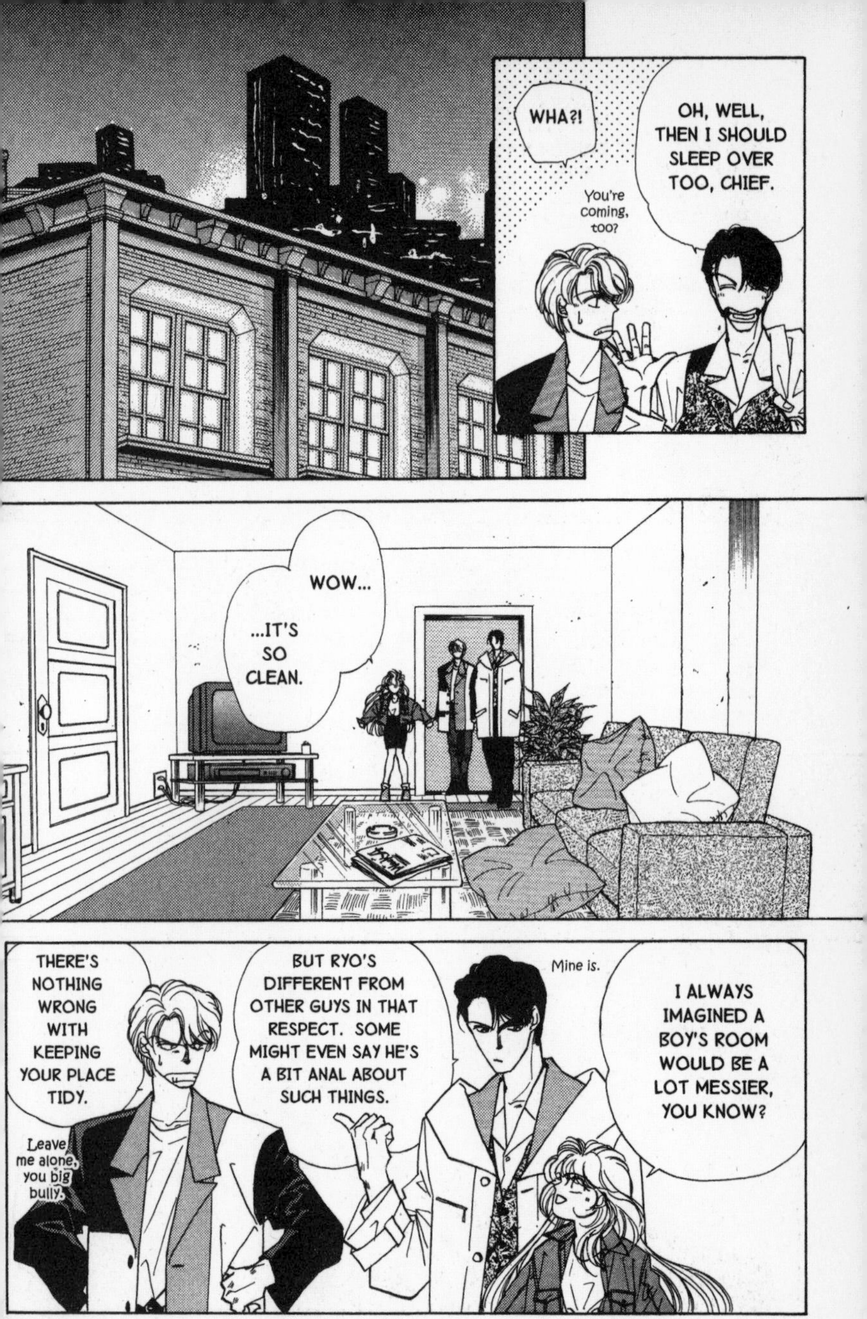
OH, WELL, THEN I SHOULD SLEEP OVER TOO, CHIEF.
WHA?!
You're coming, too?
WOW...
...IT'S SO CLEAN.
I ALWAYS IMAGINED A BOY'S ROOM WOULD BE A LOT MESSIER, YOU KNOW?
Mine is.
BUT RYO'S DIFFERENT FROM OTHER GUYS IN THAT RESPECT. SOME MIGHT EVEN SAY HE'S A BIT ANAL ABOUT SUCH THINGS.
THERE'S NOTHING WRONG WITH KEEPING YOUR PLACE TIDY.
Leave me alone, you big bully.

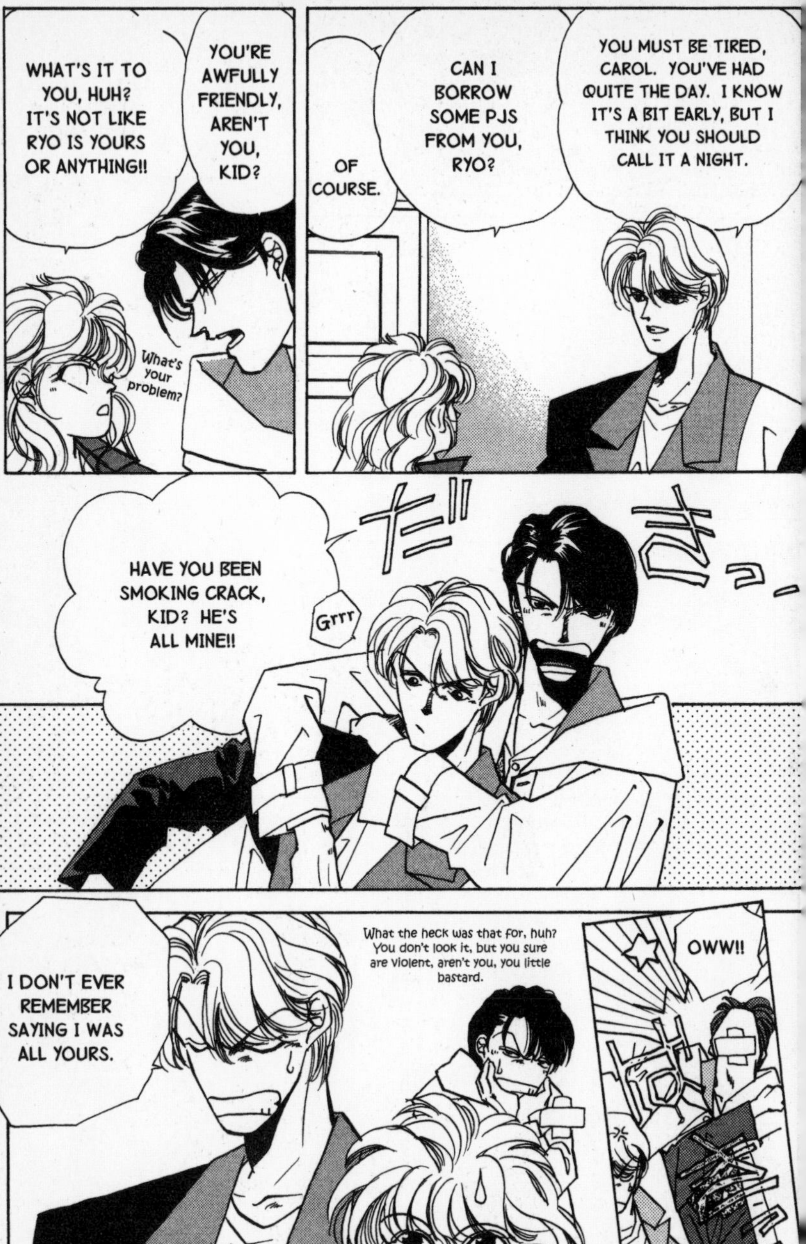
YOU MUST BE TIRED, CAROL. YOU'VE HAD QUITE THE DAY. I KNOW IT'S A BIT EARLY, BUT I THINK YOU SHOULD CALL IT A NIGHT.
CAN I BORROW SOME PJS FROM YOU, RYO?
OF COURSE.
YOU'RE AWFULLY FRIENDLY, AREN'T YOU, KID?
WHAT'S IT TO YOU, HUH? IT'S NOT LIKE RYO IS YOURS OR ANYTHING!!
What's your problem?
HAVE YOU BEEN SMOKING CRACK, KID? HE'S ALL MINE!!
Grrr
OWW!!
What the heck was that for, huh? You don't look it, but you sure are violent, aren't you, you little bastard.
I DON'T EVER REMEMBER SAYING I WAS ALL YOURS.

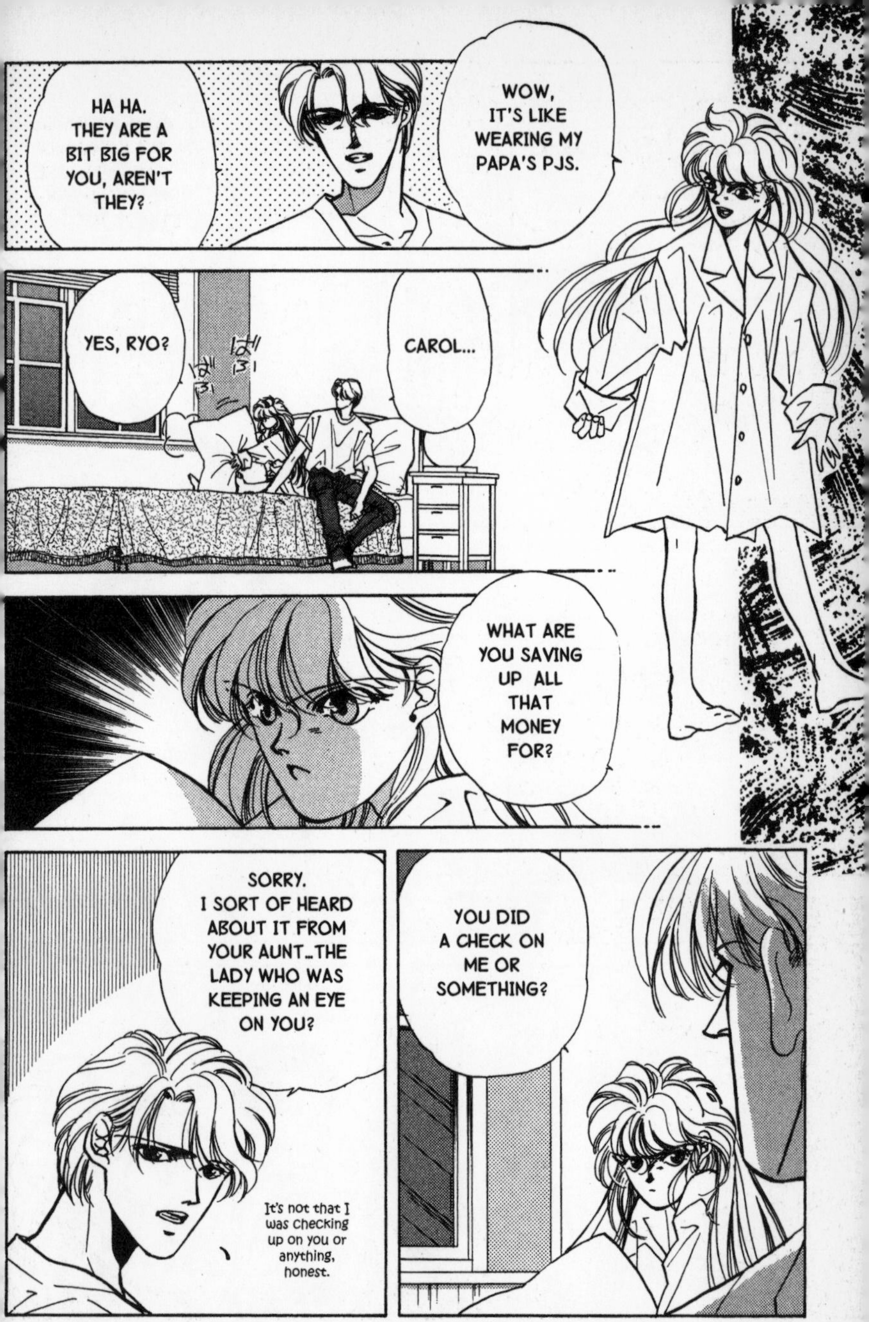
WOW, IT'S LIKE WEARING MY PAPA'S PJS.
HA HA. THEY ARE A BIT BIG FOR YOU, AREN'T THEY?
CAROL...
ばふ
ばふ
YES, RYO?
WHAT ARE YOU SAVING UP ALL THAT MONEY FOR?
YOU DID A CHECK ON ME OR SOMETHING?
SORRY. I SORT OF HEARD ABOUT IT FROM YOUR AUNT...THE LADY WHO WAS KEEPING AN EYE ON YOU?
It's not that I was checking up on you or anything, honest.

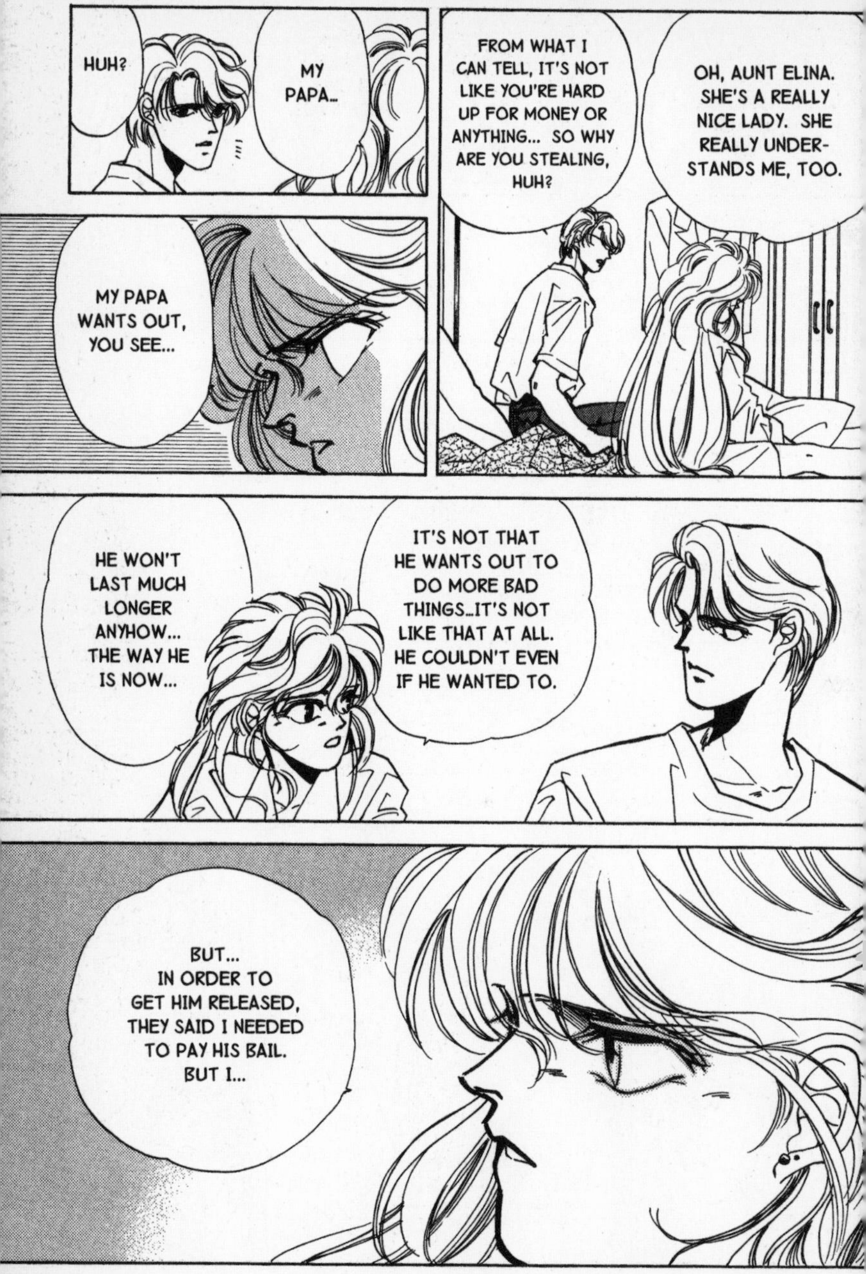
OH, AUNT ELINA. SHE'S A REALLY NICE LADY. SHE REALLY UNDER-STANDS ME, TOO.
FROM WHAT I CAN TELL, IT'S NOT LIKE YOU'RE HARD UP FOR MONEY OR ANYTHING... SO WHY ARE YOU STEALING, HUH?
MY PAPA...
HUH?
MY PAPA WANTS OUT, YOU SEE...
IT'S NOT THAT HE WANTS OUT TO DO MORE BAD THINGS...IT'S NOT LIKE THAT AT ALL. HE COULDN'T EVEN IF HE WANTED TO.
HE WON'T LAST MUCH LONGER ANYHOW... THE WAY HE IS NOW...
BUT... IN ORDER TO GET HIM RELEASED, THEY SAID I NEEDED TO PAY HIS BAIL. BUT I...

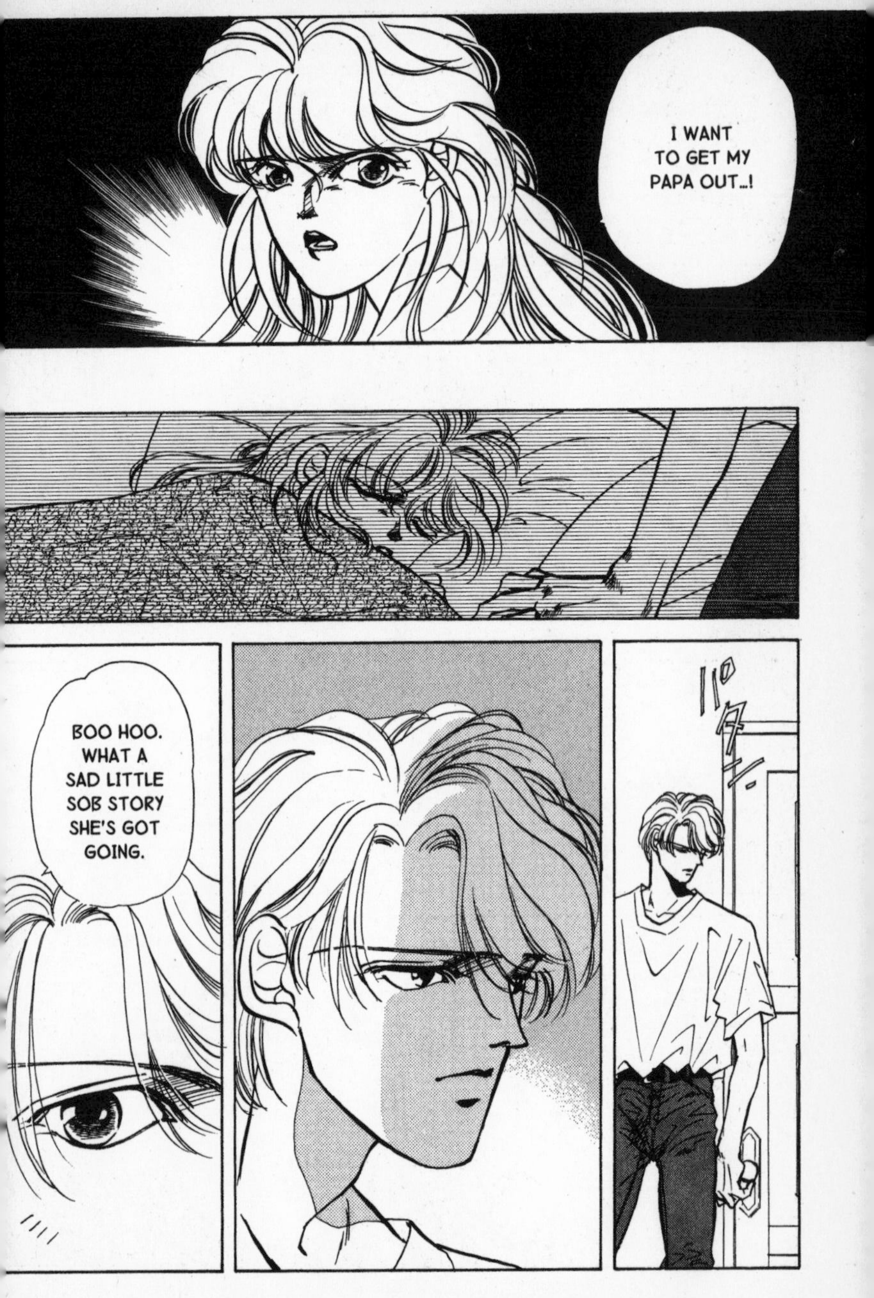
I WANT TO GET MY PAPA OUT...!
パタン
BOO HOO. WHAT A SAD LITTLE SOB STORY SHE'S GOT GOING.

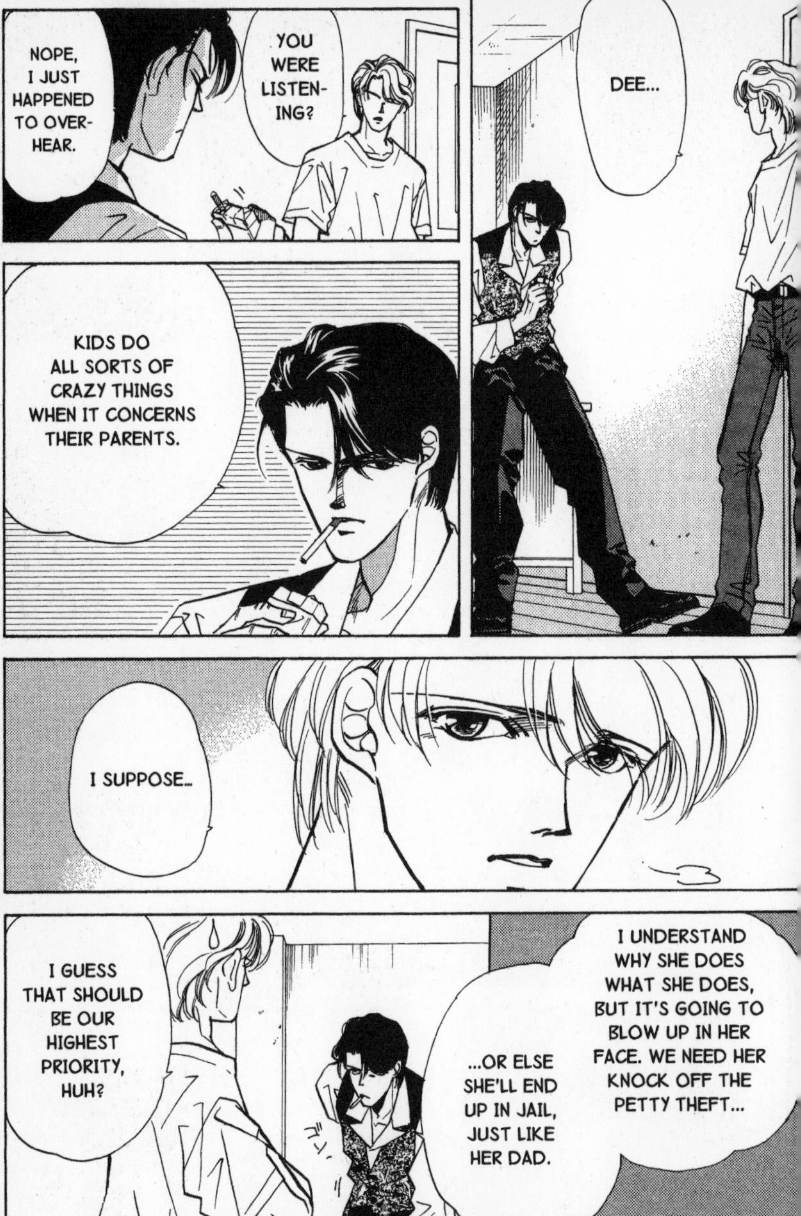
DEE...
YOU WERE LISTENING?
NOPE, I JUST HAPPENED TO OVERHEAR.
KIDS DO ALL SORTS OF CRAZY THINGS WHEN IT CONCERNS THEIR PARENTS.
I SUPPOSE...
I UNDERSTAND WHY SHE DOES WHAT SHE DOES, BUT IT'S GOING TO BLOW UP IN HER FACE. WE NEED HER KNOCK OFF THE PETTY THEFT...
...OR ELSE SHE'LL END UP IN JAIL, JUST LIKE HER DAD.
I GUESS THAT SHOULD BE OUR HIGHEST PRIORITY, HUH?

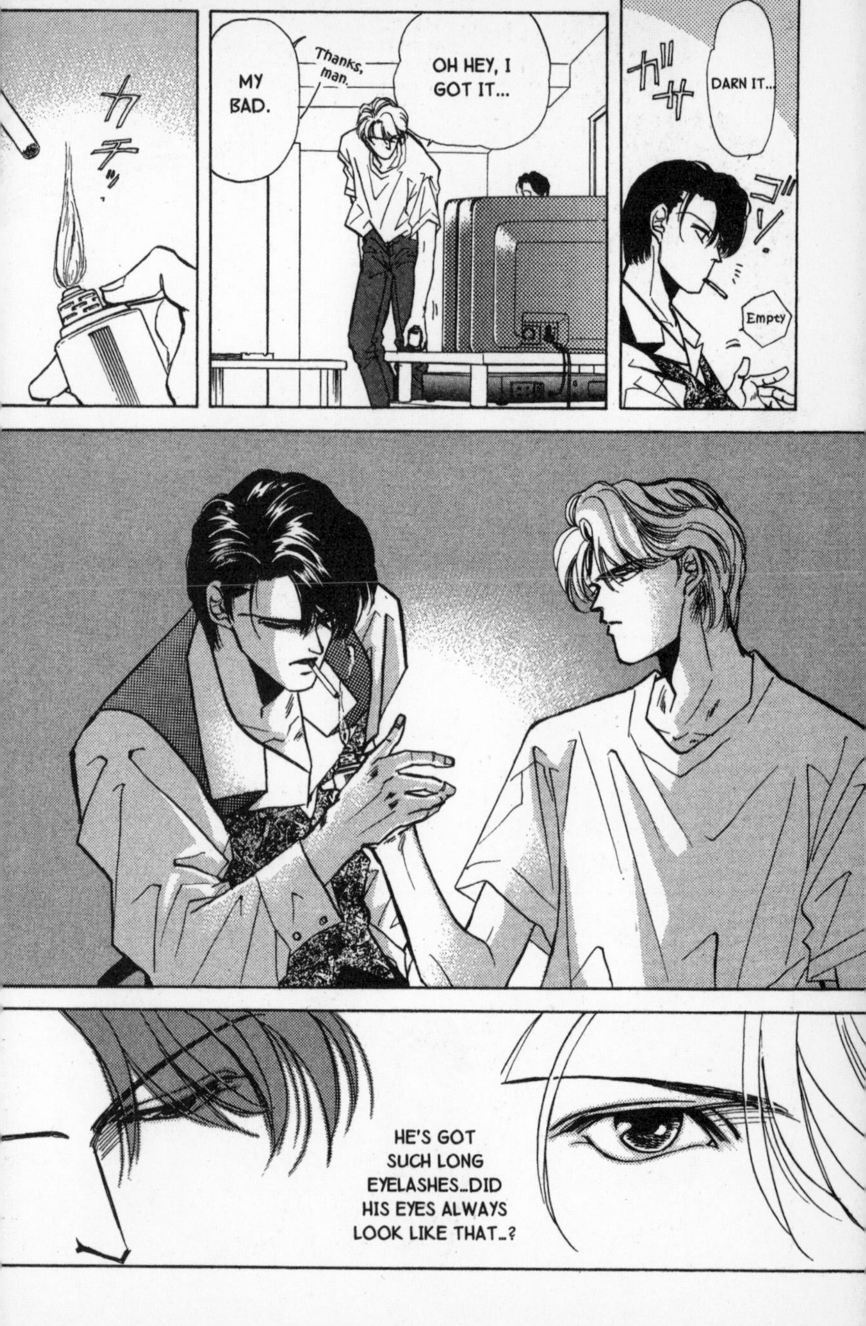
DARN IT...
Empty
OH HEY, I GOT IT...
Thanks, man.
MY BAD.
カチッ
HE'S GOT SUCH LONG EYELASHES...DID HIS EYES ALWAYS LOOK LIKE THAT...?

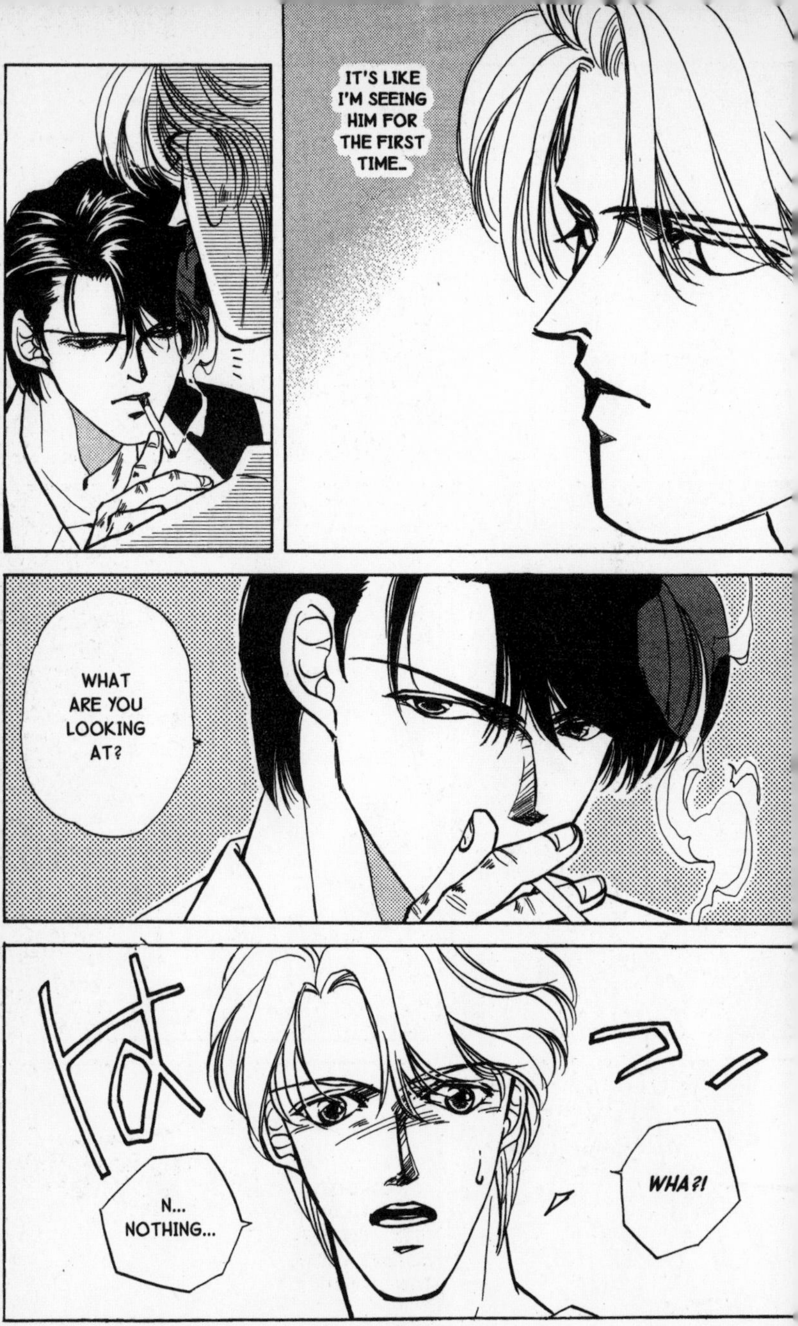
IT'S LIKE I'M SEEING HIM FOR THE FIRST TIME..
WHAT ARE YOU LOOKING AT?
WHA?!
N... NOTHING...

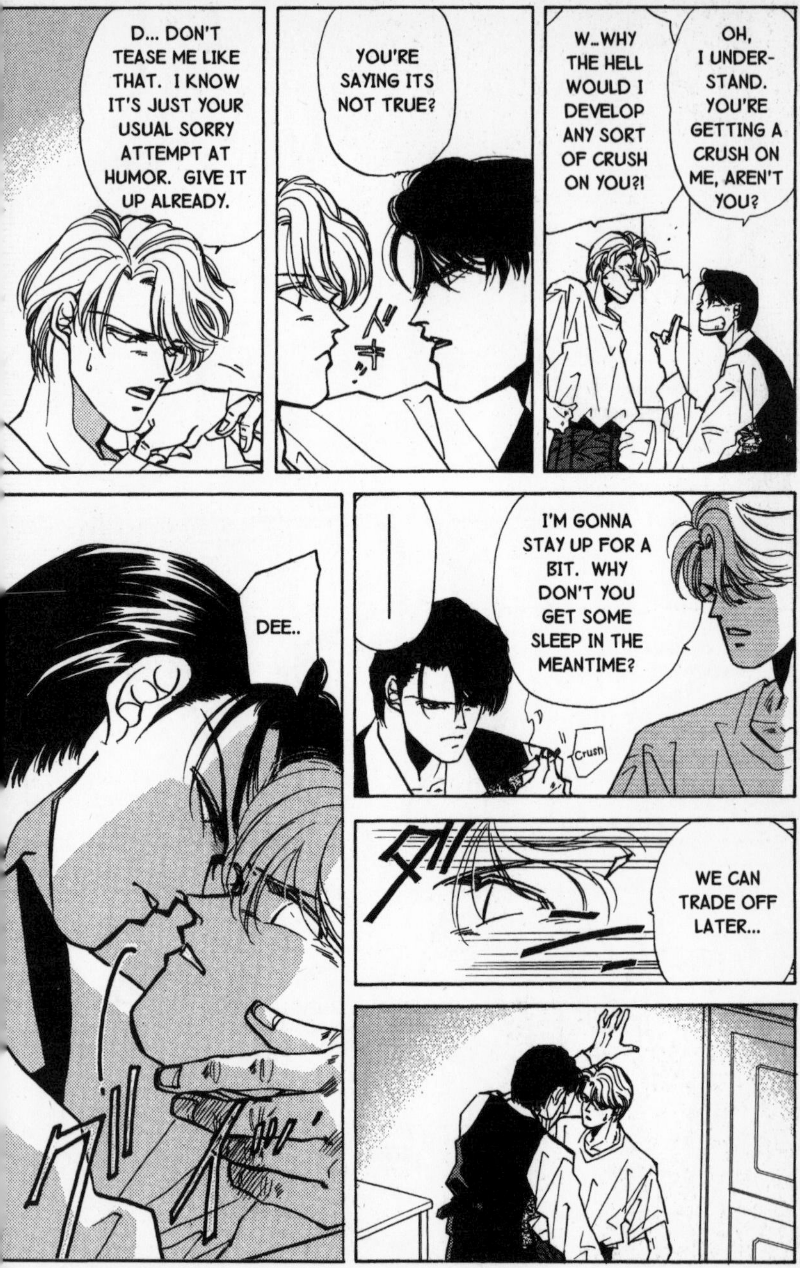
OH, I UNDER-STAND. YOU'RE GETTING A CRUSH ON ME, AREN'T YOU?
W..WHY THE HELL WOULD I DEVELOP ANY SORT OF CRUSH ON YOU?!
YOU'RE SAYING ITS NOT TRUE?
D... DON'T TEASE ME LIKE THAT. I KNOW IT'S JUST YOUR USUAL SORRY ATTEMPT AT HUMOR. GIVE IT UP ALREADY.
I'M GONNA STAY UP FOR A BIT. WHY DON'T YOU GET SOME SLEEP IN THE MEANTIME?
Crush
WE CAN TRADE OFF LATER...
DEE..

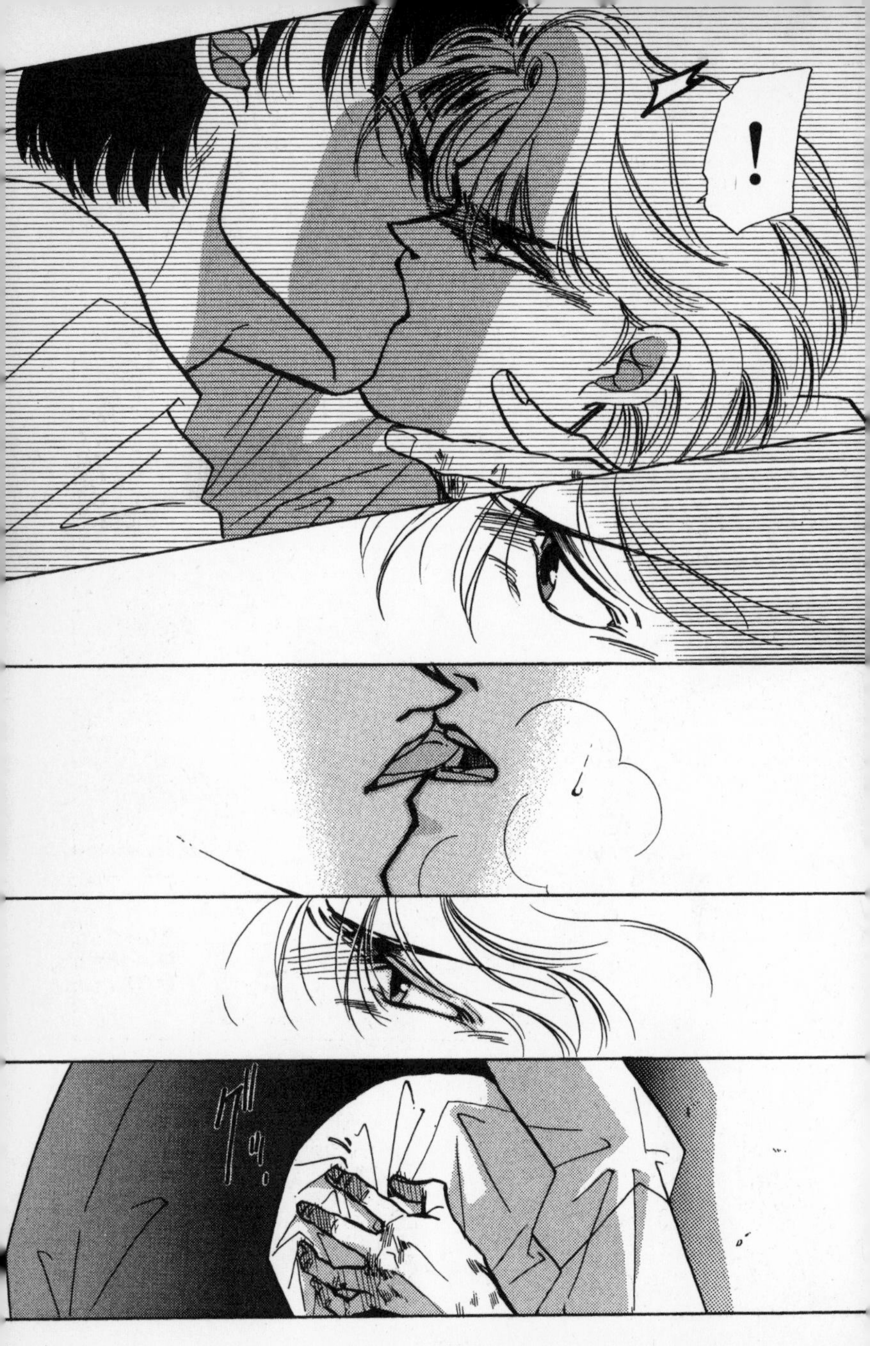
!

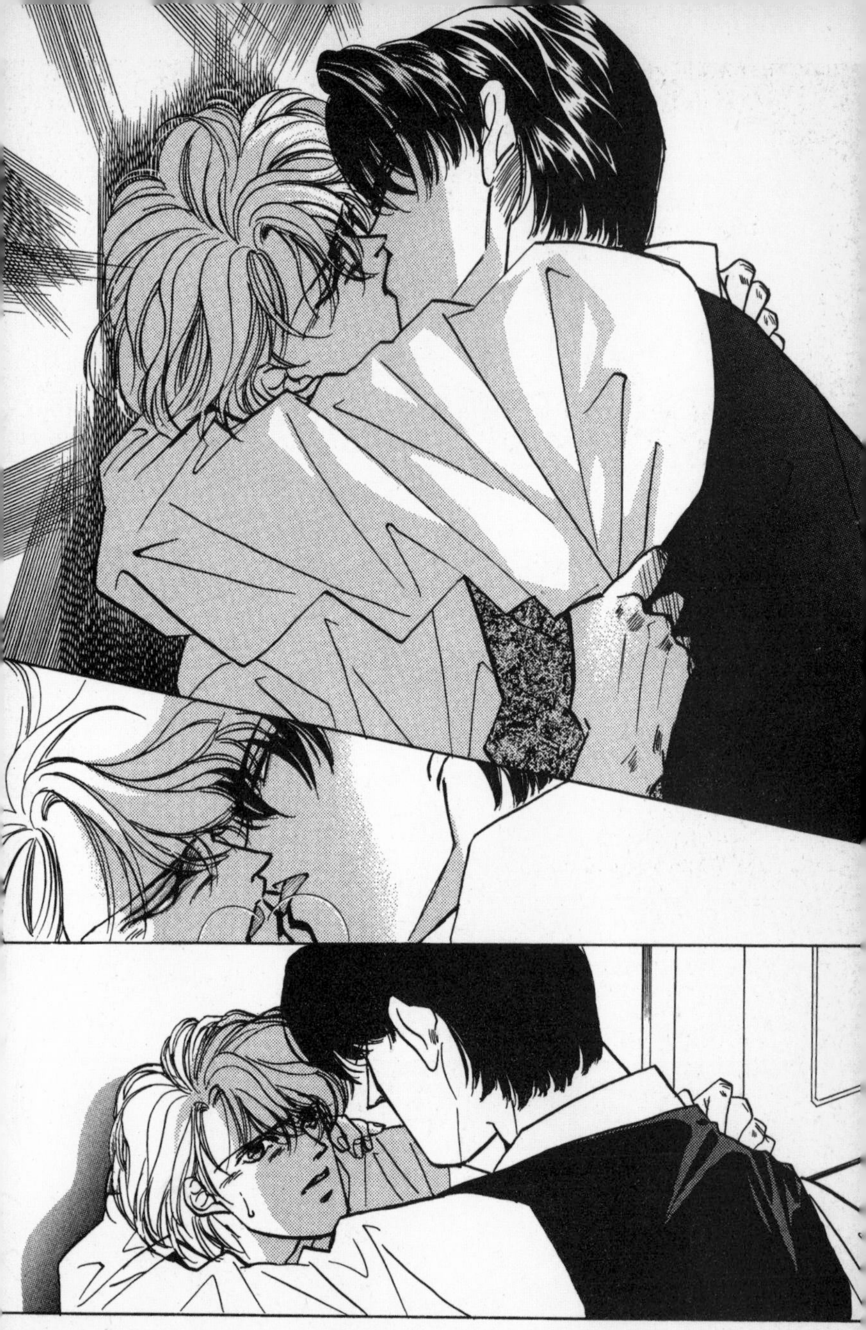

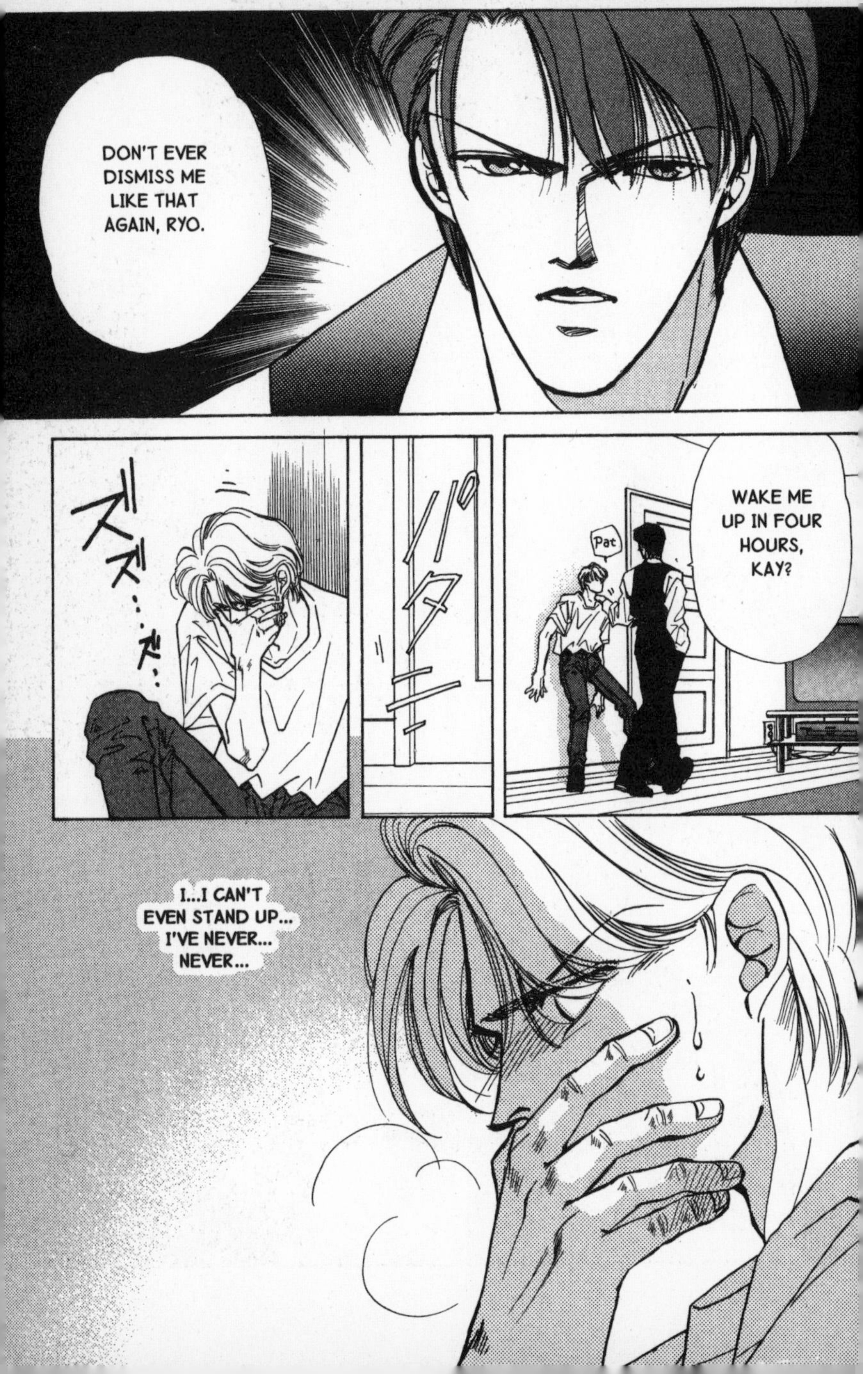
DON'T EVER DISMISS ME LIKE THAT AGAIN, RYO.
WAKE ME UP IN FOUR HOURS, KAY?
Pat
パタ
ズズ…ズ…
I...I CAN'T EVEN STAND UP... I'VE NEVER... NEVER...

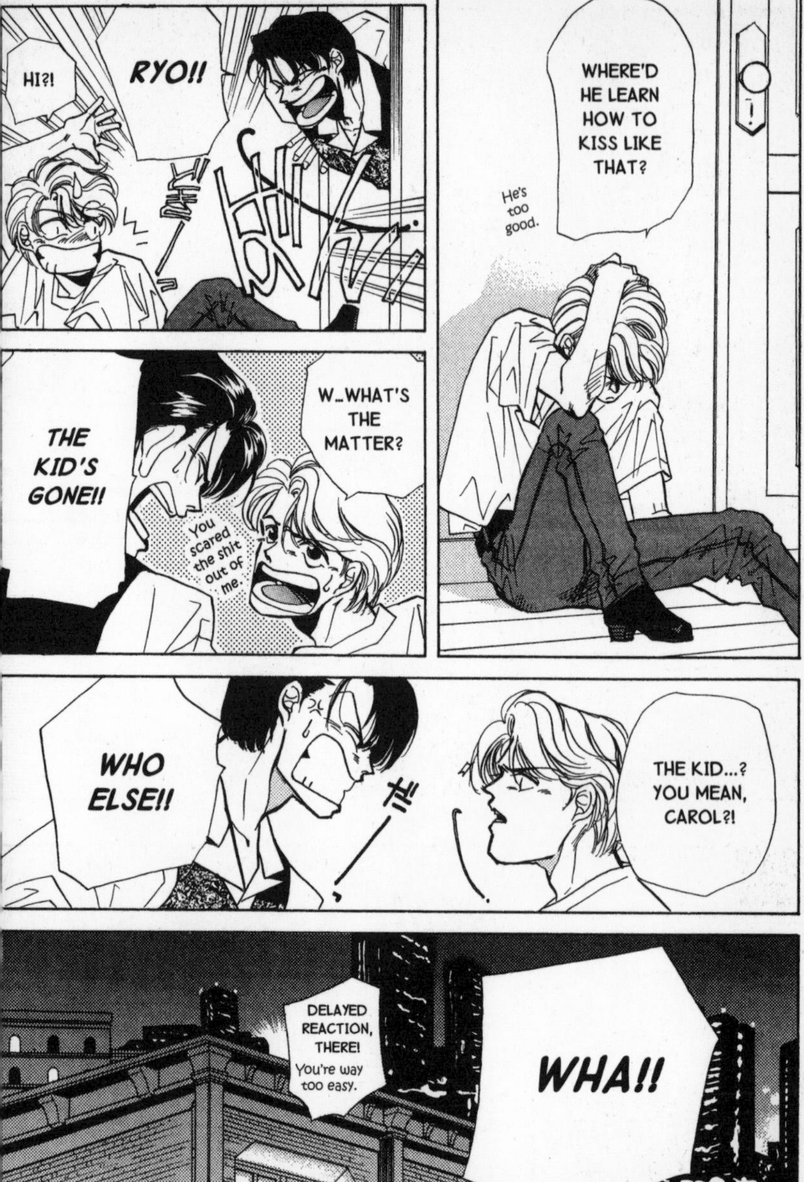
WHERE'D HE LEARN HOW TO KISS LIKE THAT?
He's too good.
RYO!!
HI?!
W...WHAT'S THE MATTER?
THE KID'S GONE!!
You scared the shit out of me.
THE KID...? YOU MEAN, CAROL?!
WHO ELSE!!
WHA!!
DELAYED REACTION, THERE!
You're way too easy.

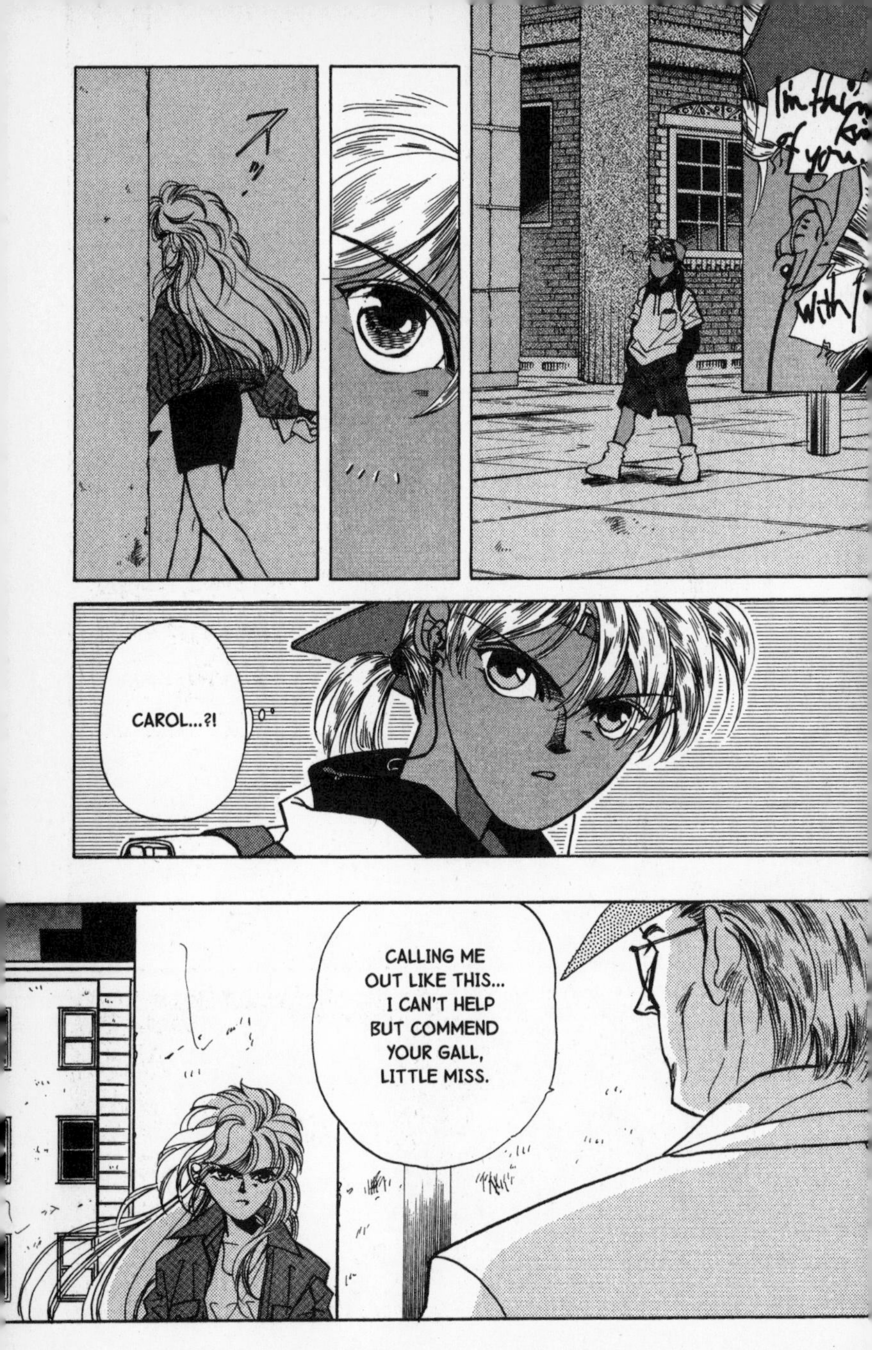
CAROL...?!
CALLING ME OUT LIKE THIS... I CAN'T HELP BUT COMMEND YOUR GALL, LITTLE MISS.

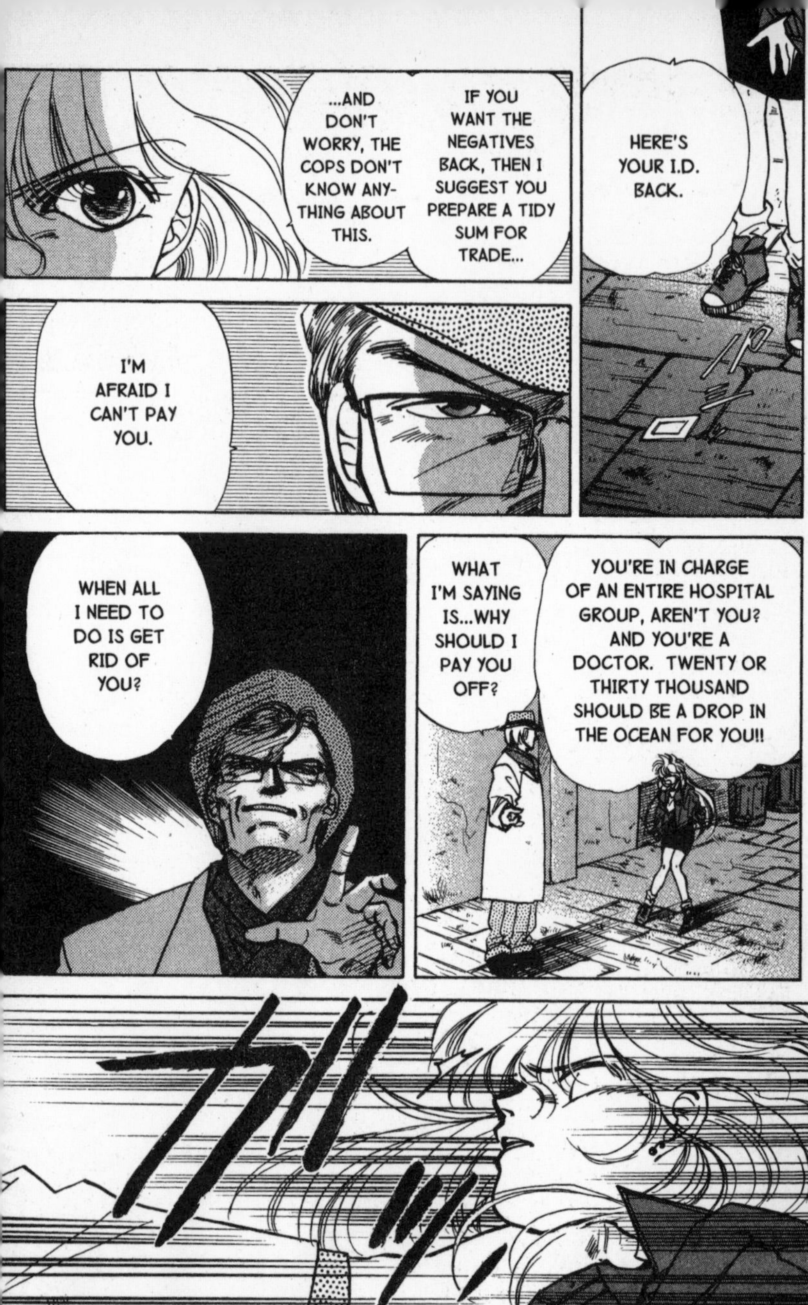
HERE'S YOUR I.D. BACK.
IF YOU WANT THE NEGATIVES BACK, THEN I SUGGEST YOU PREPARE A TIDY SUM FOR TRADE...
...AND DON'T WORRY, THE COPS DON'T KNOW ANY-THING ABOUT THIS.
I'M AFRAID I CAN'T PAY YOU.
YOU'RE IN CHARGE OF AN ENTIRE HOSPITAL GROUP, AREN'T YOU? AND YOU'RE A DOCTOR. TWENTY OR THIRTY THOUSAND SHOULD BE A DROP IN THE OCEAN FOR YOU!!
WHAT I'M SAYING IS...WHY SHOULD I PAY YOU OFF?
WHEN ALL I NEED TO DO IS GET RID OF YOU?

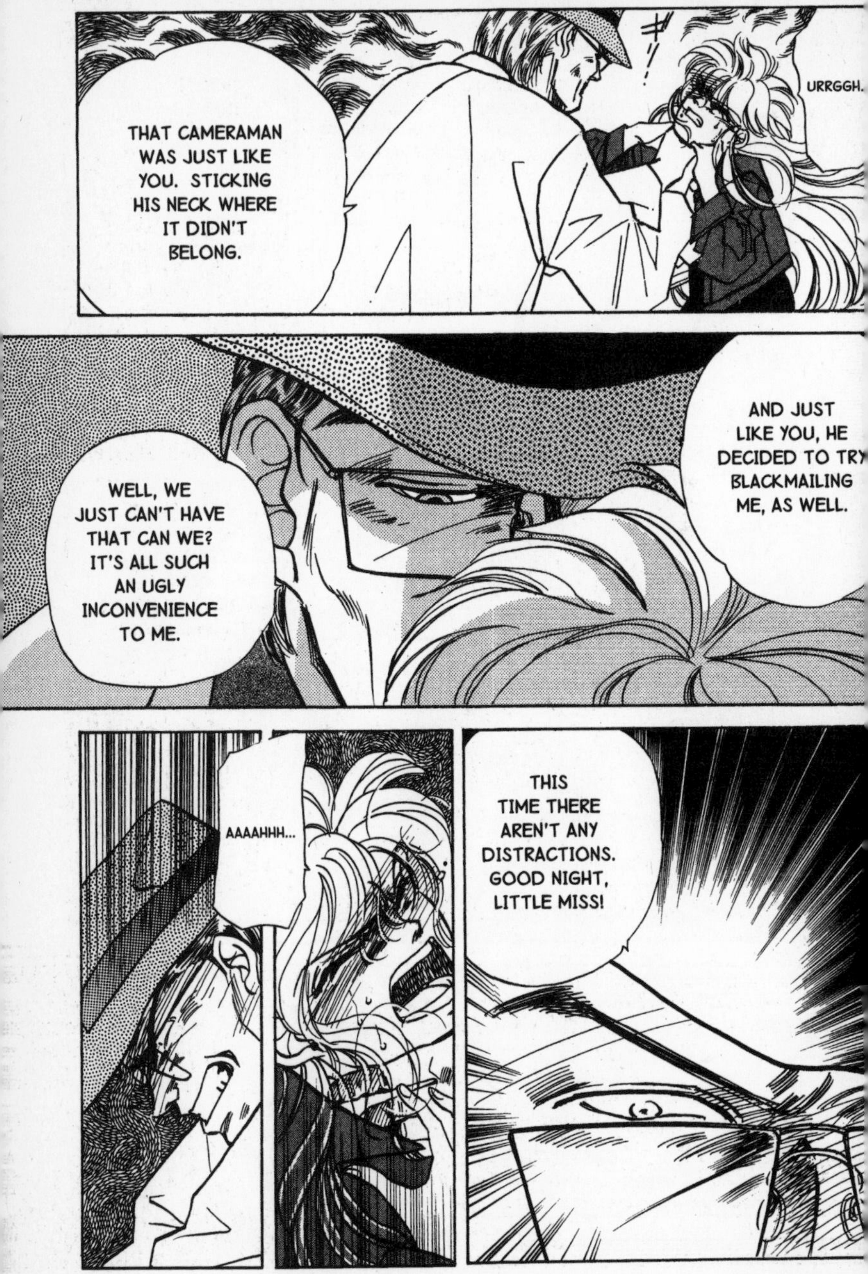
URRGGH.
THAT CAMERAMAN WAS JUST LIKE YOU. STICKING HIS NECK WHERE IT DIDN'T BELONG.
AND JUST LIKE YOU, HE DECIDED TO TRY BLACKMAILING ME, AS WELL.
WELL, WE JUST CAN'T HAVE THAT CAN WE? IT'S ALL SUCH AN UGLY INCONVENIENCE TO ME.
THIS TIME THERE AREN'T ANY DISTRACTIONS. GOOD NIGHT, LITTLE MISS!
AAAAHHH...

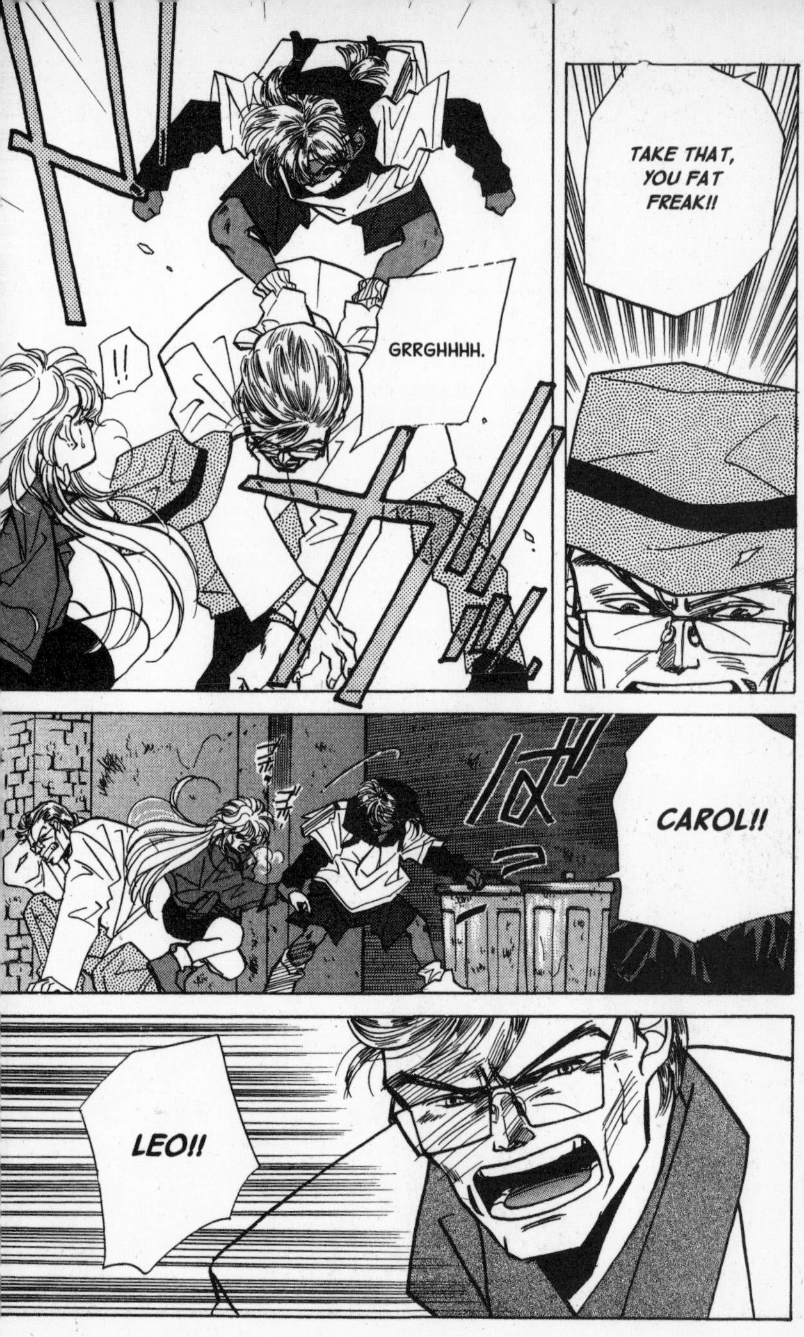
TAKE THAT, YOU FAT FREAK!!
GRRGHHHH.
!!
CAROL!!
LEO!!

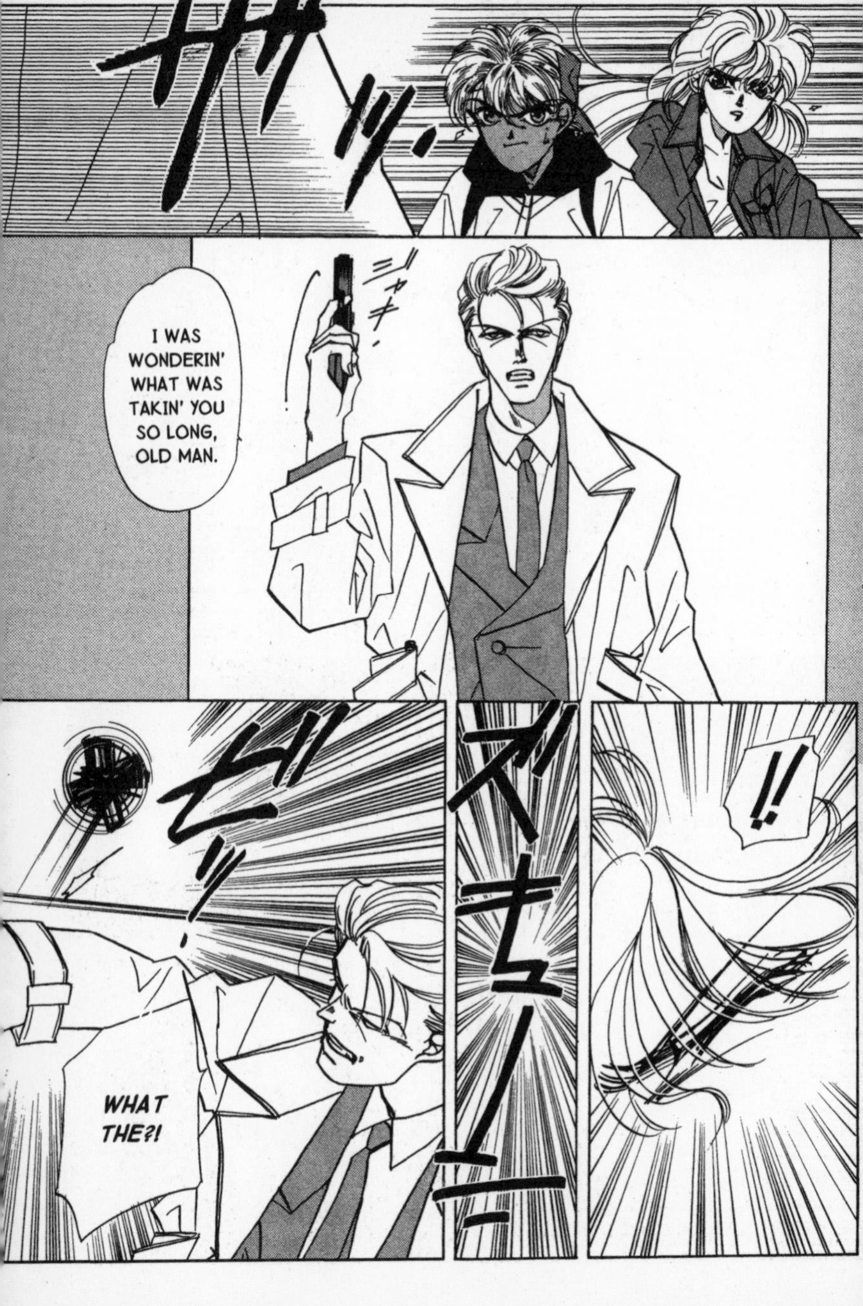
I WAS WONDERIN' WHAT WAS TAKIN' YOU SO LONG, OLD MAN.
WHAT THE?!
!!

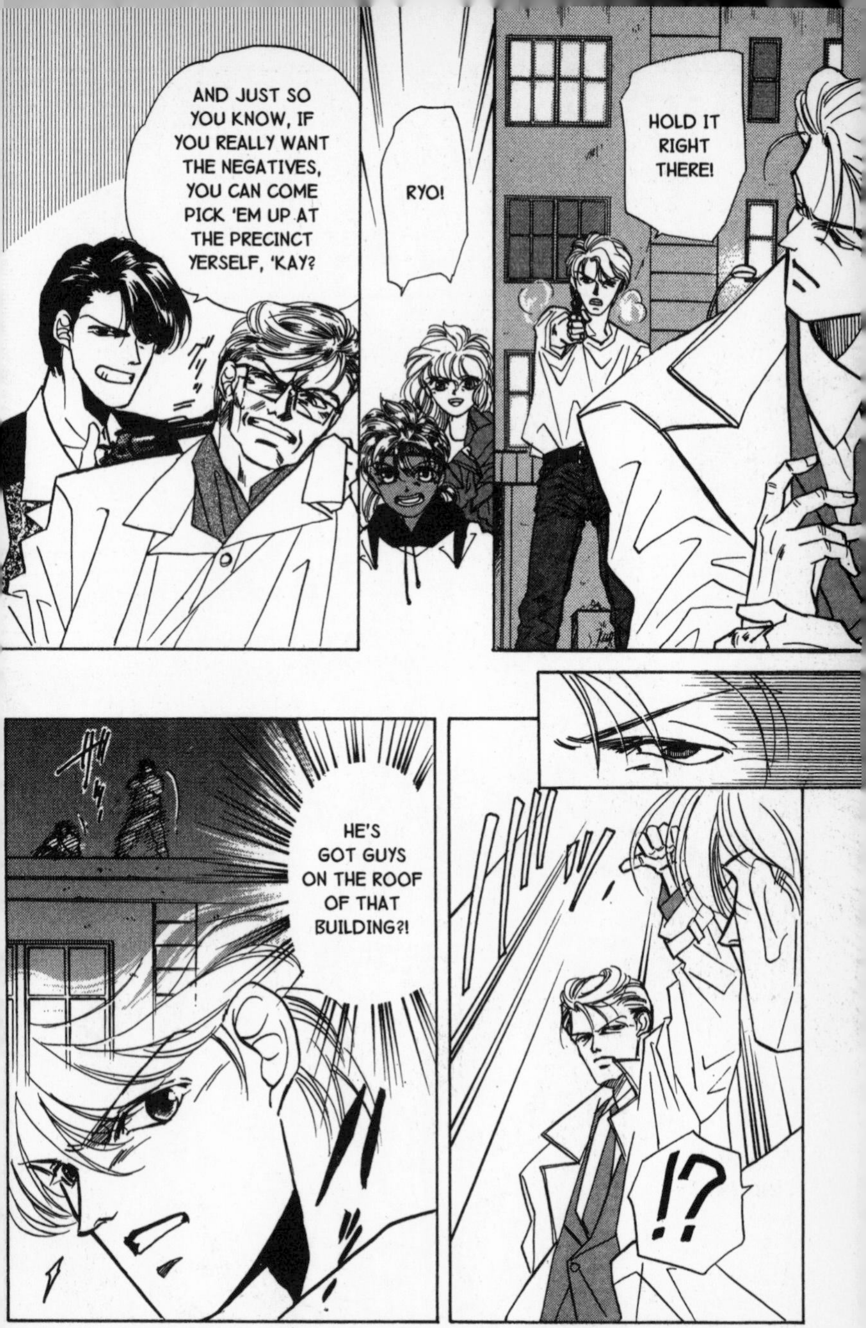
HOLD IT RIGHT THERE!
RYO!
AND JUST SO YOU KNOW, IF YOU REALLY WANT THE NEGATIVES, YOU CAN COME PICK 'EM UP AT THE PRECINCT YERSELF, 'KAY?
!?
HE'S GOT GUYS ON THE ROOF OF THAT BUILDING?!

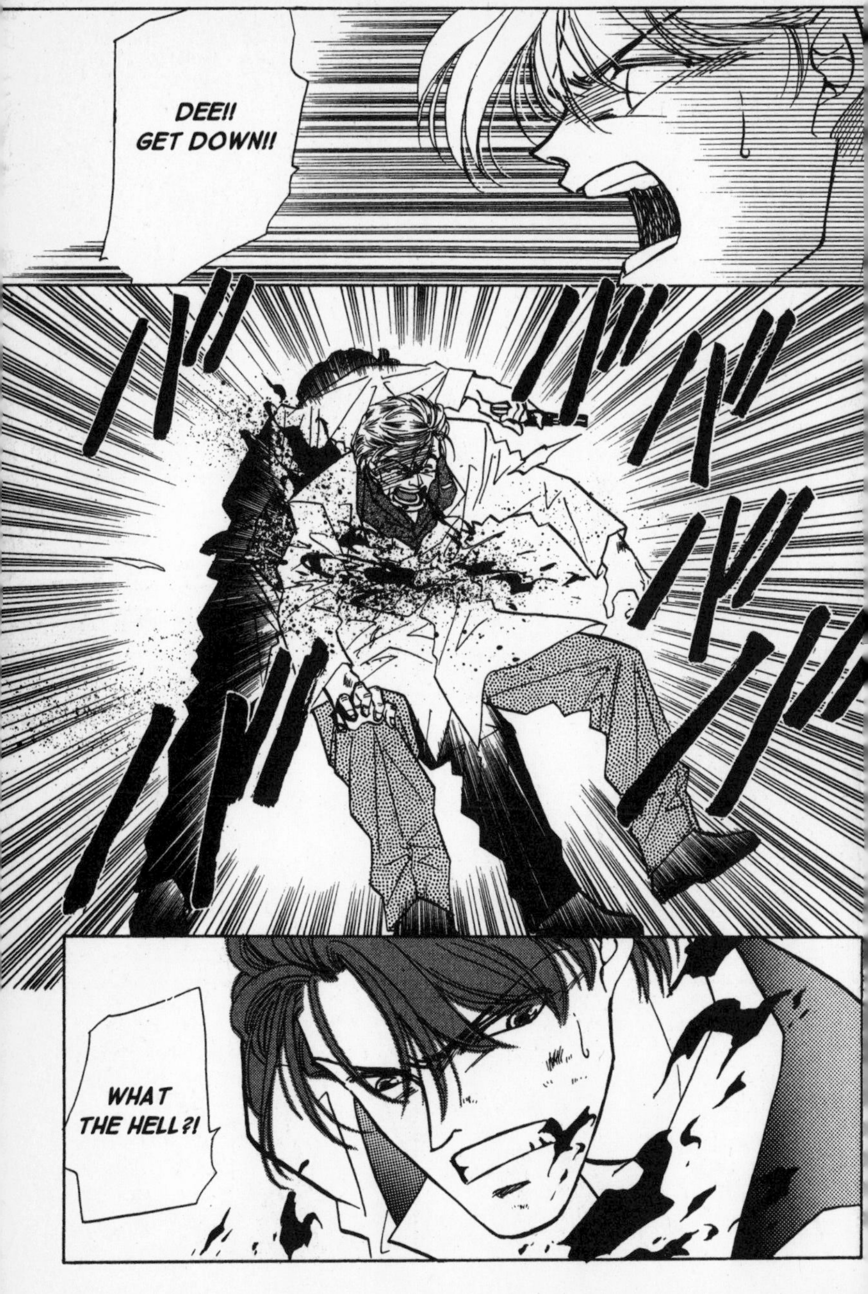
DEE!! GET DOWN!!
WHAT THE HELL?!

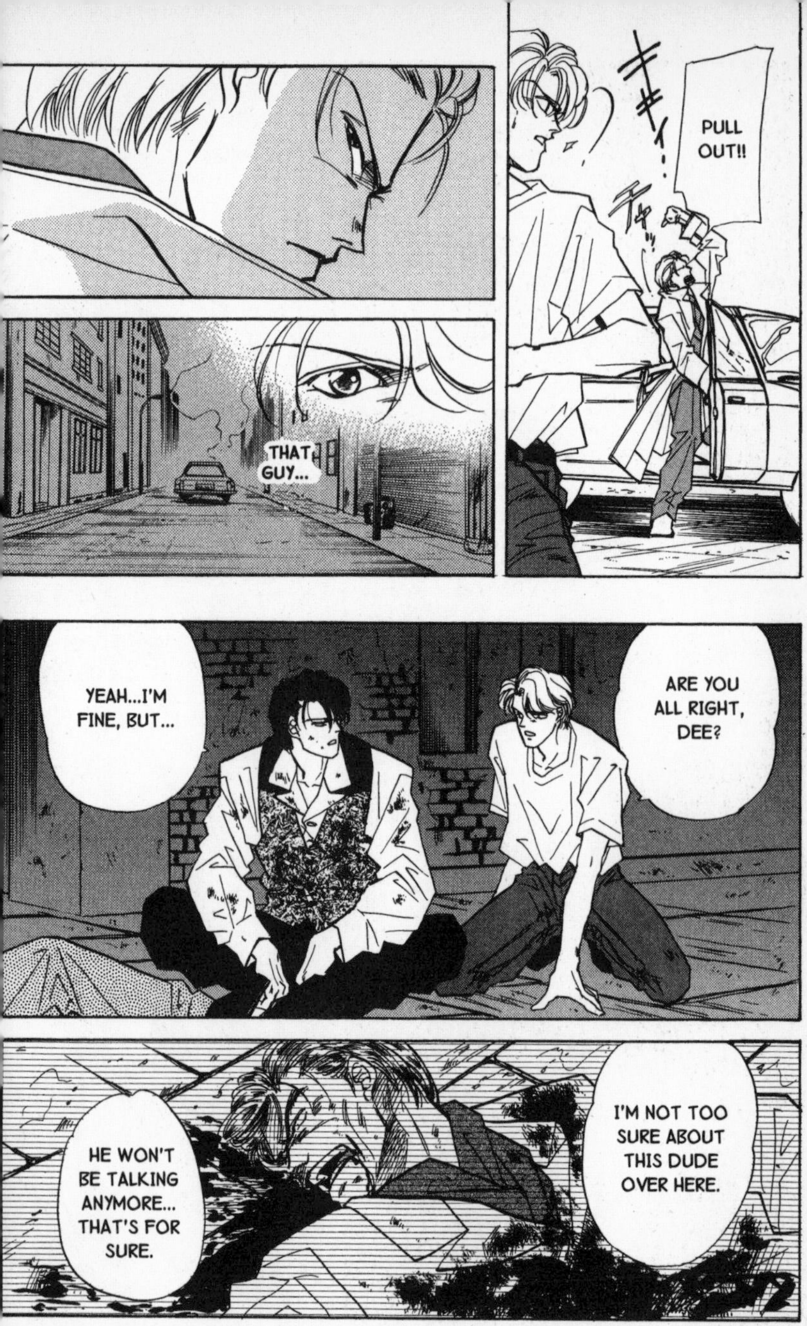
PULL OUT!!
THAT GUY...
ARE YOU ALL RIGHT, DEE?
YEAH...I'M FINE, BUT...
I'M NOT TOO SURE ABOUT THIS DUDE OVER HERE.
HE WON'T BE TALKING ANYMORE... THAT'S FOR SURE.

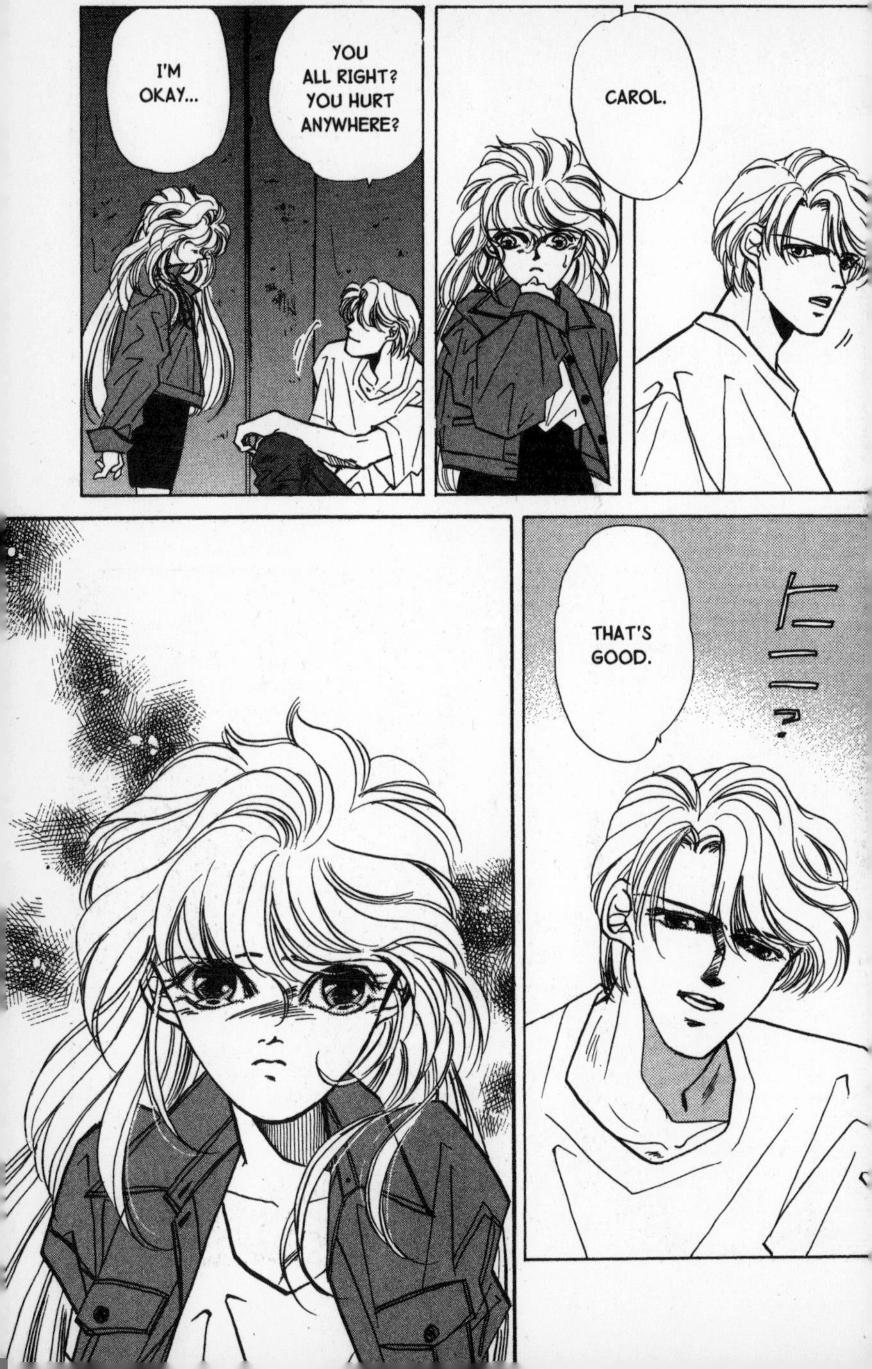
CAROL.
YOU ALL RIGHT? YOU HURT ANYWHERE?
I'M OKAY...
THAT'S GOOD.

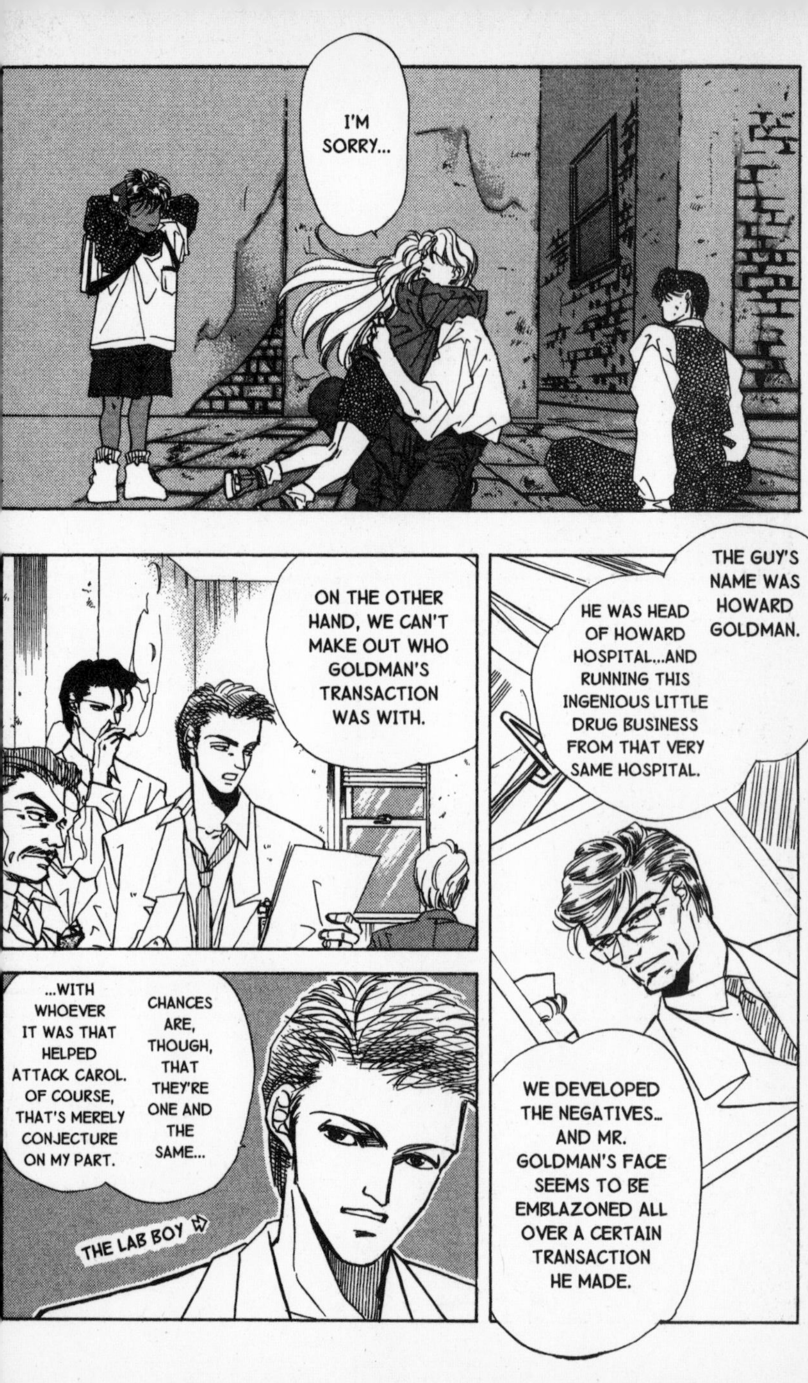
I'M SORRY...
THE GUY'S NAME WAS HOWARD GOLDMAN.
HE WAS HEAD OF HOWARD HOSPITAL...AND RUNNING THIS INGENIOUS LITTLE DRUG BUSINESS FROM THAT VERY SAME HOSPITAL.
WE DEVELOPED THE NEGATIVES... AND MR. GOLDMAN'S FACE SEEMS TO BE EMBLAZONED ALL OVER A CERTAIN TRANSACTION HE MADE.
ON THE OTHER HAND, WE CAN'T MAKE OUT WHO GOLDMAN'S TRANSACTION WAS WITH.
CHANCES ARE, THOUGH, THAT THEY'RE ONE AND THE SAME...
...WITH WHOEVER IT WAS THAT HELPED ATTACK CAROL. OF COURSE, THAT'S MERELY CONJECTURE ON MY PART.
THE LAB BOY

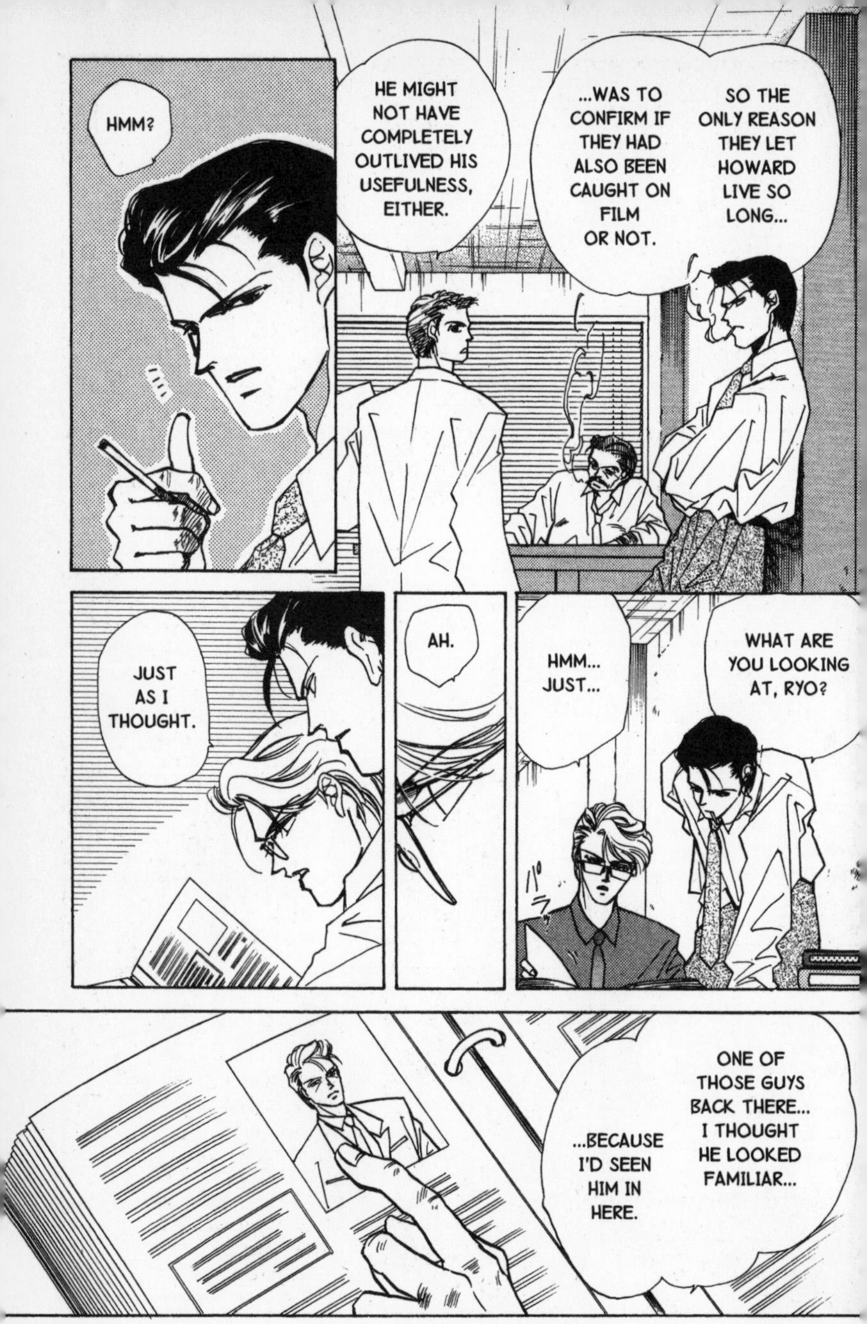
SO THE ONLY REASON THEY LET HOWARD LIVE SO LONG...
...WAS TO CONFIRM IF THEY HAD ALSO BEEN CAUGHT ON FILM OR NOT.
HE MIGHT NOT HAVE COMPLETELY OUTLIVED HIS USEFULNESS, EITHER.
HMM?
WHAT ARE YOU LOOKING AT, RYO?
HMM... JUST...
AH.
JUST AS I THOUGHT.
ONE OF THOSE GUYS BACK THERE... I THOUGHT HE LOOKED FAMILIAR...
...BECAUSE I'D SEEN HIM IN HERE.

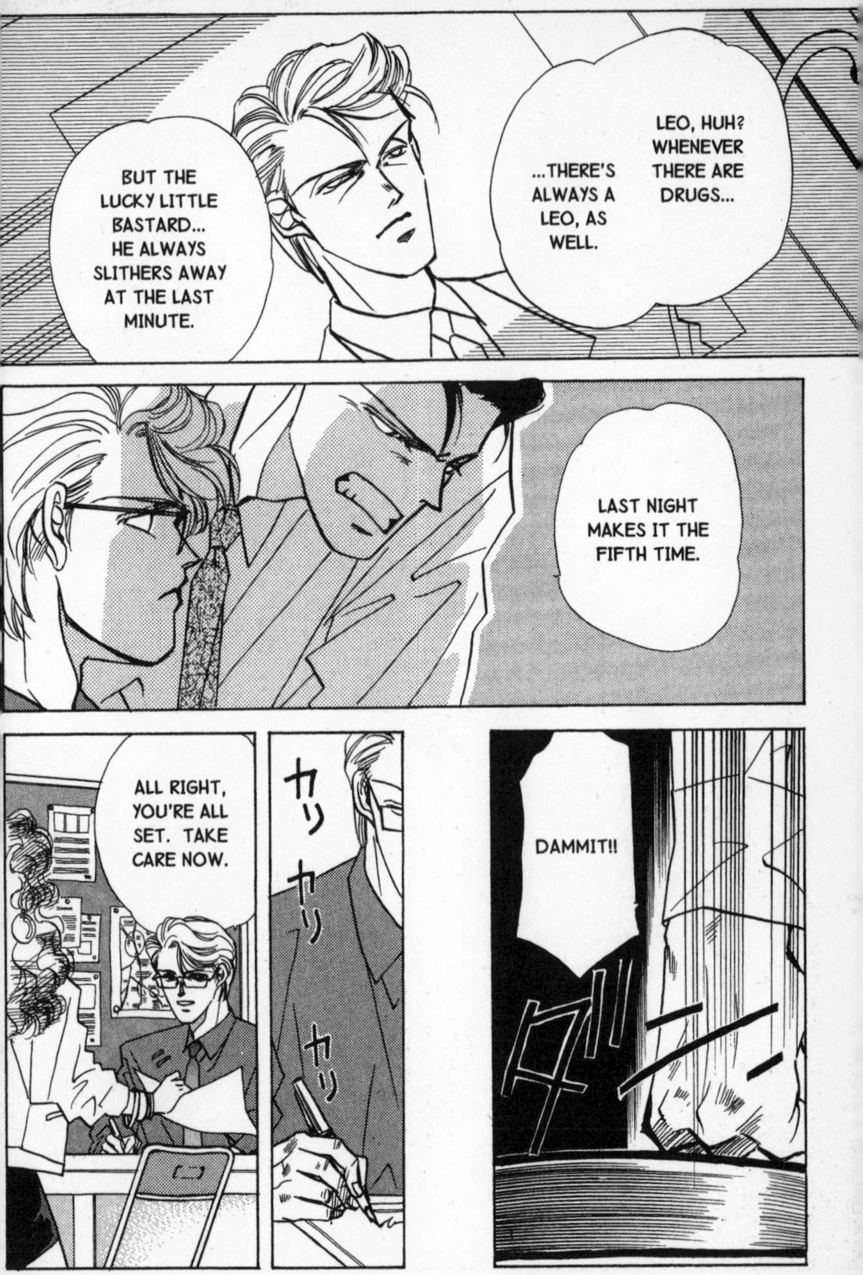
LEO, HUH? WHENEVER THERE ARE DRUGS...
...THERE'S ALWAYS A LEO, AS WELL.
BUT THE LUCKY LITTLE BASTARD... HE ALWAYS SLITHERS AWAY AT THE LAST MINUTE.
LAST NIGHT MAKES IT THE FIFTH TIME.
DAMMIT!!
カリ
カリ
カリ
ALL RIGHT, YOU'RE ALL SET. TAKE CARE NOW.

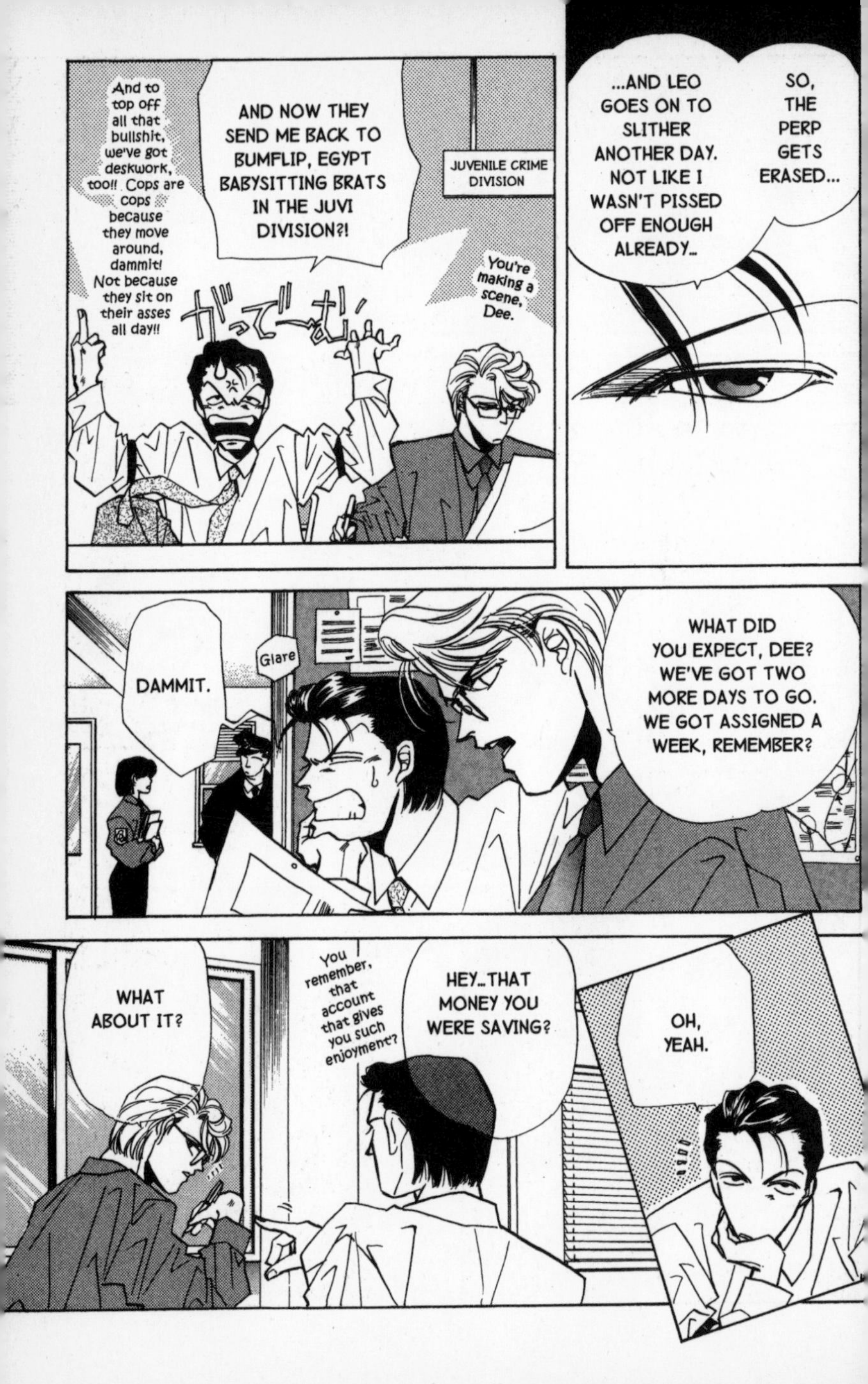
SO, THE PERP GETS ERASED...
...AND LEO GOES ON TO SLITHER ANOTHER DAY. NOT LIKE I WASN'T PISSED OFF ENOUGH ALREADY...
JUVENILE CRIME DIVISION
AND NOW THEY SEND ME BACK TO BUMFLIP, EGYPT BABYSITTING BRATS IN THE JUVI DIVISION?!
And to top off all that bullshit, we've got deskwork, too!! Cops are cops because they move around, dammit! Not because they sit on their asses all day!!
がってーむ
You're making a scene, Dee.
WHAT DID YOU EXPECT, DEE? WE'VE GOT TWO MORE DAYS TO GO. WE GOT ASSIGNED A WEEK, REMEMBER?
Glare
DAMMIT.
OH, YEAH.
HEY...THAT MONEY YOU WERE SAVING?
You remember, that account that gives you such enjoyment?
WHAT ABOUT IT?

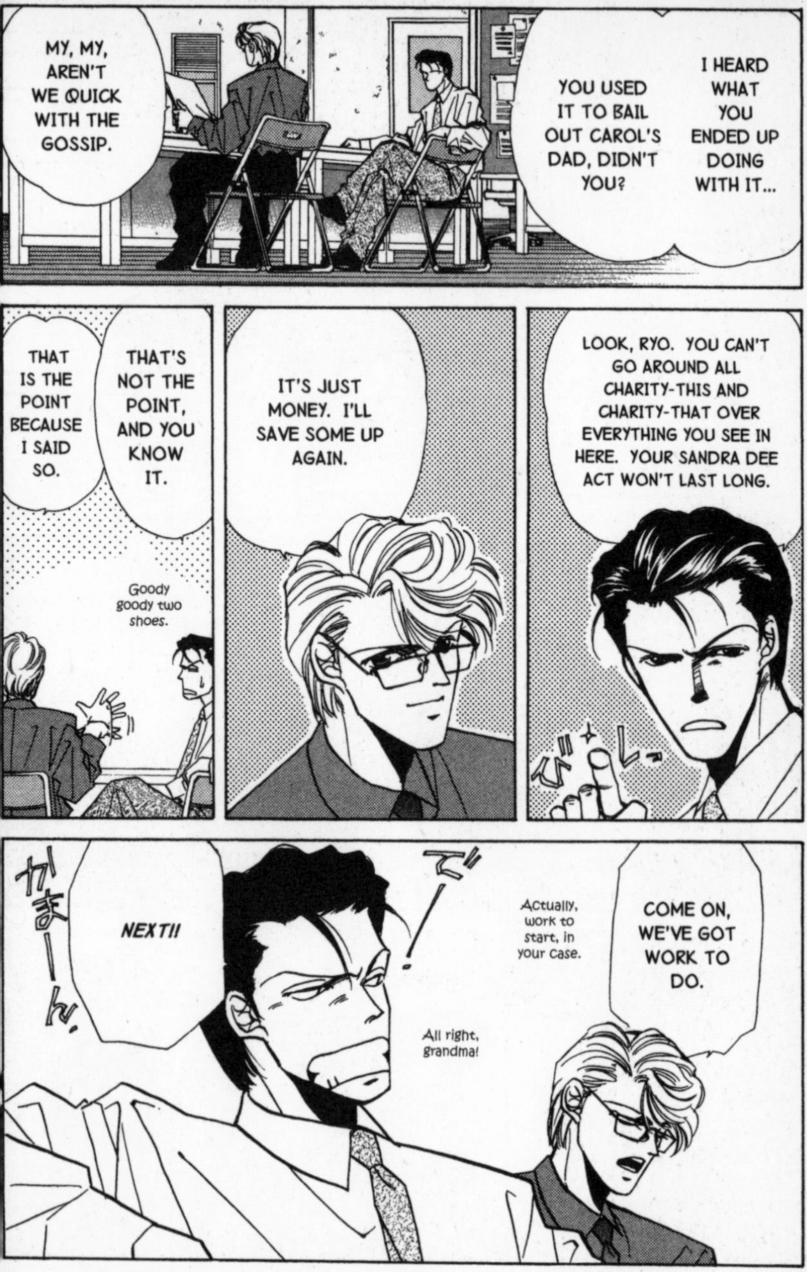
I HEARD WHAT YOU ENDED UP DOING WITH IT...
YOU USED IT TO BAIL OUT CAROL'S DAD, DIDN'T YOU?
MY, MY, AREN'T WE QUICK WITH THE GOSSIP.
LOOK, RYO. YOU CAN'T GO AROUND ALL CHARITY-THIS AND CHARITY-THAT OVER EVERYTHING YOU SEE IN HERE. YOUR SANDRA DEE ACT WON'T LAST LONG.
びしっ
IT'S JUST MONEY. I'LL SAVE SOME UP AGAIN.
THAT'S NOT THE POINT, AND YOU KNOW IT.
THAT IS THE POINT BECAUSE I SAID SO.
Goody goody two shoes.
COME ON, WE'VE GOT WORK TO DO.
Actually, work to start, in your case.
All right, grandma!
で!
NEXT!!
かまーん.

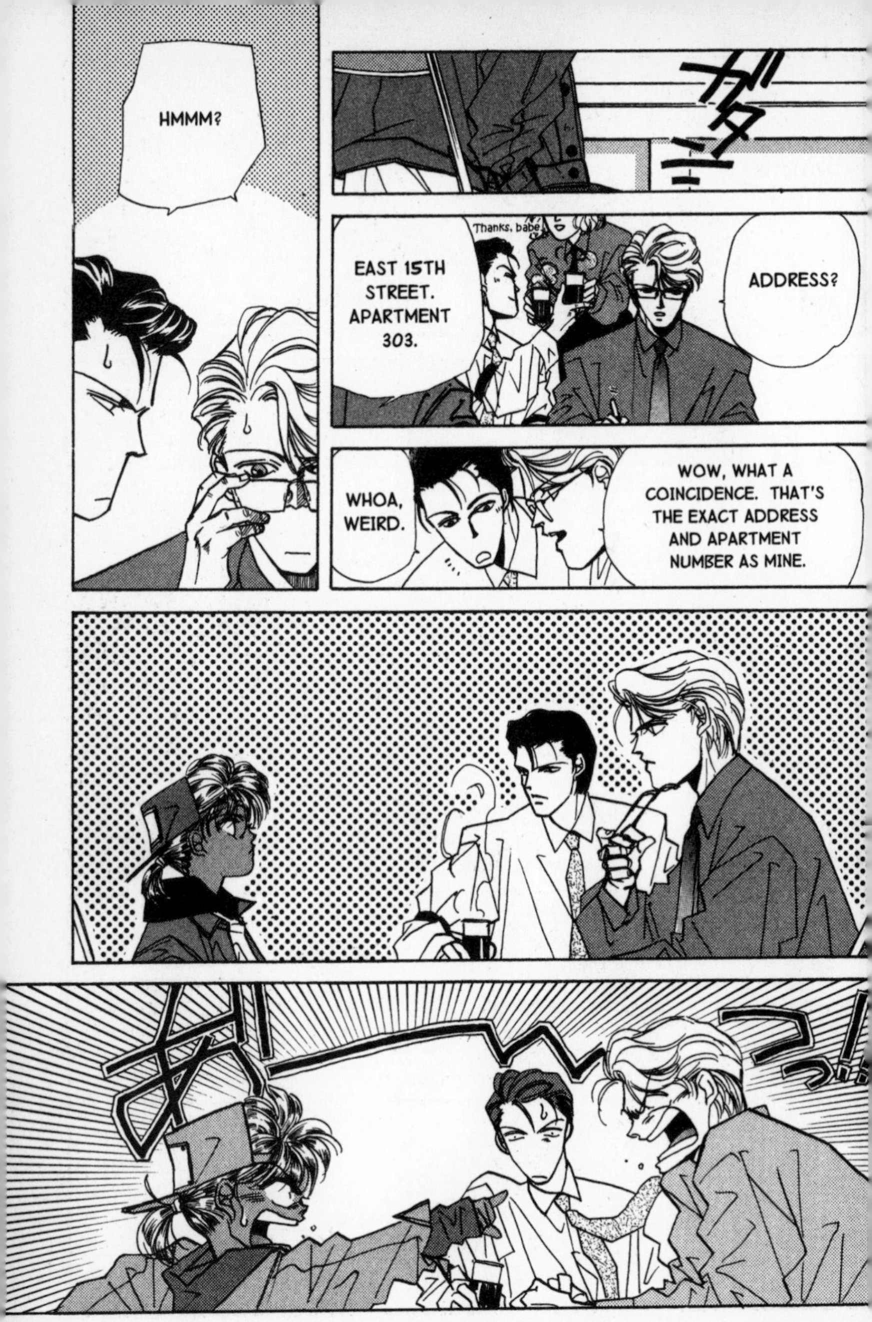
ADDRESS?
Thanks, babe
EAST 15TH STREET. APARTMENT 303.
WOW, WHAT A COINCIDENCE. THAT'S THE EXACT ADDRESS AND APARTMENT NUMBER AS MINE.
WHOA, WEIRD.
HMMM?

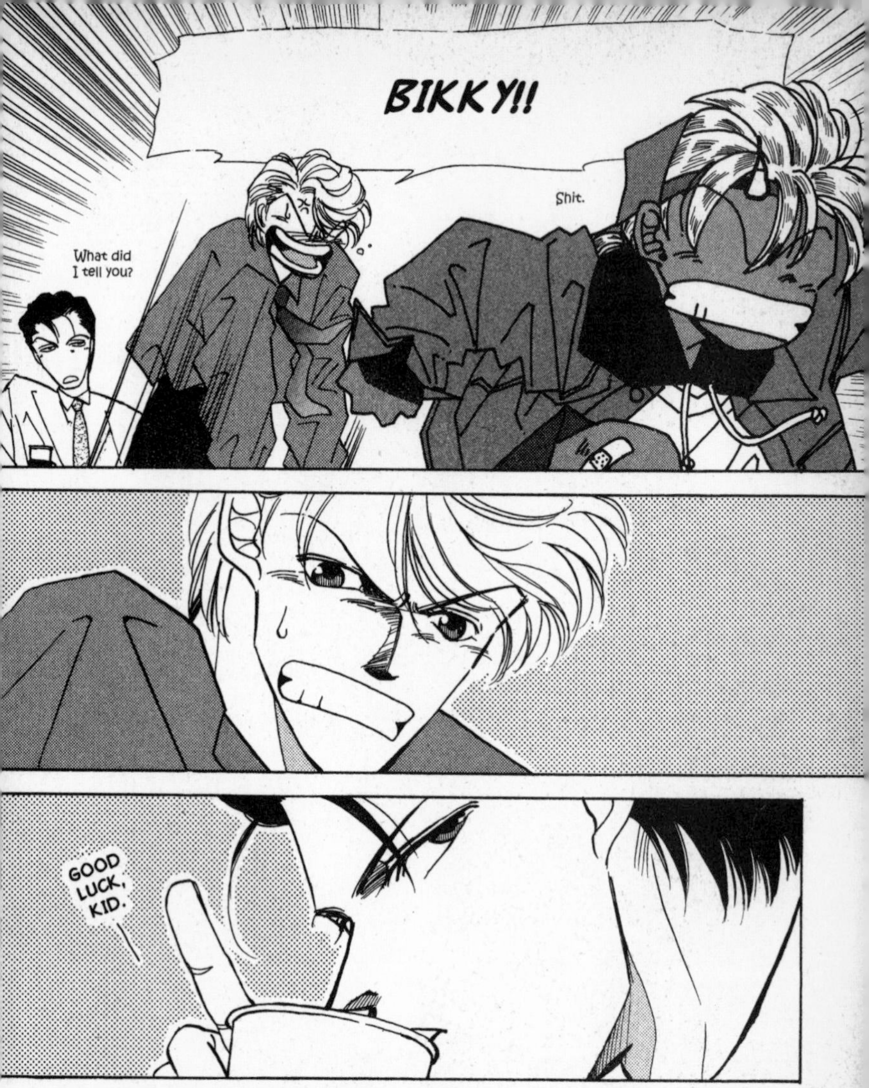
BIKKY!!
Shit.
What did I tell you?
GOOD LUCK, KID.
Sniff.
Got smacked by Ryo.
See you again

FAKE act.2/ End.

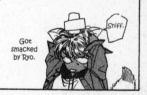

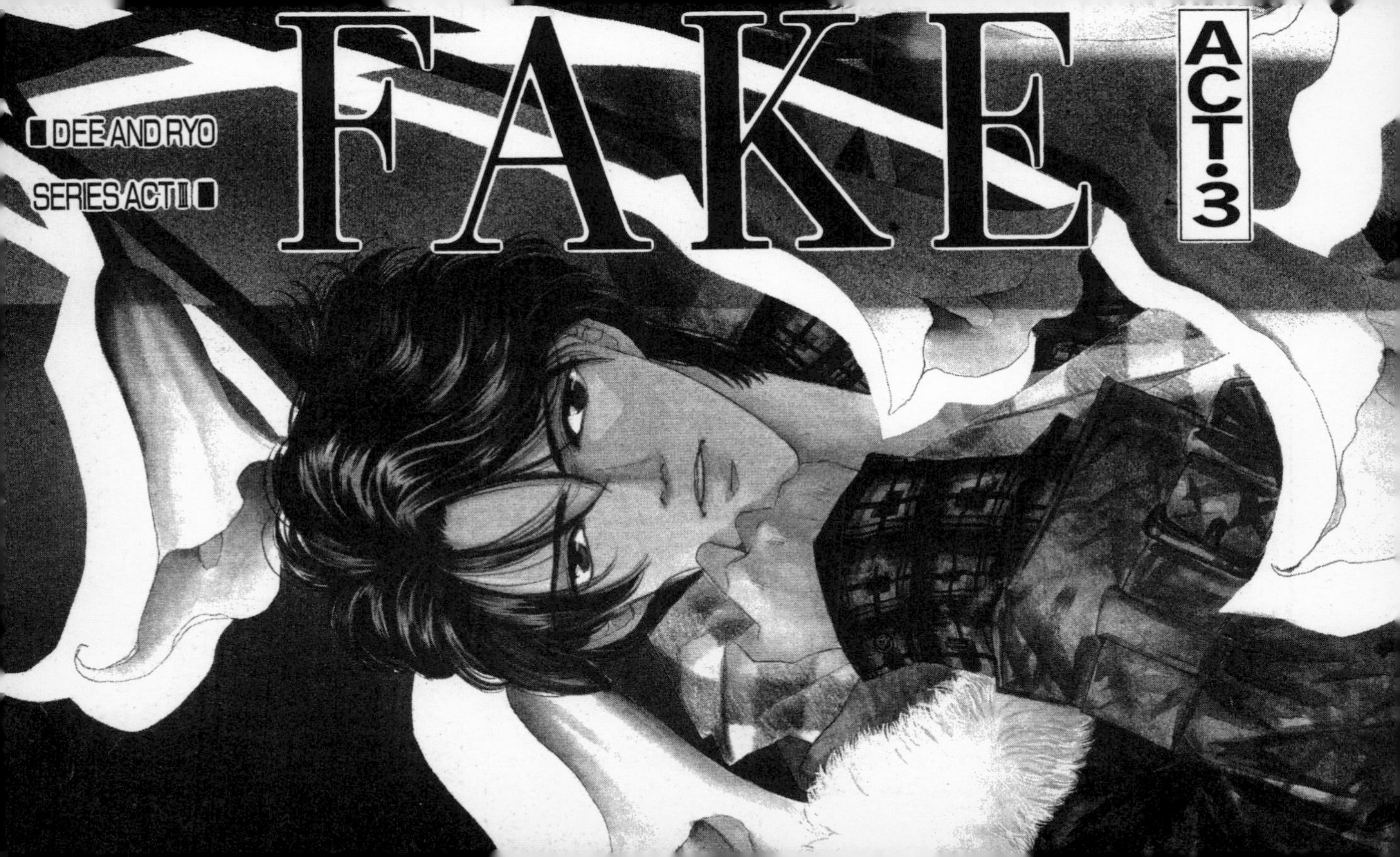
FAKE
ACT·3
DEE AND RYO
SERIES ACT III

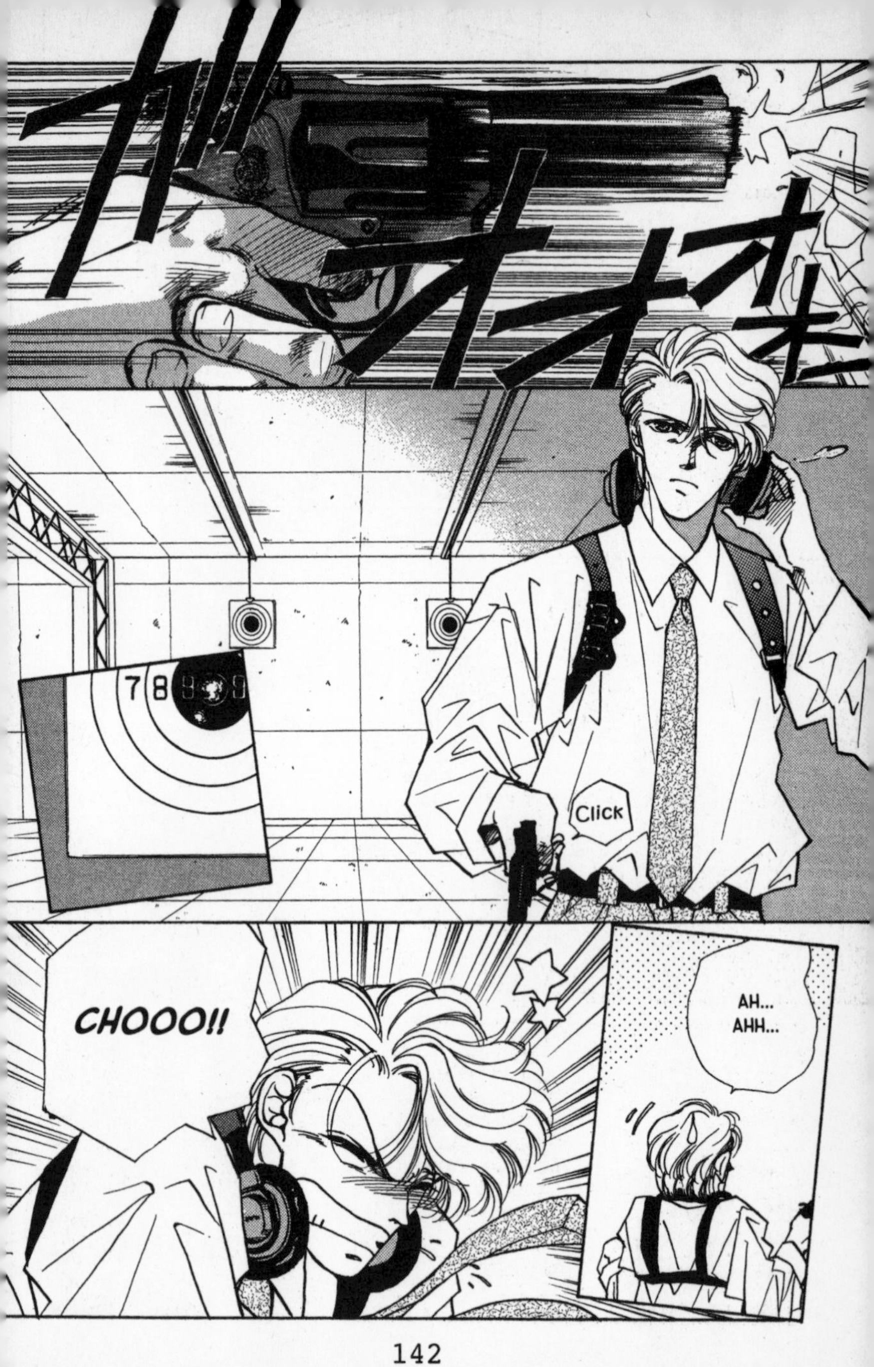
ガオオオ
Click
AH...
AHH...
CHOOO!!

WAAHH!!

RYO!!

DAMN... I THINK I HAVE A SLIGHT FEVER, TOO...

I GUESS I AM GETTING SICK AFTER ALL...

Sniffle

I'M OFF TODAY--

THIS THING RIGHT HERE.

WHAT IS?

WAY TO GO, RYO. QUITE IMPRESSIVE.

DEE.

1st.	Randy Maclean	
2nd.	Kim Lazuli	
3rd.	James Randall	
4th.	Larry McDoyal	
5th.	Dee Laytner	

IT'S THE RESULTS FROM THE STATION-WIDE SHOOTING PRACTICE SESSION WE HAD A WHILE BACK. YOU TOOK FIRST PLACE, MAN.

143

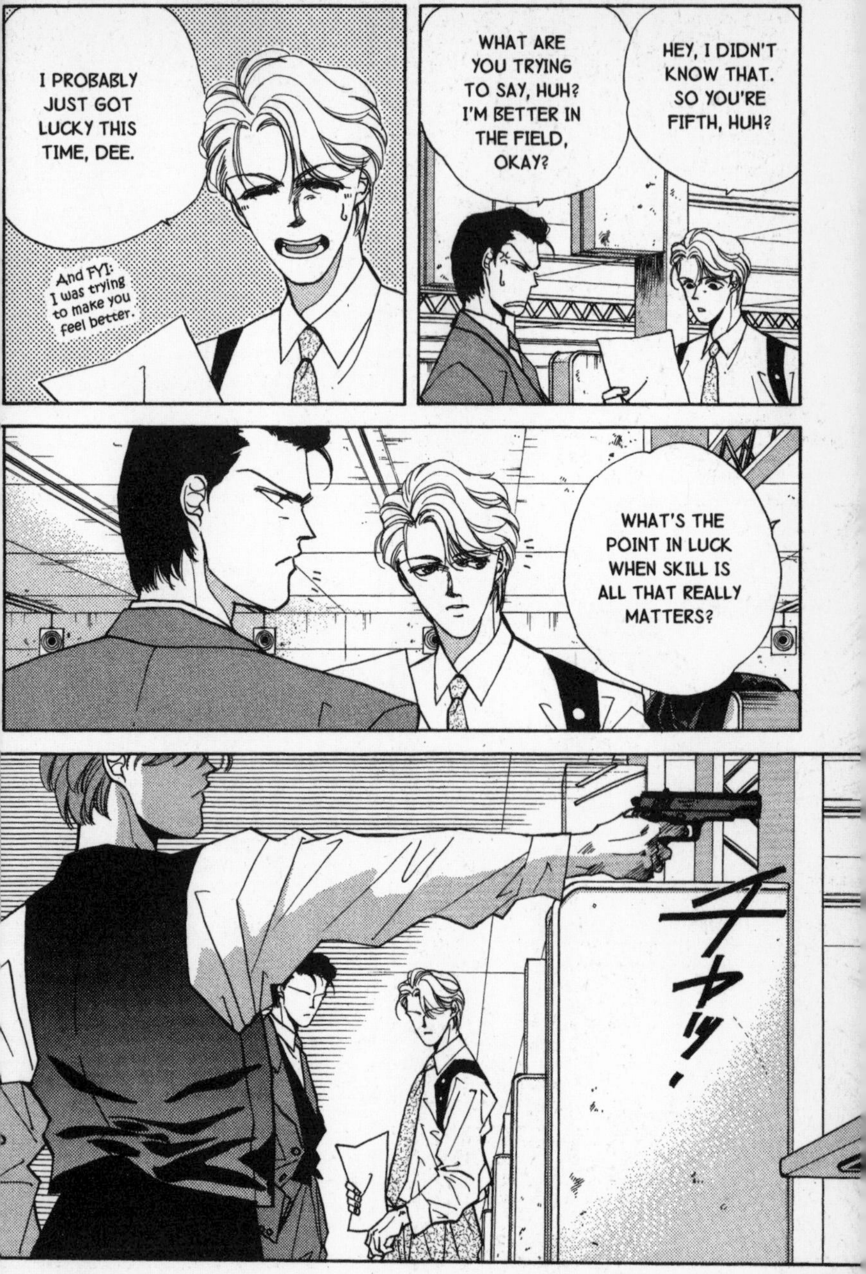
HEY, I DIDN'T KNOW THAT. SO YOU'RE FIFTH, HUH?
WHAT ARE YOU TRYING TO SAY, HUH? I'M BETTER IN THE FIELD, OKAY?
I PROBABLY JUST GOT LUCKY THIS TIME, DEE.
And FYI: I was trying to make you feel better.
WHAT'S THE POINT IN LUCK WHEN SKILL IS ALL THAT REALLY MATTERS?
チャッ!

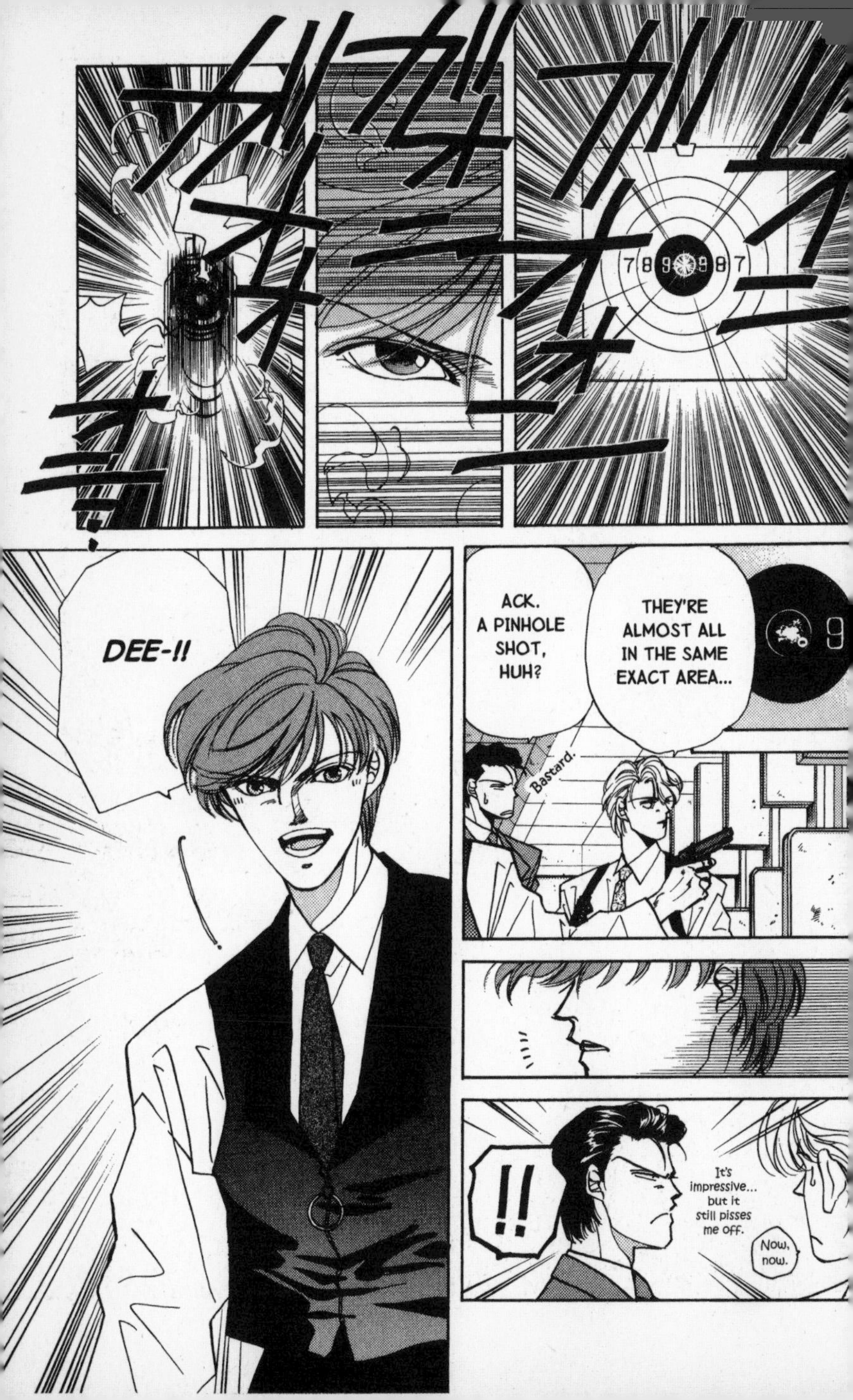
THEY'RE ALMOST ALL IN THE SAME EXACT AREA...
ACK. A PINHOLE SHOT, HUH?
Bastard.
It's impressive... but it still pisses me off.
Now, now.
!!
DEE-!!

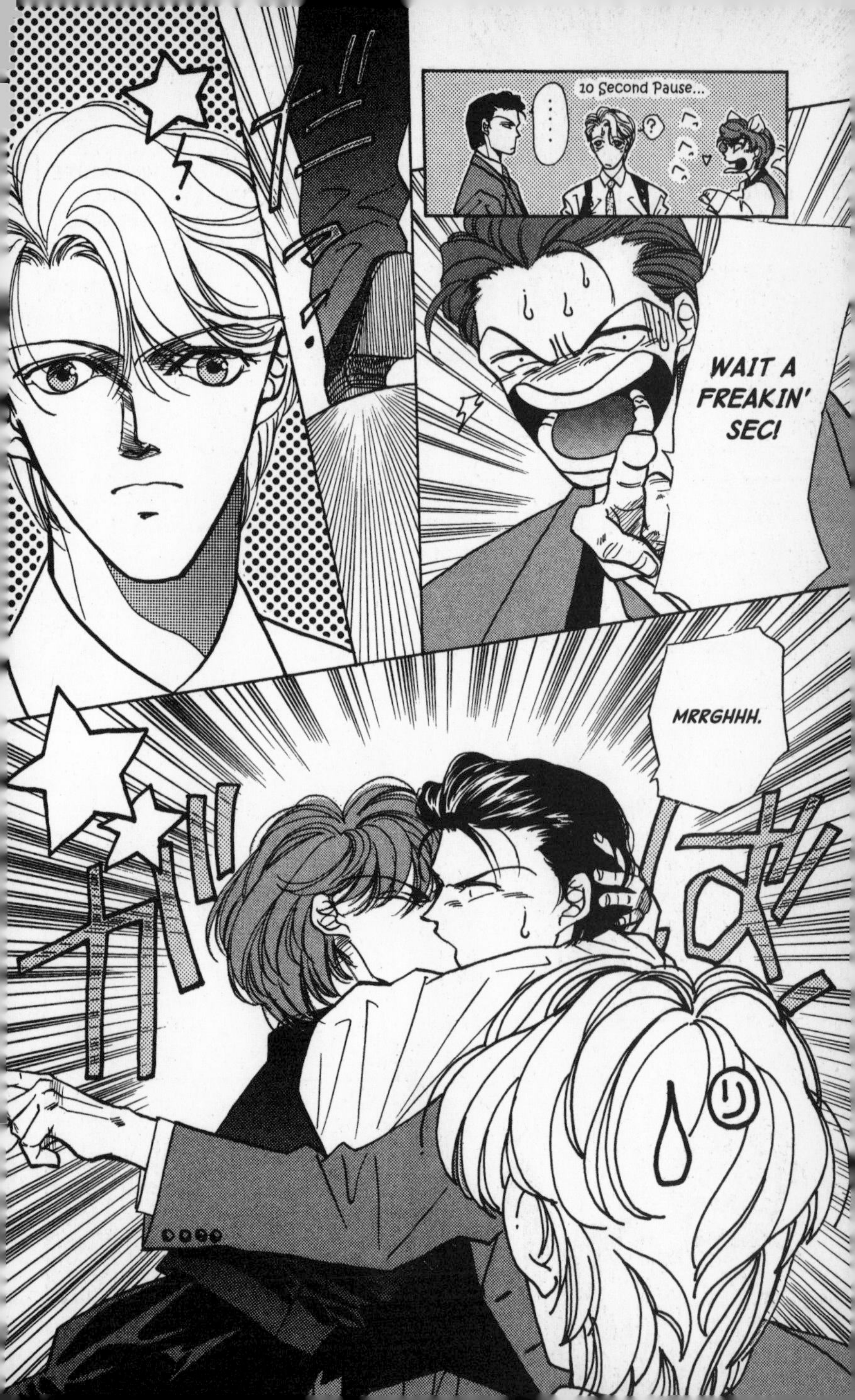
10 Second Pause...
......
WAIT A FREAKIN' SEC!
MRRGHHH.

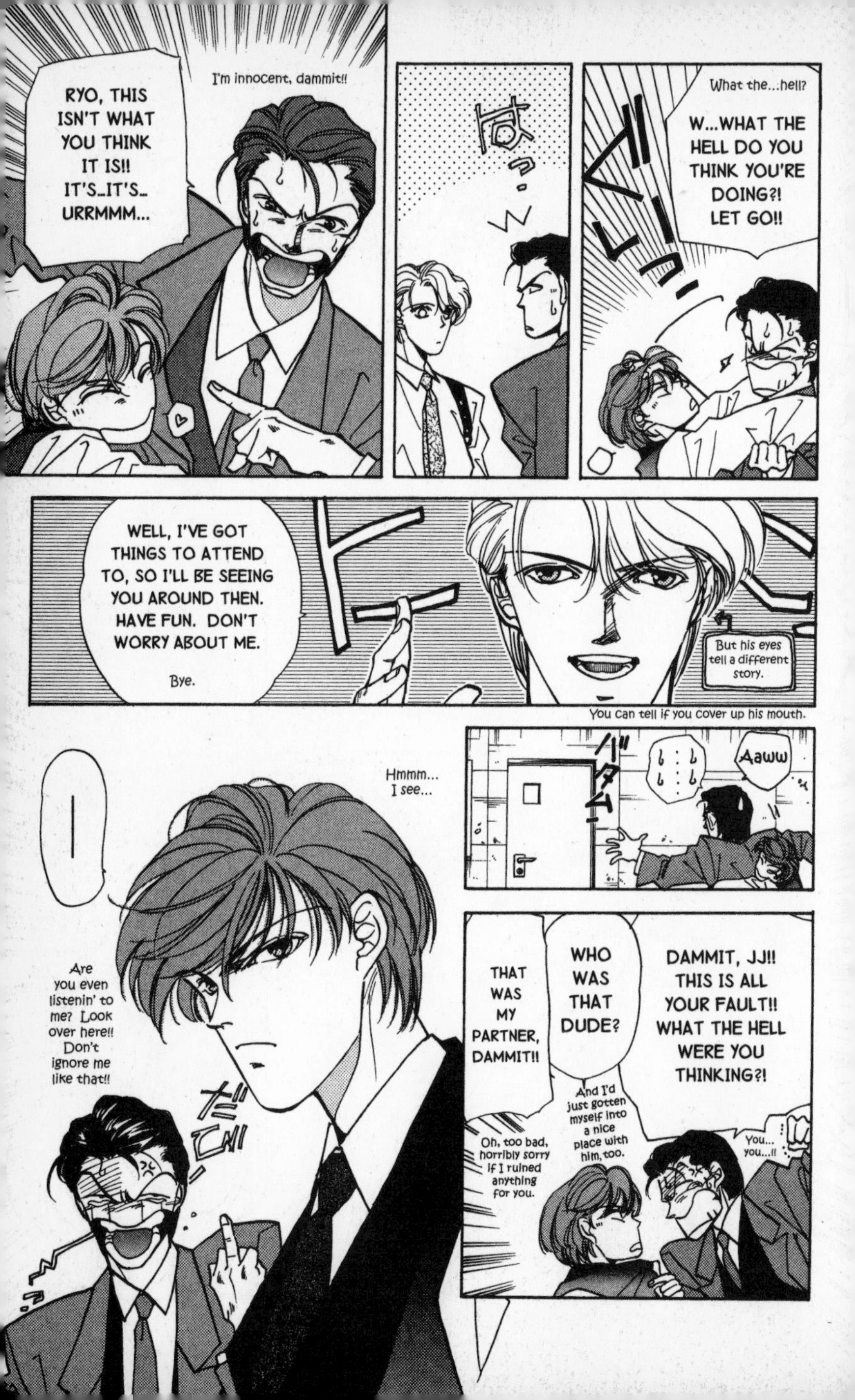
What the...hell?
W...WHAT THE HELL DO YOU THINK YOU'RE DOING?! LET GO!!
RYO, THIS ISN'T WHAT YOU THINK IT IS!! IT'S..IT'S.. URRMMM...
I'm innocent, dammit!!
WELL, I'VE GOT THINGS TO ATTEND TO, SO I'LL BE SEEING YOU AROUND THEN. HAVE FUN. DON'T WORRY ABOUT ME.
Bye.
But his eyes tell a different story.
You can tell if you cover up his mouth.
Aaww
DAMMIT, JJ!! THIS IS ALL YOUR FAULT!! WHAT THE HELL WERE YOU THINKING?!
You... you...!!
WHO WAS THAT DUDE?
And I'd just gotten myself into a nice place with him, too.
THAT WAS MY PARTNER, DAMMIT!!
Oh, too bad, horribly sorry if I ruined anything for you.
Hmmm... I see...
—
Are you even listenin' to me? Look over here!! Don't ignore me like that!!

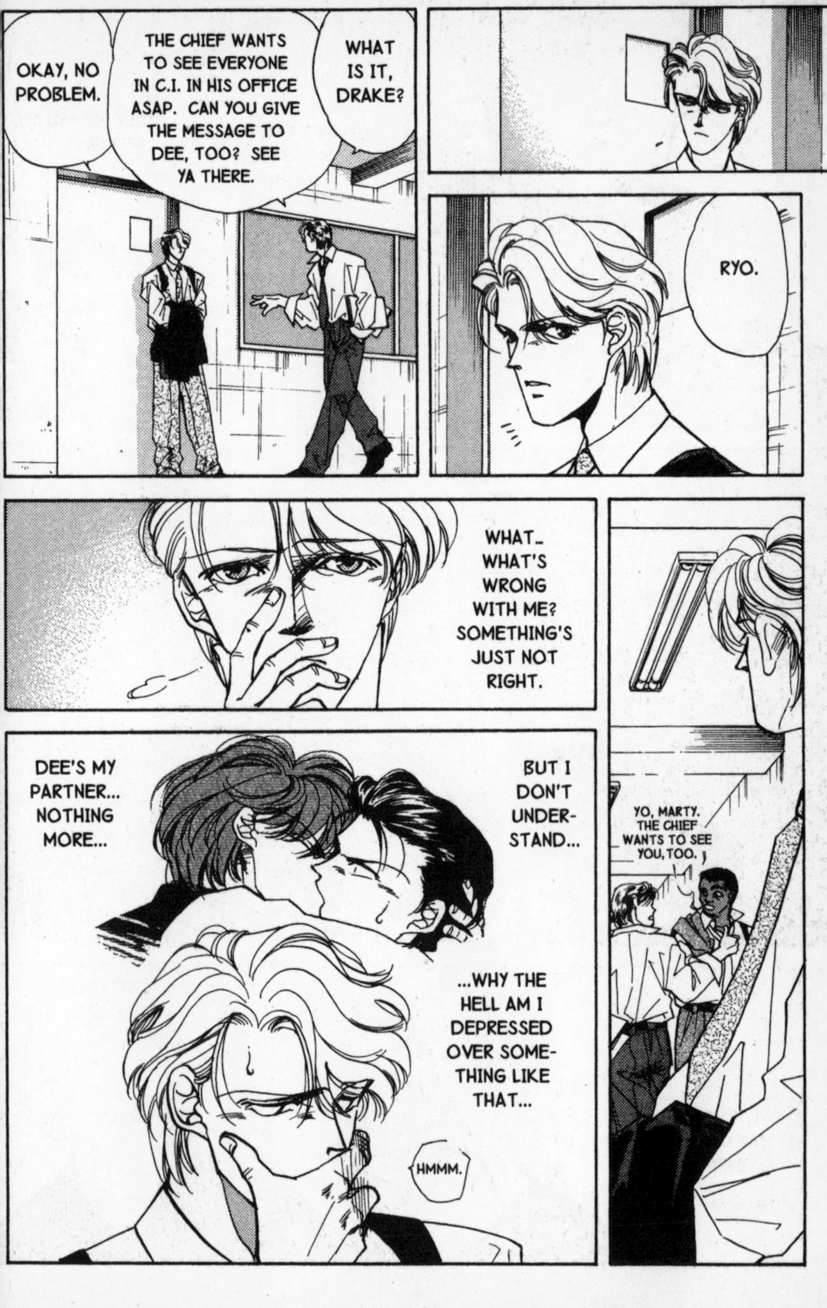
RYO.
WHAT IS IT, DRAKE?
THE CHIEF WANTS TO SEE EVERYONE IN C.I. IN HIS OFFICE ASAP. CAN YOU GIVE THE MESSAGE TO DEE, TOO? SEE YA THERE.
OKAY, NO PROBLEM.
YO, MARTY. THE CHIEF WANTS TO SEE YOU, TOO.
WHAT.. WHAT'S WRONG WITH ME? SOMETHING'S JUST NOT RIGHT.
BUT I DON'T UNDER-STAND...
DEE'S MY PARTNER... NOTHING MORE...
...WHY THE HELL AM I DEPRESSED OVER SOME-THING LIKE THAT...
HMMM.

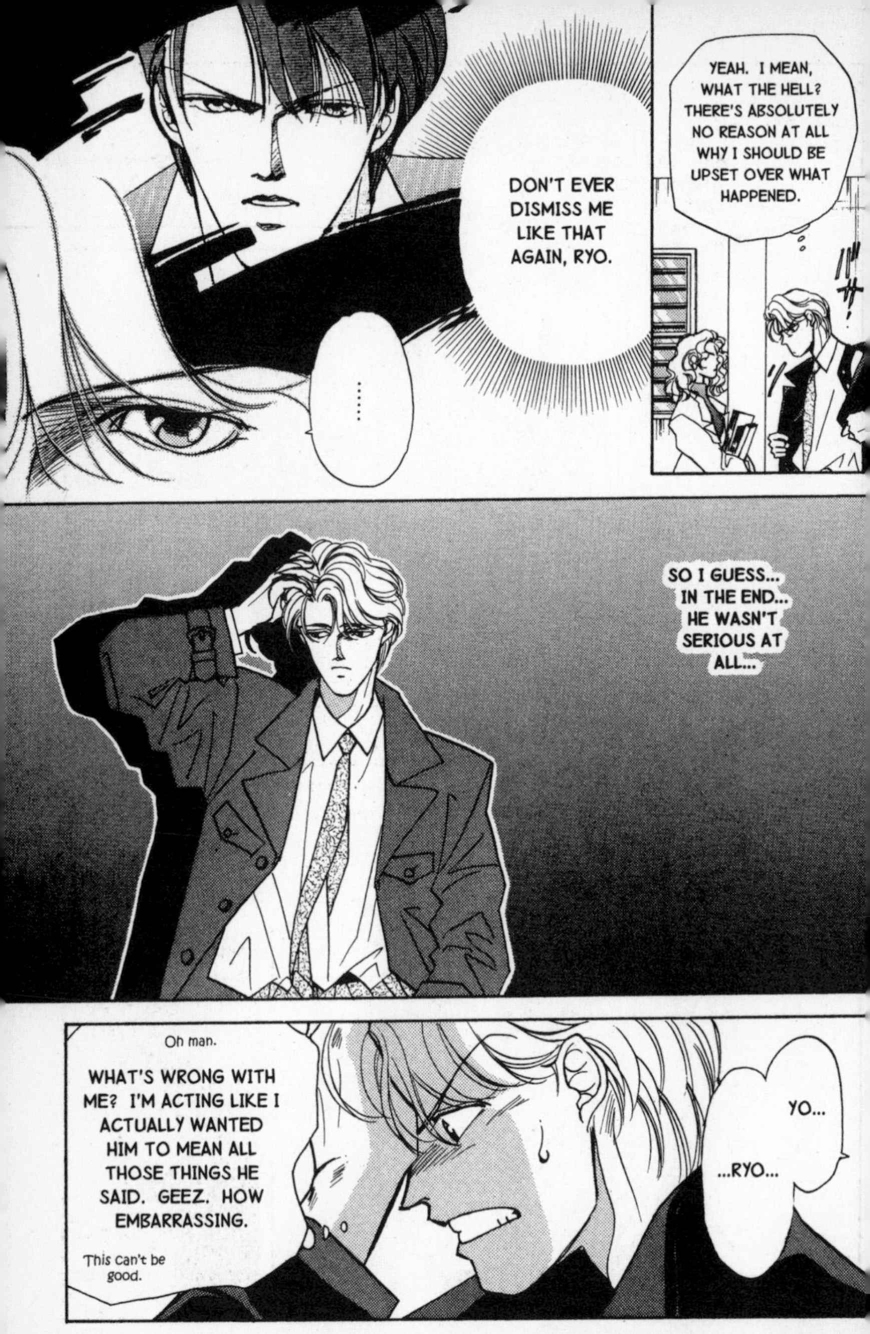
YEAH. I MEAN, WHAT THE HELL? THERE'S ABSOLUTELY NO REASON AT ALL WHY I SHOULD BE UPSET OVER WHAT HAPPENED.
DON'T EVER DISMISS ME LIKE THAT AGAIN, RYO.
......
SO I GUESS... IN THE END... HE WASN'T SERIOUS AT ALL...
YO...
...RYO...
Oh man.
WHAT'S WRONG WITH ME? I'M ACTING LIKE I ACTUALLY WANTED HIM TO MEAN ALL THOSE THINGS HE SAID. GEEZ. HOW EMBARRASSING.
This can't be good.

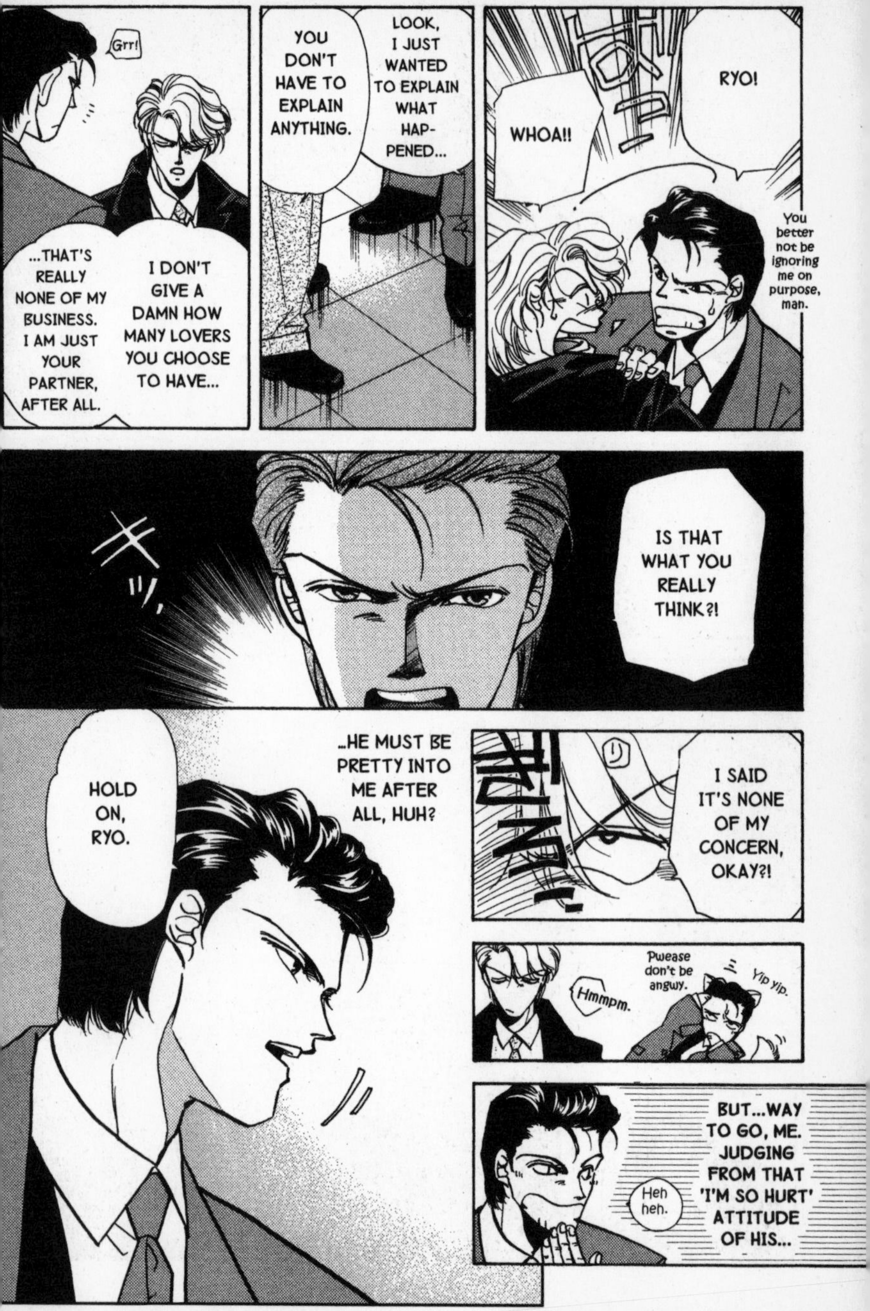
RYO!
WHOA!!
You better not be ignoring me on purpose, man.
LOOK, I JUST WANTED TO EXPLAIN WHAT HAP-PENED...
YOU DON'T HAVE TO EXPLAIN ANYTHING.
Grr!
I DON'T GIVE A DAMN HOW MANY LOVERS YOU CHOOSE TO HAVE...
...THAT'S REALLY NONE OF MY BUSINESS. I AM JUST YOUR PARTNER, AFTER ALL.
IS THAT WHAT YOU REALLY THINK?!
I SAID IT'S NONE OF MY CONCERN, OKAY?!
Yip yip.
Pwease don't be angwy.
Hmmpm.
BUT...WAY TO GO, ME. JUDGING FROM THAT 'I'M SO HURT' ATTITUDE OF HIS...
Heh heh.
...HE MUST BE PRETTY INTO ME AFTER ALL, HUH?
HOLD ON, RYO.

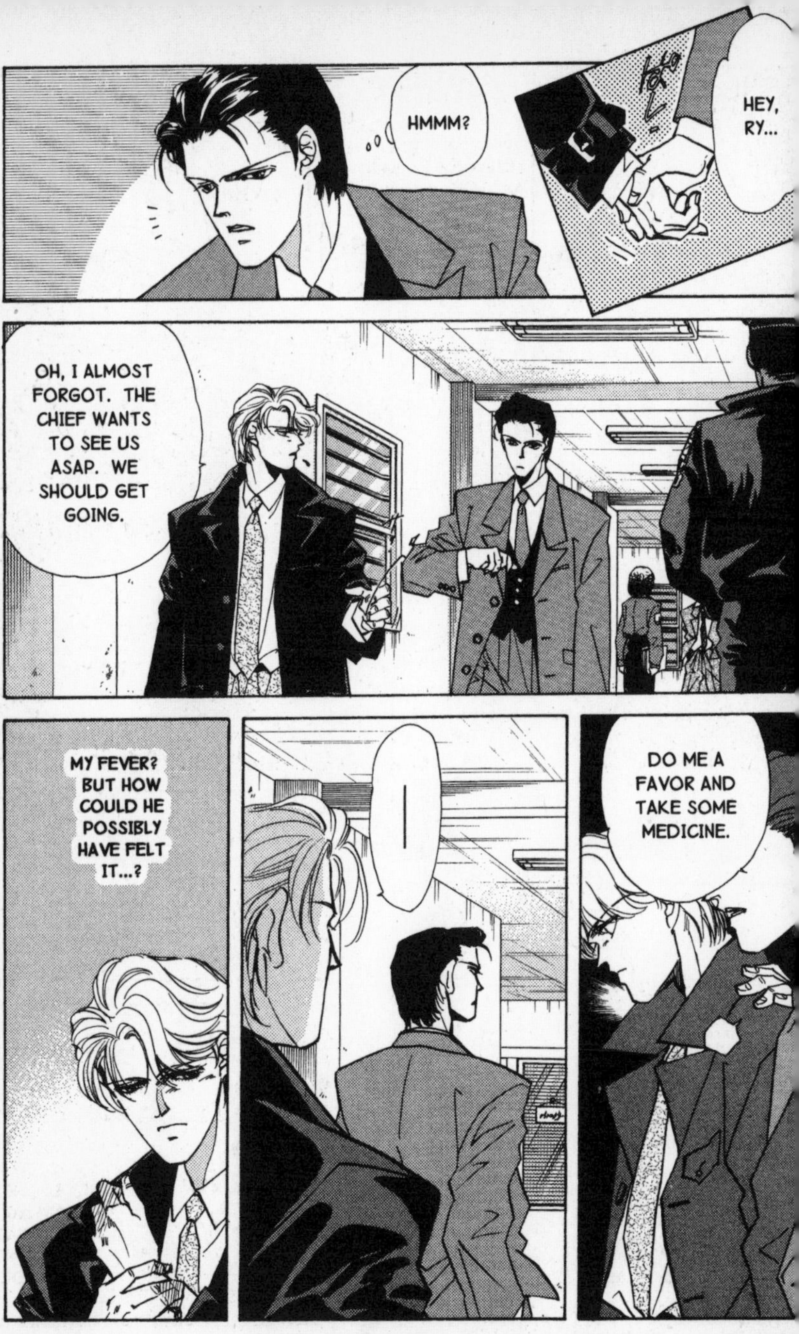
HEY, RY...
HMMM?
OH, I ALMOST FORGOT. THE CHIEF WANTS TO SEE US ASAP. WE SHOULD GET GOING.
DO ME A FAVOR AND TAKE SOME MEDICINE.
MY FEVER? BUT HOW COULD HE POSSIBLY HAVE FELT IT...?

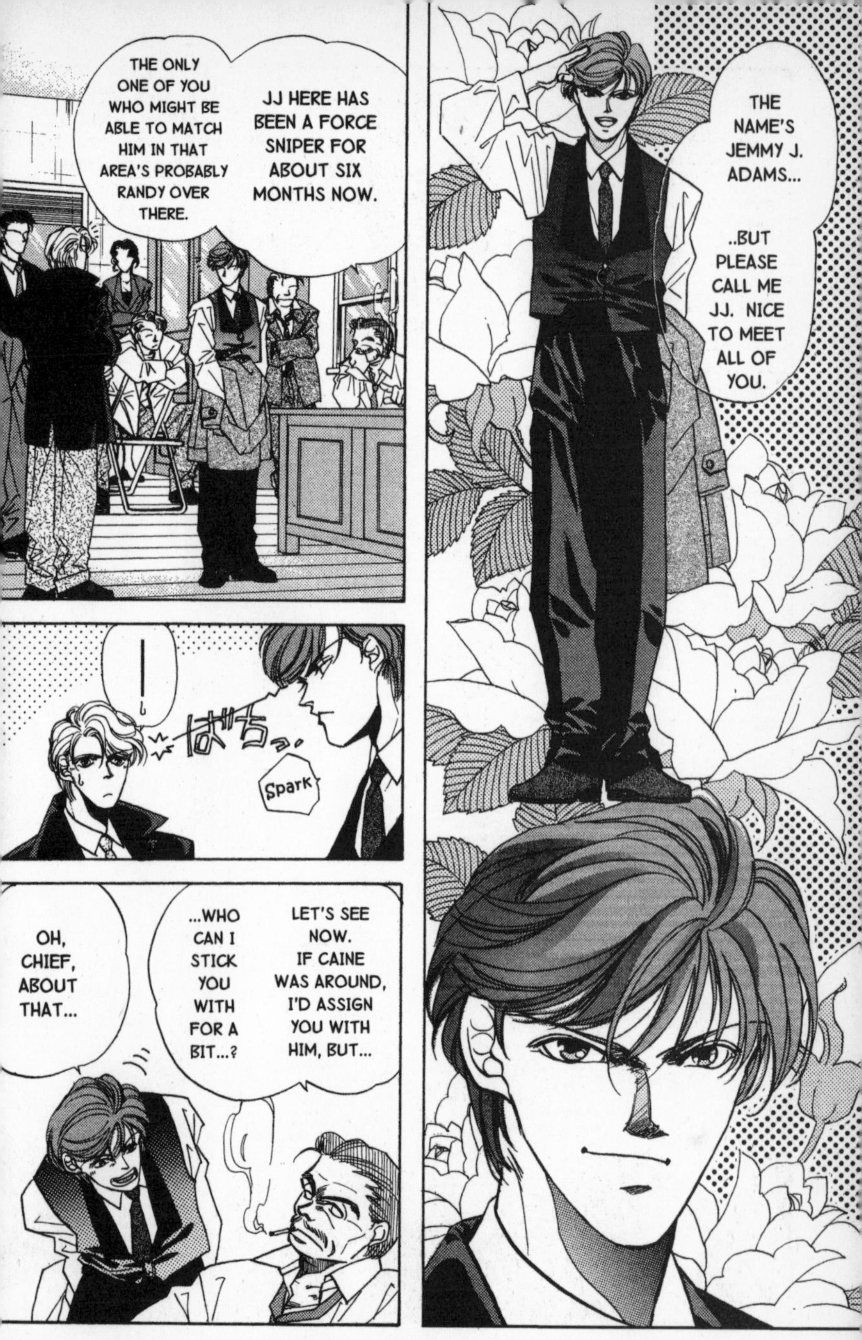
THE NAME'S JEMMY J. ADAMS...
..BUT PLEASE CALL ME JJ. NICE TO MEET ALL OF YOU.
JJ HERE HAS BEEN A FORCE SNIPER FOR ABOUT SIX MONTHS NOW.
THE ONLY ONE OF YOU WHO MIGHT BE ABLE TO MATCH HIM IN THAT AREA'S PROBABLY RANDY OVER THERE.
!
ばちっ
Spark
LET'S SEE NOW. IF CAINE WAS AROUND, I'D ASSIGN YOU WITH HIM, BUT...
...WHO CAN I STICK YOU WITH FOR A BIT...?
OH, CHIEF, ABOUT THAT...

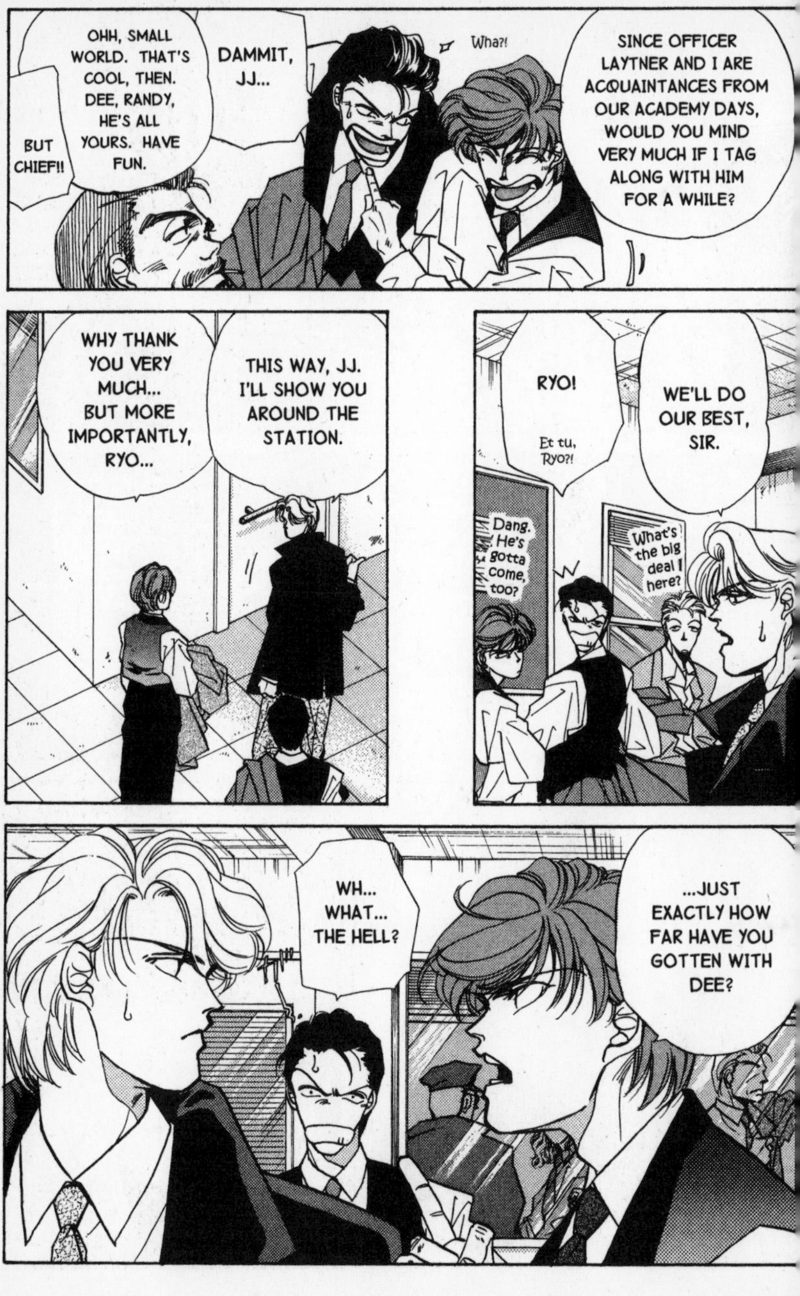
SINCE OFFICER LAYTNER AND I ARE ACQUAINTANCES FROM OUR ACADEMY DAYS, WOULD YOU MIND VERY MUCH IF I TAG ALONG WITH HIM FOR A WHILE?
Wha?!
DAMMIT, JJ...
OHH, SMALL WORLD. THAT'S COOL, THEN. DEE, RANDY, HE'S ALL YOURS. HAVE FUN.
BUT CHIEF!!
WE'LL DO OUR BEST, SIR.
RYO!
Et tu, Ryo?!
What's the big deal here?
Dang. He's gotta come, too?
THIS WAY, JJ. I'LL SHOW YOU AROUND THE STATION.
WHY THANK YOU VERY MUCH... BUT MORE IMPORTANTLY, RYO...
...JUST EXACTLY HOW FAR HAVE YOU GOTTEN WITH DEE?
WH... WHAT... THE HELL?

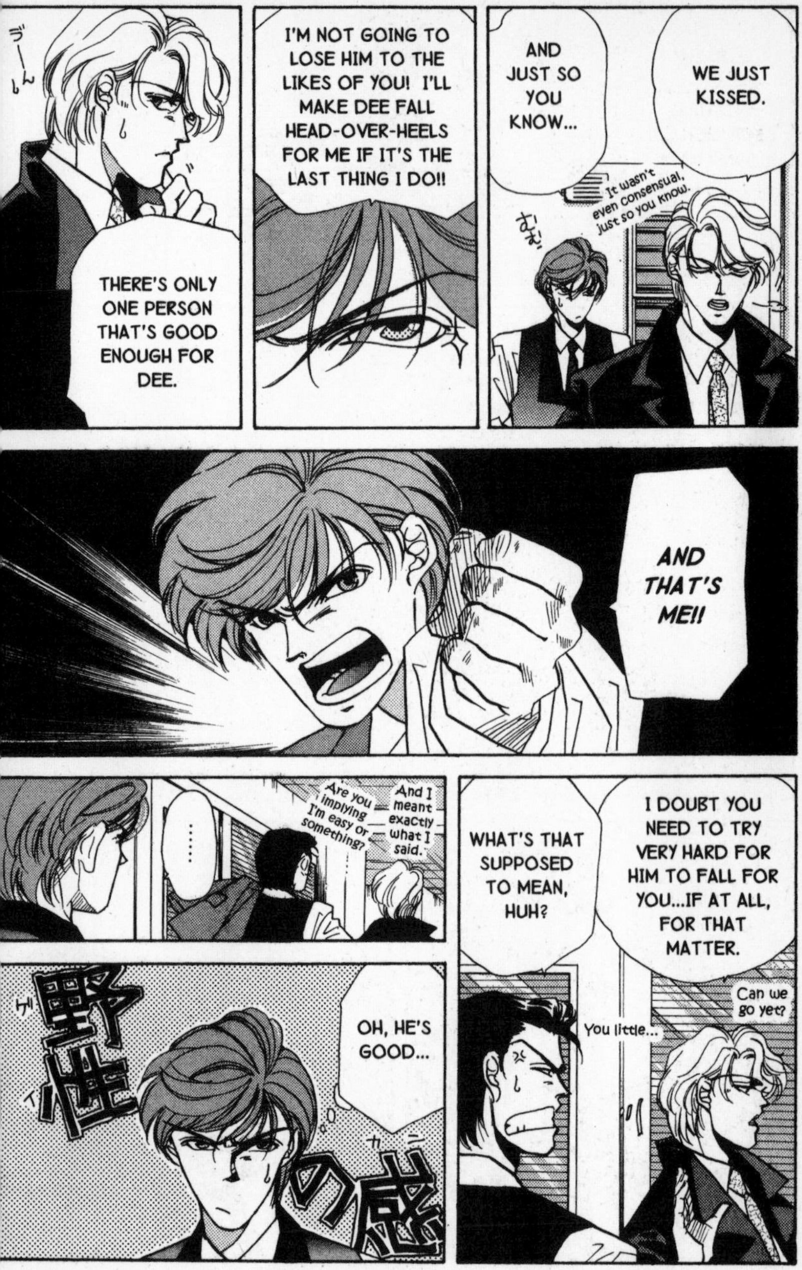
WE JUST KISSED.
AND JUST SO YOU KNOW...
It wasn't even consensual, just so you know.
むむ!
I'M NOT GOING TO LOSE HIM TO THE LIKES OF YOU! I'LL MAKE DEE FALL HEAD-OVER-HEELS FOR ME IF IT'S THE LAST THING I DO!!
ラーん
THERE'S ONLY ONE PERSON THAT'S GOOD ENOUGH FOR DEE.
AND THAT'S ME!!
I DOUBT YOU NEED TO TRY VERY HARD FOR HIM TO FALL FOR YOU...IF AT ALL, FOR THAT MATTER.
WHAT'S THAT SUPPOSED TO MEAN, HUH?
Can we go yet?
You little...
And I meant exactly what I said.
Are you implying I'm easy or something?
......
OH, HE'S GOOD...
野性の感

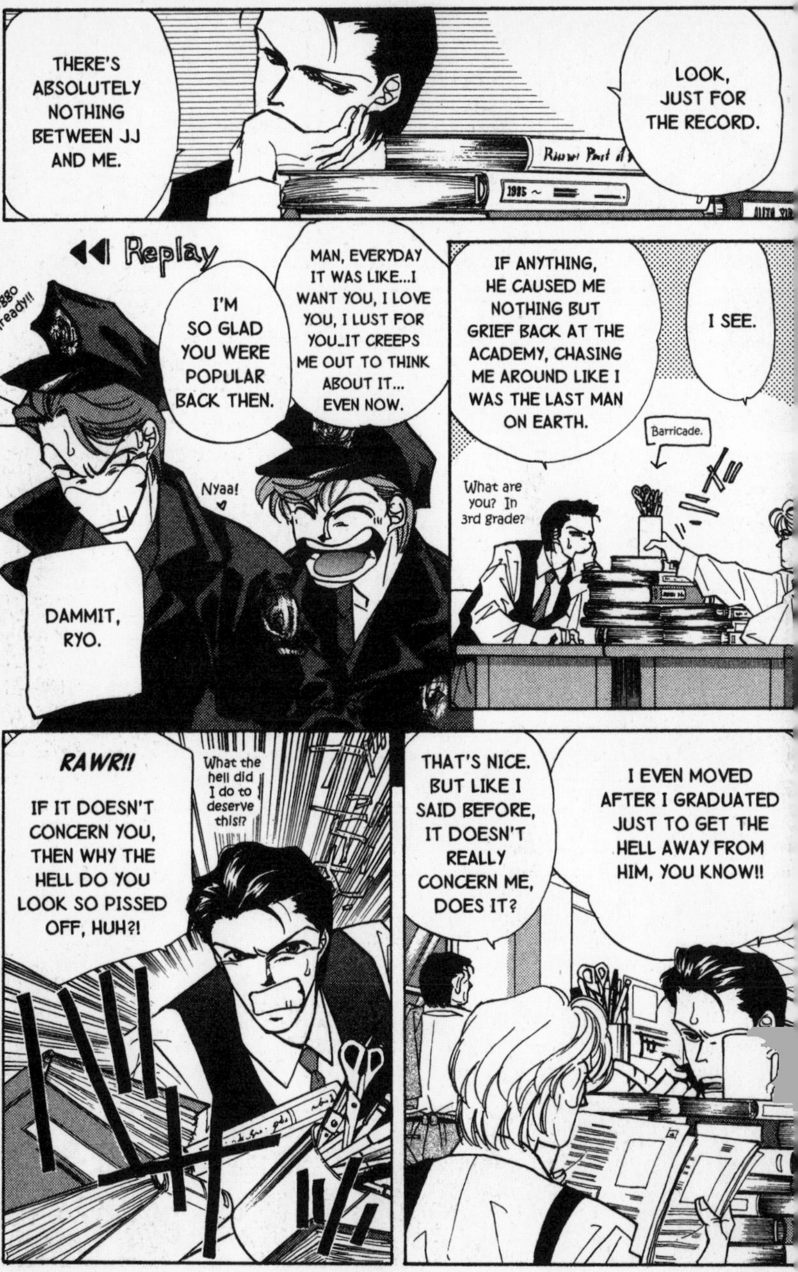
LOOK, JUST FOR THE RECORD.
THERE'S ABSOLUTELY NOTHING BETWEEN JJ AND ME.
I SEE.
IF ANYTHING, HE CAUSED ME NOTHING BUT GRIEF BACK AT THE ACADEMY, CHASING ME AROUND LIKE I WAS THE LAST MAN ON EARTH.
Barricade.
What are you? In 3rd grade?
Replay
MAN, EVERYDAY IT WAS LIKE...I WANT YOU, I LOVE YOU, I LUST FOR YOU..IT CREEPS ME OUT TO THINK ABOUT IT... EVEN NOW.
I'M SO GLAD YOU WERE POPULAR BACK THEN.
Leggo already!!
Nyaa!
DAMMIT, RYO.
I EVEN MOVED AFTER I GRADUATED JUST TO GET THE HELL AWAY FROM HIM, YOU KNOW!!
THAT'S NICE. BUT LIKE I SAID BEFORE, IT DOESN'T REALLY CONCERN ME, DOES IT?
RAWR!!
IF IT DOESN'T CONCERN YOU, THEN WHY THE HELL DO YOU LOOK SO PISSED OFF, HUH?!
What the hell did I do to deserve this!?

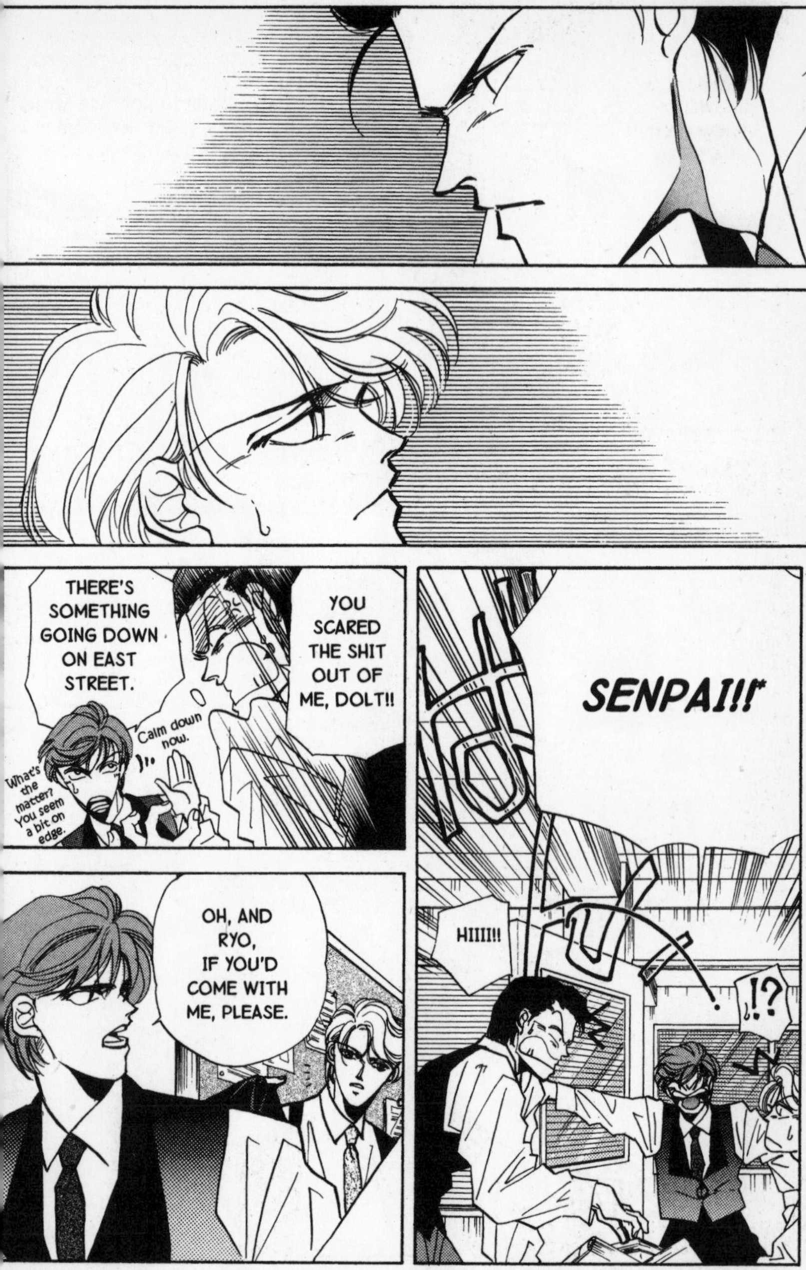
SENPAI!!*
HIIII!!
¿!?
YOU SCARED THE SHIT OUT OF ME, DOLT!!
THERE'S SOMETHING GOING DOWN ON EAST STREET.
Calm down now.
What's the matter? You seem a bit on edge.
OH, AND RYO, IF YOU'D COME WITH ME, PLEASE.

SENPAI - TERM USED TO REFER TO A CO-WORKER WHO HAS MORE SENIORITY THAN YOU; A TITLE OF RESPECT.

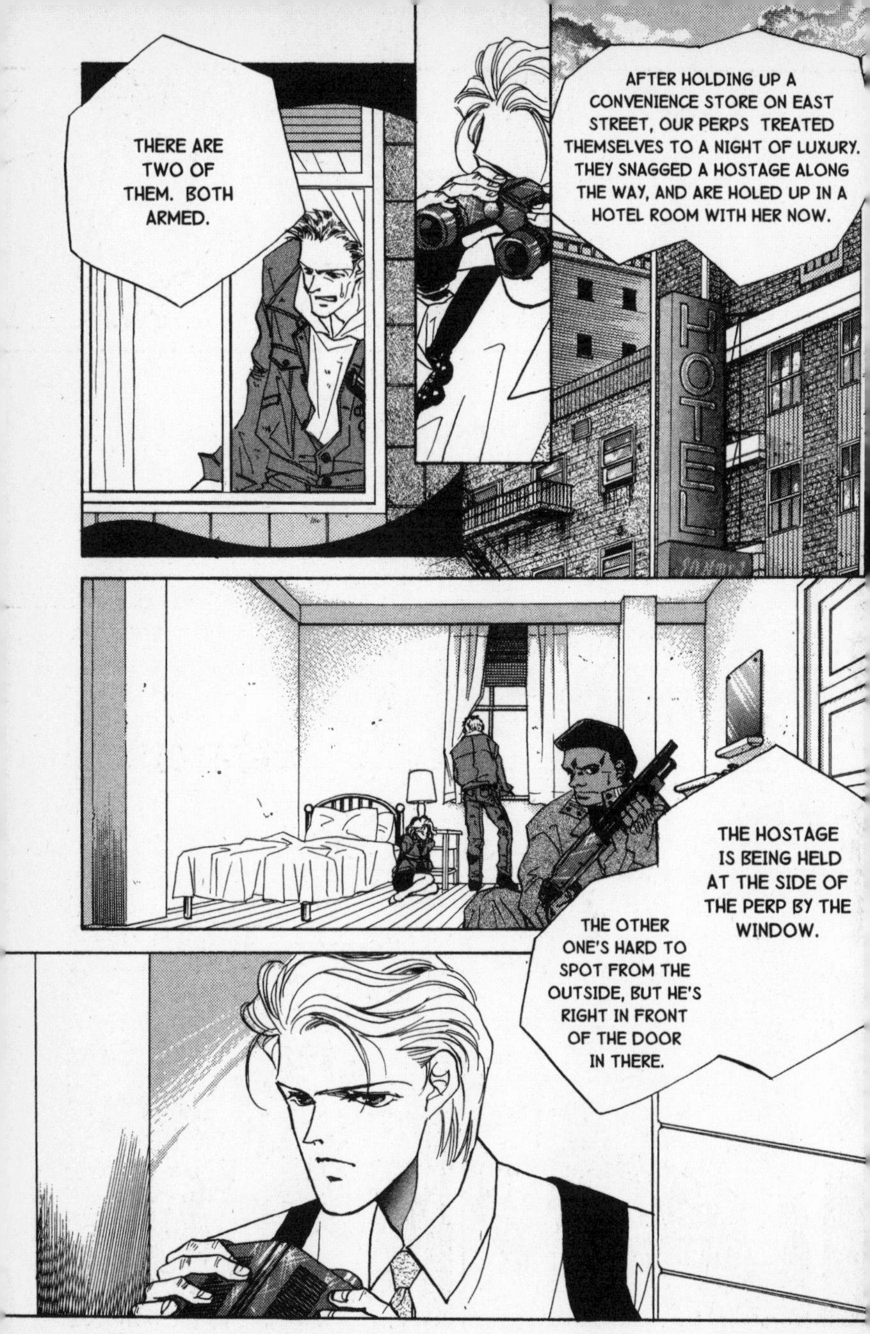
AFTER HOLDING UP A CONVENIENCE STORE ON EAST STREET, OUR PERPS TREATED THEMSELVES TO A NIGHT OF LUXURY. THEY SNAGGED A HOSTAGE ALONG THE WAY, AND ARE HOLED UP IN A HOTEL ROOM WITH HER NOW.
HOTEL
THERE ARE TWO OF THEM. BOTH ARMED.
THE HOSTAGE IS BEING HELD AT THE SIDE OF THE PERP BY THE WINDOW.
THE OTHER ONE'S HARD TO SPOT FROM THE OUTSIDE, BUT HE'S RIGHT IN FRONT OF THE DOOR IN THERE.

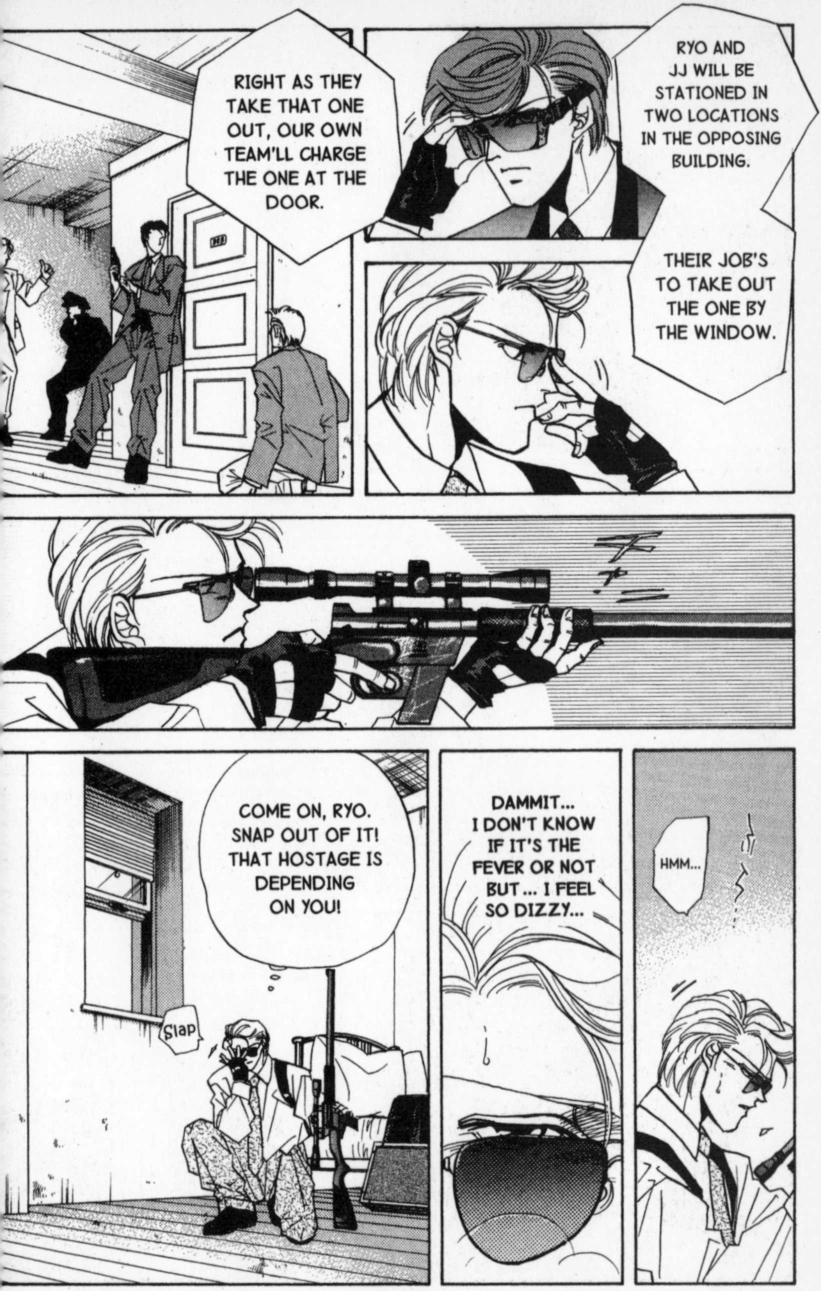
RYO AND JJ WILL BE STATIONED IN TWO LOCATIONS IN THE OPPOSING BUILDING.
THEIR JOB'S TO TAKE OUT THE ONE BY THE WINDOW.
RIGHT AS THEY TAKE THAT ONE OUT, OUR OWN TEAM'LL CHARGE THE ONE AT THE DOOR.
HMM...
DAMMIT... I DON'T KNOW IF IT'S THE FEVER OR NOT BUT ... I FEEL SO DIZZY...
COME ON, RYO. SNAP OUT OF IT! THAT HOSTAGE IS DEPENDING ON YOU!
Slap

4...

3...

5 SECONDS TO GO!

DAMMIT, THE HOSTAGE IS IN MY SHOT.

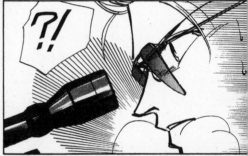

?!

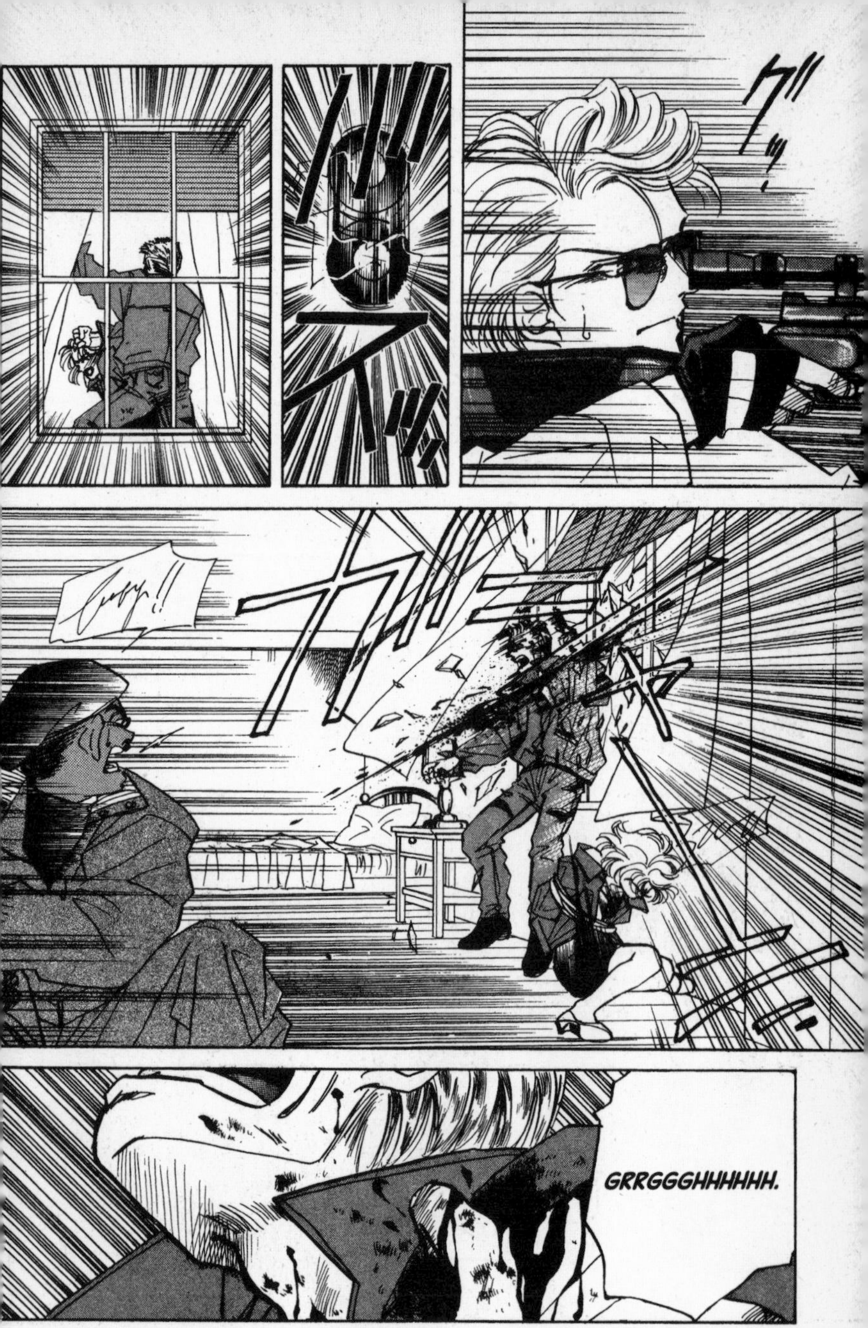
GRRGGGHHHHHH.

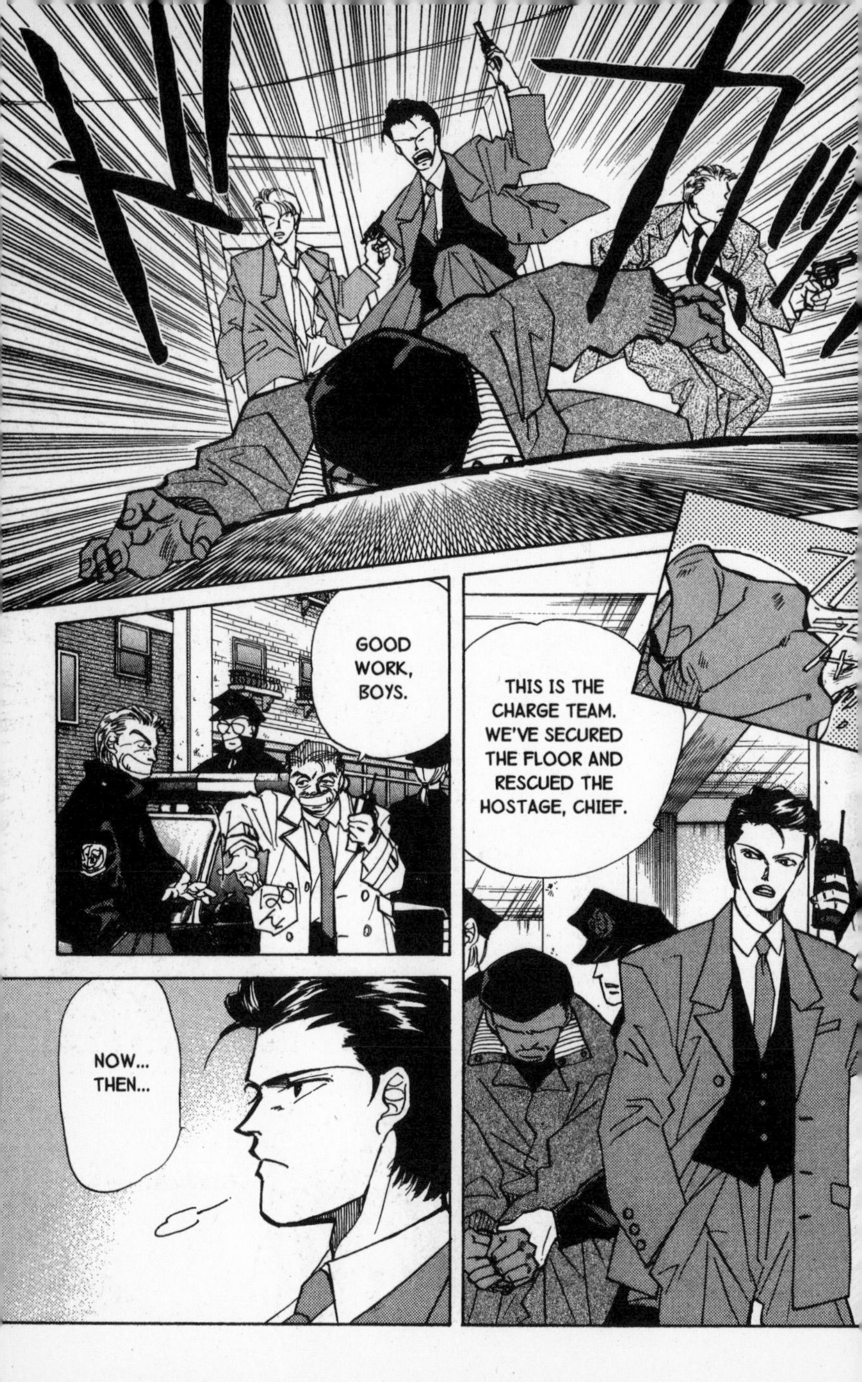
THIS IS THE CHARGE TEAM. WE'VE SECURED THE FLOOR AND RESCUED THE HOSTAGE, CHIEF.
GOOD WORK, BOYS.
NOW... THEN...

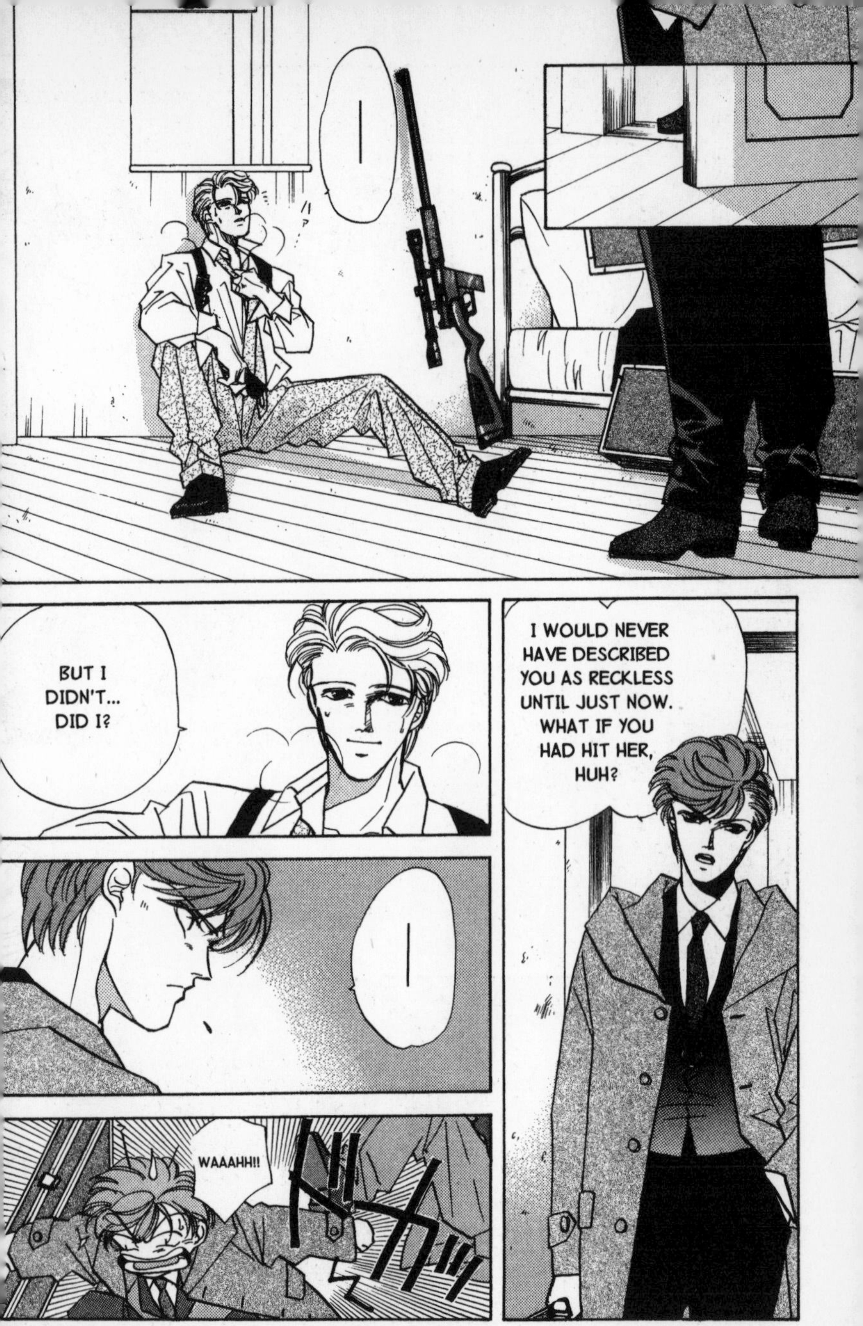
I WOULD NEVER HAVE DESCRIBED YOU AS RECKLESS UNTIL JUST NOW. WHAT IF YOU HAD HIT HER, HUH?
BUT I DIDN'T... DID I?
WAAAHH!!

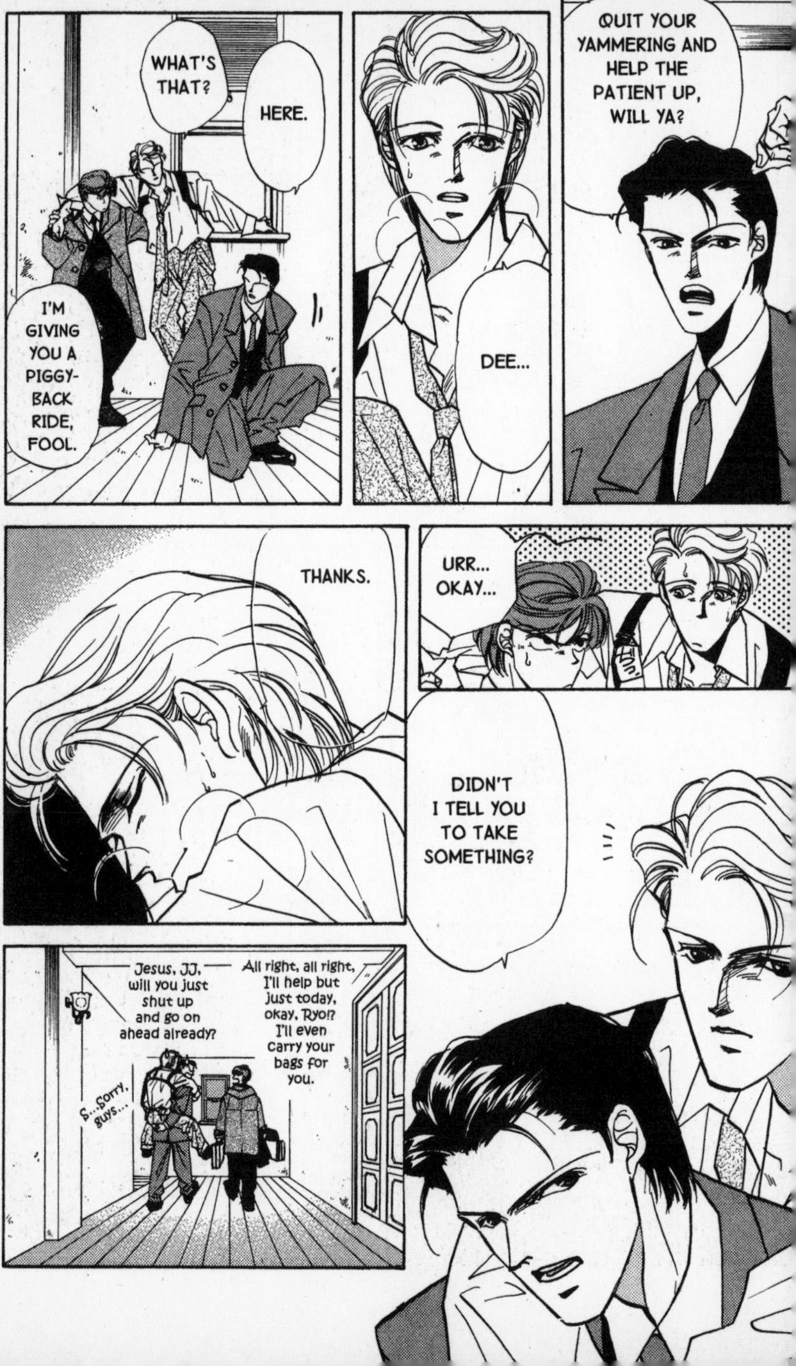
QUIT YOUR YAMMERING AND HELP THE PATIENT UP, WILL YA?
DEE...
HERE.
WHAT'S THAT?
I'M GIVING YOU A PIGGY-BACK RIDE, FOOL.
URR... OKAY...
DIDN'T I TELL YOU TO TAKE SOMETHING?
THANKS.
All right, all right, I'll help but just today, okay, Ryo!? I'll even carry your bags for you.
Jesus, JJ, will you just shut up and go on ahead already?
S...Sorry, guys...

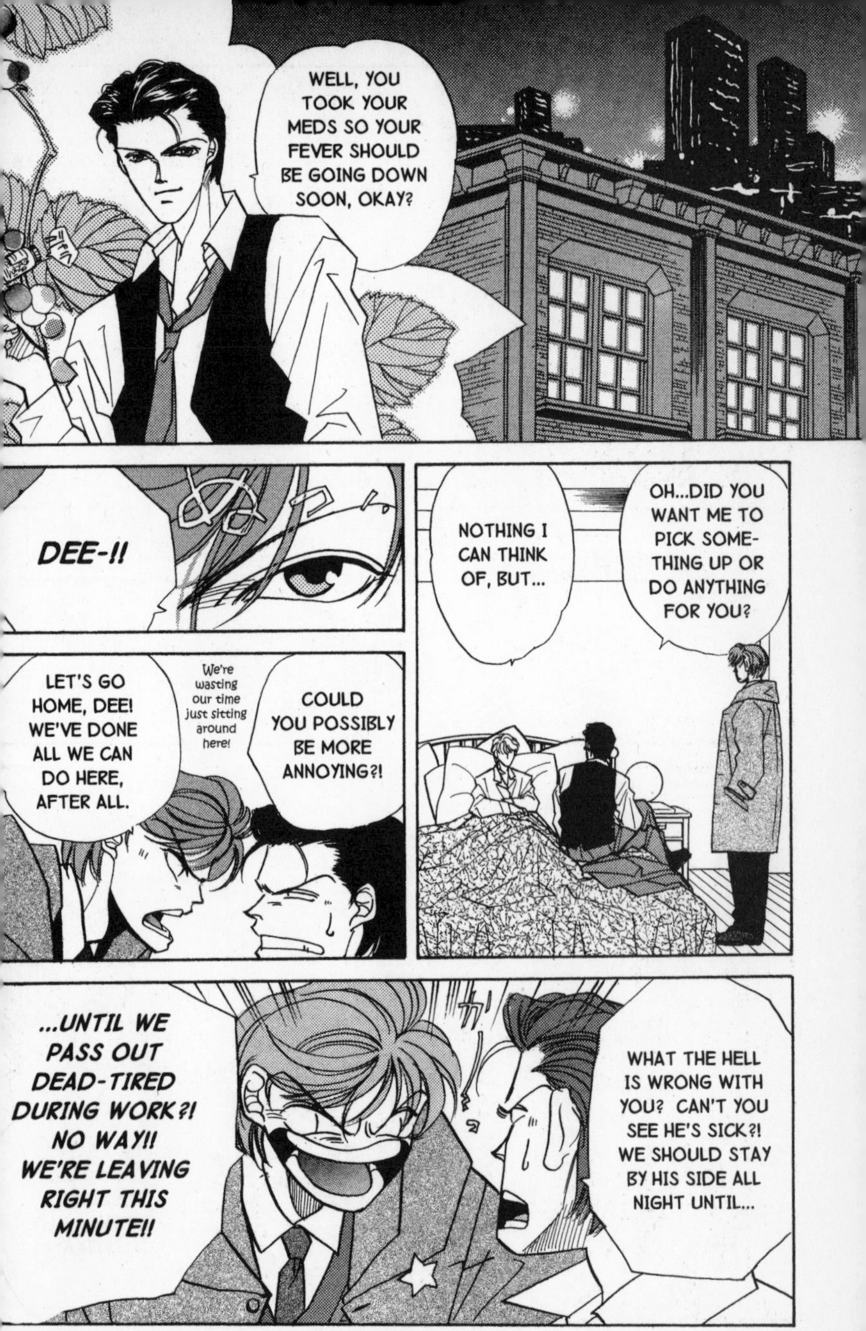
WELL, YOU TOOK YOUR MEDS SO YOUR FEVER SHOULD BE GOING DOWN SOON, OKAY?
OH...DID YOU WANT ME TO PICK SOME-THING UP OR DO ANYTHING FOR YOU?
NOTHING I CAN THINK OF, BUT...
DEE-!!
COULD YOU POSSIBLY BE MORE ANNOYING?!
We're wasting our time just sitting around here!
LET'S GO HOME, DEE! WE'VE DONE ALL WE CAN DO HERE, AFTER ALL.
WHAT THE HELL IS WRONG WITH YOU? CAN'T YOU SEE HE'S SICK?! WE SHOULD STAY BY HIS SIDE ALL NIGHT UNTIL...
...UNTIL WE PASS OUT DEAD-TIRED DURING WORK?! NO WAY!! WE'RE LEAVING RIGHT THIS MINUTE!!

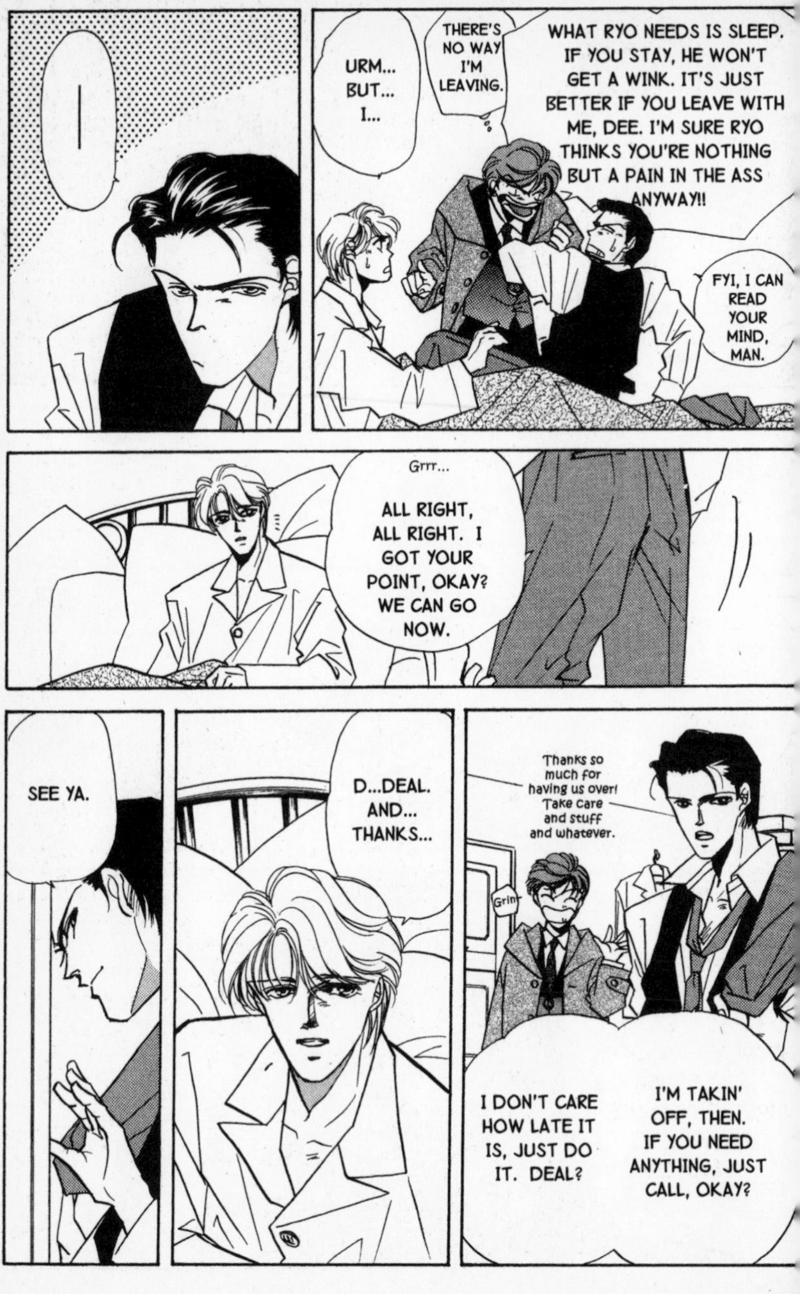
WHAT RYO NEEDS IS SLEEP. IF YOU STAY, HE WON'T GET A WINK. IT'S JUST BETTER IF YOU LEAVE WITH ME, DEE. I'M SURE RYO THINKS YOU'RE NOTHING BUT A PAIN IN THE ASS ANYWAY!!
THERE'S NO WAY I'M LEAVING.
URM... BUT... I...
FYI, I CAN READ YOUR MIND, MAN.
Grrr...
ALL RIGHT, ALL RIGHT. I GOT YOUR POINT, OKAY? WE CAN GO NOW.
Thanks so much for having us over! Take care and stuff and whatever.
Grin
I'M TAKIN' OFF, THEN. IF YOU NEED ANYTHING, JUST CALL, OKAY?
I DON'T CARE HOW LATE IT IS, JUST DO IT. DEAL?
D...DEAL. AND... THANKS...
SEE YA.

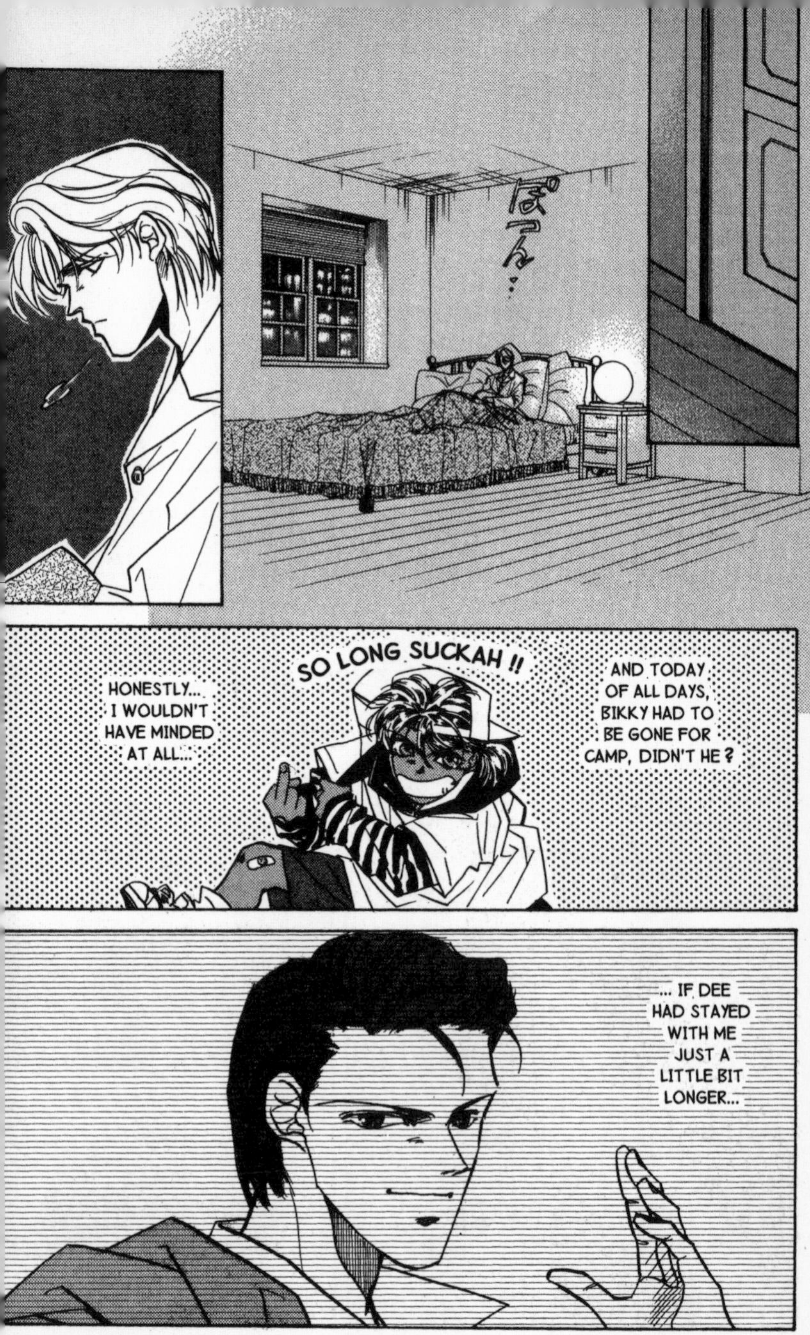
ぽつん‥
AND TODAY OF ALL DAYS, BIKKY HAD TO BE GONE FOR CAMP, DIDN'T HE?
SO LONG SUCKAH !!
HONESTLY... I WOULDN'T HAVE MINDED AT ALL...
... IF DEE HAD STAYED WITH ME JUST A LITTLE BIT LONGER...

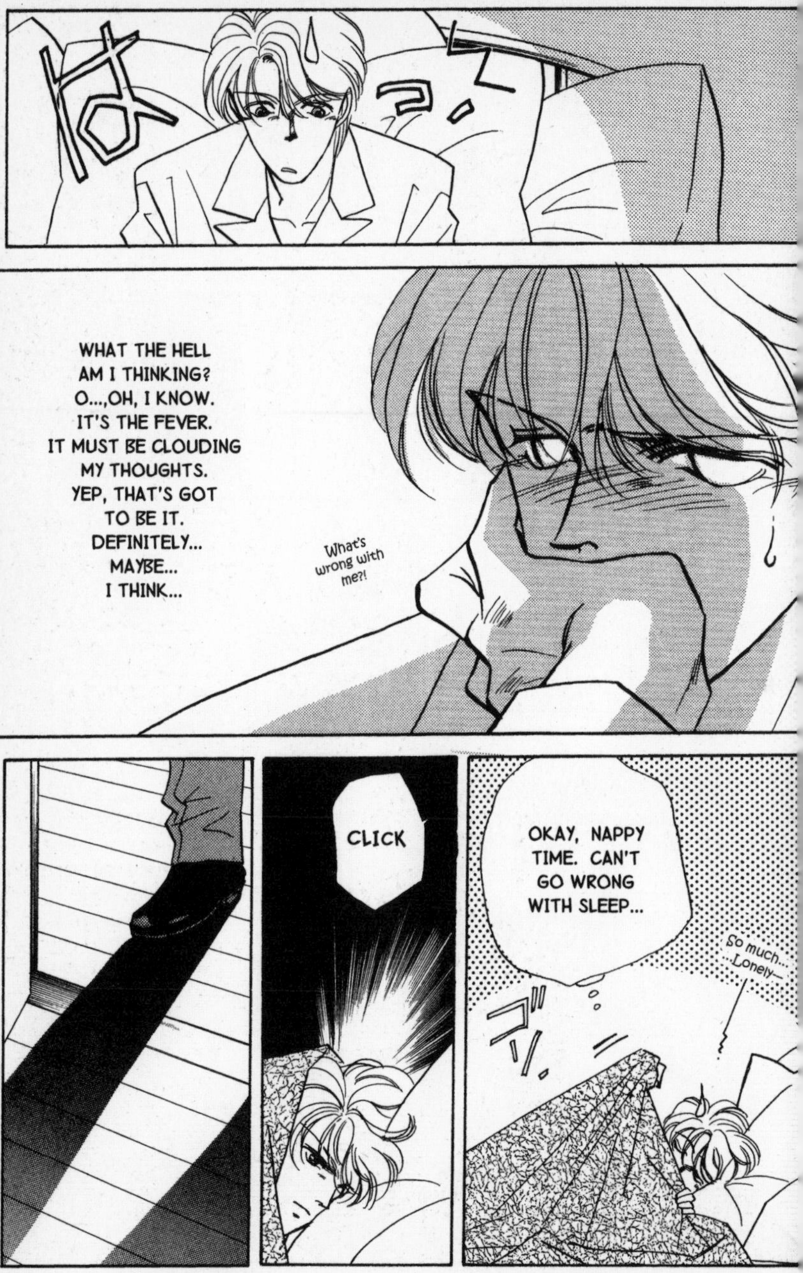
はっ
WHAT THE HELL AM I THINKING? O...,OH, I KNOW. IT'S THE FEVER. IT MUST BE CLOUDING MY THOUGHTS. YEP, THAT'S GOT TO BE IT. DEFINITELY... MAYBE... I THINK...
What's wrong with me?!
OKAY, NAPPY TIME. CAN'T GO WRONG WITH SLEEP...
So much... ...Lonely...
CLICK

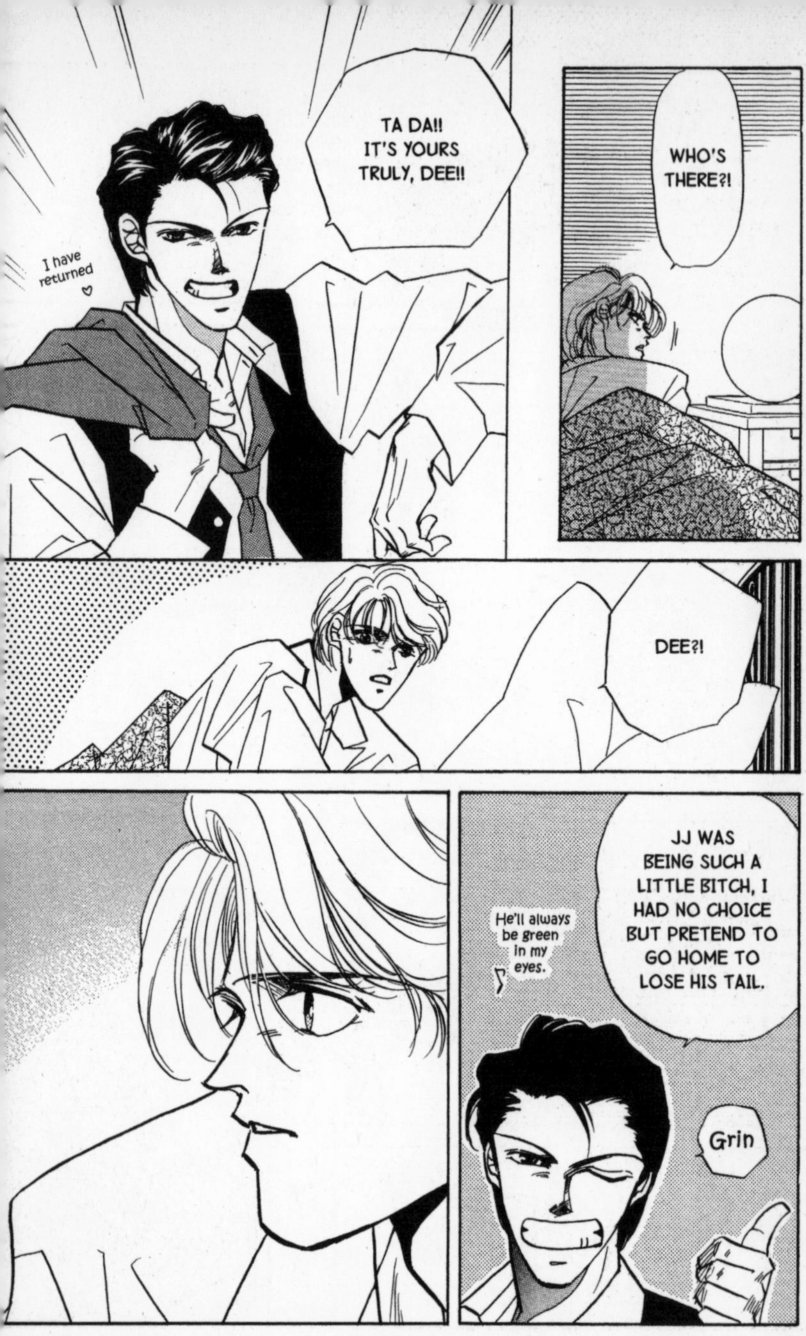
WHO'S THERE?!
TA DA!! IT'S YOURS TRULY, DEE!!
I have returned ♡
DEE?!
JJ WAS BEING SUCH A LITTLE BITCH, I HAD NO CHOICE BUT PRETEND TO GO HOME TO LOSE HIS TAIL.
He'll always be green in my eyes.
Grin

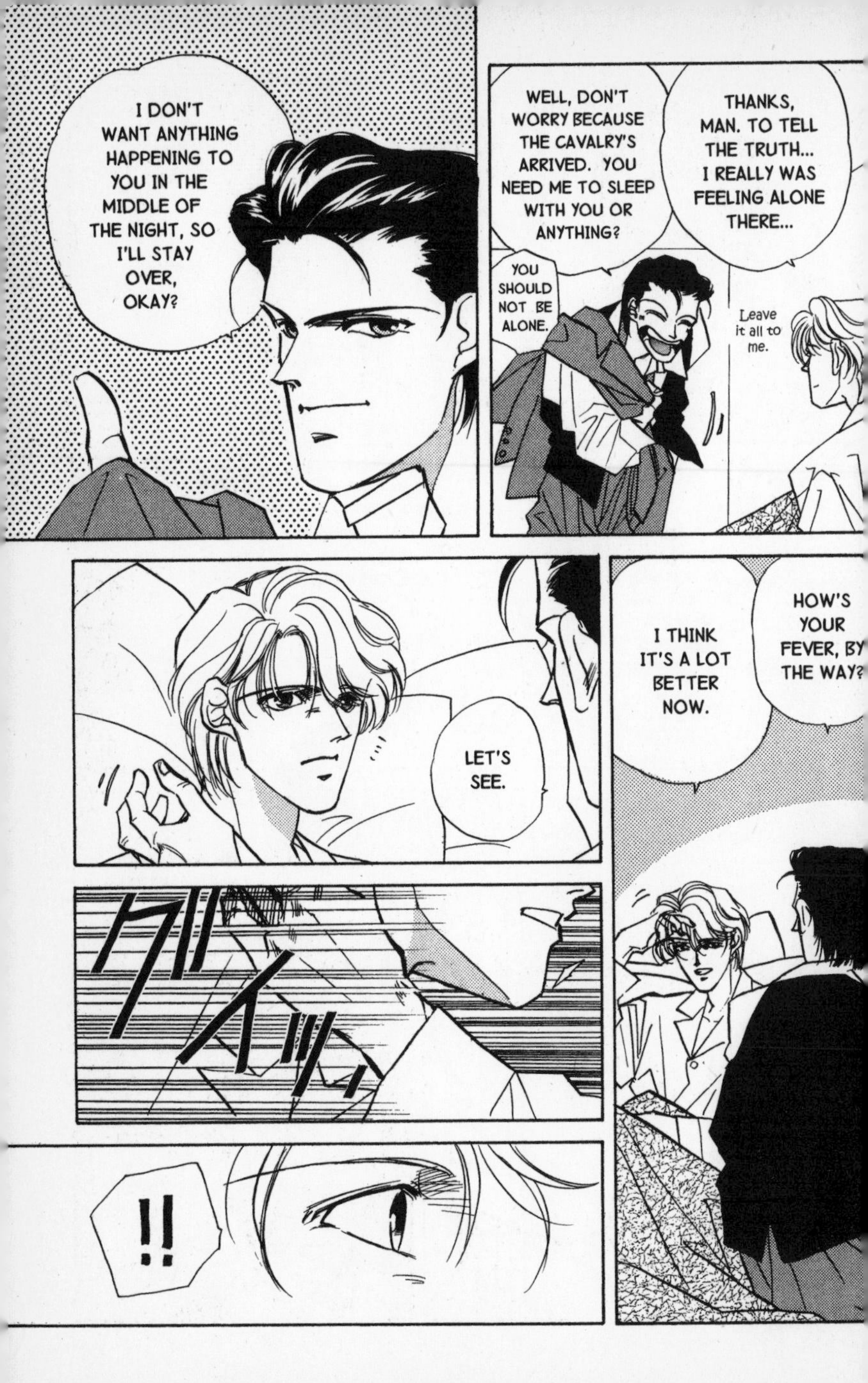
THANKS, MAN. TO TELL THE TRUTH... I REALLY WAS FEELING ALONE THERE...
WELL, DON'T WORRY BECAUSE THE CAVALRY'S ARRIVED. YOU NEED ME TO SLEEP WITH YOU OR ANYTHING?
Leave it all to me.
YOU SHOULD NOT BE ALONE.
I DON'T WANT ANYTHING HAPPENING TO YOU IN THE MIDDLE OF THE NIGHT, SO I'LL STAY OVER, OKAY?
HOW'S YOUR FEVER, BY THE WAY?
I THINK IT'S A LOT BETTER NOW.
LET'S SEE.
グイッ
!!

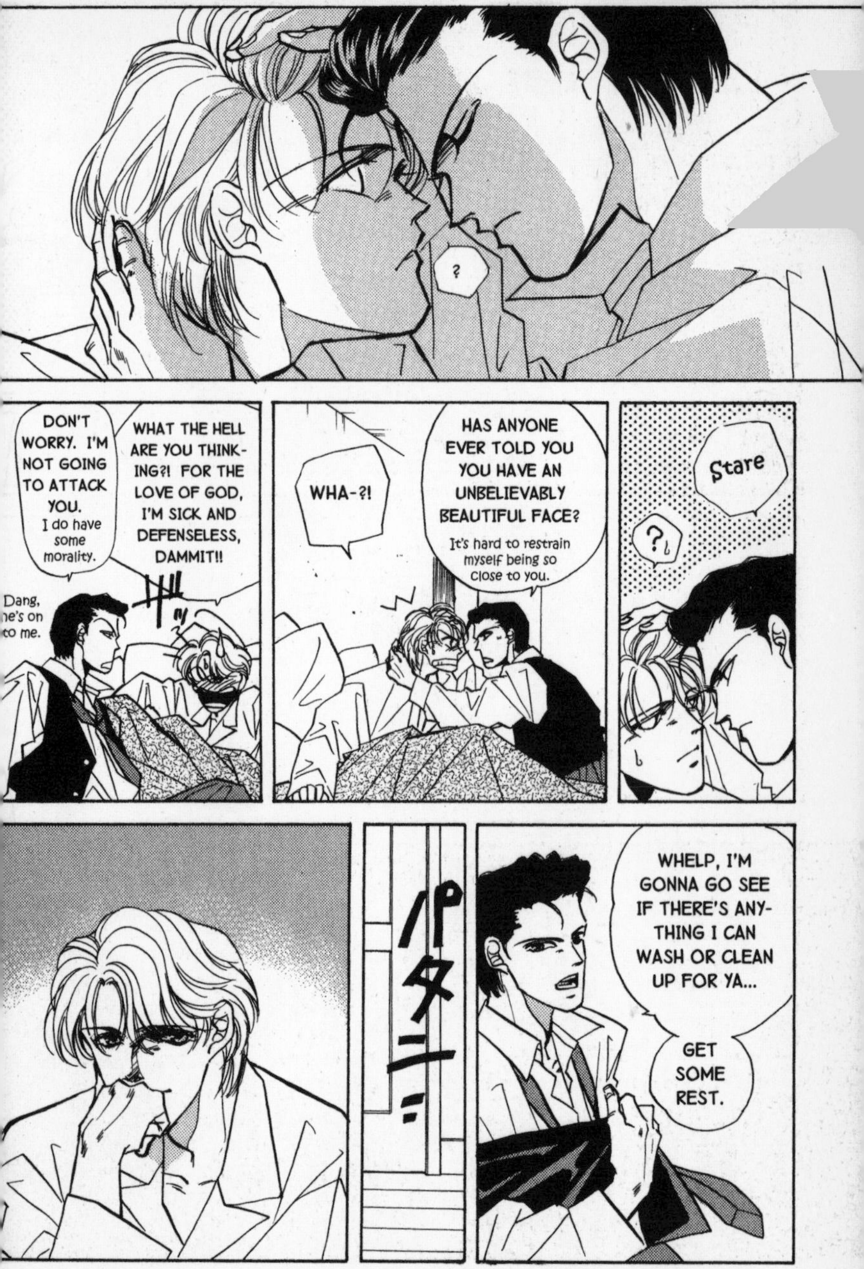
?
Stare
?
HAS ANYONE EVER TOLD YOU YOU HAVE AN UNBELIEVABLY BEAUTIFUL FACE?
It's hard to restrain myself being so close to you.
WHA-?!
WHAT THE HELL ARE YOU THINKING?! FOR THE LOVE OF GOD, I'M SICK AND DEFENSELESS, DAMMIT!!
DON'T WORRY. I'M NOT GOING TO ATTACK YOU.
I do have some morality.
Dang, he's on to me.
WHELP, I'M GONNA GO SEE IF THERE'S ANYTHING I CAN WASH OR CLEAN UP FOR YA...
GET SOME REST.
パタン

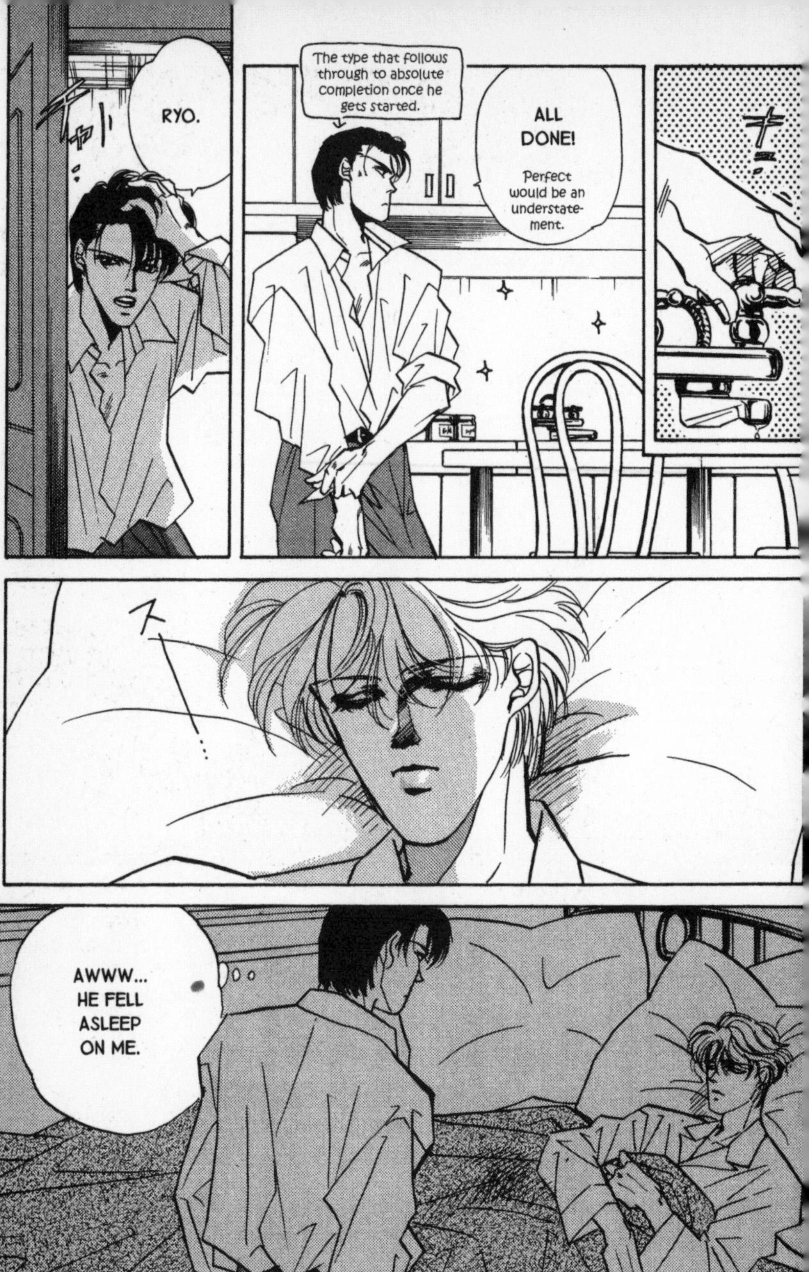
ALL DONE!
Perfect would be an understatement.
The type that follows through to absolute completion once he gets started.
RYO.
AWWW... HE FELL ASLEEP ON ME.

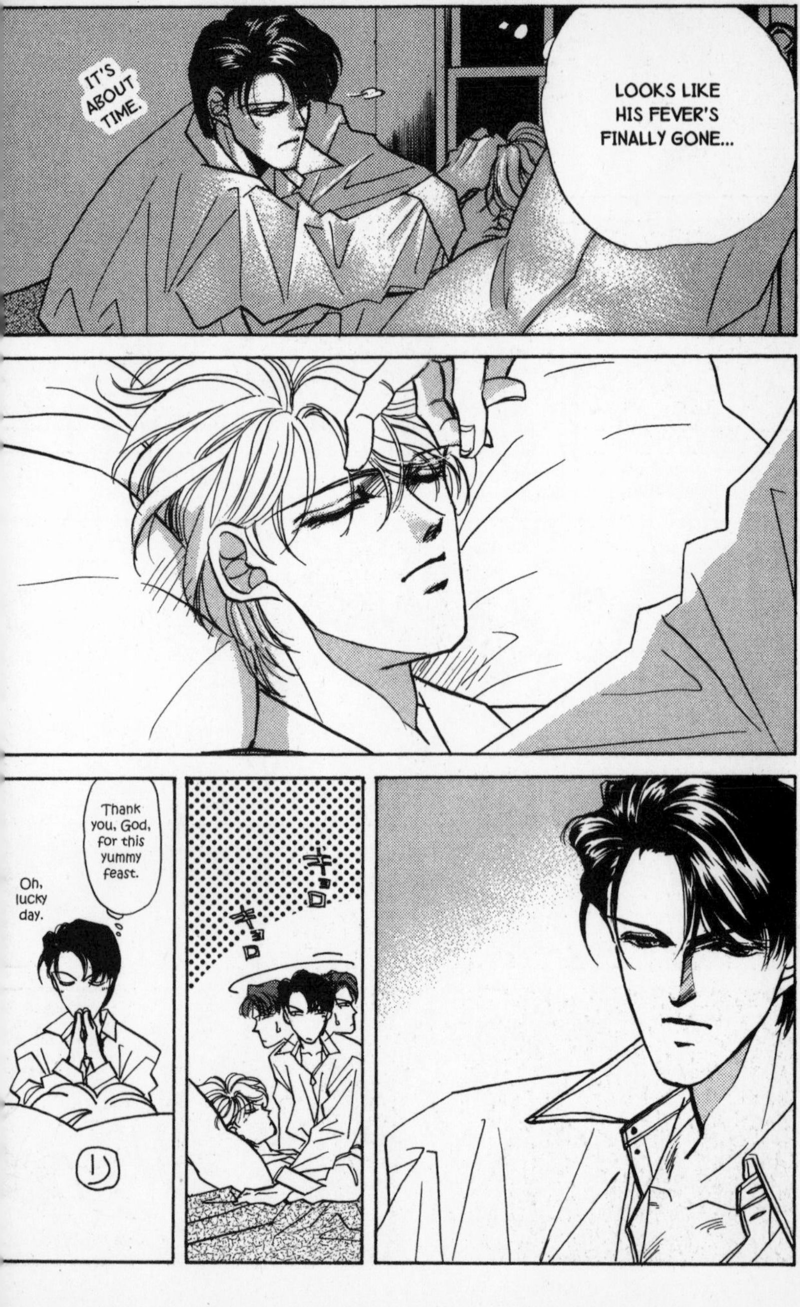
LOOKS LIKE HIS FEVER'S FINALLY GONE...
IT'S ABOUT TIME.
キョロ
キョロ
Thank you, God, for this yummy feast.
Oh, lucky day.

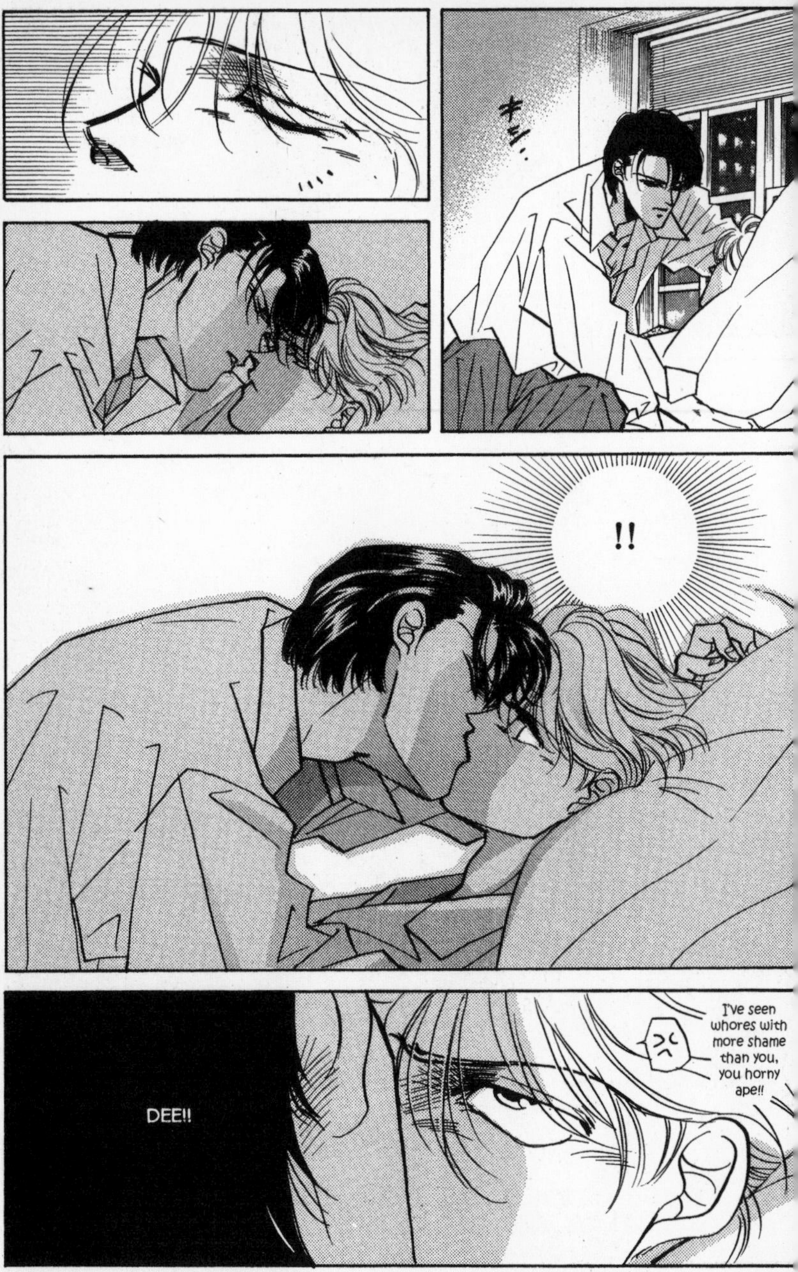
!!
I've seen whores with more shame than you, you horny ape!!
DEE!!

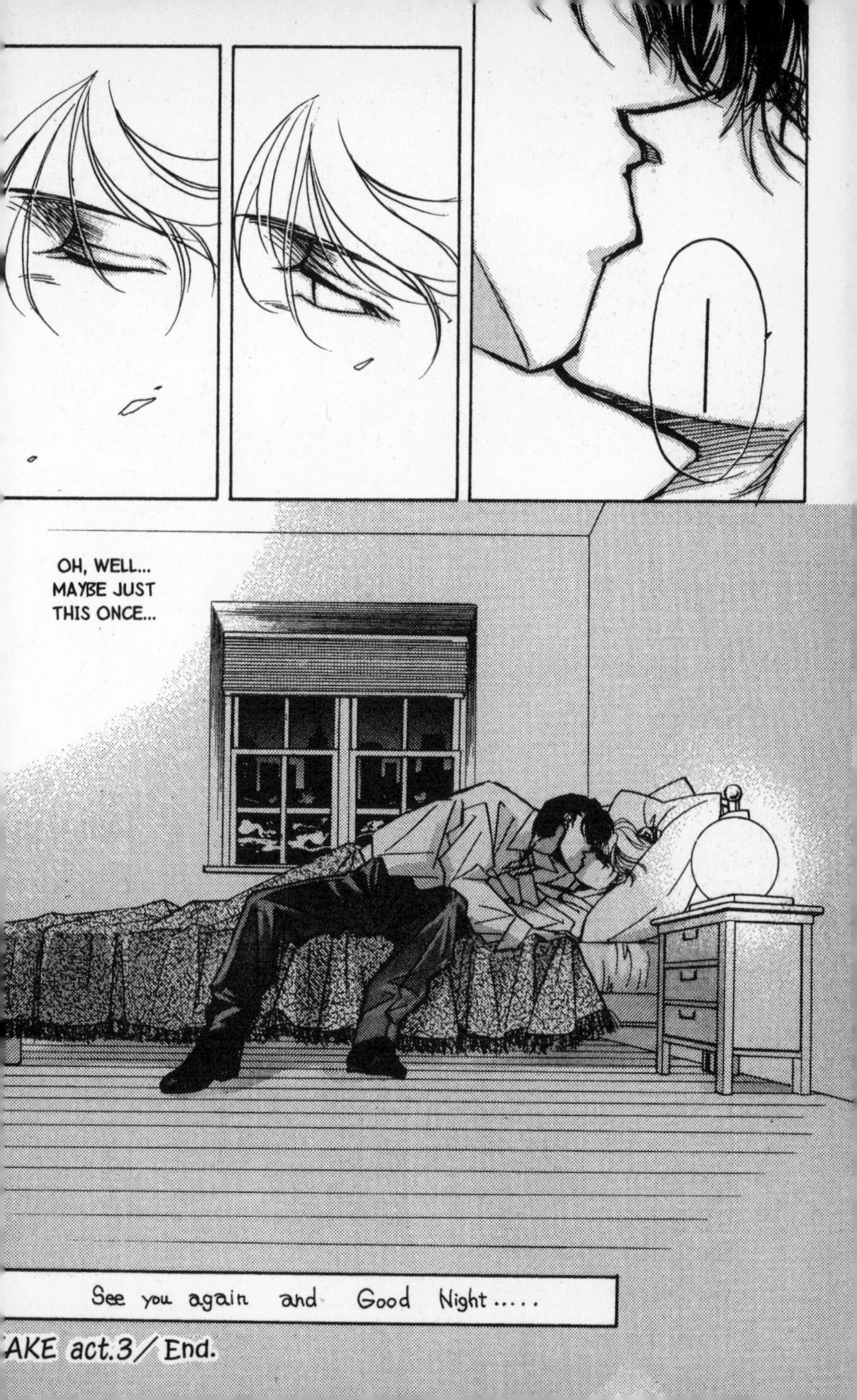
OH, WELL... MAYBE JUST THIS ONCE...
See you again and Good Night.....
AKE act.3/ End.

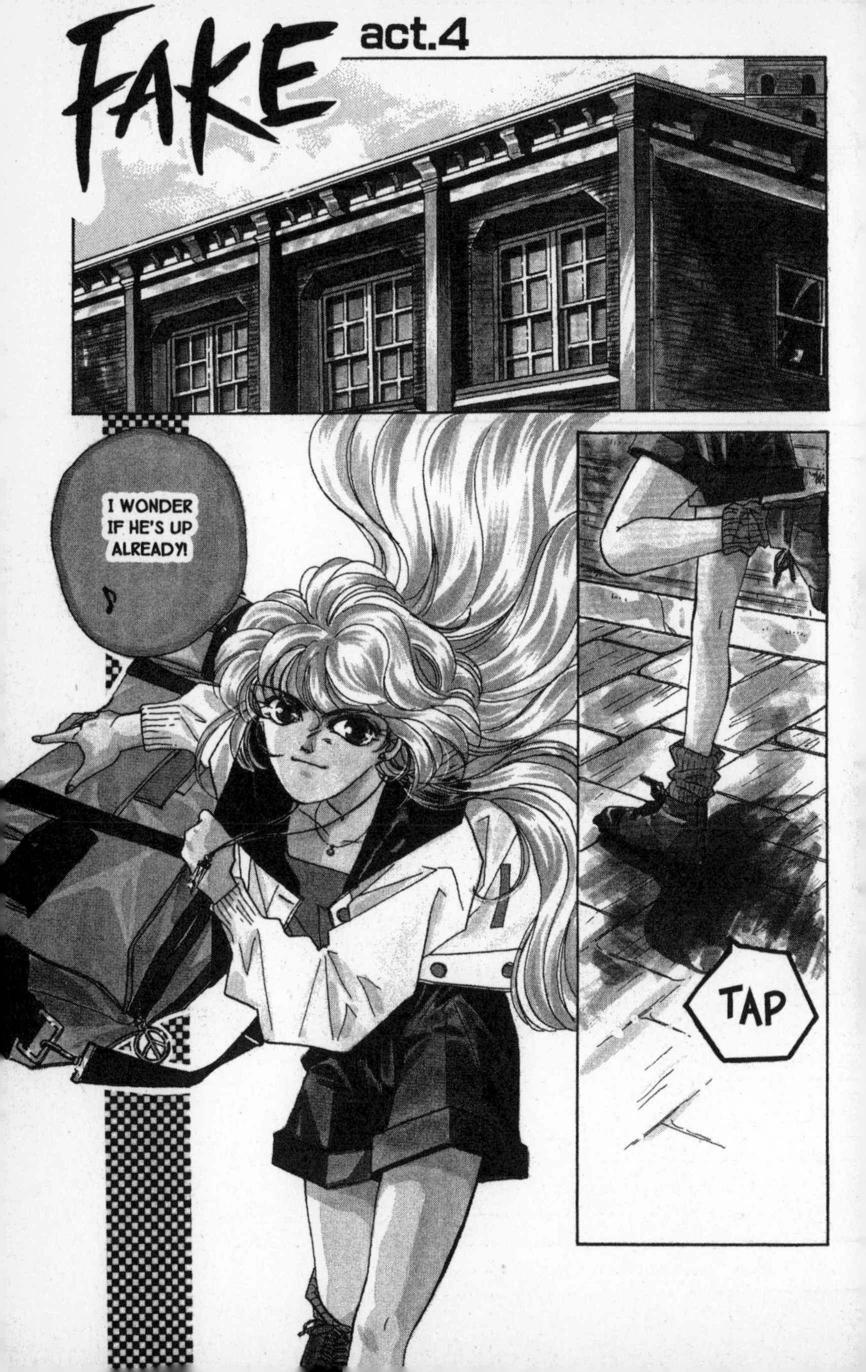
FAKE act.4
TAP
I WONDER IF HE'S UP ALREADY!

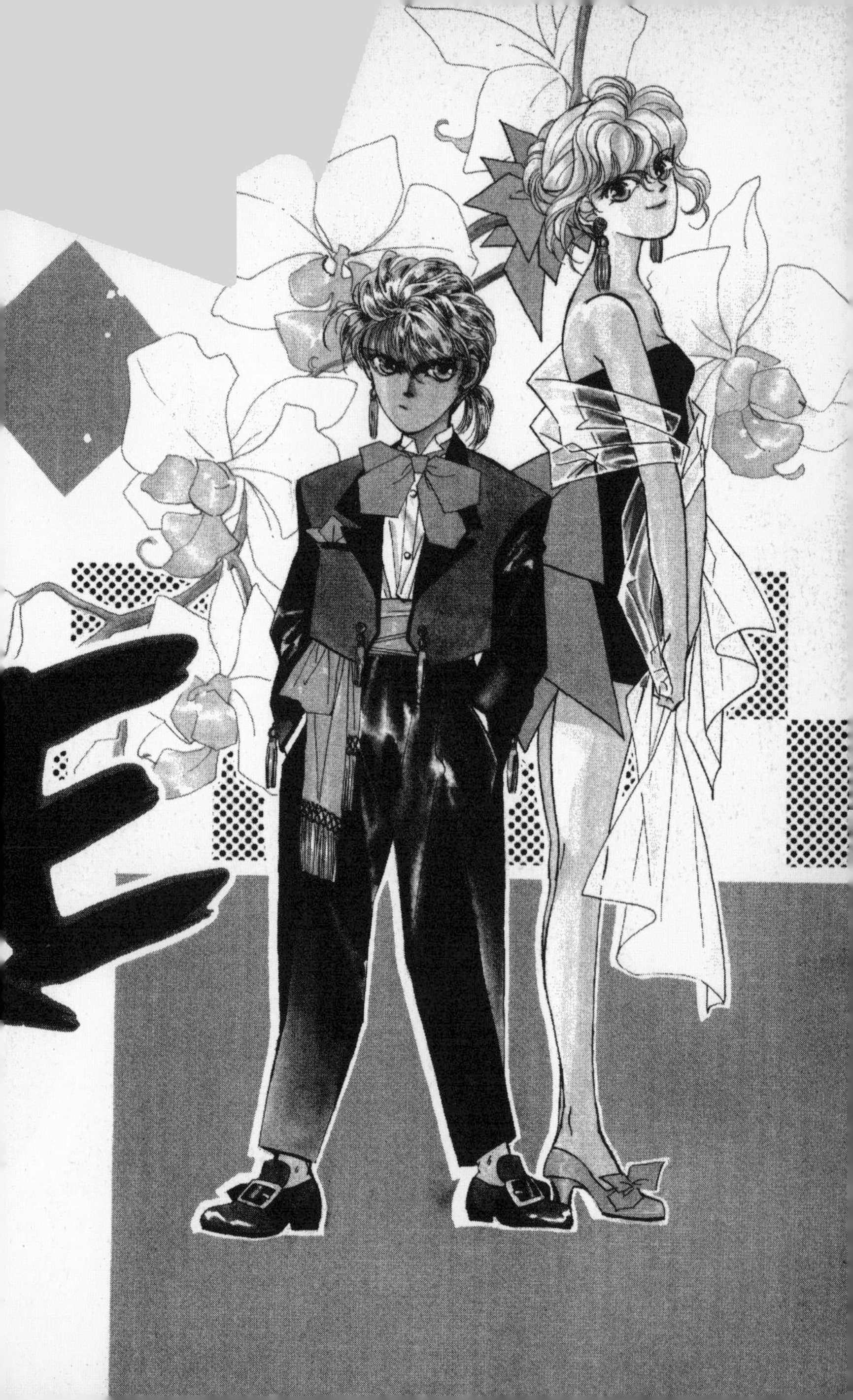

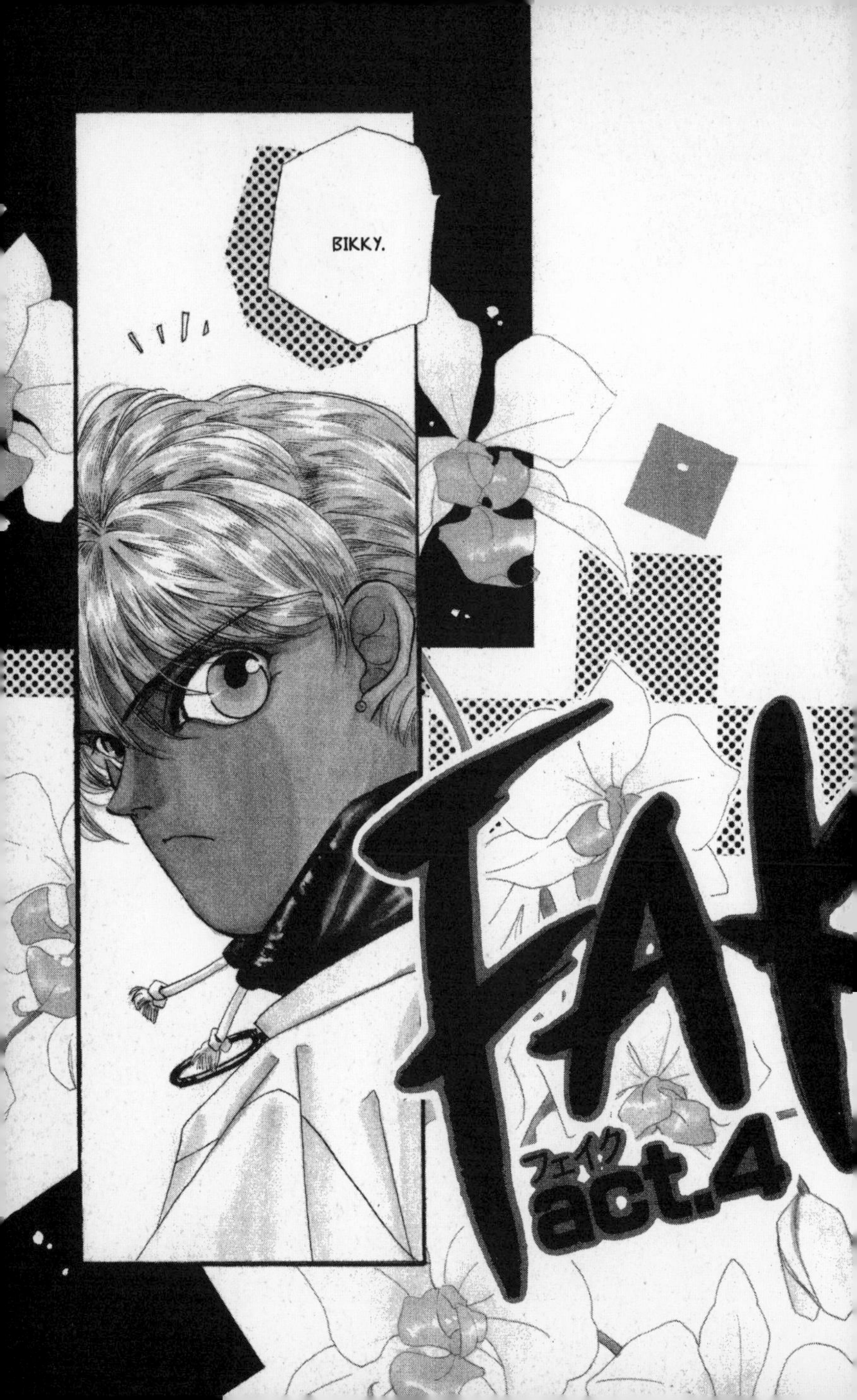
フェイク
act.4
BIKKY.

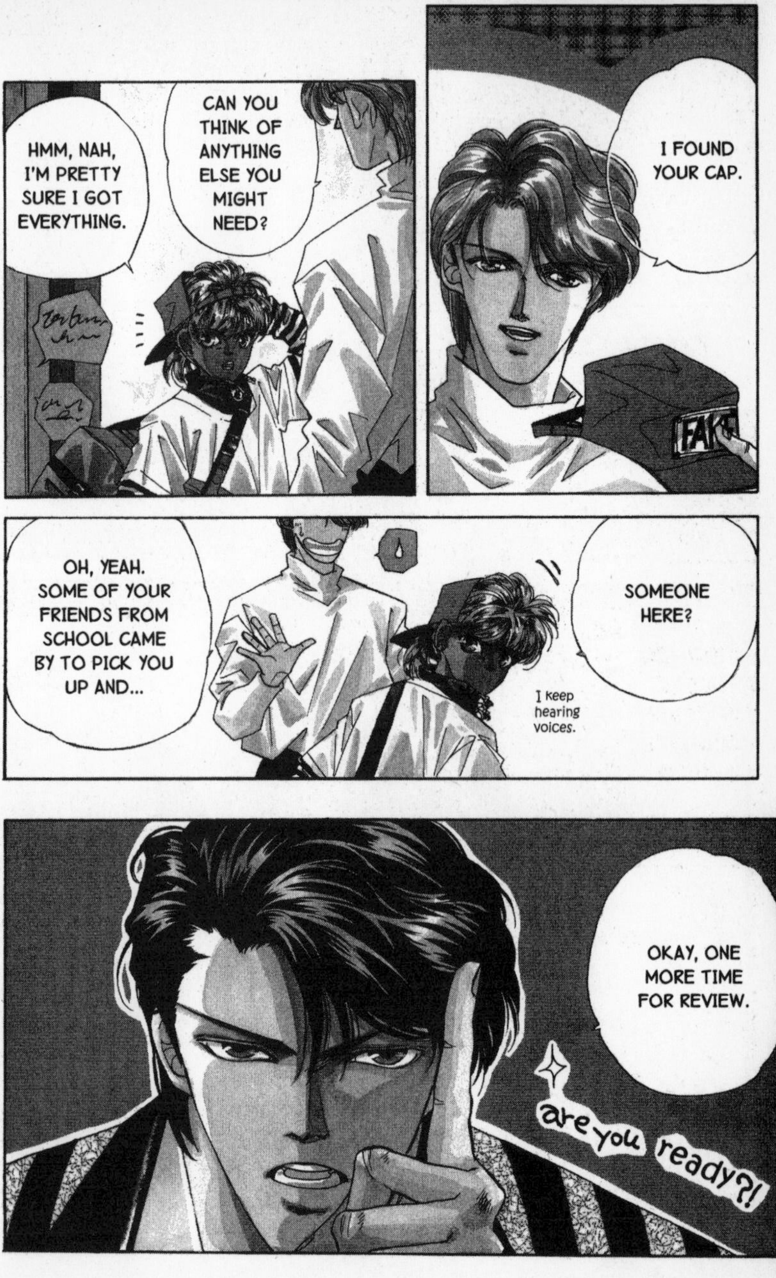
I FOUND YOUR CAP.
CAN YOU THINK OF ANYTHING ELSE YOU MIGHT NEED?
HMM, NAH, I'M PRETTY SURE I GOT EVERYTHING.
SOMEONE HERE?
I keep hearing voices.
OH, YEAH. SOME OF YOUR FRIENDS FROM SCHOOL CAME BY TO PICK YOU UP AND...
OKAY, ONE MORE TIME FOR REVIEW.
are you ready?!

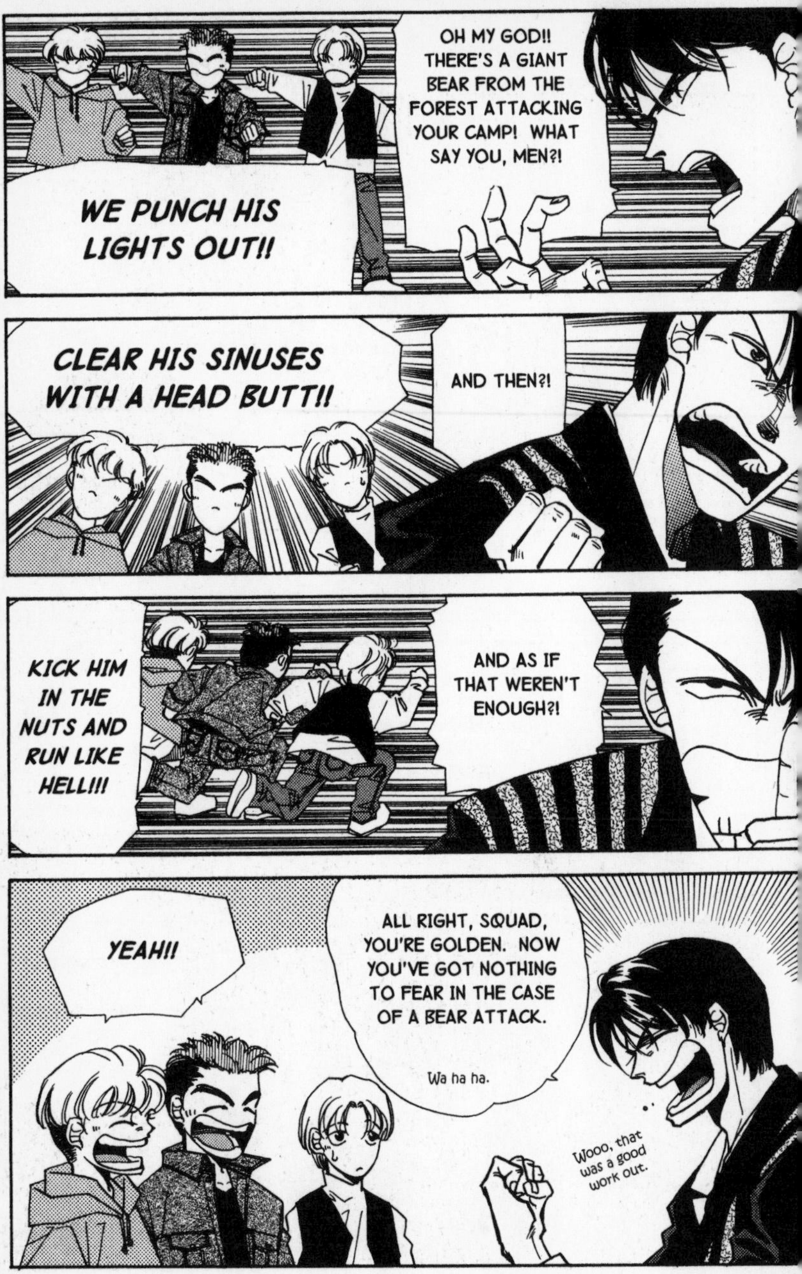
OH MY GOD!! THERE'S A GIANT BEAR FROM THE FOREST ATTACKING YOUR CAMP! WHAT SAY YOU, MEN?!
WE PUNCH HIS LIGHTS OUT!!
AND THEN?!
CLEAR HIS SINUSES WITH A HEAD BUTT!!
AND AS IF THAT WEREN'T ENOUGH?!
KICK HIM IN THE NUTS AND RUN LIKE HELL!!!
Wooo, that was a good work out.
ALL RIGHT, SQUAD, YOU'RE GOLDEN. NOW YOU'VE GOT NOTHING TO FEAR IN THE CASE OF A BEAR ATTACK.
Wa ha ha.
YEAH!!

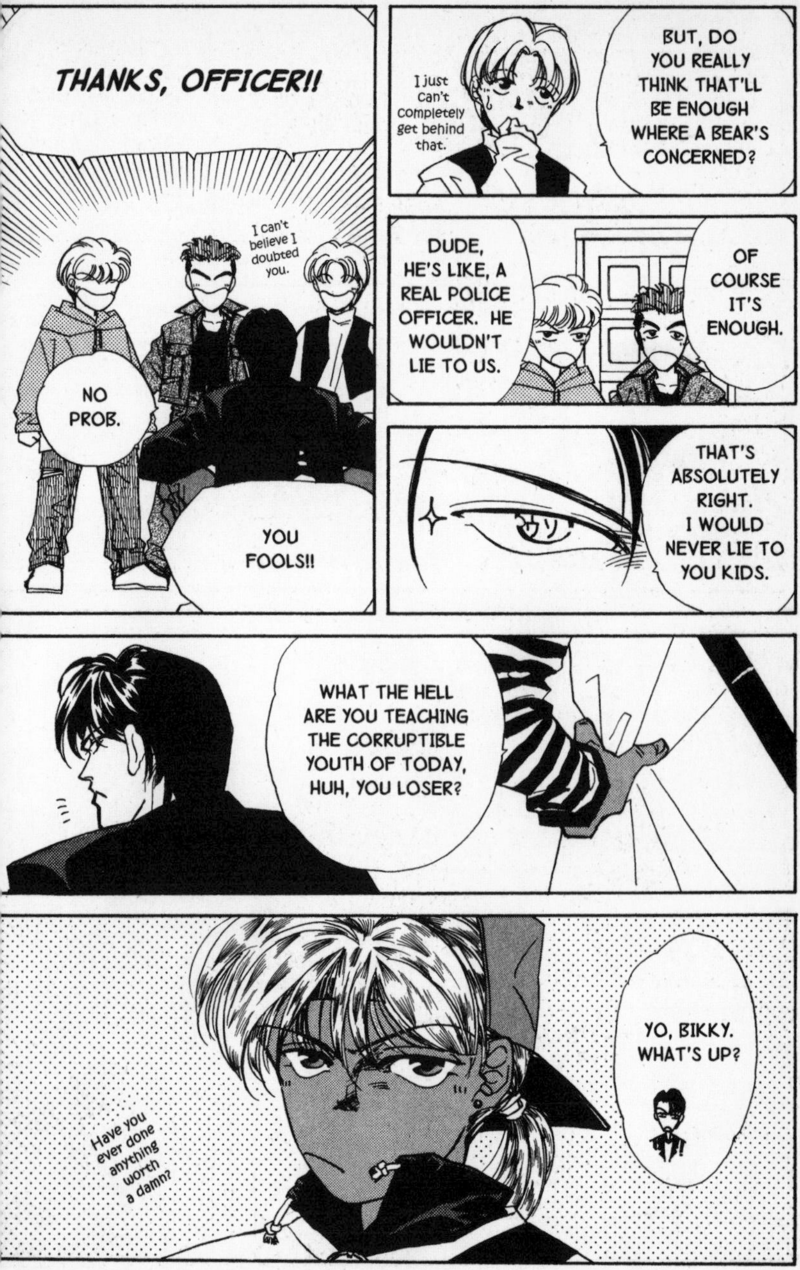
BUT, DO YOU REALLY THINK THAT'LL BE ENOUGH WHERE A BEAR'S CONCERNED?
I just can't completely get behind that.
OF COURSE IT'S ENOUGH.
DUDE, HE'S LIKE, A REAL POLICE OFFICER. HE WOULDN'T LIE TO US.
THAT'S ABSOLUTELY RIGHT. I WOULD NEVER LIE TO YOU KIDS.
THANKS, OFFICER!!
I can't believe I doubted you.
NO PROB.
YOU FOOLS!!
WHAT THE HELL ARE YOU TEACHING THE CORRUPTIBLE YOUTH OF TODAY, HUH, YOU LOSER?
YO, BIKKY. WHAT'S UP?
Have you ever done anything worth a damn?

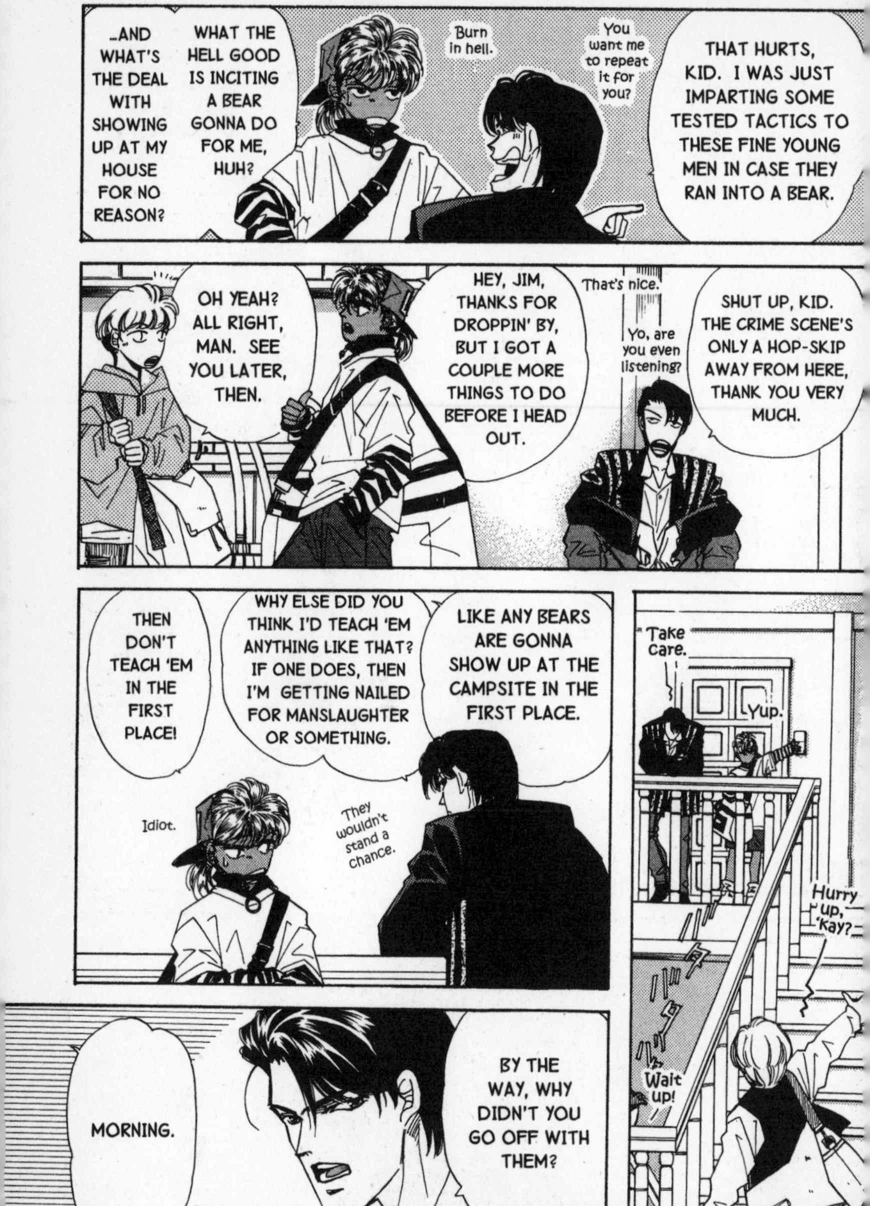
THAT HURTS, KID. I WAS JUST IMPARTING SOME TESTED TACTICS TO THESE FINE YOUNG MEN IN CASE THEY RAN INTO A BEAR.
You want me to repeat it for you?
Burn in hell.
WHAT THE HELL GOOD IS INCITING A BEAR GONNA DO FOR ME, HUH?
...AND WHAT'S THE DEAL WITH SHOWING UP AT MY HOUSE FOR NO REASON?
SHUT UP, KID. THE CRIME SCENE'S ONLY A HOP-SKIP AWAY FROM HERE, THANK YOU VERY MUCH.
Yo, are you even listening?
That's nice.
HEY, JIM, THANKS FOR DROPPIN' BY, BUT I GOT A COUPLE MORE THINGS TO DO BEFORE I HEAD OUT.
OH YEAH? ALL RIGHT, MAN. SEE YOU LATER, THEN.
Take care.
Yup.
Hurry up, 'kay?
Wait up!
MUSIC
LIKE ANY BEARS ARE GONNA SHOW UP AT THE CAMPSITE IN THE FIRST PLACE.
WHY ELSE DID YOU THINK I'D TEACH 'EM ANYTHING LIKE THAT? IF ONE DOES, THEN I'M GETTING NAILED FOR MANSLAUGHTER OR SOMETHING.
They wouldn't stand a chance.
THEN DON'T TEACH 'EM IN THE FIRST PLACE!
Idiot.
BY THE WAY, WHY DIDN'T YOU GO OFF WITH THEM?
MORNING.

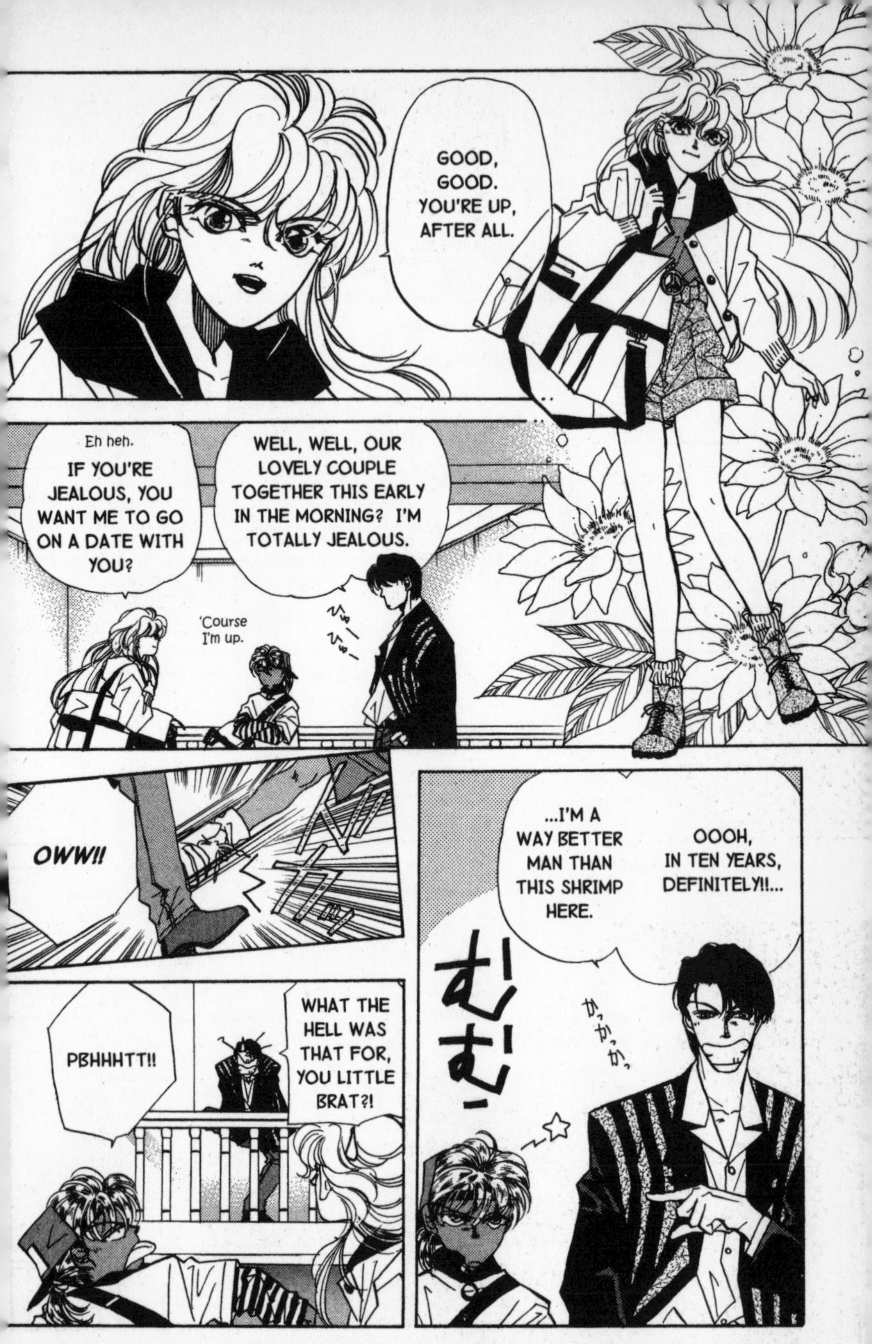
GOOD, GOOD. YOU'RE UP, AFTER ALL.
WELL, WELL, OUR LOVELY COUPLE TOGETHER THIS EARLY IN THE MORNING? I'M TOTALLY JEALOUS.
Eh heh. IF YOU'RE JEALOUS, YOU WANT ME TO GO ON A DATE WITH YOU?
ひゅーひゅー
'Course I'm up.
OOOH, IN TEN YEARS, DEFINITELY!!...
...I'M A WAY BETTER MAN THAN THIS SHRIMP HERE.
むむー
かっかっか
OWW!!
WHAT THE HELL WAS THAT FOR, YOU LITTLE BRAT?!
PBHHHTT!!

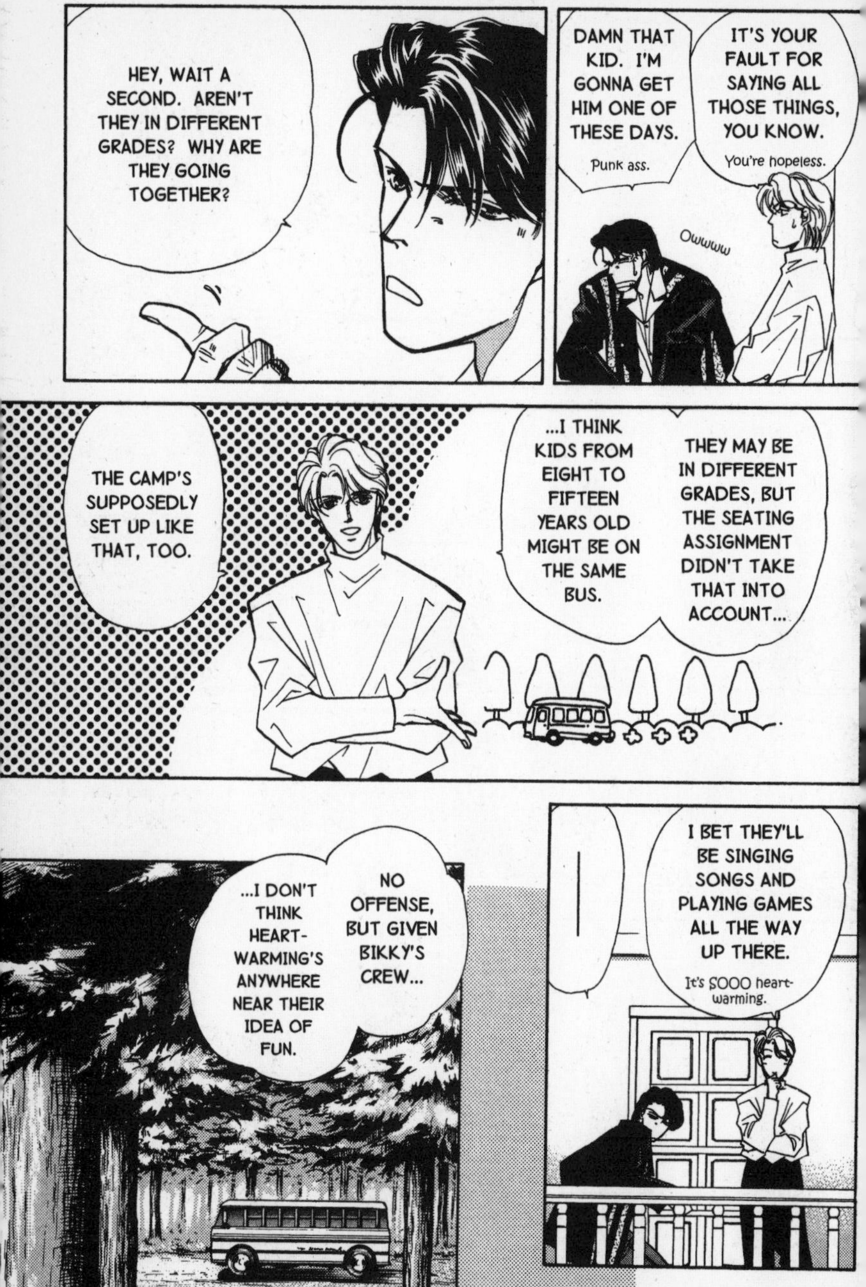
IT'S YOUR FAULT FOR SAYING ALL THOSE THINGS, YOU KNOW.
You're hopeless.
DAMN THAT KID. I'M GONNA GET HIM ONE OF THESE DAYS.
Punk ass.
Owwww
HEY, WAIT A SECOND. AREN'T THEY IN DIFFERENT GRADES? WHY ARE THEY GOING TOGETHER?
THEY MAY BE IN DIFFERENT GRADES, BUT THE SEATING ASSIGNMENT DIDN'T TAKE THAT INTO ACCOUNT...
...I THINK KIDS FROM EIGHT TO FIFTEEN YEARS OLD MIGHT BE ON THE SAME BUS.
THE CAMP'S SUPPOSEDLY SET UP LIKE THAT, TOO.
I BET THEY'LL BE SINGING SONGS AND PLAYING GAMES ALL THE WAY UP THERE.
It's SOOO heart-warming.
NO OFFENSE, BUT GIVEN BIKKY'S CREW...
...I DON'T THINK HEART-WARMING'S ANYWHERE NEAR THEIR IDEA OF FUN.

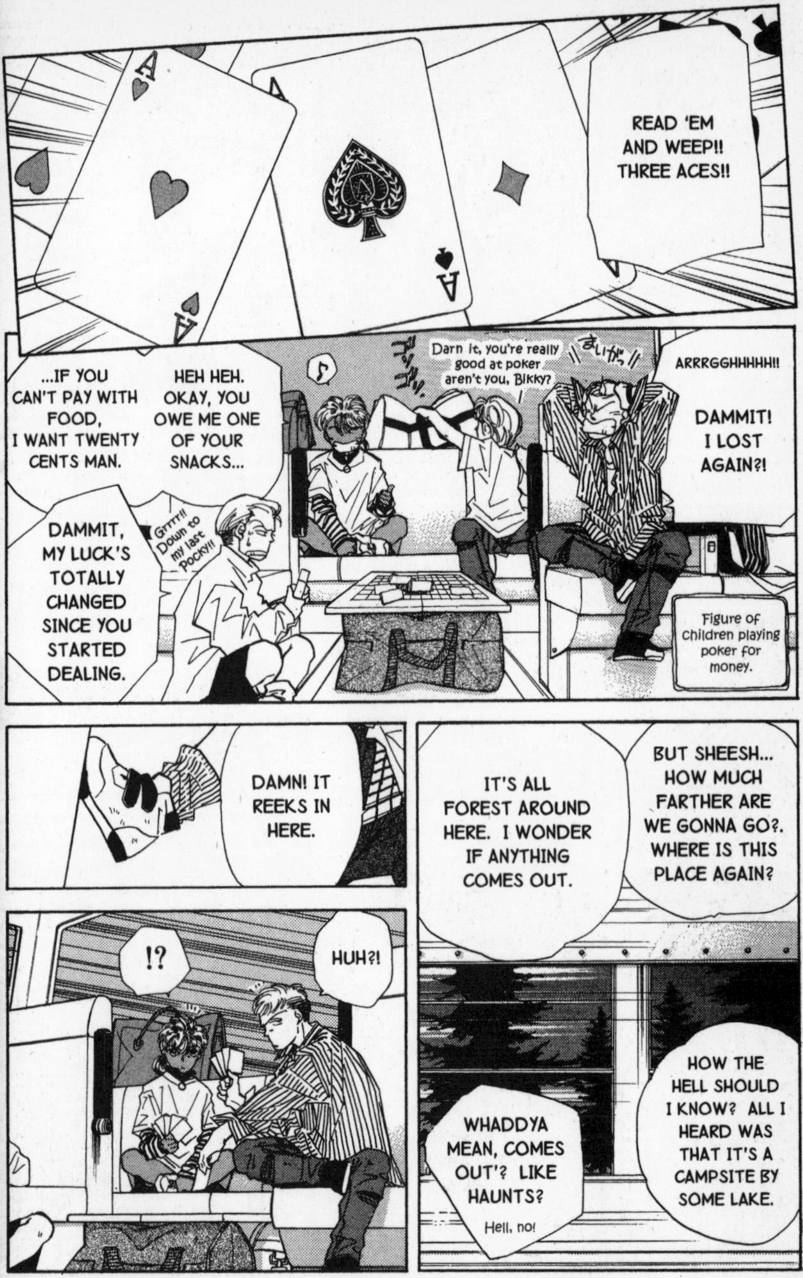
READ 'EM AND WEEP!! THREE ACES!!
ARRRGGHHHHH!!
DAMMIT! I LOST AGAIN?!
Figure of children playing poker for money.
Darn it, you're really good at poker aren't you, Bikky?
♪
HEH HEH. OKAY, YOU OWE ME ONE OF YOUR SNACKS...
...IF YOU CAN'T PAY WITH FOOD, I WANT TWENTY CENTS MAN.
Grrrr!! Down to my last Pocky!!
DAMMIT, MY LUCK'S TOTALLY CHANGED SINCE YOU STARTED DEALING.
BUT SHEESH... HOW MUCH FARTHER ARE WE GONNA GO?. WHERE IS THIS PLACE AGAIN?
IT'S ALL FOREST AROUND HERE. I WONDER IF ANYTHING COMES OUT.
HOW THE HELL SHOULD I KNOW? ALL I HEARD WAS THAT IT'S A CAMPSITE BY SOME LAKE.
WHADDYA MEAN, COMES OUT'? LIKE HAUNTS?
Hell, no!
DAMN! IT REEKS IN HERE.
HUH?!
!?

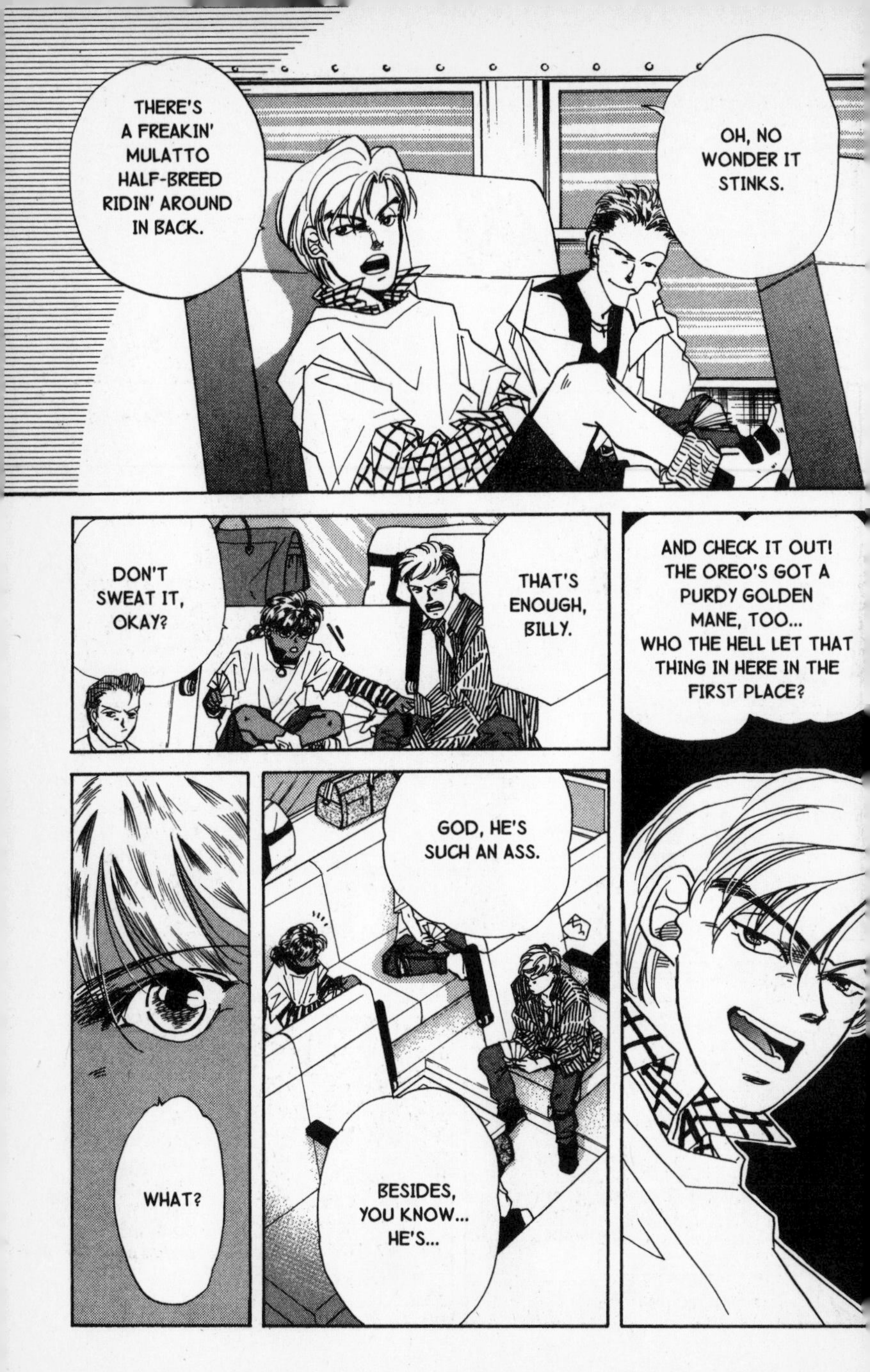
OH, NO WONDER IT STINKS.
THERE'S A FREAKIN' MULATTO HALF-BREED RIDIN' AROUND IN BACK.
AND CHECK IT OUT! THE OREO'S GOT A PURDY GOLDEN MANE, TOO... WHO THE HELL LET THAT THING IN HERE IN THE FIRST PLACE?
THAT'S ENOUGH, BILLY.
DON'T SWEAT IT, OKAY?
GOD, HE'S SUCH AN ASS.
BESIDES, YOU KNOW... HE'S...
WHAT?

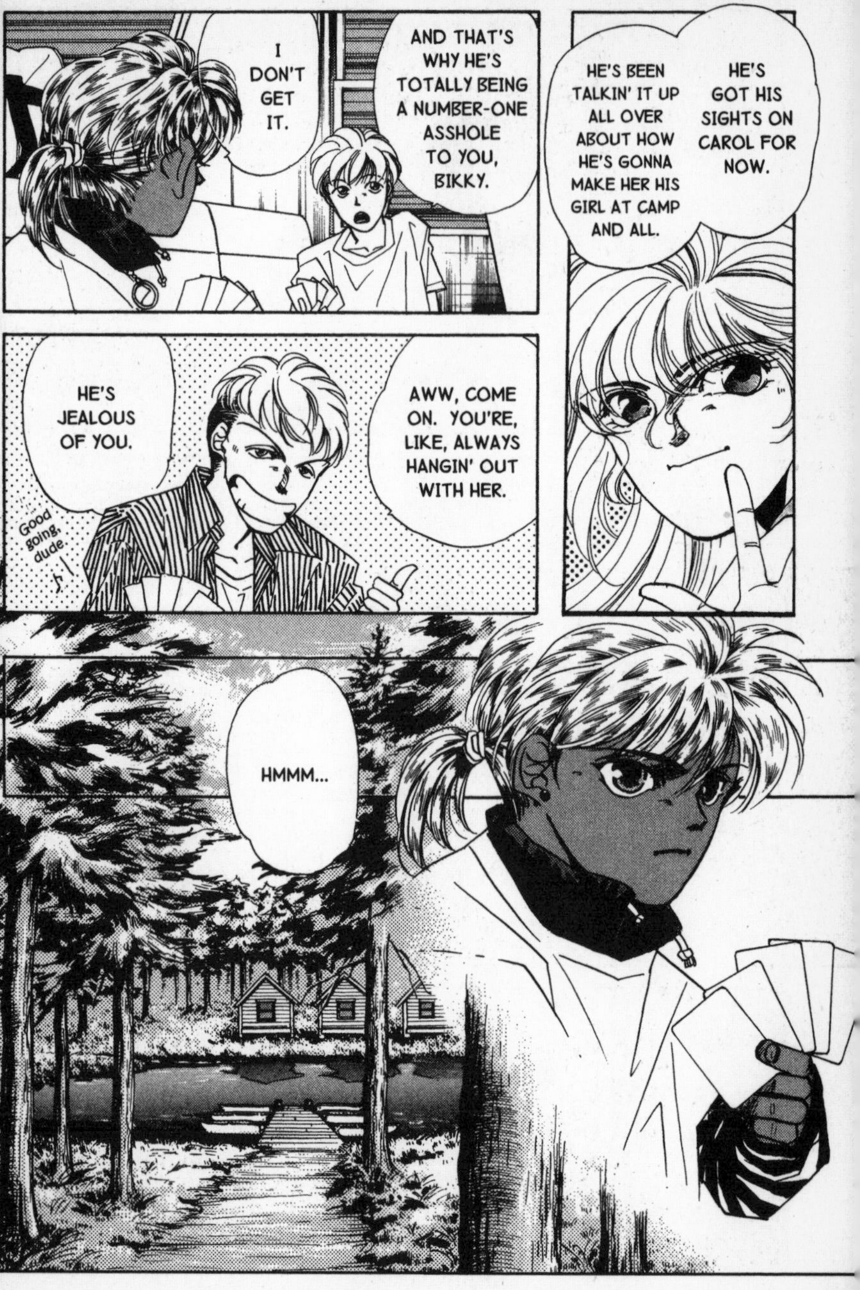
HE'S GOT HIS SIGHTS ON CAROL FOR NOW.
HE'S BEEN TALKIN' IT UP ALL OVER ABOUT HOW HE'S GONNA MAKE HER HIS GIRL AT CAMP AND ALL.
AND THAT'S WHY HE'S TOTALLY BEING A NUMBER-ONE ASSHOLE TO YOU, BIKKY.
I DON'T GET IT.
AWW, COME ON. YOU'RE, LIKE, ALWAYS HANGIN' OUT WITH HER.
HE'S JEALOUS OF YOU.
Good going, dude.
HMMM...

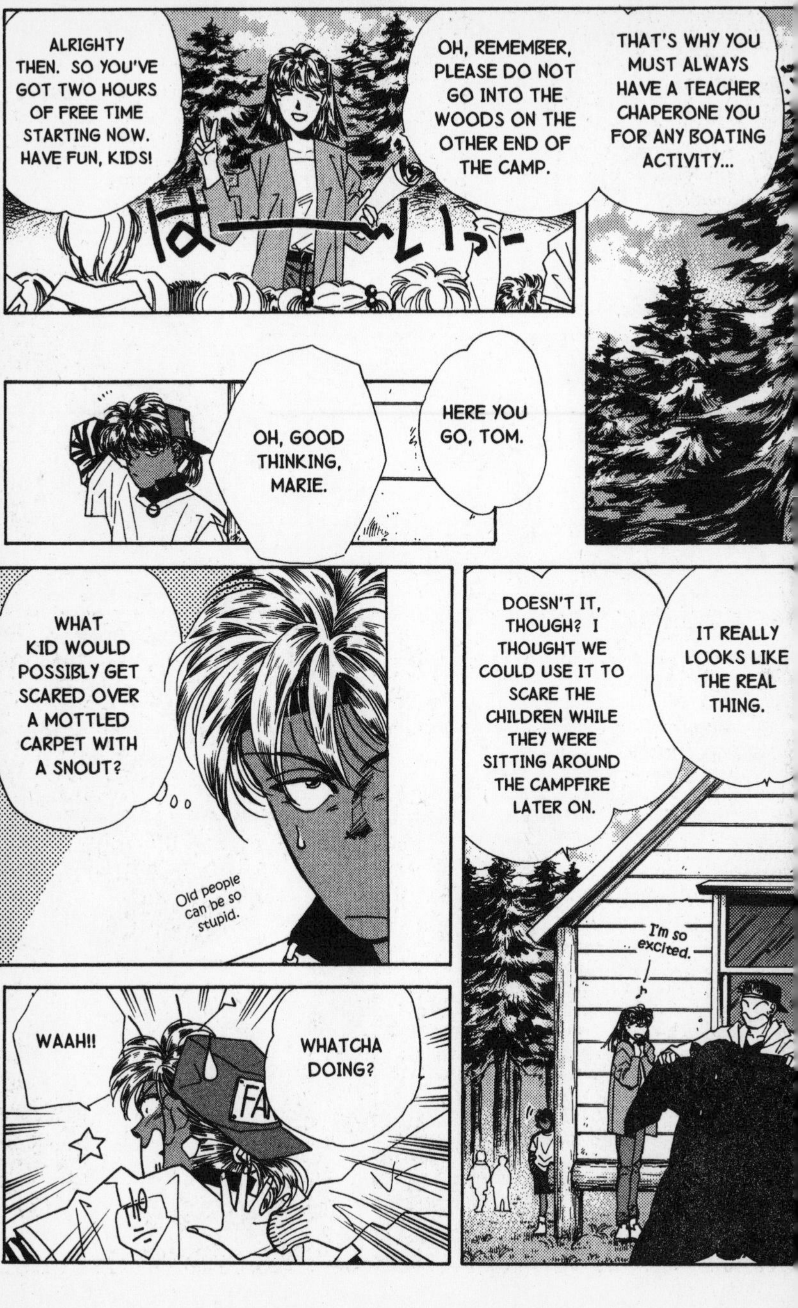
THAT'S WHY YOU MUST ALWAYS HAVE A TEACHER CHAPERONE YOU FOR ANY BOATING ACTIVITY...
OH, REMEMBER, PLEASE DO NOT GO INTO THE WOODS ON THE OTHER END OF THE CAMP.
ALRIGHTY THEN. SO YOU'VE GOT TWO HOURS OF FREE TIME STARTING NOW. HAVE FUN, KIDS!
はーーーい
HERE YOU GO, TOM.
OH, GOOD THINKING, MARIE.
IT REALLY LOOKS LIKE THE REAL THING.
DOESN'T IT, THOUGH? I THOUGHT WE COULD USE IT TO SCARE THE CHILDREN WHILE THEY WERE SITTING AROUND THE CAMPFIRE LATER ON.
I'm so excited.
WHAT KID WOULD POSSIBLY GET SCARED OVER A MOTTLED CARPET WITH A SNOUT?
Old people can be so stupid.
WHATCHA DOING?
WAAH!!

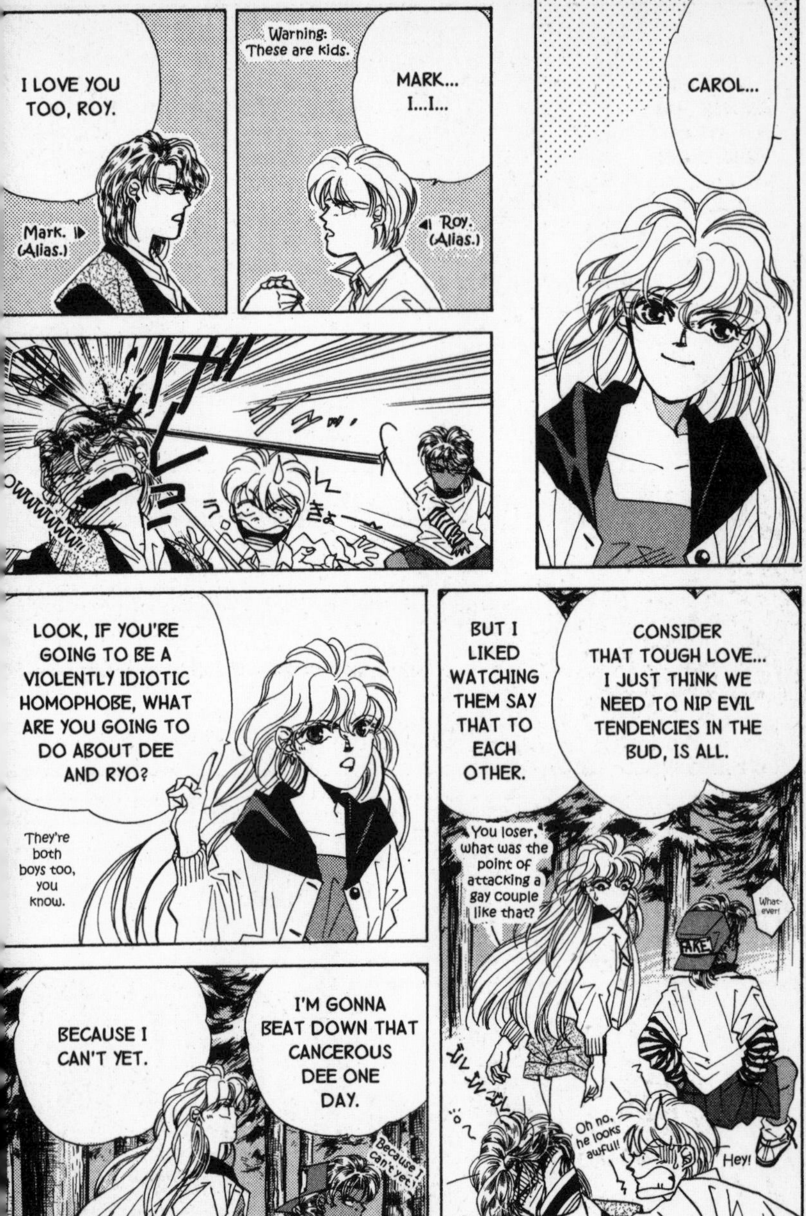
CAROL...
Warning: These are kids.
MARK... I...I...
Roy. (Alias.)
I LOVE YOU TOO, ROY.
Mark. (Alias.)
Owwwwwwww
CONSIDER THAT TOUGH LOVE... I JUST THINK WE NEED TO NIP EVIL TENDENCIES IN THE BUD, IS ALL.
BUT I LIKED WATCHING THEM SAY THAT TO EACH OTHER.
Whatever!
You loser, what was the point of attacking a gay couple like that?
Hey!
Oh no, he looks awful!
I'm hurt!
LOOK, IF YOU'RE GOING TO BE A VIOLENTLY IDIOTIC HOMOPHOBE, WHAT ARE YOU GOING TO DO ABOUT DEE AND RYO?
They're both boys too, you know.
I'M GONNA BEAT DOWN THAT CANCEROUS DEE ONE DAY.
Because I can't yet!
BECAUSE I CAN'T YET.

Well, this really is a girls' comic, after all...

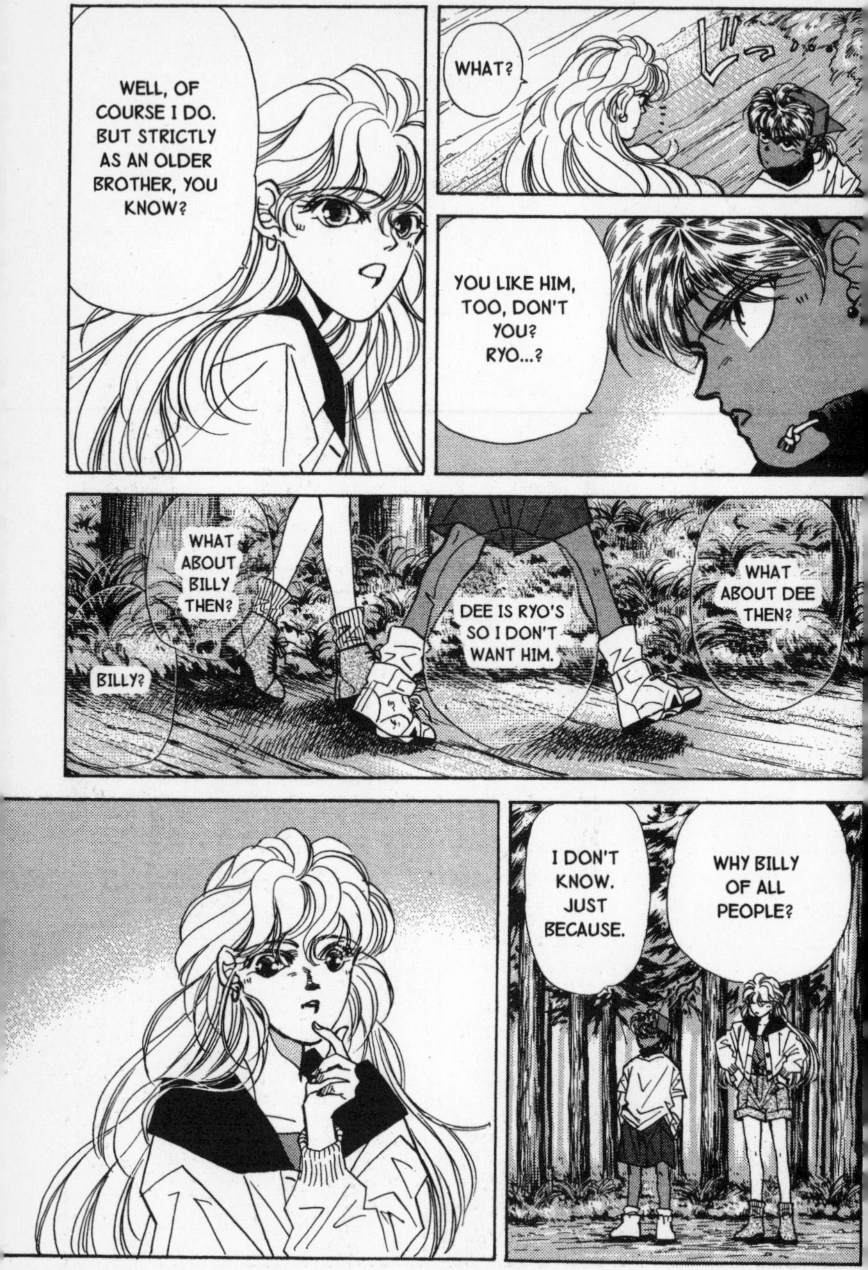
WHAT?
YOU LIKE HIM, TOO, DON'T YOU? RYO...?
WELL, OF COURSE I DO. BUT STRICTLY AS AN OLDER BROTHER, YOU KNOW?
WHAT ABOUT DEE THEN?
DEE IS RYO'S SO I DON'T WANT HIM.
WHAT ABOUT BILLY THEN?
BILLY?
WHY BILLY OF ALL PEOPLE?
I DON'T KNOW. JUST BECAUSE.

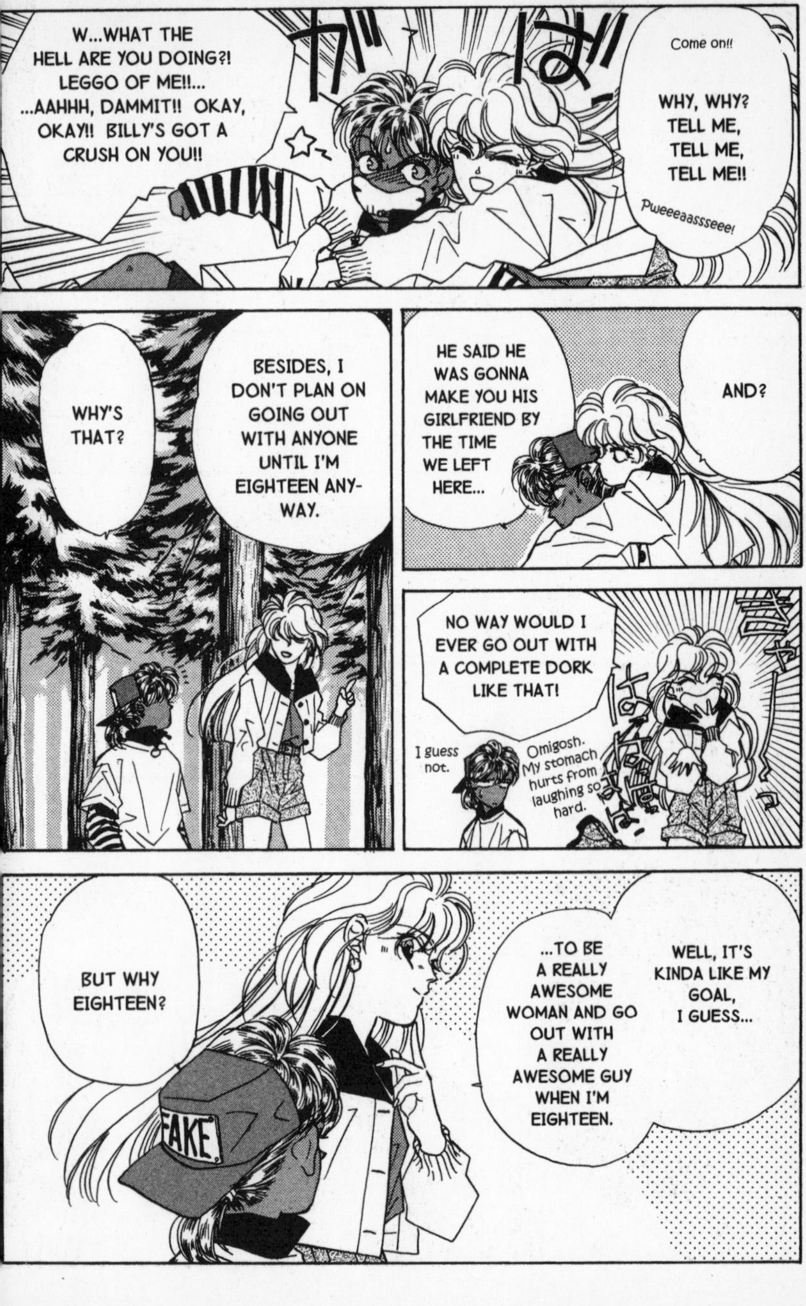
Come on!!
WHY, WHY? TELL ME, TELL ME, TELL ME!!
Pweeeaassseee!
W...WHAT THE HELL ARE YOU DOING?! LEGGO OF ME!!... ...AAHHH, DAMMIT!! OKAY, OKAY!! BILLY'S GOT A CRUSH ON YOU!!
AND?
HE SAID HE WAS GONNA MAKE YOU HIS GIRLFRIEND BY THE TIME WE LEFT HERE...
NO WAY WOULD I EVER GO OUT WITH A COMPLETE DORK LIKE THAT!
Omigosh. My stomach hurts from laughing so hard.
I guess not.
BESIDES, I DON'T PLAN ON GOING OUT WITH ANYONE UNTIL I'M EIGHTEEN ANY-WAY.
WHY'S THAT?
WELL, IT'S KINDA LIKE MY GOAL, I GUESS...
...TO BE A REALLY AWESOME WOMAN AND GO OUT WITH A REALLY AWESOME GUY WHEN I'M EIGHTEEN.
BUT WHY EIGHTEEN?
FAKE

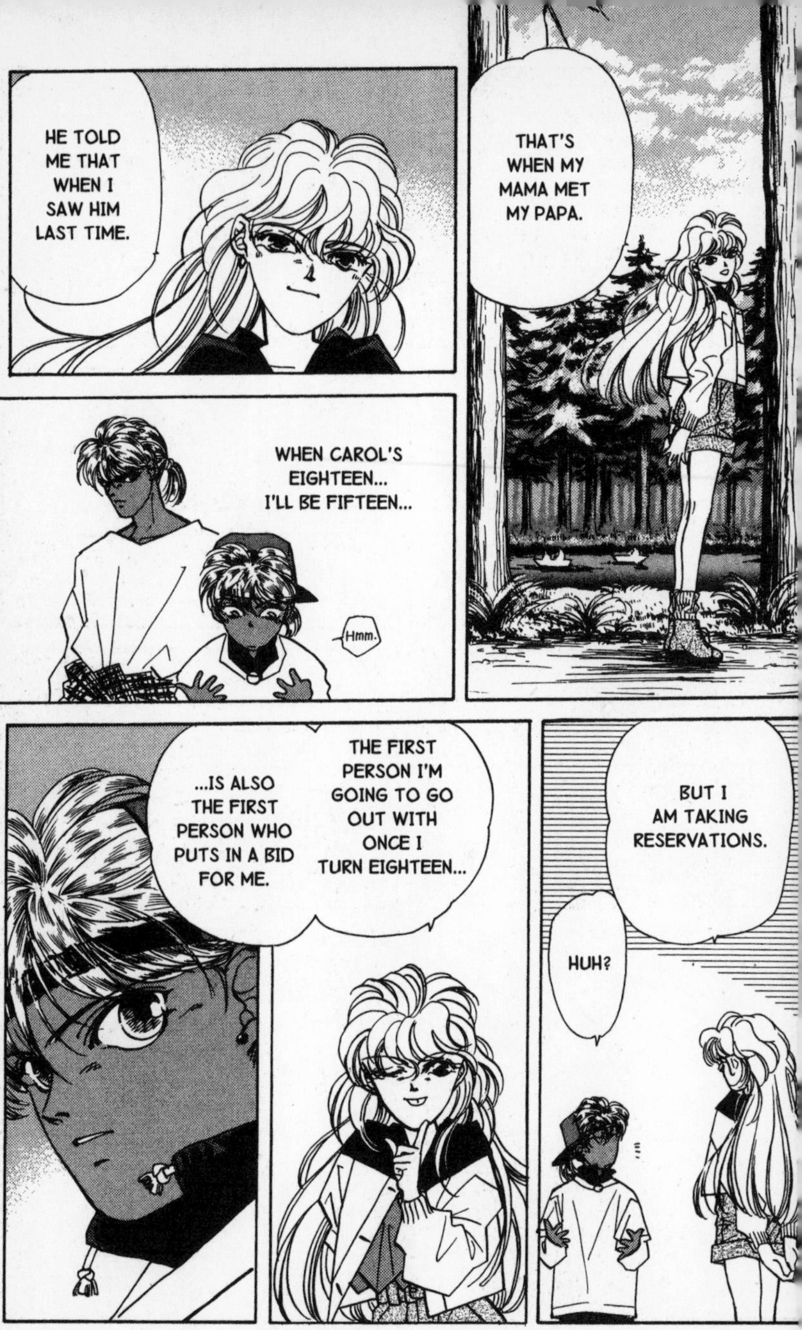
THAT'S WHEN MY MAMA MET MY PAPA.
HE TOLD ME THAT WHEN I SAW HIM LAST TIME.
WHEN CAROL'S EIGHTEEN... I'LL BE FIFTEEN...
Hmm.
BUT I AM TAKING RESERVATIONS.
HUH?
THE FIRST PERSON I'M GOING TO GO OUT WITH ONCE I TURN EIGHTEEN...
...IS ALSO THE FIRST PERSON WHO PUTS IN A BID FOR ME.

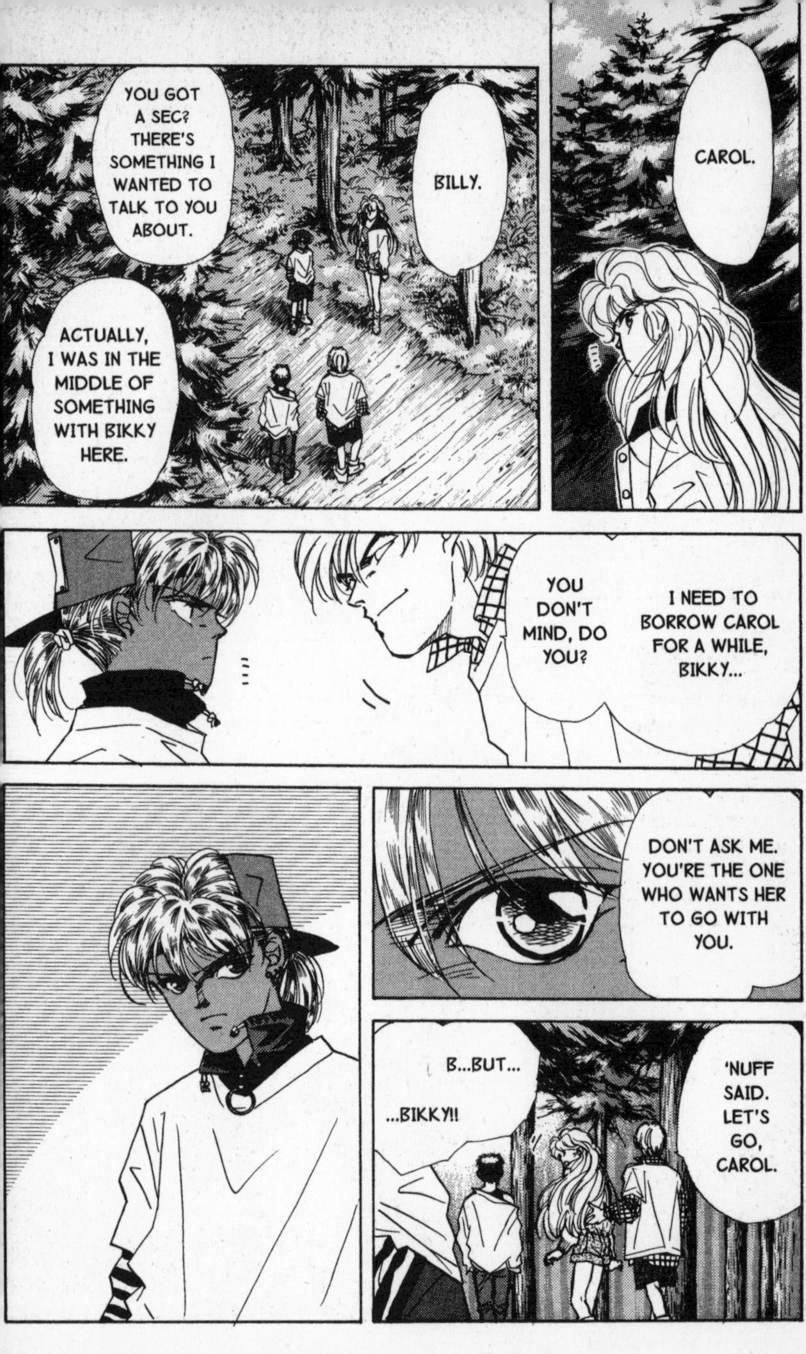
CAROL.
BILLY.
YOU GOT A SEC? THERE'S SOMETHING I WANTED TO TALK TO YOU ABOUT.
ACTUALLY, I WAS IN THE MIDDLE OF SOMETHING WITH BIKKY HERE.
I NEED TO BORROW CAROL FOR A WHILE, BIKKY...
YOU DON'T MIND, DO YOU?
DON'T ASK ME. YOU'RE THE ONE WHO WANTS HER TO GO WITH YOU.
'NUFF SAID. LET'S GO, CAROL.
B...BUT...
...BIKKY!!

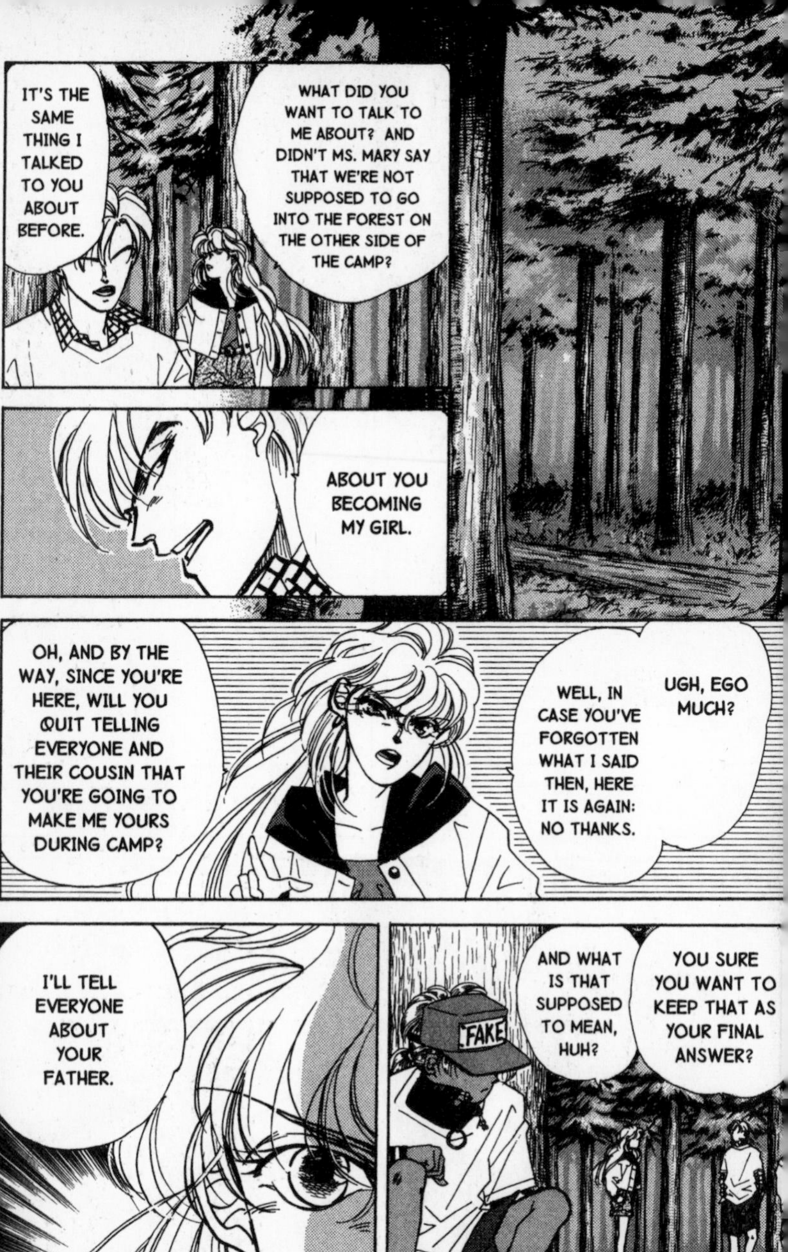
WHAT DID YOU WANT TO TALK TO ME ABOUT? AND DIDN'T MS. MARY SAY THAT WE'RE NOT SUPPOSED TO GO INTO THE FOREST ON THE OTHER SIDE OF THE CAMP?
IT'S THE SAME THING I TALKED TO YOU ABOUT BEFORE.
ABOUT YOU BECOMING MY GIRL.
UGH, EGO MUCH?
WELL, IN CASE YOU'VE FORGOTTEN WHAT I SAID THEN, HERE IT IS AGAIN: NO THANKS.
OH, AND BY THE WAY, SINCE YOU'RE HERE, WILL YOU QUIT TELLING EVERYONE AND THEIR COUSIN THAT YOU'RE GOING TO MAKE ME YOURS DURING CAMP?
YOU SURE YOU WANT TO KEEP THAT AS YOUR FINAL ANSWER?
AND WHAT IS THAT SUPPOSED TO MEAN, HUH?
FAKE
I'LL TELL EVERYONE ABOUT YOUR FATHER.

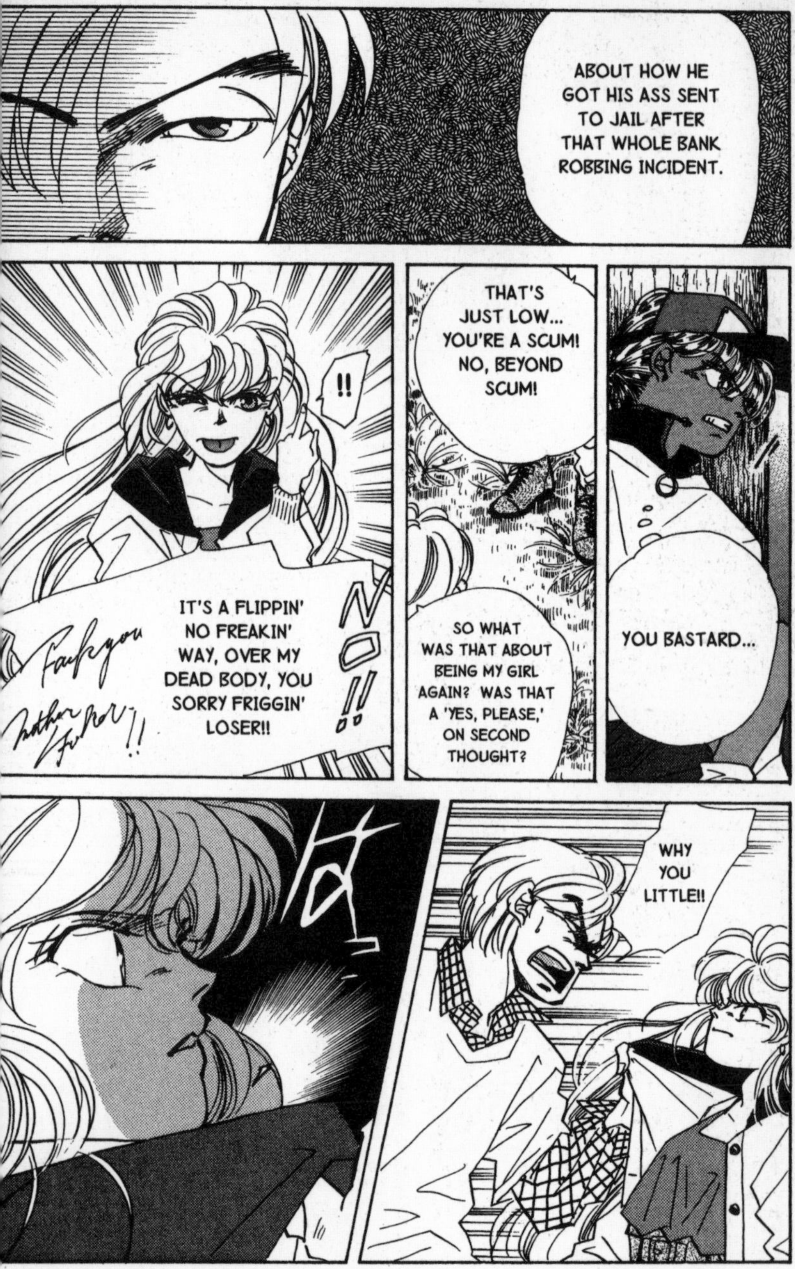
ABOUT HOW HE GOT HIS ASS SENT TO JAIL AFTER THAT WHOLE BANK ROBBING INCIDENT.
YOU BASTARD...
THAT'S JUST LOW... YOU'RE A SCUM! NO, BEYOND SCUM!
SO WHAT WAS THAT ABOUT BEING MY GIRL AGAIN? WAS THAT A 'YES, PLEASE,' ON SECOND THOUGHT?
!!
IT'S A FLIPPIN' NO FREAKIN' WAY, OVER MY DEAD BODY, YOU SORRY FRIGGIN' LOSER!!
NO!!
Fuck you
Mother Fucker!!
WHY YOU LITTLE!!

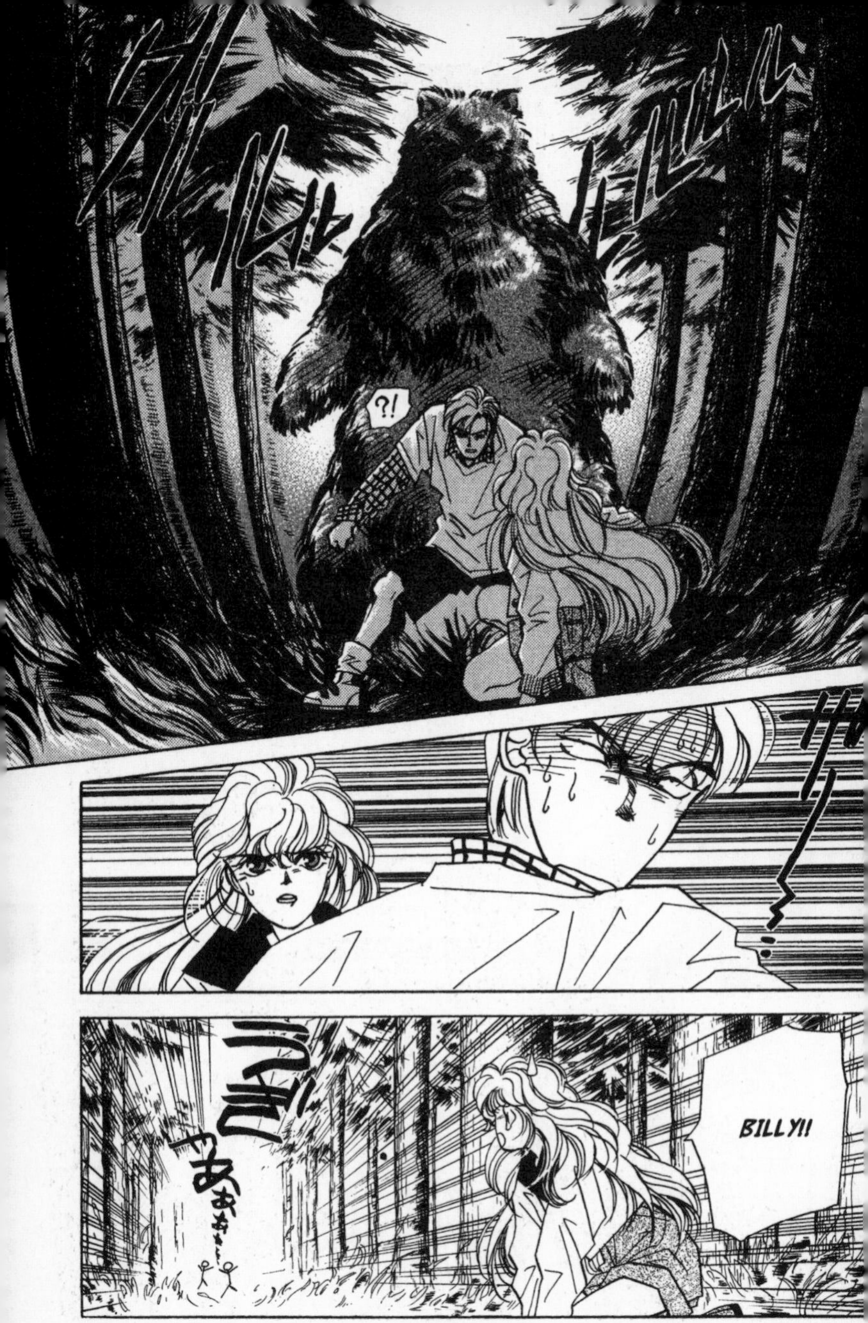
?!
BILLY!!

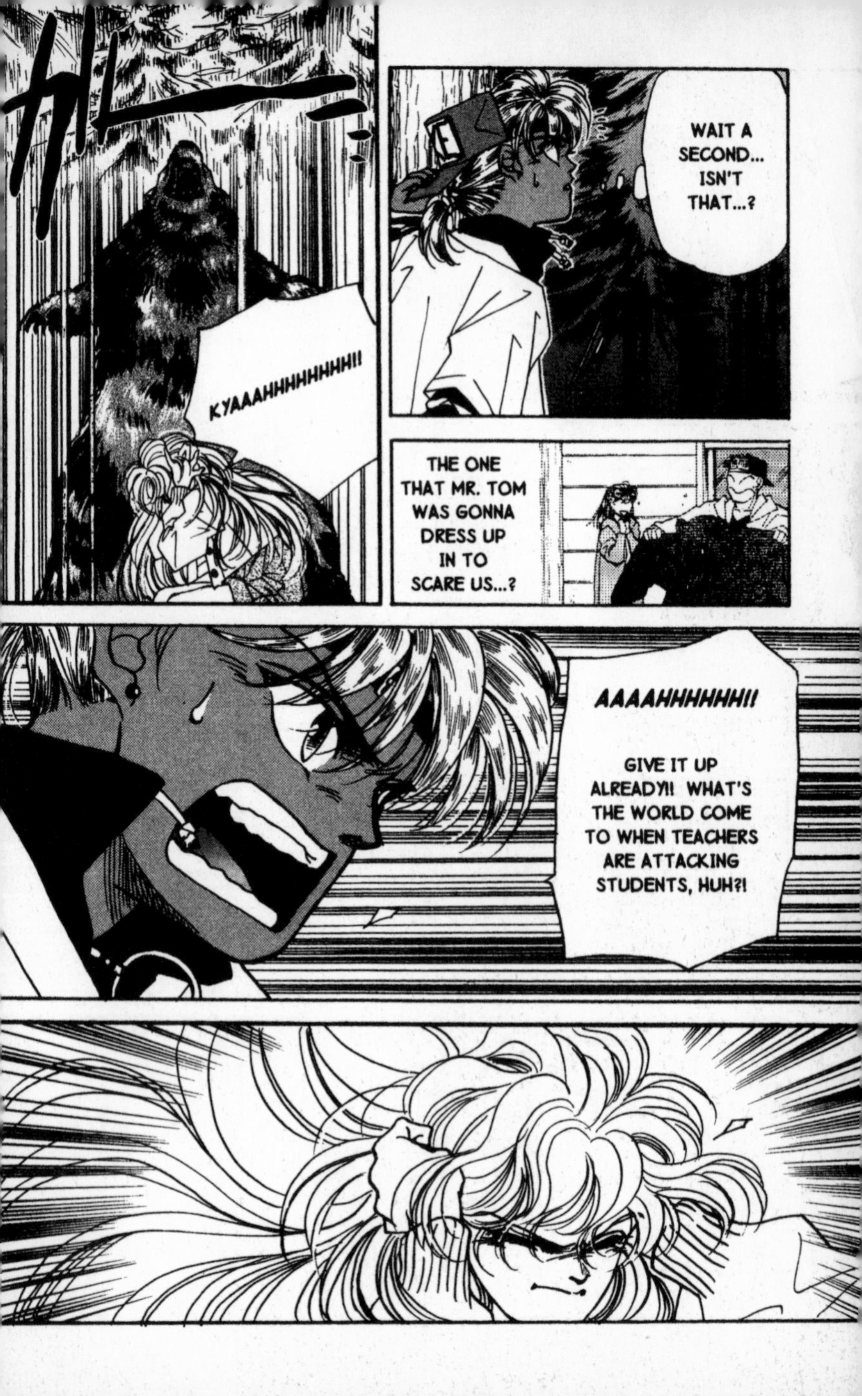
WAIT A SECOND... ISN'T THAT...?
THE ONE THAT MR. TOM WAS GONNA DRESS UP IN TO SCARE US...?
KYAAAHHHHHHHH!!
AAAAHHHHHH!!
GIVE IT UP ALREADY!! WHAT'S THE WORLD COME TO WHEN TEACHERS ARE ATTACKING STUDENTS, HUH?!

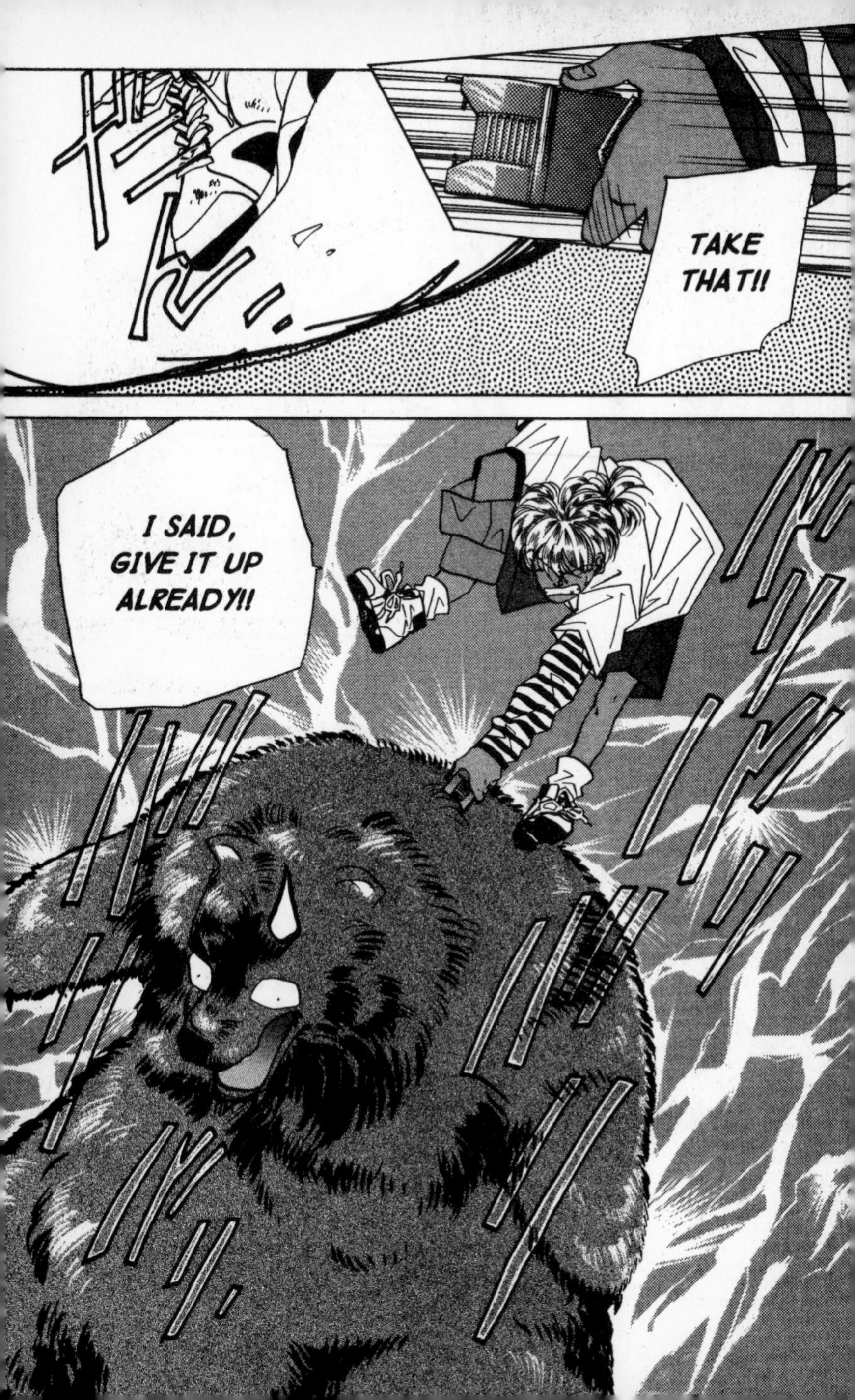
TAKE THAT!!
I SAID, GIVE IT UP ALREADY!!

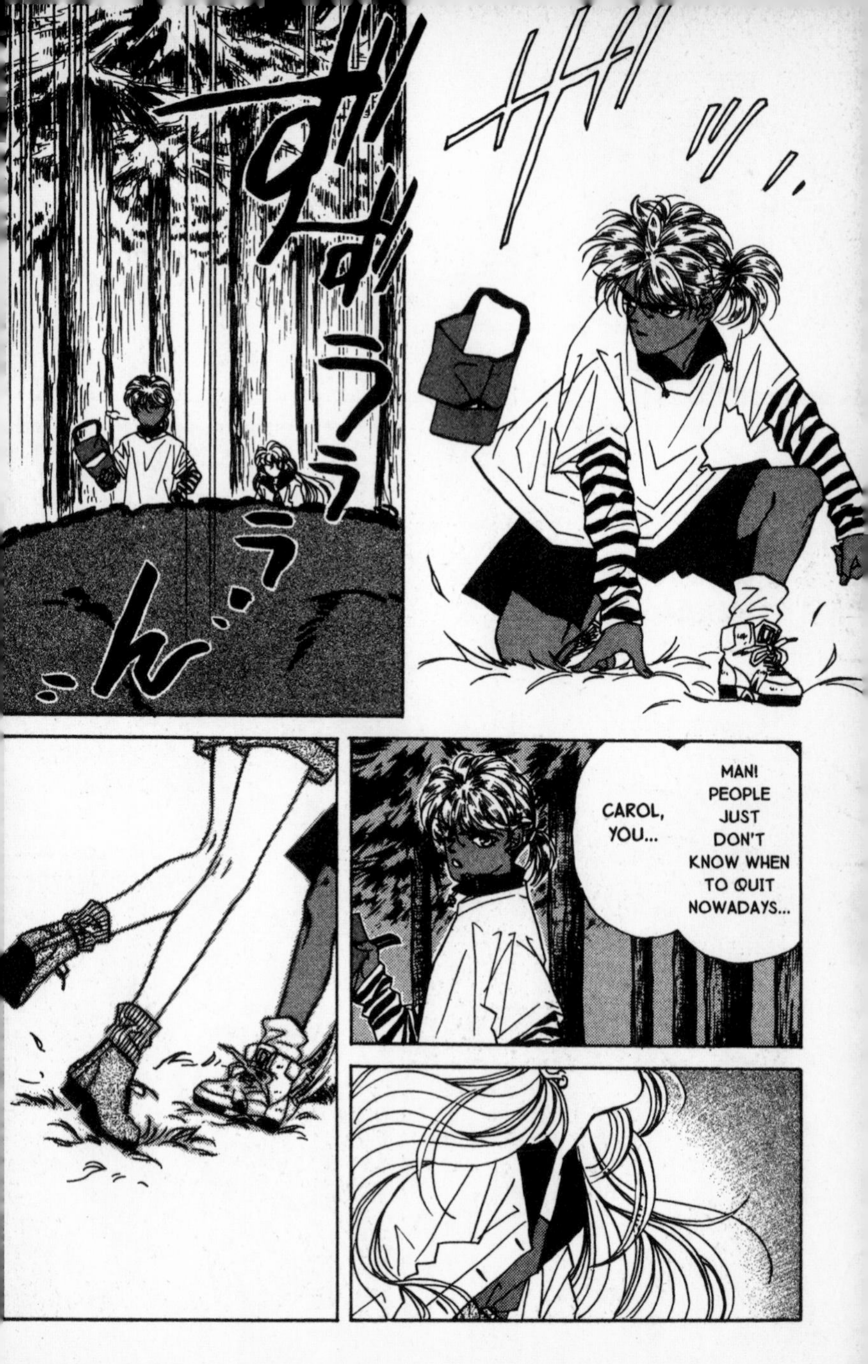
MAN! PEOPLE JUST DON'T KNOW WHEN TO QUIT NOWADAYS...
CAROL, YOU...

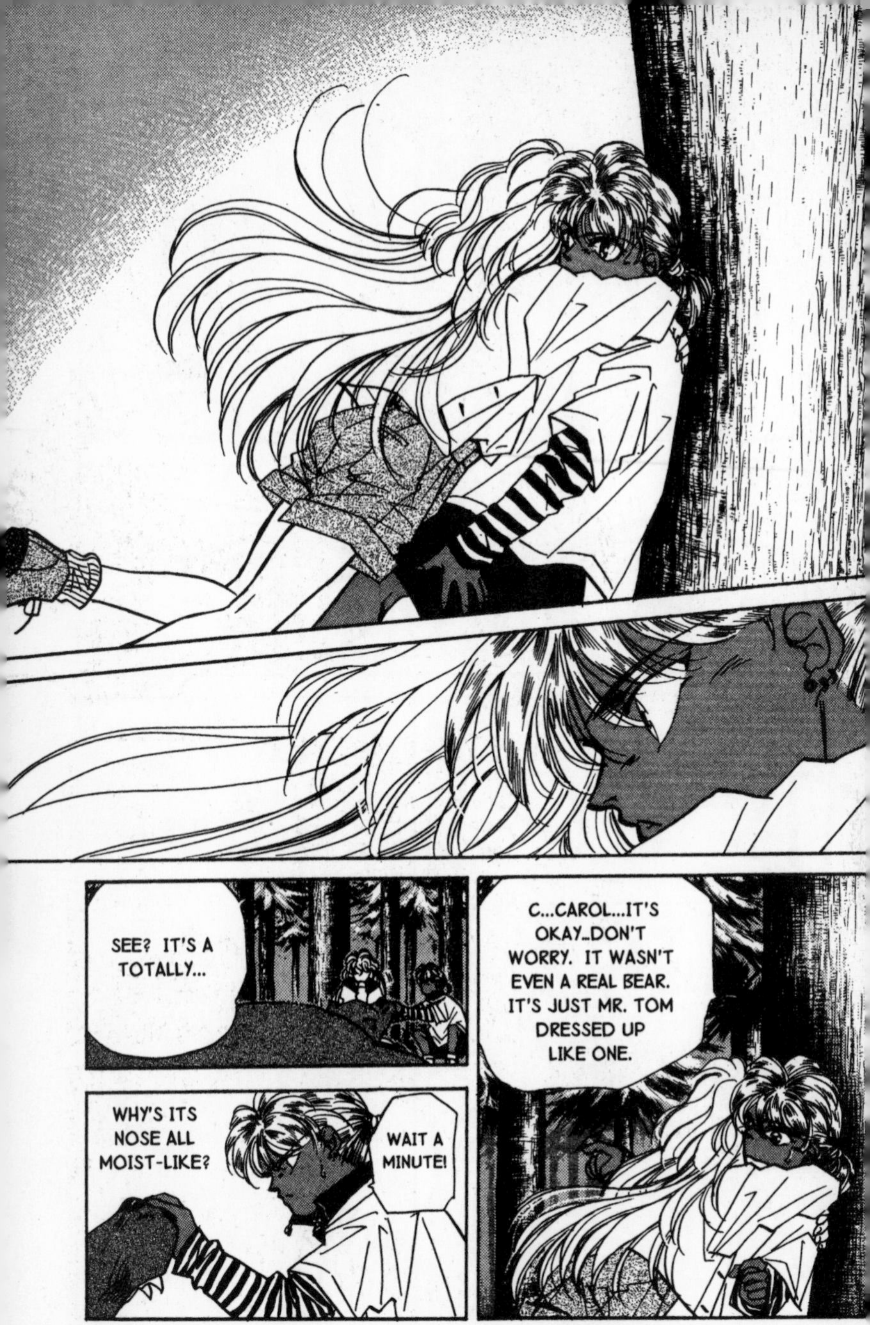
C...CAROL...IT'S OKAY..DON'T WORRY. IT WASN'T EVEN A REAL BEAR. IT'S JUST MR. TOM DRESSED UP LIKE ONE.
SEE? IT'S A TOTALLY...
WAIT A MINUTE!
WHY'S ITS NOSE ALL MOIST-LIKE?

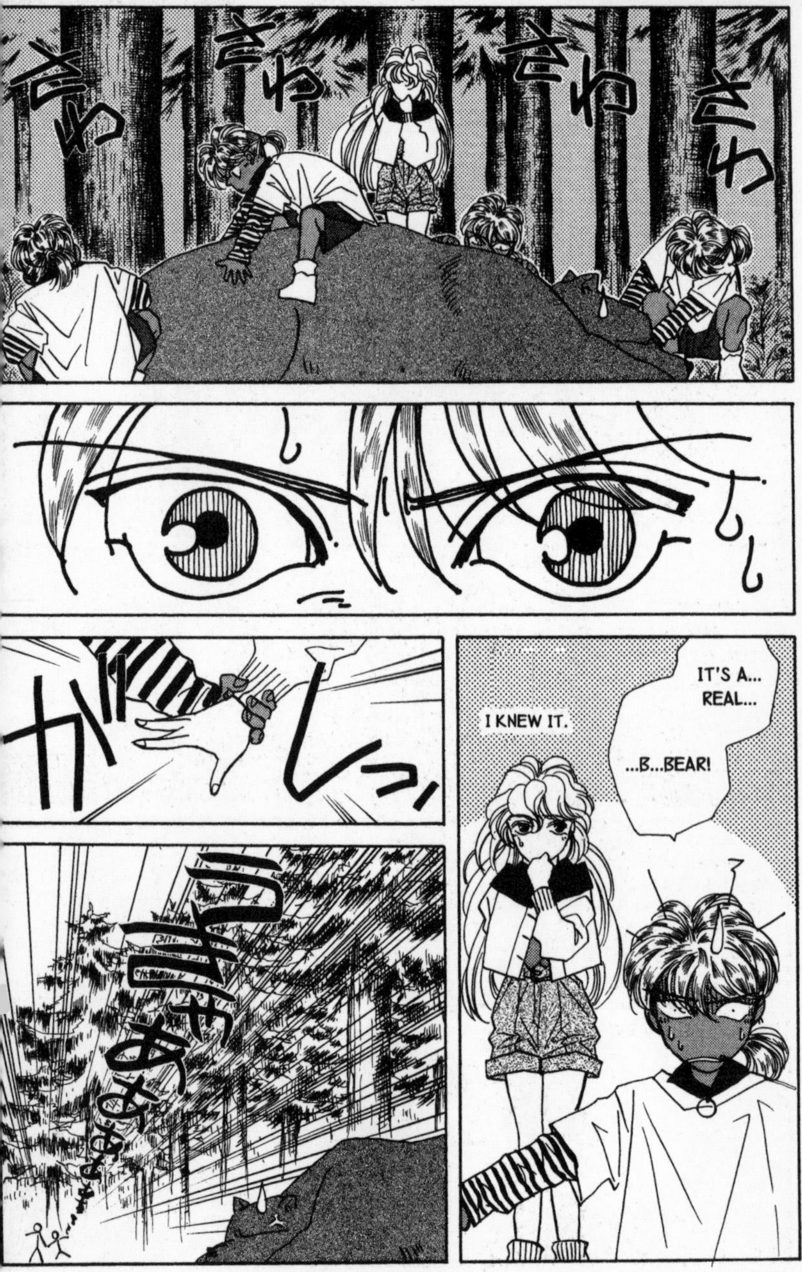
さわ さわ さわ さわ
IT'S A... REAL... ...B...BEAR!
I KNEW IT.
ガバしっ
うぎゃああああ

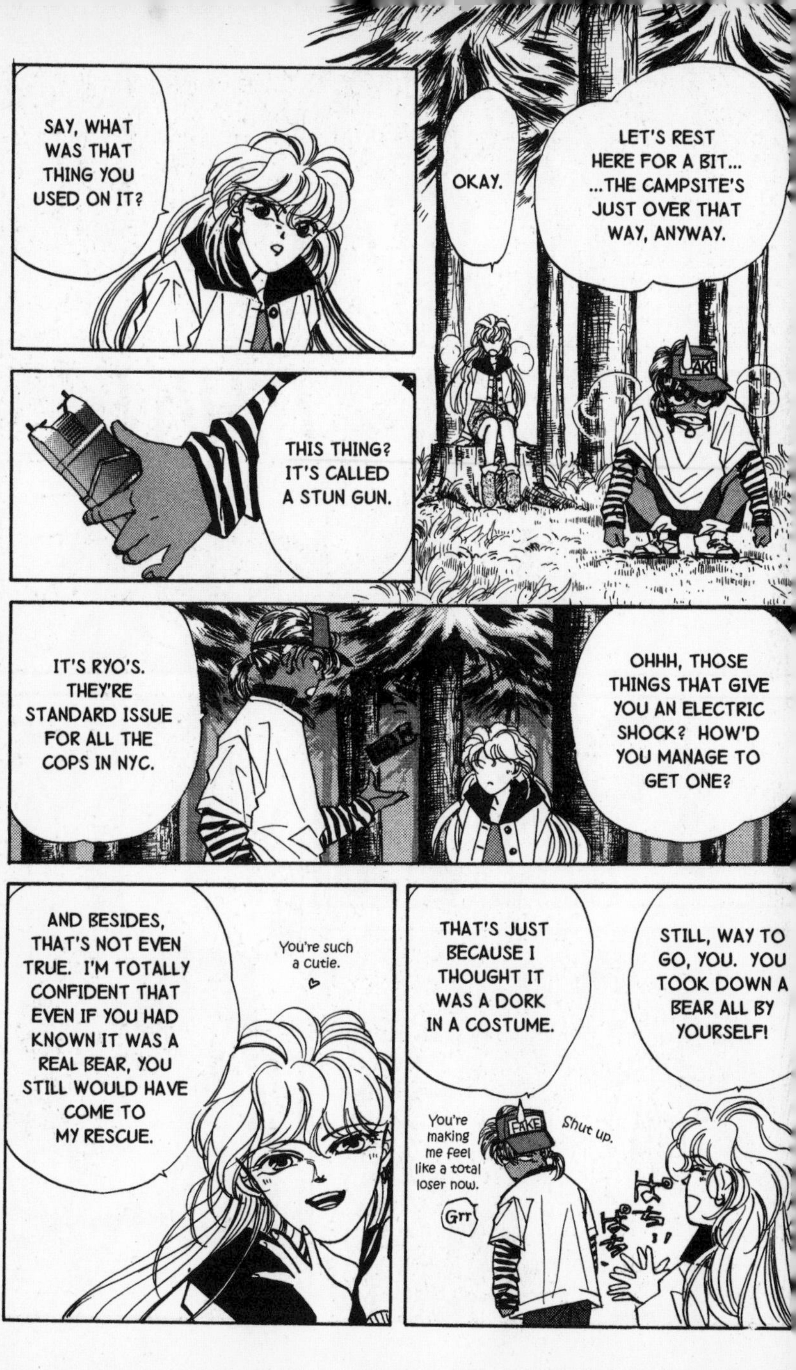
LET'S REST HERE FOR A BIT... ...THE CAMPSITE'S JUST OVER THAT WAY, ANYWAY.
OKAY.
SAY, WHAT WAS THAT THING YOU USED ON IT?
THIS THING? IT'S CALLED A STUN GUN.
OHHH, THOSE THINGS THAT GIVE YOU AN ELECTRIC SHOCK? HOW'D YOU MANAGE TO GET ONE?
IT'S RYO'S. THEY'RE STANDARD ISSUE FOR ALL THE COPS IN NYC.
STILL, WAY TO GO, YOU. YOU TOOK DOWN A BEAR ALL BY YOURSELF!
THAT'S JUST BECAUSE I THOUGHT IT WAS A DORK IN A COSTUME.
Shut up.
You're making me feel like a total loser now.
Grr
AND BESIDES, THAT'S NOT EVEN TRUE. I'M TOTALLY CONFIDENT THAT EVEN IF YOU HAD KNOWN IT WAS A REAL BEAR, YOU STILL WOULD HAVE COME TO MY RESCUE.
You're such a cutie.

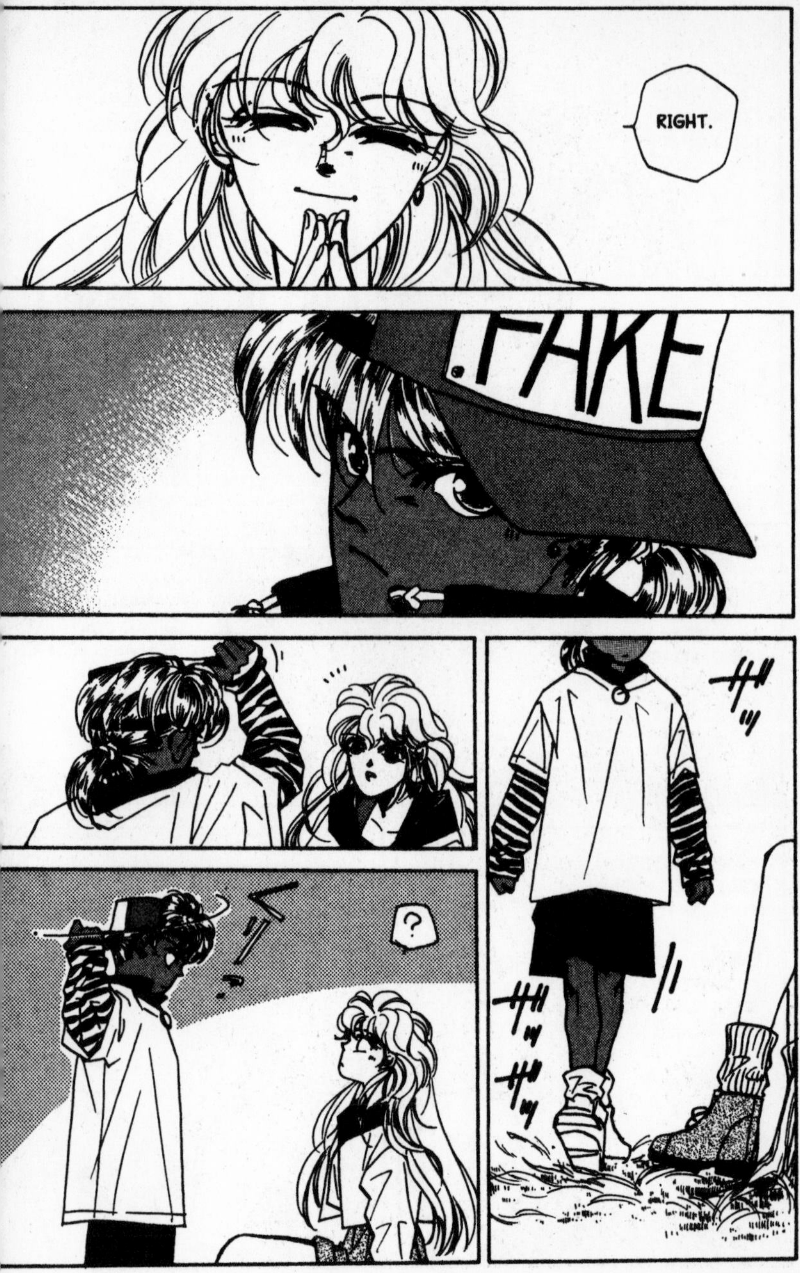
RIGHT.
FAKE
?

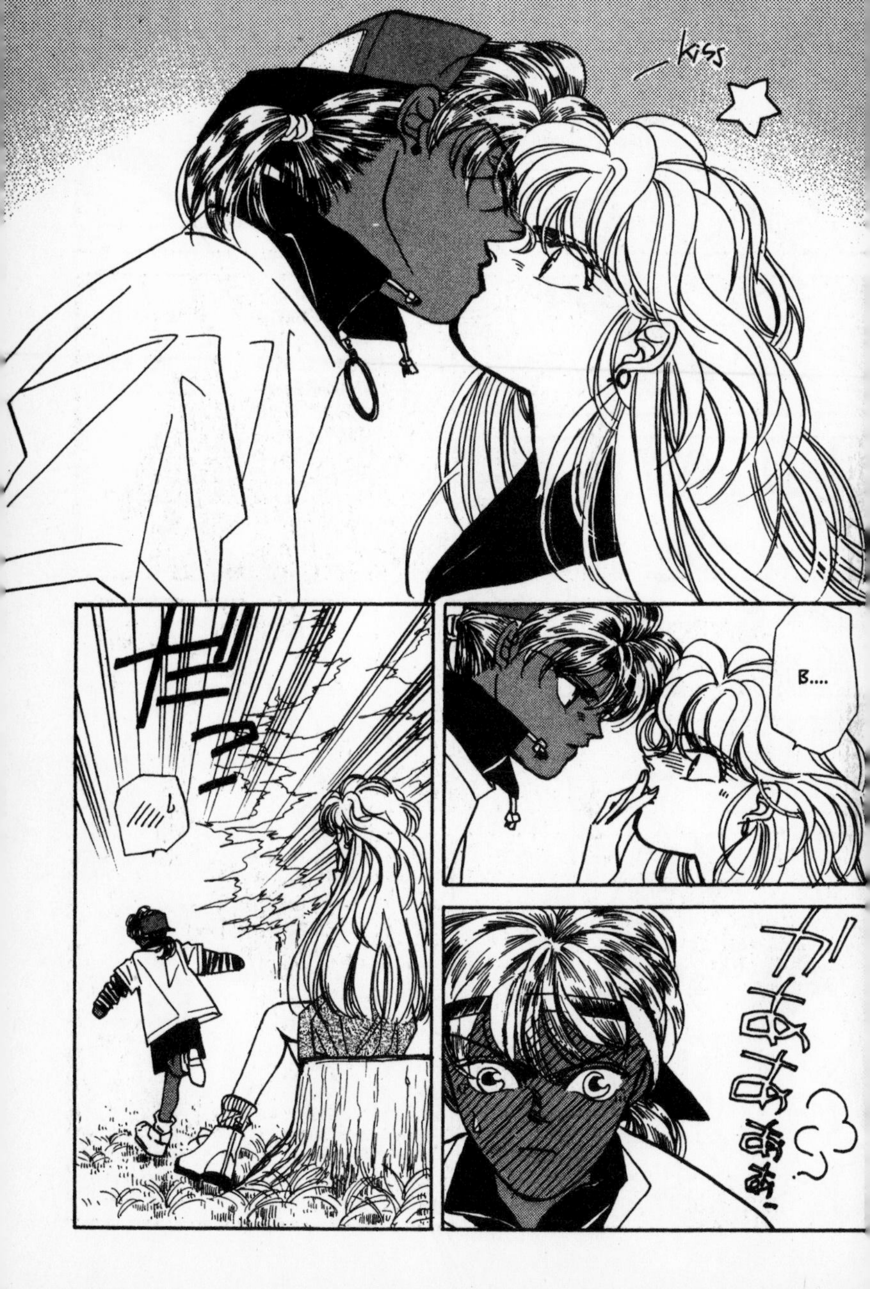
kiss
B....

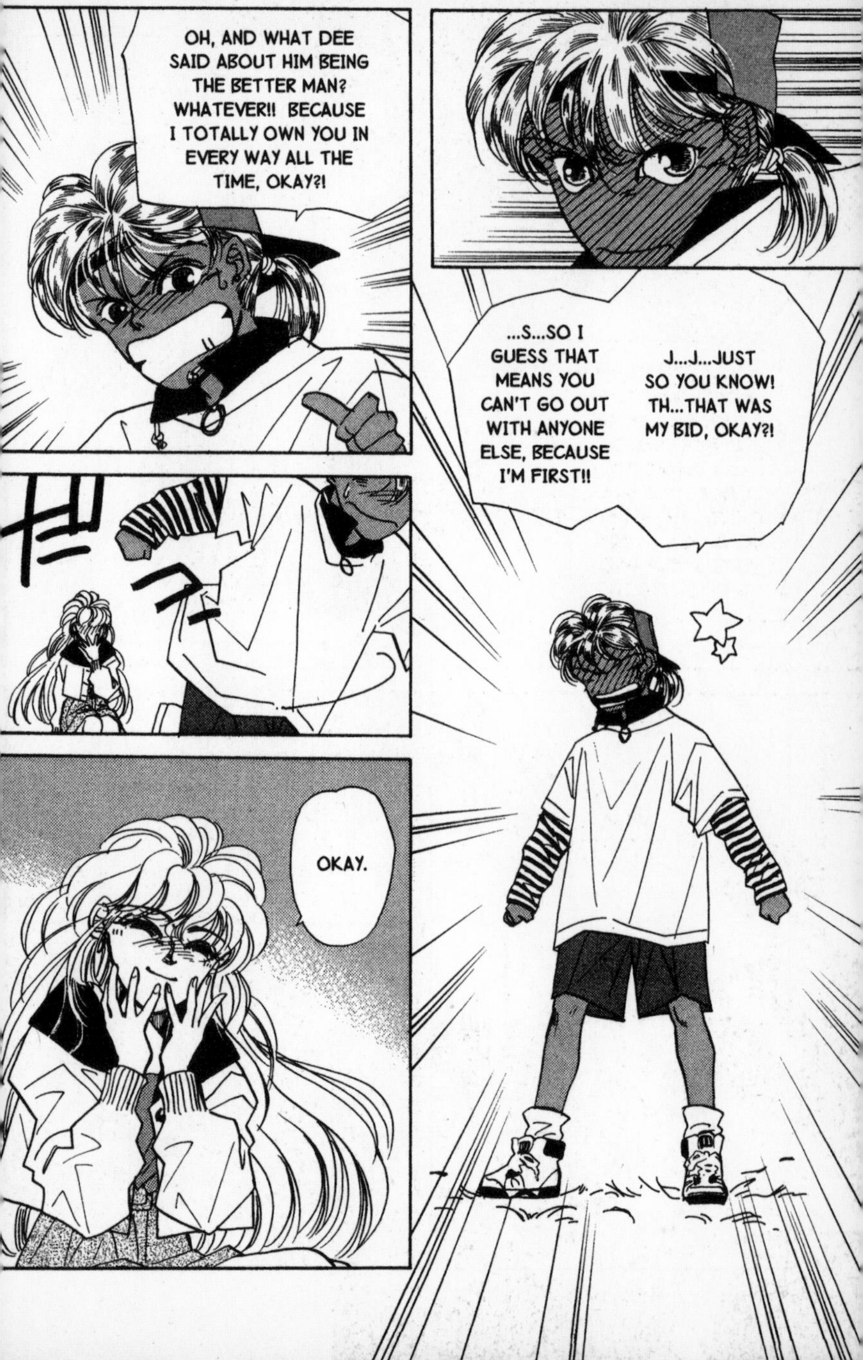
OH, AND WHAT DEE SAID ABOUT HIM BEING THE BETTER MAN? WHATEVER!! BECAUSE I TOTALLY OWN YOU IN EVERY WAY ALL THE TIME, OKAY?!
J...J...JUST SO YOU KNOW! TH...THAT WAS MY BID, OKAY?!
...S...SO I GUESS THAT MEANS YOU CAN'T GO OUT WITH ANYONE ELSE, BECAUSE I'M FIRST!!
OKAY.

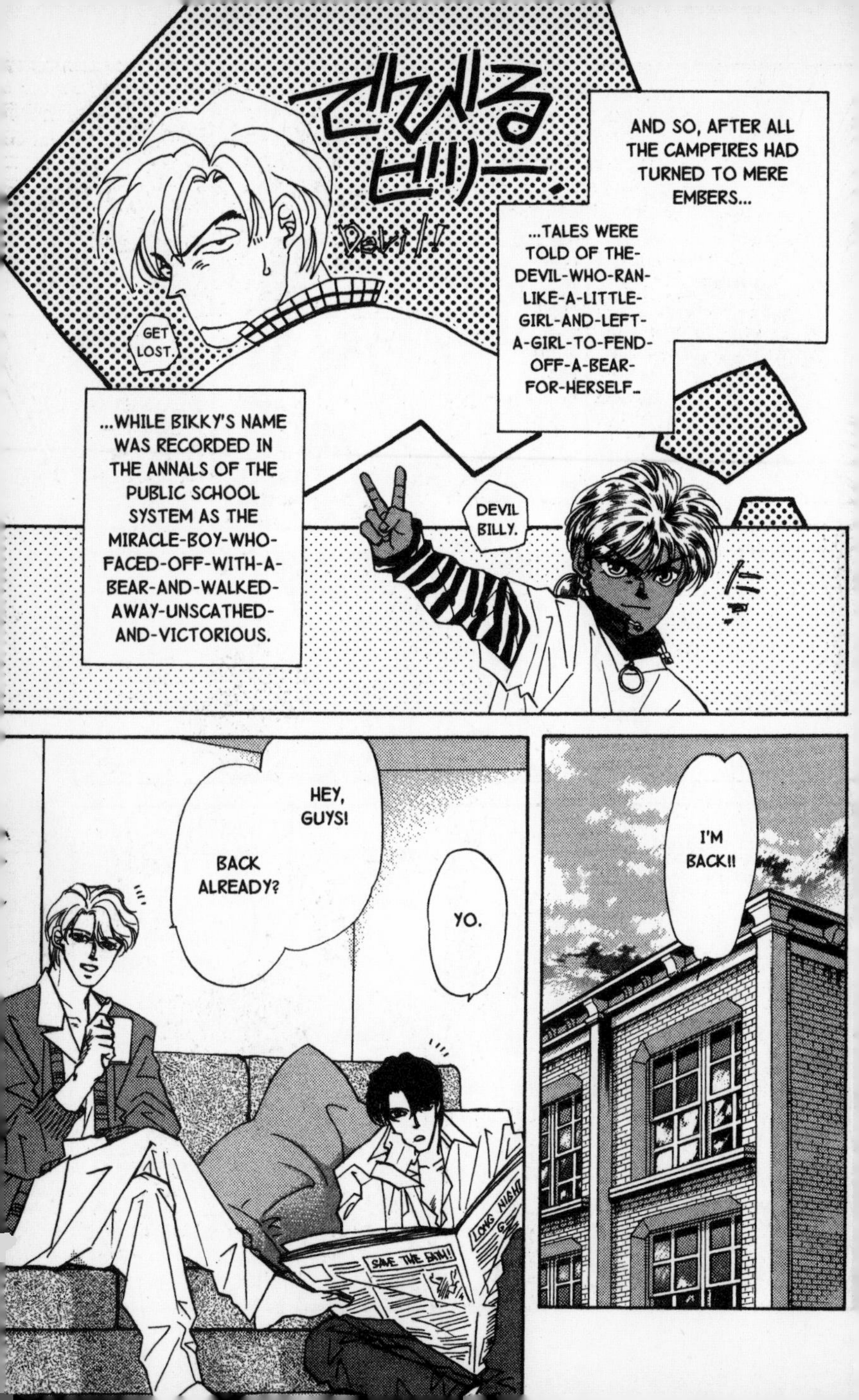
AND SO, AFTER ALL THE CAMPFIRES HAD TURNED TO MERE EMBERS...
...TALES WERE TOLD OF THE-DEVIL-WHO-RAN-LIKE-A-LITTLE-GIRL-AND-LEFT-A-GIRL-TO-FEND-OFF-A-BEAR-FOR-HERSELF..
でびるビリー.
Devil!!
GET LOST.
...WHILE BIKKY'S NAME WAS RECORDED IN THE ANNALS OF THE PUBLIC SCHOOL SYSTEM AS THE MIRACLE-BOY-WHO-FACED-OFF-WITH-A-BEAR-AND-WALKED-AWAY-UNSCATHED-AND-VICTORIOUS.
DEVIL BILLY.
I'M BACK!!
HEY, GUYS!
BACK ALREADY?
YO.
SAVE THE BATH!

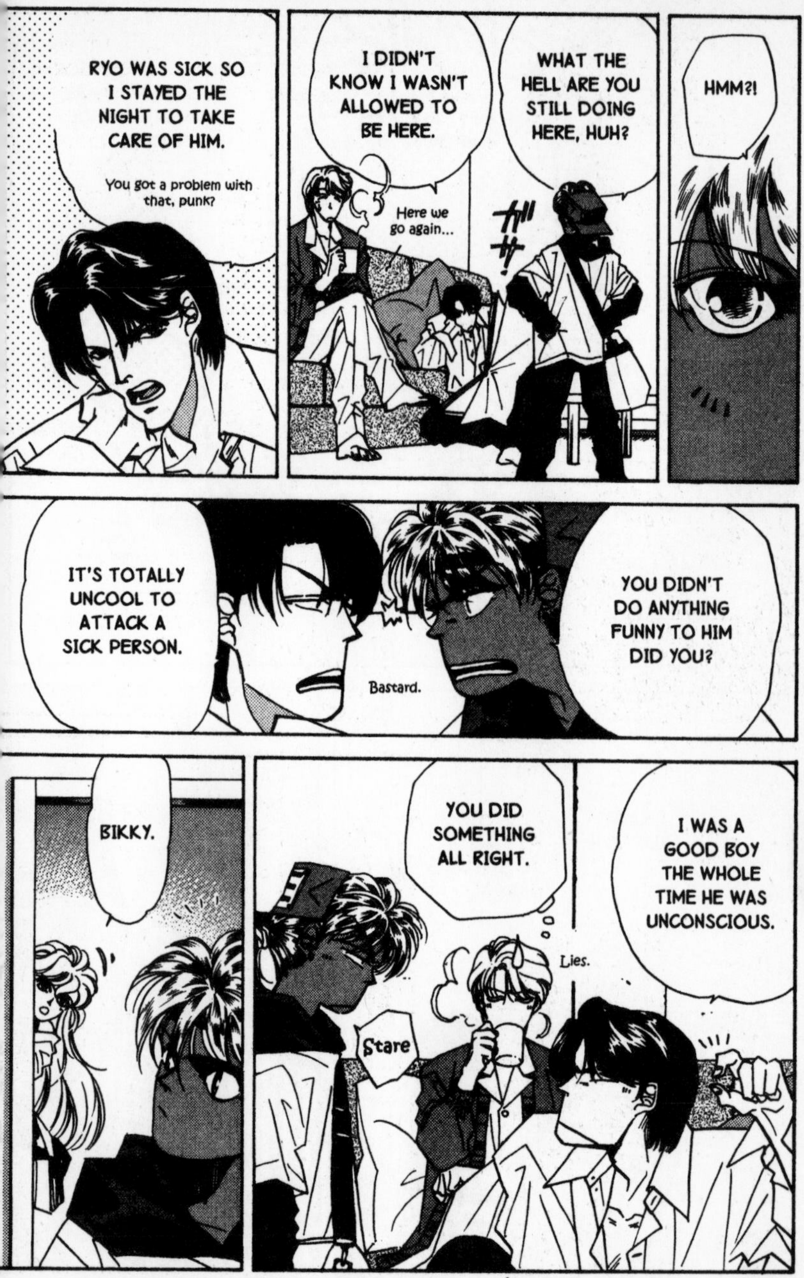
HMM?!
WHAT THE HELL ARE YOU STILL DOING HERE, HUH?
I DIDN'T KNOW I WASN'T ALLOWED TO BE HERE.
Here we go again...
RYO WAS SICK SO I STAYED THE NIGHT TO TAKE CARE OF HIM.
You got a problem with that, punk?
YOU DIDN'T DO ANYTHING FUNNY TO HIM DID YOU?
Bastard.
IT'S TOTALLY UNCOOL TO ATTACK A SICK PERSON.
I WAS A GOOD BOY THE WHOLE TIME HE WAS UNCONSCIOUS.
YOU DID SOMETHING ALL RIGHT.
Lies.
Stare
BIKKY.

↑ Refer to FAKE Act 3 and you'll understand.

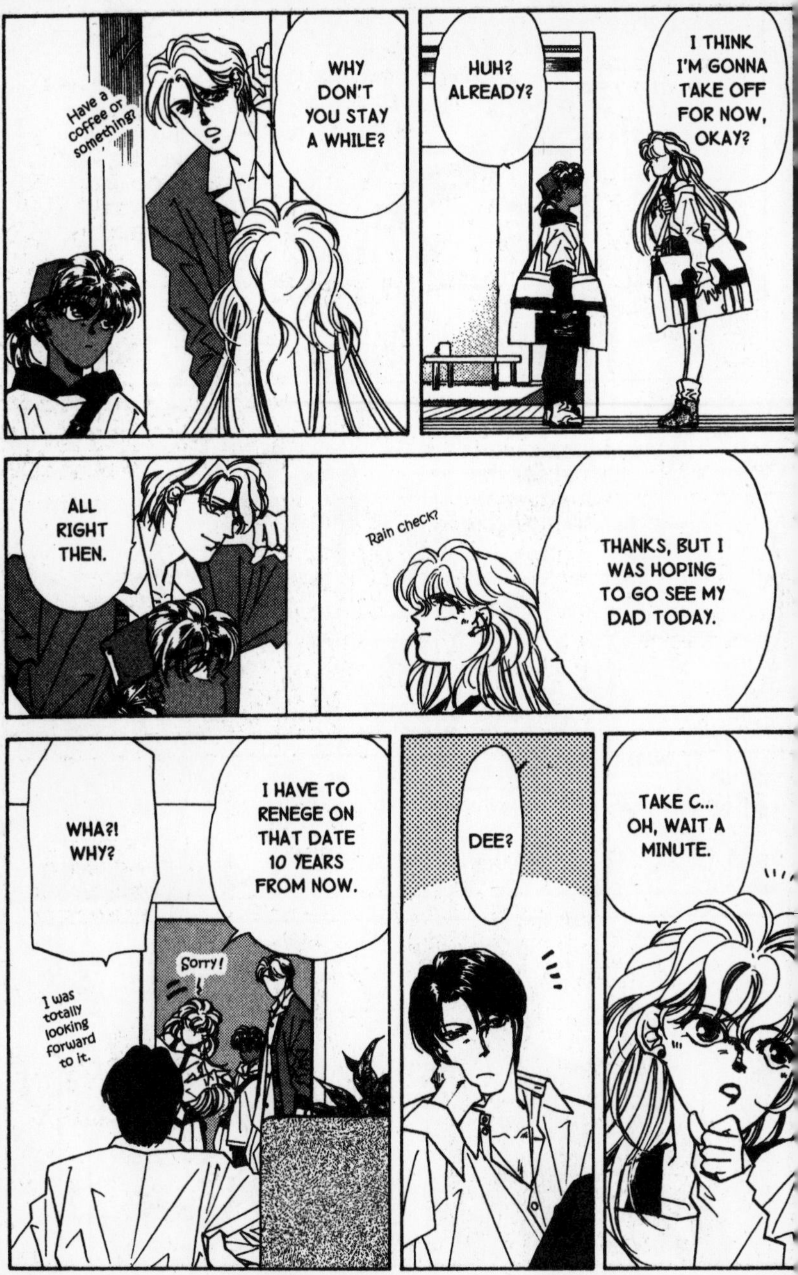
I THINK I'M GONNA TAKE OFF FOR NOW, OKAY?
HUH? ALREADY?
WHY DON'T YOU STAY A WHILE?
Have a coffee or something?
THANKS, BUT I WAS HOPING TO GO SEE MY DAD TODAY.
Rain check?
ALL RIGHT THEN.
TAKE C... OH, WAIT A MINUTE.
DEE?
I HAVE TO RENEGE ON THAT DATE 10 YEARS FROM NOW.
WHA?! WHY?
Sorry!
I was totally looking forward to it.

Please don't look forward to something like that...

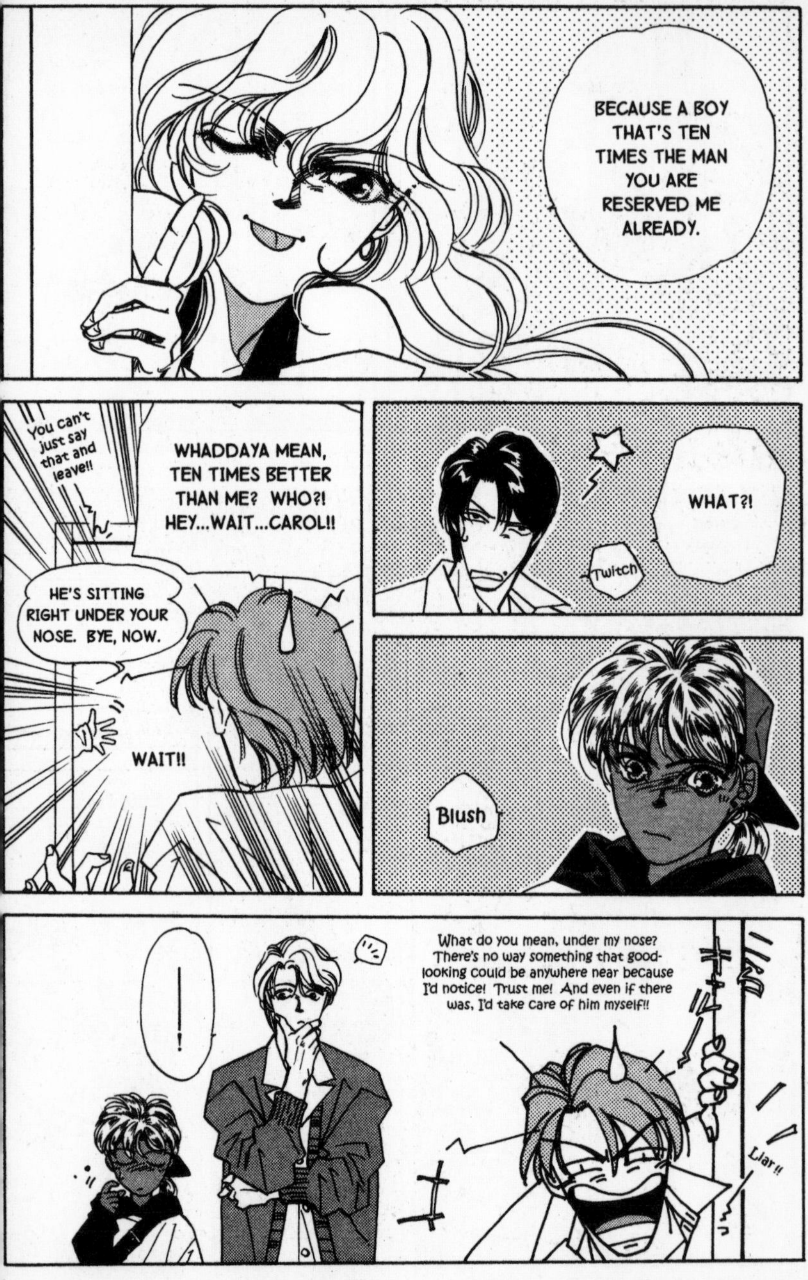
BECAUSE A BOY THAT'S TEN TIMES THE MAN YOU ARE RESERVED ME ALREADY.
WHAT?!
Twitch
Blush
WHADDAYA MEAN, TEN TIMES BETTER THAN ME? WHO?! HEY...WAIT...CAROL!!
You can't just say that and leave!!
HE'S SITTING RIGHT UNDER YOUR NOSE. BYE, NOW.
WAIT!!
What do you mean, under my nose? There's no way something that good-looking could be anywhere near because I'd notice! Trust me! And even if there was, I'd take care of him myself!!
Liar!!
!

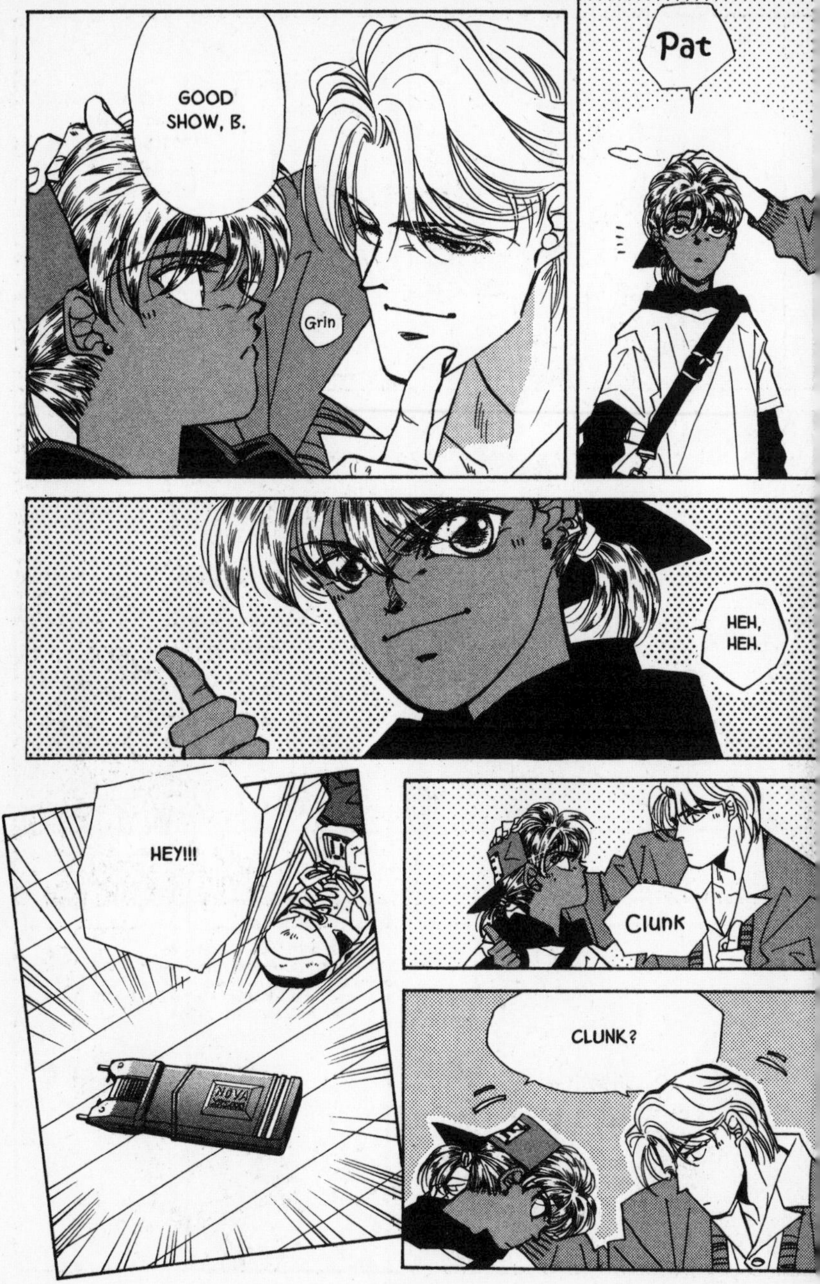
Pat
GOOD SHOW, B.
Grin
HEH, HEH.
Clunk
CLUNK?
HEY!!!

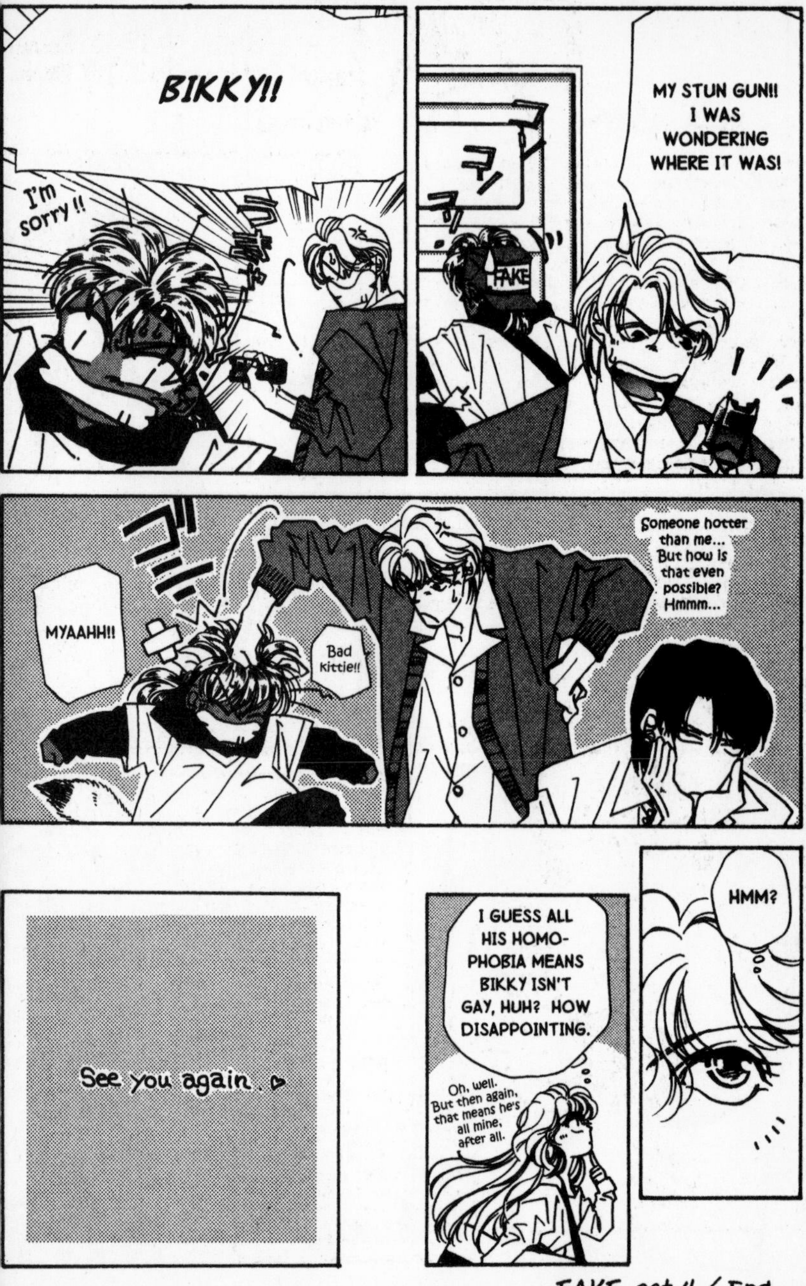
MY STUN GUN!! I WAS WONDERING WHERE IT WAS!
BIKKY!!
I'm sorry!!
Someone hotter than me... But how is that even possible? Hmmm...
Bad kittie!!
MYAAHH!!
HMM?
I GUESS ALL HIS HOMO-PHOBIA MEANS BIKKY ISN'T GAY, HUH? HOW DISAPPOINTING.
Oh, well. But then again, that means he's all mine, after all.
See you again. ♡

FAKE act.4/ End.

FAKE After-Talk ▶ By Sanami Matoh.

Comics and CD ▶

It's been some time now since I've done a comic. This is also my first work published through Biblos, and I think it's been almost a year since I began the FAKE series in the first place!! Since I've got quite a few other works going on simultaneously, FAKE kinda ended up with a "when I feel like it" pace, so please forgive me. But it sure is worth it to continue a series sometimes, as Movic has decided to create a CD based on this series. Actually, the first time the idea of a CD was brought up was when the ad for Part 1 of the first act of Fake had just hit the presses! (Way too early!!) Of course, nothing really came of those talks since no one was really sure how the series was even going to do—not to mention the fact I hadn't even drawn part one yet. So they pretty much sent me packing with me begging them to "call me about it anytime—if you remember!" And they remembered, so thank you very much, Movic!!

I was able to be present for the CD recording session and all I can say is that I'm completely satisfied with how everything went. It was sooo fun, so please please take a listen to it if you get the chance.

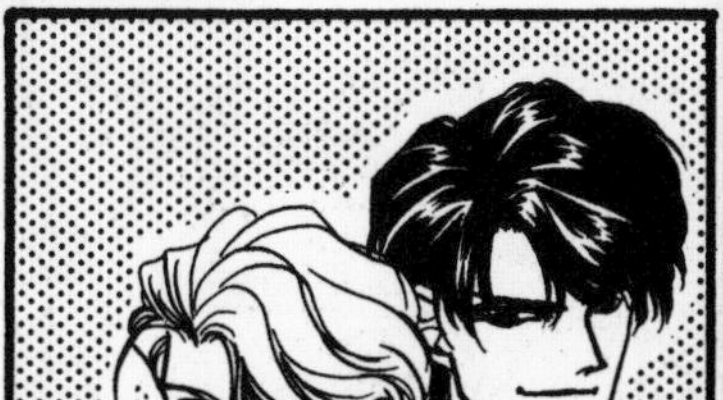

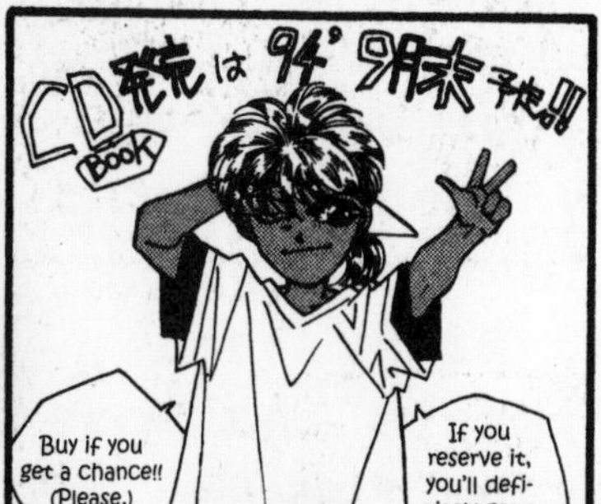
CD BOOK 発売は 94' 9月末予定!!
If you reserve it, you'll definitely get a copy.
Buy if you get a chance!! (Please.)
For reservations, contact a bookstore or specialty store.

Cast: Ryo. Nobuo Tobita.
He had a soft and kind delivery. I was very happy that we decided to go with him. (And thank you so much for talking with me about all sorts of useless things afterwards as well.)
Cast: Dee. Tomokazu Seki.
He's got all of Dee's 'cool' scenes and his 'dorky' scenes right on the money. I'm very happy with the result. (He was such a down-to-earth guy, and I had a blast with him. I might have been just a bit too comfy with him. If so, sorry!)

NEXT CAST ▶

CAST: Bikky. Rika Matsumoto.
I'm so happy that she made Bikky into such a cute and lovable character. Thank you very much! (Ms. Matsumoto was so beautiful that I couldn't help but be very nervous around her. Darn, I wish I could go back and talk to her some more now!!)

(Baddie.) Feldman: Kenji Uchiumi.
The Chief: Yohsuke Akimoto.
Janet: Masako Katsuo.
(Another baddie.)
Killer: Kazuhiro Nakata.
(And another.)
Snake: Mitsuaki Hoshino.

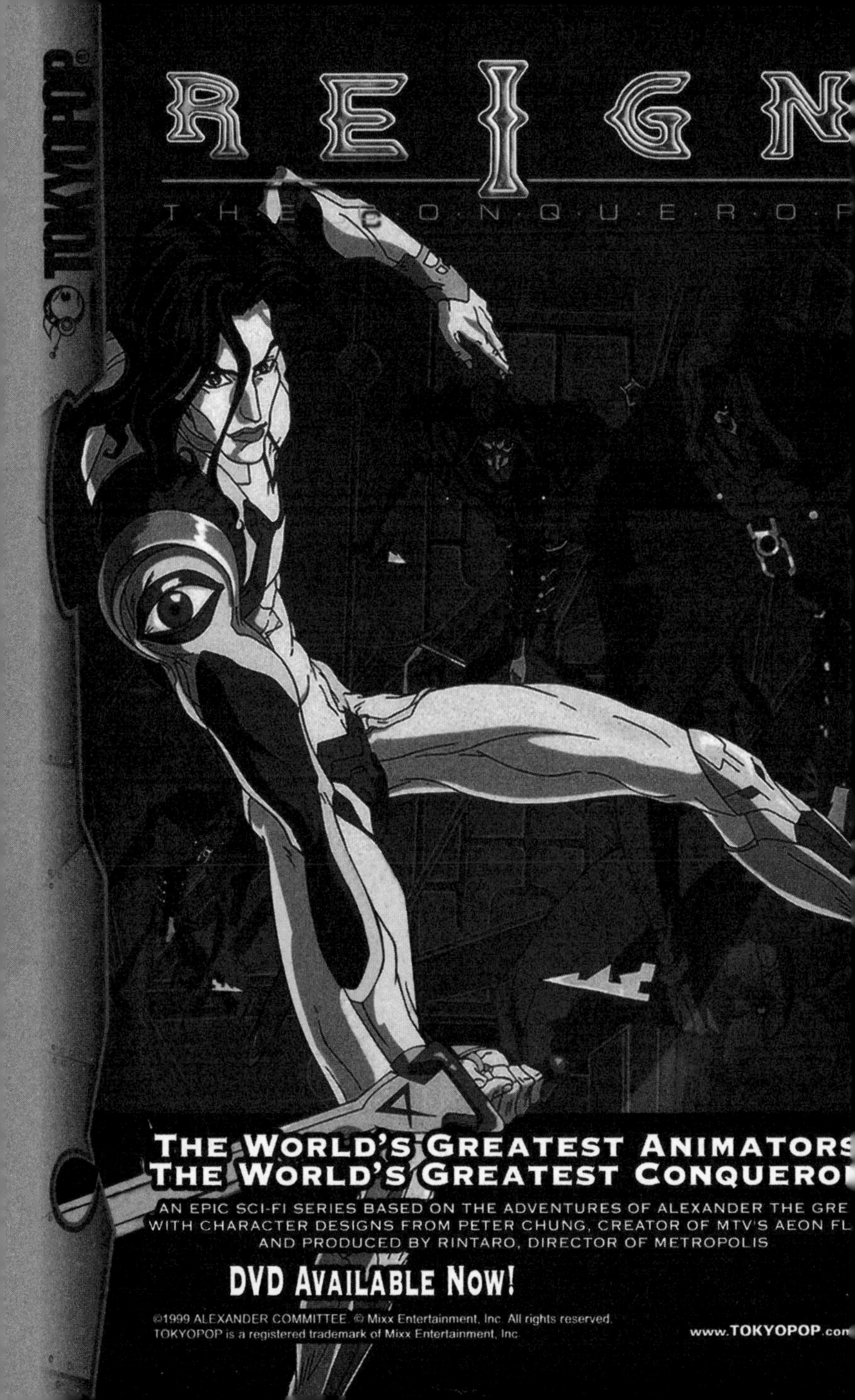
TOKYOPOP
REIGN
THE CONQUEROR
THE WORLD'S GREATEST ANIMATORS
THE WORLD'S GREATEST CONQUERO
AN EPIC SCI-FI SERIES BASED ON THE ADVENTURES OF ALEXANDER THE GRE
WITH CHARACTER DESIGNS FROM PETER CHUNG, CREATOR OF MTV'S AEON FL
AND PRODUCED BY RINTARO, DIRECTOR OF METROPOLIS
DVD AVAILABLE NOW!
©1999 ALEXANDER COMMITTEE © Mixx Entertainment, Inc. All rights reserved.
TOKYOPOP is a registered trademark of Mixx Entertainment, Inc.
www.TOKYOPOP.com

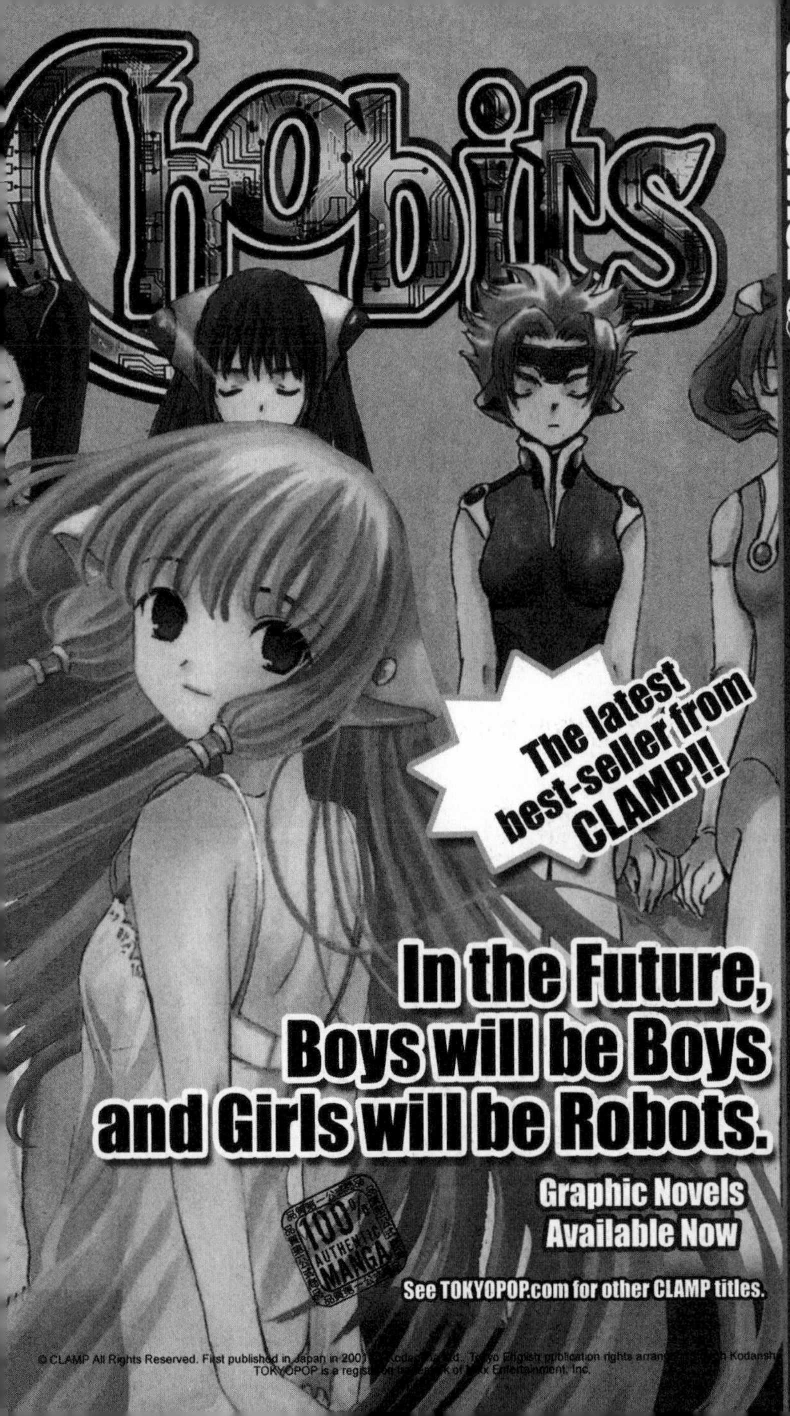
Chobits
The latest best-seller from CLAMP!!
In the Future, Boys will be Boys and Girls will be Robots.
100% AUTHENTIC MANGA
Graphic Novels Available Now
See TOKYOPOP.com for other CLAMP titles.
© CLAMP All Rights Reserved. First published in Japan in 2001

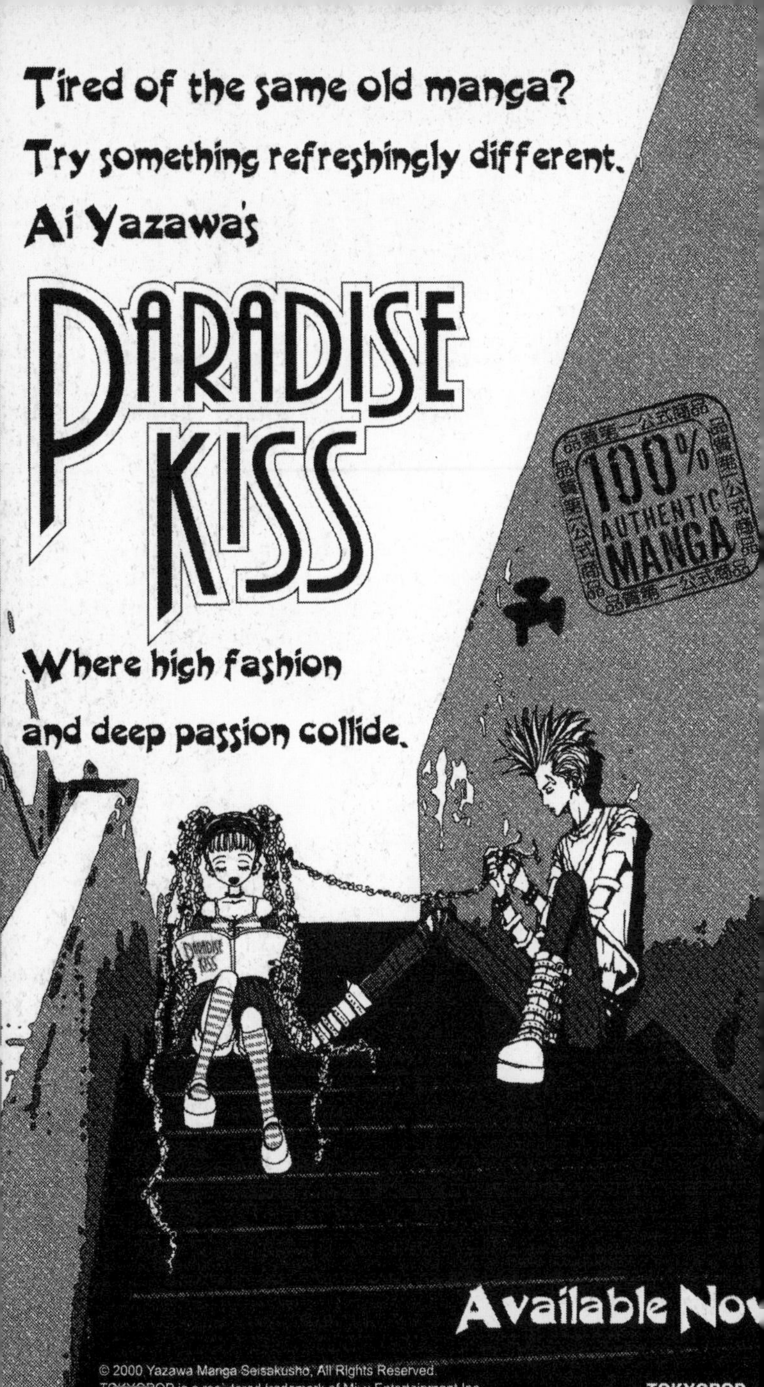

Tired of the same old manga?
Try something refreshingly different.
Ai Yazawa's
PARADISE KISS
100% AUTHENTIC MANGA
PARADISE KISS
Where high fashion
and deep passion collide.
Available No
© 2000 Yazawa Manga Seisakusho, All Rights Reserved.

STOP!

This is the back of the book.
You wouldn't want to spoil a great ending!

This book is printed "manga-style," in the authentic Japanese right-to-left format. Since none of the artwork has been flipped or altered, readers get to experience the story just as the creator intended. You've been asking for it, so TOKYOPOP® delivered: authentic, hot-off-the-press, and far more fun!

DIRECTIONS

If this is your first time reading manga-style, here's a quick guide to help you understand how it works.

It's easy... just start in the top right panel and follow the numbers. Have fun, and look for more 100% authentic manga from TOKYOPOP®!